Events Marketing Management

This textbook provides students with an essential introduction to the theoretical underpinnings and practicalities of managing the marketing of events.

In order to market events effectively, it is vital to consider marketing of events from the organiser's perspective and to link it to that of the consumers attending events. As such, this is the first book on the topic which reflects the unique characteristics of marketing in the events industry by exploring both sides of the marketing coin – the supply and the demand – in the specific context of events. The book takes the reader from core marketing mix principles to exploring the event marketing landscape, and from consumer experience and involvement with event marketing to strategies and tactics employed to manage the marketing activities related to events. The use of technology and the importance of sponsorship and PR are also considered. International case studies are integrated throughout to show practical realities of marketing and managing events and a range of useful learning aids are incorporated to assist navigation throughout the book, spur critical thinking and further students' knowledge.

This accessible and comprehensive account of Events Marketing Management is essential reading for all students and future managers.

Ivna Reic is currently Senior Lecturer in Events Management at the University of Northampton's Faculty of Business and Law where she teaches on the BA Events Management programme. Before moving to Northampton, Ivna was Course Leader for the BA Events Management programmes at London Metropolitan University, where she also taught on postgraduate programmes related to events management and events marketing. Her academic interests include events marketing and consumer psychology, corporate events, as well as exploring the application of general management theories within the area of events management, most notably theories relating to stakeholder management and sustainability.

D0322773

Events Marketing Management

A consumer perspective

Ivna Reic

Routledge
Taylor & Francis Group

LONDON AND NEW YORK

First published 2017
by Routledge
2 Park Square, Milton Park, Abingdon, Oxon, OX14 4RN

and by Routledge
711 Third Avenue, New York, NY 10017

Routledge is an imprint of the Taylor & Francis Group, an informa business

British Library Cataloguing in Publication Data
A catalogue record for this book is available from the British Library

Library of Congress Cataloging in Publication Data
Names: Reic, Ivna, author.
Title: Events marketing management : a consumer perspective / Ivna Reic.
Description: New York, NY : Routledge, 2016. | Includes bibliographical
references and index.
Identifiers: LCCN 2016010252| ISBN 9780415533577 (hbk) | ISBN
9781138901810 (pbk) | ISBN 9780415533584 (ebk)
Subjects: LCSH: Special events--Marketing. | Special events--Management.
Classification: LCC GT3405 .R45 2016 | DDC 394.2--dc23
LC record available at https://lccn.loc.gov/2016010252

ISBN: 978-0-415-53357-7 (hbk)
ISBN: 978-0-415-53358-4 (pbk)
ISBN: 978-0-203-11414-8 (ebk)

Typeset in Iowan Old Style
by Saxon Graphics Ltd, Derby
Printed in Great Britain by Ashford Colour Press Ltd

This book is dedicated to my two boys, Deji and David, without whom my life would be truly dreary indeed, and to my parents, Nera and Gauro, without whom I wouldn't be where I am today – with love and appreciation.

Contents

Figures

Tables

Vignettes

Acknowledgements

This book is a product of years of discussions, challenges and mulling over of theoretical concepts and how these transpire in events marketing practice. On a more practical level special thanks is due to:

My colleague and mentor, Justin Lance – for sparking my interest specifically in events marketing and for his input which paved the way for the ideas presented in this book.

Sara and Henrik Linden, Zoe Aris, Daniela Chialoufas, Kevin Lane, Matilda Kelly, Jasmin Reeve and Eve Robinson, as well as the University of Northampton Marketing Department – for their contribution to case studies and illustrations in this volume.

Present and former colleagues at the University of Northampton, London Metropolitan University and Middlesex University – working alongside you has been an absolute pleasure.

Present and former students – for pushing me to be my best and for always trying to have an answer.

Olympia London for their permission to use some of their digital properties for illustration purposes.

Chapter **1**

About this book

In the spring of 2010 I had been teaching events management for about a year and found myself particularly drawn to the area of events marketing. In late 2009, having completed my master's degree in Events Marketing Management after about five years spent in events and marketing/advertising, I came across *Buyology*, an insightful and thought-provoking book by Martin Lindstrom, a branding expert and avid consumer educator (who would have thought that the two worlds could so easily be combined in one person!). The book was a revelation and sparked my interest in consumer psychology, particularly in relation to events. I scoured the event management literature on offer at the time and all the books I opened were filled with conventional marketing thought. Moreover, marketing as a function of event management seemed to be under-represented in the literature, which was not surprising considering how young this subject area is. As I tried to reconcile the 'traditional' notion of marketing and promotion with the new and exciting concepts Lindstrom talked about in his work, the idea for this book was born. It took a while for it to crystallise and find its own voice, but in December 2011 my publisher, Taylor & Francis, decided they wanted in on the action. Fast-forward four years and the fruit of this (and much other) labour is now in your hands.

What is event marketing?

Steve Jobs, the iconic former CEO of Apple, one of the world's leading creative technology brands, is attributed with saying: 'To me, marketing is all about values. This is a complicated world, it's a noisy world, and we're not going to get the chance to get people to remember much about us – no company is, so we have to be really clear on what we want them to know about us.'

In the marketing classes I teach I often start by asking my students the question in the title of this section: 'What is event marketing?' The variety of answers I receive to this question always impresses me, particularly as students from different countries always add another dimension to the answer. In reality, there is no one true answer – the word 'marketing' has a slightly different meaning to every single person and every company has a different way of defining and designing their 'marketing'.

Current academic literature largely discusses event marketing through the classic marketing lens of McCarthy's (1960) concept of the Marketing Mix, more commonly known as the 4Ps, and Booms and Bitner's (1982) concept of the 7Ps – marketing mix for services. The majority of authors discussing event marketing (see Bowdin *et al.*, 2011; Getz, 2005; Allen *et al.*, 2010) adapt one of the two concepts and try to fit event marketing within the parameters already given. These have been discussed in depth in Chapter 4. As we will see in Chapter 2, events as a phenomenon are an amalgamation of products and services, with a particular impact of the time constraint that heavily influences the marketing aspect. Thus, event marketing as a business function is a more fluid concept that cannot fit neatly into marketing mix 'boxes', however many Ps one chooses to adapt. This book introduces a new model which reframes the popular notions of the marketing mix and, I feel, is more intuitive and more responsive to the almost amorphous nature of events.

Another specificity of event marketing is the aspect of time. Whilst marketing of products and services does need to fit within a particular timeline, there is some space for flexibility with the start, end and duration of marketing campaigns. Time is an important and integral aspect of events as a market offering. As events themselves are time-constrained, this creates an invisible boundary line within which marketing activities must fit – if an event is happening on the first weekend in May, then there is not much space to be flexible with when the marketing of the event will be done. There must be no delays or missed opportunities for marketing the event, otherwise it could negatively impact not just the event's media exposure, but also attendee numbers, brand awareness and (ultimately) revenues and profits.

There are three key things the reader should know before going any further with this book. First, this book is the first comprehensive text focusing on managing the marketing processes within the events industry. It critically evaluates the various 'traditional' marketing ideas and concepts within the context of the events industry; it looks at the practicalities of planning, implementing and evaluating marketing communications strategies and also explores their antecedents. Second, this book provides a strong overview of the key concepts of consumer behaviour discussed in the context of events, which is something little other event marketing literature offers. And finally, it introduces key concepts offered by contemporary marketing and business authors, such as Martin Lindstrom, Malcolm Gladwell, Daniel Pink, Dan Ariely and others, and outlines their place in the evolving nature of event marketing.

The book itself is arranged thematically.

The first section deals with defining events. Chapter 2 discusses the events industry and its characteristics, ways of classifying events and the role and impact of seasonality in driving the industry forward. Chapter 3 outlines the evolution of dominant economic paradigms which led to the prominence of events in the economy and introduces where the value lies in events and the role of the event experience in building this value. Chapter 4 dissects the notion of the Marketing Mix and discusses its applicability in the context of events.

The next section presents the key concepts that define the events marketing landscape. Chapter 5 presents frameworks for the analysis of the external environment and differentiation and positioning strategies for events, and Chapter 6 discusses segmentation.

The following two chapters focus on the events consumers. Chapter 7 explores the key economic concepts of demand and supply and evaluates the notion of the Economic Man in the consumption of leisure experiences which are events. Chapter 8 introduces the notions of identity, authenticity and being human, which are at the heart of the consumers' decision-making process, and discusses their relationship to the motivation of consumers to attend events.

The next chapters delve into the practicalities of marketing communications for events. Chapter 9 introduces the generic marketing strategies that provide the overall direction for any marketing plan. Chapter 10 evaluates the role of traditional marketing tactics in the marketing of events, whilst Chapter 11 talks about the changing role of public relations and explores how new PR tactics work in the twenty-first century. Chapter 12 discusses a key new strand of marketing communications – e-marketing (or digital marketing). Chapter 13 presents the marketing planning function and the increasingly important role of integrating marketing communications for events. It outlines the recommendations for financial and other control of the event marketing process.

The final chapter, Chapter 14, represents a sort of conclusion, if you will; it presents a new model for event marketing that puts the consumer centre stage. The model presents an alternative to the current concept of the Marketing Mix, not so much by abandoning the Ps but, rather, by reframing the Ps within a new framework, more suitable to the nature of events as specific market offerings.

The theoretical frameworks and concepts discussed within this book are supported with a variety of practical examples throughout, as well as more extensive vignettes presenting the practical application of the key concepts more in depth. Furthermore, each chapter concludes with a practical case study which encourages the reader to engage with the theory presented in the chapter and to see how it is (or can be) applied in an industry context. Case studies, which are international and varied, highlight the challenges posed by the specific nature of events and provide ample food for thought. Additionally, each chapter is also accompanied by an event management scenario, which allows the reader to assume the role of an events marketer and come up with practical solutions to the scenarios in their own specific local context. For those eager to learn more about the theory behind the chapter, a useful list of books, journals and other resources is also provided at the end of each chapter, to entice the inner researcher in you.

As the author of this book, I am hoping that the book will be interesting to a wide variety of audiences, not only related to events, but also to other areas of the creative industries. However, my primary focus is on those studying and working in, or otherwise connected to, the events sector. Therefore, this book is for you if:

- You are a student on any of the event management vocational, undergraduate or postgraduate programmes.

- You are an events management educator.

- You are an events management practitioner or considering entering the industry.

Additionally, this book can be used by anyone interested in gaining a fresh perspective on the management of marketing activities within the events sector.

About the author

Ivna Reic is an early career academic, who has been teaching events management in the UK higher education since early 2009. She is currently Senior Lecturer in Events Management at the University of Northampton's Faculty of Business and Law where she teaches on the BA Events Management programme and is Programme Leader for the BA (Hons) Events Management Top Up. Before moving to Northampton, Ivna was the Programme Leader for the BA Events Management programmes at London Metropolitan University, where she also taught on postgraduate programmes related to events management and events marketing. After six years of working in events and advertising, Ivna completed her master's degree in Events Marketing Management and is now preparing to start her doctoral studies. Her academic interests include events marketing and consumer psychology, and corporate events, as well as (to a lesser extent, perhaps) exploring the application of general management theories within the area of events management, most notably theories relating to stakeholder management and sustainability. In January 2014 Ivna was awarded Fellowship of the UK Higher Education Academy and in May 2014 she received the student-led teaching award from the University of Northampton Students Union, which she is particularly proud of. Ivna remains committed to ensuring the next generation of event managers educated at the University of Northampton's Faculty of Business and Law gain not only the relevant academic skills, but also personal and professional skills that will take them through their career and enable them to become genuine lifelong learners.

References

Allen, J., O'Toole, W., Harris, R. and McDonnell, I. 2010. *Festival and Special Event Management*, 5th Edition, Milton: John Wiley & Sons Australia.

Booms, B.H. and Bitner, M.J. 1982. Marketing services by managing the environment, *The Cornell Hotel and Restaurant Administration Quarterly*, 23(May), pp. 35–39.

Bowdin, G.A.J., Allen, J., O'Toole, W., Harris, R. and McDonnell, I. 2011. *Events Management*, 3rd Edition, Oxford: Butterworth-Heinemann.

Getz, D. 2005. *Event Management and Event Tourism*, Putnam Valley, NY: Cognizant Communication Corporation.

McCarthy, E. J. 1960. *Basic Marketing: A managerial approach*, Homewood, IL: Richard D. Irwin.

Chapter **2**

Defining the event industry for events marketing

LEARNING OUTCOMES

By the end of the chapter, students should be able to:

- Identify the characteristics of the event industry and the range and variety of event types

- Compare and contrast the differences in event purpose according to the type of event ownership

- Use the Event Categorisation model for the definition of events and understand its relevance to the marketing of events

- Critically explain the significance of demand and seasonality to the management of events

- Critically evaluate the Product Life Cycle model in the context of the event industry

- Describe the characteristics of the supply chain within the events industry

The events industry contributes to exports, inward investment, infrastructure development, cultural appreciation, civic and national pride and community cohesion, to the shaping of destination identity, creative enterprise, innovation, knowledge transfer, professional development, and tourism.

Business Visits and Events Partnership (2014)

Introduction

Ever since events have emerged as a legitimate area of academic inquiry, the debate around the nature of events has been centre stage: are events products or services? If events are products, how are they defined, produced and delivered? If events are services, how are they best packaged for maximum impact?

Why is there such interest in the nature of events? As we will see further on in Chapter 4, classifying events as either products or services will have a big impact on their marketing. For the purpose of this book, we define events as unique market offerings that represent an amalgamation of products and services and which support the delivery of the event experience. As such, events do not neatly fit into the dominant definitions of products and services.

Events do, however, share all of the inherent characteristics of services (as identified by Grönroos, 2000), namely:

> *Intangibility* – events (or, rather, the event experience) cannot be touched, they are not physical objects.

> *Inseparability* – in order for the event to exist, the person experiencing it needs to be present at a specific location at a specific time.

> *Variability (heterogeneity)* – every event is a unique occurrence and even events which are traditional, long-standing and happen in a particular cycle (e.g. on an annual or monthly basis) are never the same. This may be influenced by the change of time frame (and/or location) and the people involved in the delivery of the event and consumption of the event experience.

> *Perishability* – events do not (at least technically speaking) exist outside of their official start and end times.

This chapter introduces the nature and structure of the event industry and their implications for successful events marketing. We pay particular attention to the concept of the Product Life Cycle with events, as well as the role that seasonality and demand play in determining the life cycle of each particular event. These initial concepts represent the backbone upon which are built the notions of value creation in events discussed in Chapter 3, the marketing mix for events explored in Chapter 4, the nature of event customers defined in Chapters 7 and 8 and the new model for the marketing of event experience presented in Chapter 14.

It is the role of events marketing to extend the life of an event by engaging event audiences (attendees as well as other stakeholders) before and after the event has happened. This is done through the use of various channels, which we discuss more in detail in Chapters 9–12.

Event 'products'

In the event management literature, the term 'event product' (Bowdin *et al.*, 2011) can often be found to denote the market offering of an event, thus, this notion of 'production' and 'consumption' is still very much embedded in the nature of events. Events, however, are 'produced' and 'consumed' simultaneously, which is a significant factor determining the

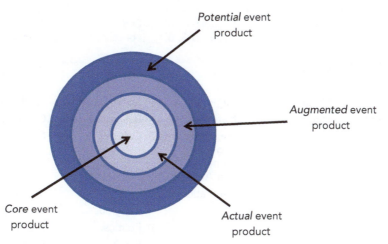

Figure 2.1 Levels of event product

Source: Adapted from Brassington and Pettitt (2003), Robinson *et al.* (2010), McCabe (2009), and Tersine and Hummingbird (1995)

flow of their marketing efforts. Additionally, the notion of the event experience (Robinson *et al.*, 2010) adds a further complexity in defining the actual event product. Figure 2.1 outlines the four levels of event product as follows:

Core event product – is the actual consumer need or want that the event is fulfilling.

Actual event product – is the totality of the event format and content; it is also known in literature as the tangible product.

Augmented event product – comprises all the 'extras' that are offered to the event consumers, which help deliver the event experience.

Potential event product – identifies opportunities to further develop the event in the future, either in terms of redefining the event concept or in terms of supplementing the current concept with additional features (e.g. new technologies, additional physical features within the event, etc.).

Event categorisation

One of the contributing factors to the confusion in defining the nature of events is the fact that events are so many and varied. Figure 2.2 provides a framework for the categorisation of events. It takes into account the type, size, geographical reach, content and format of the event.

It can be seen that, in terms of the sector within which they occur, events can be organised for private (for-profit) businesses, charitable (non-profit) organisations/causes or governmental (public) departments or bodies. The nature of the sector within which an event is being organised will have implications for the objectives and management of the event. For example, events organised in the public sector will usually be focusing on addressing particular issues which are of public interest and apply to or involve a broad range of audiences. These events will likely need to demonstrate their immediate impact and will

Events by sector	Events by size	Events by geographical reach	Events by content	Events by format
Private (for-profit)	Micro	Local	Musical	Trade show
Public	Minor	Regional	Sporting	Exhibition
Non-profit	Major	National	Business	Conference
	Hallmark	Pan-continental (e.g. pan-European, pan-African)	Cultural	Convention
	Mega	International	Arts	Meeting
			Religious	Training
			Political	Team building
			Family	Festival
			Generational	Performance
			Fundraising	Fair
				Summit
				Party
				Awards ceremony
				Product launch
				Gala
				Celebration
				Competition
				Showcase

Figure 2.2 Event categorisation matrix
Source: Adapted from Bowdin *et al.* (2011) and Getz (2007)

be governed in their financial management by the purchasing policies of the public bodies on behalf of which they are organisers. Events in the for-profit sector will largely focus on achieving company or organisational objectives and maximising positive impact for the company which is organising the event. The impact will usually be measured in the amount of profit made or objectives achieved by the event or its sponsors and other key stakeholders. Events in the 'third' sector (non-profit) will usually have a strong fundraising component which will imply a focus on maximising profits and/or awareness raised via the event and driving the organisational costs down. Of particular importance in this sector is the notion of in kind sponsorship, which we discuss more in detail in Chapter 11.

The usual division of events by size into minor, major, hallmark and mega-events (Getz, 2008) is here supplemented with the introduction of another category – *micro* events, which encompass the important personal milestone events on an individual level – a category not previously explored (or indeed mentioned) within event management literature. Examples of this could include weddings, anniversaries, birthday parties, etc. The remaining three criteria (geographical reach, content and format) are fairly self-explanatory and will, therefore, not be discussed in any particular depth.

Whilst there is no 'perfect' solution for categorising events, simply due to their heterogeneous nature, this tool should at least allow for most events to be categorised and defined in terms of their broad characteristics. It is important to note that determining the exact category of a particular event will have certain implications for its marketing. For instance, it is likely that a for-profit hallmark music festival will attract a completely (or at least sufficiently) different target audience than a non-profit minor local cultural festival. In addition to the difference in target audiences, there will also be a difference in the available budgets for the marketing of these events, as well as a difference in the mix of communications channels used to promote these events.

VIGNETTE 2.1

International sporting events in Africa

African Games are a major non-profit pan-African sporting competition. The games have been held since 1965 and have, since their inception, been officially recognised by the International Olympic Committee.

Initially organised and supported by the political body Supreme Council for Sports in Africa (SCSA) since 1966, in 2011 the event changed owners and is now entrusted to the non-profit Association of National Olympic Committees of Africa (ANOCA), which is reflected in the nature of the event and its primary objectives. Whilst in the first four decades the event served as a platform to promote the governmental policies of the organising countries (which also impacted on the types of sports that were included in each particular edition of the games), since the change of ownership there has been much more freedom in determining the scope of the event in accordance with the general popularity of the sports on a more global scale.

Throughout their 50-year history, the African Games have been used to promote the sporting values of participation, togetherness and striving for excellence in order to develop sports in the participating nations. However, they have also served as a platform to promote African achievements in sport on a global level.

Complementing the African Games, the African Youth Games are a youth-focused international multi-sport event which has sprung out of the need to involve African youth in sports in order to support the general development of sport throughout Africa. The event focuses on investing in young athletes aged 14–18 and building them up in order to develop sports within the participating African nations. Organised for the first time in Rabat, Morocco, in 2010, the event is already set as a qualifier for the World Youth Olympic Games, which raises its profile internationally. The second edition was organised in Gaborone, Botswana, in 2014 and the bid for the 2018 event has recently been awarded to the city of Algiers in Algeria. Preparations are currently underway for securing private sponsorship in order to be able to deliver the event successfully.

More information about the Association of National Olympic Committees of Africa can be found on their webpage www.africaolympic.net.

More information about Associations of National Olympic Committees generally can be found on www.acnolympic.org.

The role of seasonality in events

Similarly to retail, the events industry is strongly influenced by seasonality. Think about the following: when do Christmas parties usually take place? When do UK music festivals take place? When do agricultural fairs take place?

Seasonality is ingrained in the very origins of the events industry. Bowdin *et al.* (2011) refer to the early folk festivals such as Plough Monday, May Day, Midsummer Day and Harvest Home, which frame the annual agricultural cycle and serve as its seasonal benchmarks. Similarly, Christmas and New Year's celebrations always happen at the same time every year and celebrate the ending of one cycle and the beginning of the next.

Depending on their nature and profile, events are heavily influenced by seasonality, although today it is not only a matter of the actual calendar season, but also business season or cycle of operations pertinent to particular industries, and thus events. For example, the UK music festival season runs from early June to late August/early September, primarily due to the fact that most music festivals take place outdoors and are highly dependent on the weather conditions. Some large sporting competitions, such as the FIFA World Cup or the Olympics, run on a four-year season; others, such as the NBA, run on a one-year season. Christmas parties only take place in November and December and are heavily influenced by the holiday season. Thus, we can establish the following causes of seasonality in events:

- Natural seasonality – dependent on climate conditions.

- Calendar seasonality – dependent on particular seasonal demands.

- Traditional seasonality – influenced by established social customs and tradition.

- Tourism seasonality – geographically framed.

- Institutionalised seasonality – taking into account public holidays.

- Sporting seasonality – dependent on the competition cycle for a particular sport.

- Economic seasonality – driven by a particular industry's business cycle and/or customs.

- Devotional (religious) seasonality – coinciding with various religious holidays and cycles.

- Social seasonality – influenced by the social calendar of a particular location, fashion and other social trends, as well as peer pressure.

It is also important to note that seasonality in everything, including the events industry, is highly specific to the geographical location in which that industry operates. For example, whilst the music festival season, highly dependent on the weather conditions, in the UK runs only for four months during the year, this might not necessarily be an influencing factor in areas with a warmer climate, such as parts of Australia, Africa or southern American states.

Apart from the forms of seasonality mentioned above, there is one more important form of seasonality which frames events on a more personal level: individual seasonality. This type of seasonality influences the landmark events in an individual's life – their birthday parties (landmark 'sweet sixteen' or twenty-first birthday celebrations), personal religious ceremonies (such as naming ceremonies, baptism or confirmation ceremonies, bar and bat mitzvahs, etc.), weddings, funerals, graduation and awards ceremonies, as well as other types of anniversaries and celebrations. Getz (2007) emphasises the role of these highly personal events in marking important personal occasions and celebrating good and bad times by including the individual's social circles.

It is, thus, clear that seasonality is one of the key factors that impact on the nature of an event. It influences the type of the event, its content and the profile of the event's audiences. For commercial (for-profit) events, seasonality will influence the strength of and competitiveness within the industry. For example, Christmas fairs and celebrations will be limited by the short time-frame which is 'traditional' for such events and their supply needs to be balanced well with the limited demand for such events in a particular location. It follows, then, that seasonality is itself specific to a particular geographical location.

VIGNETTE 2.2

Seasonality in the fashion industry

The fashion industry is one that is highly influenced by trends and seasonality. Since the early twentieth century retailers of women's clothes, particularly large department stores, have traditionally been organising events which showcased their latest designs, trying to entice their customers and boost sales through emphasising exclusivity. Towards the end of World War II, New York Fashion Week was born, more through necessity than through creative forethought. This was due to the fact that, at the time, Paris was the centre of fashion creativity – clothes may have been produced in America, but the creative designs came from Paris. With the inability to travel to Paris during the war for their annual dose of fashion inspiration came a need to find and showcase home-grown designer talent. The first New York Fashion Week (then called Press Week) was held in 1943 and was later followed by the fashion weeks in Paris (mid-late 1940s), Milan (mid-1970s) and London (1984).

These four events are the largest and longest-running events, which represent the staple of the industry and are often referred to as the 'Big Four'. The purpose of the fashion weeks is to provide an opportunity for members of the fashion press, fashion buyers and celebrities to preview the trends for the upcoming season. The events take place twice-yearly: the September/early October events showcase the trends for the following Spring/Summer season, whilst the February/early March editions focus on the upcoming Autumn/Winter collections. This half-a-year lead-in time allows the retailers to create marketing materials featuring the new designs and also allows the buyers to order required quantities of particular designs for their retail outlets in preparation for the new retail season.

Aside from the 'Big Four', which dictate the pace of the industry, a large number of Fashion Weeks that have sprung up all over the globe over the past 15 years or so follow the same seasonal pattern: twice-yearly events held around the same time or immediately after the 'Big Four'. This pattern can be seen in Table 2.1.

Table 2.1 Seasonality of global Fashion Week events

Name of event	Location	Autumn/Winter 2013 edition	Spring/Summer 2014 edition
New York Fashion Week	USA	7–14 February 2013	5–12 September 2013
London Fashion Week	United Kingdom	15–19 February 2013	13–17 September 2013
Madrid Fashion Week	Spain	18–22 February 2013	13–17 September 2013
Milan Fashion Week	Italy	20–26 February 2013	18–23 September 2013
Paris Fashion Week	France	26 February–6 March 2013	24 September–2 October 2013
Johannesburg Fashion Week	South African Republic	7–9 March 2013	3–7 October 2013
Los Angeles Fashion Week	USA	8–17 March 2013	3–24 October 2013
Istanbul Fashion Week	Turkey	12–16 March 2013	7–11 October 2013
Shanghai Fashion Week	China	11–16 April 2013	16–25 October 2013
Toronto Fashion Week	Canada	13–28 March 2013	16–26 October 2013
Tokyo Fashion Week	Japan	19–25 March 2013	14–19 October 2013
Jakarta Fashion Week	Indonesia	14–17 February 2013	19–25 October 2013
Sao Paulo Fashion Week	Brazil	18–22 March 2013	28 October–1 November 2013

Certainly, with the strong popularity of fashion as an element of defining one's identity, fashion weeks are becoming increasingly popular in all corners of the globe. There are, of course, other fashion weeks not mentioned in Table 2.1 which take place outside of the 'norms' set by the 'Big Four'. For example, Miami Fashion Week takes place in May, Berlin Fashion Week, Amsterdam Fashion Week and Bangalore Fashion Week happen in July and Copenhagen Fashion Week and Buenos Aires Fashion Week are organised in August. However, the official industry business still operates on a six-month cycle, dictating the timeline for the most relevant fashion week events around the globe.

Event supply chain

Supply chain is an integral part of the delivery of any product or service – it represents a link between the producers of a particular product or service and the end users (customers) of these products and services. Johnston and Clark (2008) emphasise the role of successful relationship management for the efficient management of the supply chain. Whilst in the traditional product marketing the supply chain is a linear and sequential structure (Figure 2.3), with events it takes up a more matrix-like structure (see Figure 2.4). Thus, it may be wise to note that the term 'supply chain' does not really accurately reflect the complexities of the supply concept for events and terms such as 'supply matrix' or 'supply network' would probably be more appropriate within this particular industry.

Figure 2.3 Product supply chain

Source: Author's own

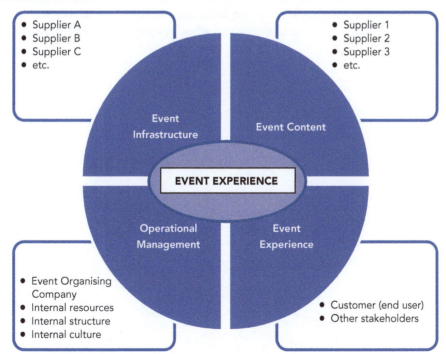

Figure 2.4 Event supply network – a very simplified example

Source: Author's own

It is important to note that both Figure 2.3 and Figure 2.4 represent a very simplified version of the product supply chain and event supply network, respectively. In reality, the event supply network that supports the construction of the event experience will depend on the number of suppliers (dependant on its scope and complexity). In addition to traditional suppliers, there will always exist a variety of other stakeholders that influence the delivery of the event, thus impacting on the overall event experience. Supply chain is particularly important in creating and delivering value – we discuss this further in Chapter 3. Of particular importance with events is also the extent to which consumers (end users) participate in the creation of the event experience and their role in the event supply network. We discuss consumers and their role in the delivery and marketing of events more in detail in Chapter 7.

Event Product Life Cycle

The Product Life Cycle (PLC) model outlines the key characteristics of a product or service in each of the 'life stages' of its existence (Brassington and Pettitt, 2003; Clow and Baack, 2010). There is very little discussion of the event product life cycle in the current event management literature. O'Toole (2011) refers to the 'event life cycle' which encompasses the stages of managing a specific edition of an event, from the initial concept development to the shutdown stage. In this book, however, we talk about a strategic role of the product life cycle concept in the long-term management of (mostly) recurring events. As such, we need to go back to the drawing board and see how the original concept presented by Levitt (1965) applies in general event marketing practice, as broadly indicated by Walle (1994).

The generic PLC model is presented in Figure 2.5a. First introduced by Levitt (1965), the model is based on the biological cycle of living beings. Since its introduction the model has been widely used in the general marketing literature and is one of the key notions any marketer in any sector needs to keep in mind when designing marketing strategies in a specific context.

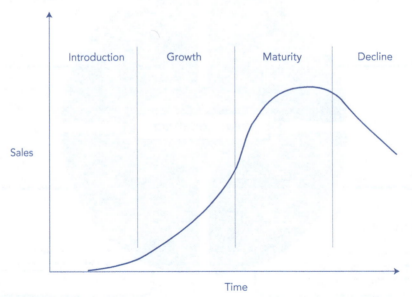

Figure 2.5a The generic Product Life Cycle model

Source: Adapted from Brassington and Pettitt (2003), Kotler *et al.* (2003) and Blythe (2013)

Kotler *et al.* (2003) highlight the fact that each of these stages will require a different approach to running the marketing communications of a product or service. In the *Introduction stage*, the sheer novelty may influence the audiences to attend the event, although the profit margin for the organisers may be quite low, or even negative. This is due to the relatively high costs of putting an event on for the very first time, without having a solid customer base which has already demonstrated an interest in an event of this sort. In the *Growth stage*, the demand for the event picks up, as the event becomes more known and the increase in demand helps profits rise as well. In the *Maturity stage*, the event has reached the maximum number of attendees interested in attending and profits are at their maximum. Events that are highly popular may decide to restrict the number of tickets offered, which can lead them to a state of constant maturity (see Figure 2.5b). The *Decline stage* is characterised by falling sales and profits, which signals the need for change. This change can be managed in three ways:

1   Complete event relaunch

Figure 2.5c represents the product life cycle of an event that has relaunched. The element of novelty is crucial in the introductory stage of any event – it is novelty that sparks the target audiences' interest in attending the event and helps the event to build a strong client base. However, as with everything in life, the novelty will, at one point or another, wear off. When this starts to happen, the event enters the decline stage. For recurring events, which are of strategic importance to a company, individual or an organisation, the complete relaunch of the event and the introduction of a new event format and/or features is one of the ways to reel the existing audiences back in, or to expand the pool of potential target audiences, thus creating more space for future event growth. For example, the low-carbon motoring exhibition, EcoVelocity, was scheduled to be relaunched in 2013 as the Future Drive Motor Show. The new event title came with a format adjustment based on market research conducted with previous visitors of the event, which revealed

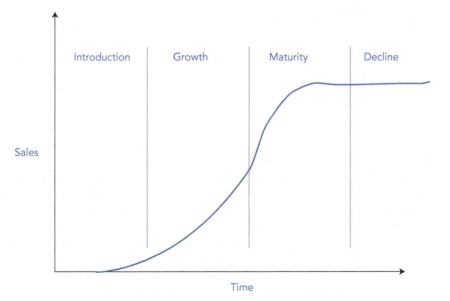

Figure 2.5b Product life cycle of an event with restricted numbers of tickets
Source: Adapted from Blythe (2013)

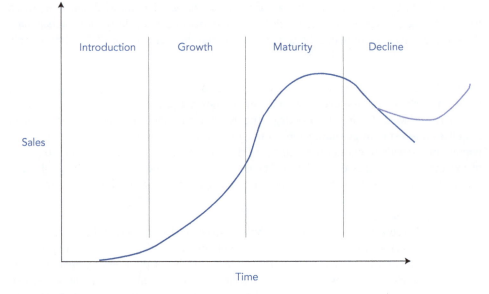

Figure 2.5c Product life cycle – event relaunch
Source: Adapted from Blythe (2013)

that one of the primary motives for attending a show of this type was having the opportunity to test-drive particular vehicles, which has since become the most prominent feature within the event. The event was finally cancelled the month before the advertised dates, with blame being put on poor interest from potential exhibitors, due to reduced marketing budgets as a result of the global recession.

2   Artificial abandonment of the event
Figure 2.5d depicts the product life cycle of an event that is strategically abandoned for a limited period of time. Reasons for this can relate to efforts to keep the novelty going and sustain the demand for an event by enforcing temporary scarcity, or they can be the result of factors in the external environment which are impacting on the delivery of an event. For example, in 2012 amidst the strong political tensions in Tibet, the Miss Tibet Pageant was cancelled for a year, but it resumed operation in 2013.

3   Natural abandonment of the event
The product life cycle of an event that is naturally abandoned is shown in Figure 2.5e. The natural abandonment can be effected by the management team based on a variety of reasons, which can include: poor financial performance of the event, the lack of event-brand fit, overwhelming negative impacts of the event on its stakeholders or unfavourable conditions in the external environment which would endanger the safety and the success of the event. For example, the natural smoothie company Innocent cancelled their brand event Fruitstock in 2007 after four very successful years due to the fact that its growth was becoming increasingly difficult to manage, both operationally and financially. The event would have had to look for external sponsorship in the following years and this was seen by the management as unfavourable to the image of the parent company – Innocent. The company abandoned this event and launched a new one on a much smaller scale – the Innocent Village Fete. Another good (albeit sad) example of the natural abandonment of

an event is the 2010 Love Parade in Duisburg, whose organising and support services teams had demonstrated extremely poor management of the health and safety aspects, which led to the deaths of over twenty attendees. Needless to say, that was the end of the Love Parade as a brand and the event has not been held since.

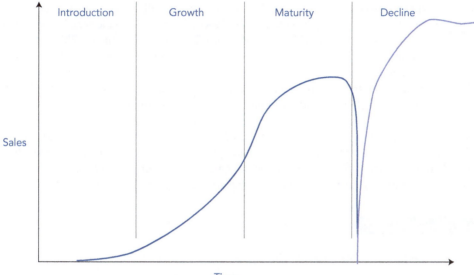

Figure 2.5d Product life cycle – artificial abandonment of an event
Source: Adapted from Blythe (2013)

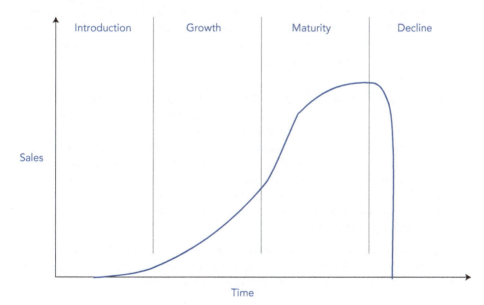

Figure 2.5e Product life cycle – natural abandonment of an event
Source: Adapted from Blythe (2013)

Exploring and understanding the concept of the product life cycle within the events industry is particularly important, as this industry is highly dependent on social trends and seasonality. It is a dynamic industry in which changes occur rapidly and require agility and forethought to be successfully managed. Note the choice of variables used to design the PLC graphs – they demonstrate the flow of sales over a period of time. It is important, however, to point out that, whilst time is a key element of the product life cycle, PLC graphs do not need to be restricted to sales only. This is particularly true of events, the 'life' of which can be measured in a variety of terms, most notably changes in profit, attendance, sponsorship, or other variables relevant to a particular event type. Blythe (2013) highlights several weaknesses of the PLC model, which may limit its usefulness in the day-to-day management of the product. The main issues that arise are the model's ineffectiveness in predicting the length of each particular phase, as well as any future trends that might affect these. Additionally, as this is a two-variable-only model, it is impossible to account for changes in the marketing approach which respond to changing societal trends or address the weaknesses of a particular stage within the product life cycle. Additionally, the original generic Product Life Cycle model had not taken into account the various options open to event managers and marketers in its decline stage, but this has been accounted for in adapted Figures 2.5b–2.5e.

CASE STUDY

Glastonbury Festival Product Life Cycle

Glastonbury is one of the longest-running 'modern' festivals in the world, having originated just one year after the landmark Woodstock festival, which marked a new era in the music industry. As a hallmark event, it has become synonymous with its location, which has been the same since the introduction of the festival in 1970 – the Worthy farm near Pilton, Somerset, UK. The originator of the festival, Worthy farm owner Michael Eavis, launched the event in 1970 inspired by the 'free festival' ethics of Woodstock and the impressive performance by some of the leading bands of the decade at the Bath Festival of Blues and Progressive Music held in the same year.

Since its modest beginnings in the second half of the twentieth century, Glastonbury Festival has grown considerably and demonstrated an impressive resilience in the face of a number of difficulties the organisers have encountered over the decades. It is a particularly pertinent example of the benefits of artificial abandonment of an event as a strategic tool in sustaining its longevity. Whilst there may have been some uncertainties in the first decade of the event's history, which meant that the event was suspended between 1972 and 1977 (inclusive), from 1978 onwards Glastonbury has grown steadily, as demonstrated by attendance figures outlined in Table 2.2.

Over its 30-odd-year history, there were a number of editions of the event that had been suspended. This artificial abandonment of the event was sometimes dictated by developments in the external environment, although there were also times

Table 2.2 Attendance figures for Glastonbury Festival

Year	Attendance	Year	Attendance	Year	Attendance
1970	1,500	1990	70,000	2003	150,000
1971	12,000	1991	gap year	2004	150,000
1978	500	1992	70,000	2005	153,000
1979	12,000	1993	80,000	2006	gap year
1981	18,000	1994	80,000	2007	135,000
1982	25,000	1995	80,000	2008	134,000
1983	30,000	1996	gap year	2009	135,000
1984	35,000	1997	90,000	2010	135,000
1985	40,000	1998	105,000	2011	135,000
1986	60,000	1999	100,500	2012	gap year
1987	60,000	2000	100,000	2013	135,000
1988	gap year	2001	gap year		
1989	65,000	2002	140,000		

Source: Figures compiled from Glastonbury website (www.glastonburyfestivals.co.uk), BBC News (www.bbc.co.uk) and *The Guardian* (www.guardian.co.uk).

Note: The attendance numbers identified here refer only to weekend tickets being sold for the event. Since 2007 the event has amended its ticketing structure to include 37,500 passes for staff, performers and VIPs and roughly 5,000 Sunday tickets in addition to 135,000 weekend tickets (as stated above).

when this was a conscious and strategic decision by the event's management team. In the period of 1979 to 1987 the event attendance had almost quadrupled, from the initial 12,000 to an impressive 60,000 people, which forced the organisers to take a year out in 1988 in order to regroup and address the issue of event size, which was important for the organisation and management of the event site. The gap year in 1991 was a result of disturbances experienced during the twentieth anniversary of the event in 1990, when the police confronted the travellers who were looting the emptying event site, resulting in 235 arrests and £50,000 worth of damage to property. In the early 1990s the event attendance increased to 80,000, which meant that the festival was beginning to take its toll on the natural environment, prompting the organisers to pick 1996 as a year of recovery for the event site. By 2000, the festival reached an attendance of 100,000. This was also the year in which attendance numbers started being licensed, meaning the event could not legally accept more people even though it had the potential to accommodate more. In this year, there were a number of instances of gate crashing, which led to the event organisers being fined £5,000 for breach of licensed attendance and £1,000 for noise offences. Following this, 2001 was used by the organisers to regroup and address the safety issues related to the increase in attendee numbers. By the year 2005 the festival had grown by over 50 per cent to 153,000, which again put additional strain on the organisers, both in terms of operational challenges of delivering such a large-scale event, and in terms of the impacts an event of that size had on the environment and local community, so 2006 was again picked as a recovery year for the organisers and the event site. From 2007 onwards, the licensed attendance has remained steady at roughly 135,000 people, which has provided some stability in terms of operational management and maintaining the high health and safety standards of the event. The following gap year, which was originally planned for 2011, was moved to 2012 due to the delivery of the London 2012 Olympic Games causing a serious shortage of police officers to support other events. In 2013 all of the 135,000 tickets were sold out within 1 hour and 40 minutes of being released on sale, demonstrating the value of artificial abandonment in sustaining the demand for an event.

The figures in Table 2.2 have been used to design the product life cycle graph for the event, shown in Figure 2.6.

In addition to rising attendance, Glastonbury organisers have also been mindful of the evolution of the event concept and content. What began as a small, local music festival utilising an improvised stage in an open field in the 1970s has now developed into the largest global greenfield festival, attracting 135,000 people to a semi-purpose-built location (the famous Pyramid stage has been a permanent structure since 1981 and doubles as a cowshed and animal food store for the remainder of the year). Aside from the music, the festival now also incorporates other aspects of the performing arts and is titled Glastonbury Festival of Contemporary Performing Arts.

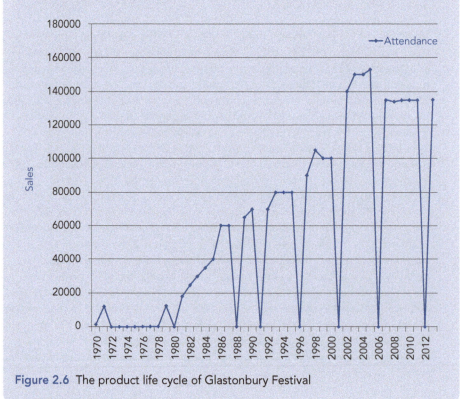

Figure 2.6 The product life cycle of Glastonbury Festival

Whilst the graph in Figure 2.6 provides an outline of the historical performance of the event, it does not offer enough relevant information that would be useful for the future management of the event. It does, however, demonstrate that facing challenges head-on and quickly and competently responding to issues arising in the process of event delivery allow for the sustained growth and financial prosperity of an event.

Case study questions

1 What do you think should be the future direction of Glastonbury Festival? How would you make it happen if you were the event manager of this event?

2 What would be the implications of increasing attendee numbers in the future? Would this require the event to be repositioned?

3 Discuss the benefits and drawbacks of artificial event abandonment in this context.

SUMMARY

This chapter has discussed the key characteristics of events as market offerings, particularly their ambiguity in terms of conforming to the rather rigid definitions of products and services. It has contextualised events within the three sectors of the economy and has offered a framework for the classification of events according to a number of different criteria, which may prove to be useful in determining the direction for the future management and marketing of the event. The impact of seasonality within the events industry has been highlighted, including the ways in which it is embedded in the nature of events. Additionally, this chapter sought to explore the applicability of the Product Life Cycle model to the events industry and has offered a number of variations of the model, dependent on the type and nature of the event being examined. Whilst there may be limitations to the usefulness of the Product Life Cycle model in the day-to-day planning and delivery of an event, the tool is nonetheless beneficial as a historical overview of the impact of management decisions on the economic sustainability of the event in question.

REVIEW QUESTIONS

1 Are events products or services? Argue your position.

2 Why is it important to have a tool for classifying events? What criteria have we identified in this chapter? What other criteria do you think might be useful to categorise events?

3 What are the three sectors in which events can be organised? Outline the benefits and drawbacks for event marketers operating within each of these.

4 Discuss the relevance of seasonality in the events industry? What are the key things event marketers need to take into consideration?

5 What is the relevance of the Product Life Cycle model in contemporary event marketing?

> ### EVENT MARKETING SCENARIO
>
> You are the owner of a small event production agency which, although small, has developed an impressive portfolio of events since its inception seven years ago. You started out as a 'one-man band' co-ordinating subcontractors, but today your agency employs 20 people and runs an average of 75 events per year, across the three sectors: private, public and non-profit. Your most lucrative client is the local government who has contracted you to run their annual jobs fair, alongside some smaller celebrations, conferences and trainings; these are currently in the early growth stage. Your non-profit work focuses on a portfolio of fundraising galas, which seem to be in the decline stage. Your commercial contracts comprise a variety of events, spanning business conferences, awards ceremonies and team building events, which bring in a reliable and steady income and most of which are in the maturity stage of the product life cycle. Your overall company profits over the past two years have been declining slightly, although the situation is not yet alarming. Map out your events on a PLC chart and discuss how you would manage your portfolio over the coming year. Which sectors would you focus on and why? Would you focus on expanding your portfolio of events, your target audiences, or both? Justify your decision by considering the conditions within your local marketing environment.

Further reading

Books

Getz, D. 2012. *Event Studies: Theory, research and policy for planned events*, 2nd Edition, Oxford: Butterworth-Heinemann
This is the second edition of the excellent comprehensive text which explores the contextualisation of events within society from an academic perspective. It provides a wealth of information that will help the reader understand how events have evolved over time, as well as how that evolution was influenced by a range of different areas, such as psychology, sociology, politics and others. It is a must-read for anyone starting out in event studies.

O'Toole, W. 2011. *Events Feasibility and Development: From strategy to operations*, Oxford: Butterworth-Heinemann
Although this book only briefly mentions the event life cycle from the concept development to the shutdown stage, it also offers some useful information about different event types within the three sectors we mention in this chapter.

Shone, A. and Parry, B. 2013. *Successful Event Management: A practical handbook*, 4th Edition, Andover: Cengage Learning, EMEA
This is a useful resource which presents events from a very practical perspective. Particularly useful are the initial chapters which contextualise events as an industry within the wider business and economic context.

Journals

Getz, D. 2008. Event tourism: Definition, evolution and research, *Tourism Management*, 29(3), pp. 403–428
This is a useful article by one of the leading authors in the field which explores the complexities of event classification and is a good starting point for an exploration of event classification.

Levitt, T. 1965. Exploit the product life cycle, *Harvard Business Review*, 43, November–December, pp. 81–94
This is the seminal work which introduces the concept of the product life cycle and should be the starting point for anyone wishing to develop an in-depth understanding of the concept.

Walle, A.H. 1994. The festival life cycle and tourism strategies: The case of the Cowboy Poetry Gathering, *Festival Management and Event Tourism*, 2, pp. 85–94
This is one of the few articles explicitly discussing the application of the product life cycle concept within the tourism and event industries.

Other resources

Berneman, C. and Petit, C. 2006. Festivals and product life cycle, in the *Proceedings of 5th International Marketing Trends Conference*, 2006, Paris–Venice: Trends Marketing Association
Whilst this paper explores the concept of the product life cycle within a very specific area of the events industry – that of cultural festivals – it nonetheless puts forward some interesting ideas in terms of how marketing can influence the extension of an event's life cycle, which is one of the key concerns for any event marketer.

Business Visits and Events Partnership www.businesstourismpartnership.com/
This is the UK's umbrella organisation representing key players in the UK business visits and events sector (trade and professional organisations, government agencies and other significant influencers). It is a useful source for exploring the dynamics between different players and the impact of the overall societal context on the development of the sector.

References

Blythe, J. 2013. *Consumer Behaviour*, 2nd Edition, London: SAGE.
Bowdin, G., Allen, J., O'Toole, W., Harris, R. and McDonnell, I. 2011. *Event Management*, 3rd Edition, Oxford: Butterworth-Heinemann.
Brassington, F. and Pettitt, S. 2003. *Principles of Marketing*, 3rd Edition, Harlow: FT Prentice Hall.
Business Visits and Events Partnership. 2014. Events are Great Britain, BVEP [Online]. Available at: www.businesstourismpartnership.com// [Accessed 1 July 2014].
Clow, K.E. and Baack, D. 2010. *Marketing Management: A customer-oriented approach*, London: SAGE.
Getz, D. 2007. *Event Studies: Theory, research and policy for planned events*, Oxford: Butterworth-Heinemann.
Getz, D. 2008. Event tourism: Definition, evolution and research, *Tourism Management*, 29(3), pp. 403–428.
Grönroos, C. 2000. *Service Management and Marketing: A customer relationship management approach*, Chichester: John Wiley & Sons.
Johnston, R. and Clark, G. 2008. *Service Operations Management: Improving service delivery*, 3rd Edition, Harlow: Pearson Education Ltd.
Kotler, P., Bowen, J. and Makens, J. 2003. *Marketing for Hospitality and Tourism*, 3rd Edition, Harlow: Pearson Education Ltd.

Levitt, T. 1965. Exploit the product life cycle, *Harvard Business Review*, 43, November–December, pp. 81–94.

McCabe, S. 2009. *Marketing Communications in Tourism and Hospitality: Concepts, strategies and cases*, Oxford: Butterworth-Heinemann.

O'Toole, W. 2011. *Events Feasibility and Development: From strategy to operations*, Oxford: Butterworth-Heinemann.

Robinson, P., Wale, D. and Dickson, G. 2010. *Events Management*, Wallingford: CABI.

Tersine, R.J. and Hummingbird, E.A. 1995. Lead-time reduction: The search for competitive advantage, *International Journal of Operations and Production Management*, 15(2), pp. 8–18.

Walle, A.H. 1994. The festival life cycle and tourism strategies: The case of the Cowboy Poetry Gathering, *Festival Management and Event Tourism*, 2, pp. 85–94.

Chapter **3**

Creating value
The marketing of the event experience

LEARNING OUTCOMES

By the end of the chapter, students should be able to:

- Explain the various emerging economies and associated theories and concepts that underpin and contribute to the concept of the experience economy

- Define the relationship between the experience economy, event experience and event marketing

- Describe the characteristics of the value chain within the events industry

- Explain the relationship between the value chain and the event experience in creating value

Create the change before it creates you

Michael Eisner (former CEO of Disney)

Introduction

This chapter provides a brief introduction to the value creation theory relevant to events. In Chapter 2 we've defined the nature and characteristics of events. We now turn our attention to how events fit within the contemporary value creation theories that have been shaping modern business thought for the past couple of decades. Grönroos (2000, pp. 195–196) emphasises the importance of a service-oriented approach to management. He highlights that, in order to really deliver value, a company has to understand:

1 Customers' perceptions of quality and value.

2 The process of creating that value.

3 Efficient and effective management of resources to achieve this value creation.

More recently, Chaffey and Ellis-Chadwick (2012) define the value proposition as the set of 'benefits or value a brand offers to customers in its products and services', whilst Kotler *et al.* (2013) emphasise the role of differentiation and positioning in the definition of value for consumers. We discuss differentiation and positioning later on in Chapter 5 of this book. For now, we turn our attention to the natural evolution of events as value-creating entities and present what exactly it is that defines value for events.

Emerging economic theories: From an agrarian to an emotion economy

In Chapter 4 we present briefly the evolution of marketing philosophies throughout the twentieth century, in which we outline the evolution from an industrial to a marketing-oriented economy. At the turn of the twenty-first century, however, two seemingly unrelated works shifted the focus from the then-dominant marketing paradigm towards a more aspirational and inspirational direction for communicating with consumers. The two works were *The Experience Economy* by Pine and Gilmore (1999) and *The Dream Society* by Danish futurist Rolf Jensen (2001).

The experience economy and the role of imagineering

Pine and Gilmore's (1999) book was the very first business management publication that actually verbalised the notion of experiences in an economic context. Although the notion of experience is nothing new – indeed, according to Boswijk *et al.* (2007), it dates all the way back to ancient Greek and Roman times – it seemed to have gone largely unnoticed and unformalised in the context of product and service creation and delivery, with the exception of Toffler's (1970) *Future Shock*, a forward-looking manifesto in which the famous futurologist anticipated the dematerialisation of the economy and within it the prominent role of experiences (Boswijk *et al.*, 2007). Interestingly, Toffler's subsequent work, in particular his article from 1990 in *Industry Week*, anticipated another extension of the experience and the key role of instant communication in the wealth creation of the twenty-first century. As we have observed over the past 20 years, the internet has become an unavoidable part of our everyday lives and is the key channel of communication, participation and co-creation – all the processes designed to deliver the emotion economy of the third millennium.

Pine and Gilmore's (1999) view of the progression of economic value is outlined in Figure 3.1.

Figure 3.1 charts the evolution of economic value over time (outlined at the top of the figure) and the dominant philosophies that have accompanied this within the business and marketing context. The agricultural economy was focused on planting, sowing, growing and turning raw commodities into goods via simple engineering processes (e.g. production of sugar or soap). The industrial age brought with it the concept of mass production and advertising developed as a tool for pushing the mass-produced products to a wide customer base. With

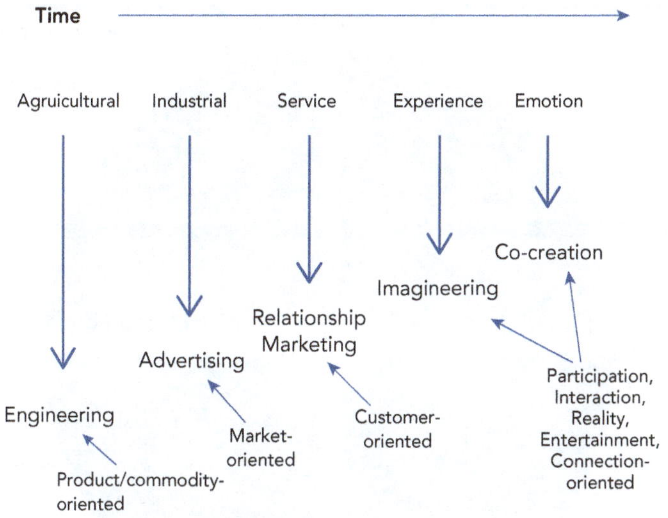

Figure 3.1 Progression of economic value
Source: Adapted from Pine and Gilmore (1999)

the proliferation of service industries, such as financial services, hospitality, tourism and others, more attention has been put on creating a quality service experience which will support good long-term relationships with consumers. However, since the mid-1990s, the role of experiences and emotions in supporting consumption of products and services has become more and more prominent. The new paradigm requires a new approach to marketing, as consumers are no longer just passively waiting for a quality service to be delivered to them – they are very much taking an active role in facilitating the creation of this service and thus notions of imagineering, participation and co-creation have emerged as vehicles of delivering this new type of value.

Pine and Gilmore (1999) framed their concept of experience within their 4E framework, in which all experiences balance between passive to active participation on one axis and between basic absorption to complete immersion on the other axis, as can be seen in Figure 3.2.

Entertainment is usually experienced passively, where the spectator has no actual impact on the 'performance'. Think of a classical music concert at London's Royal Albert Hall or a ballet performance at the New York's Metropolitan Opera House as examples of an entertaining experience.

Education is usually a result of active participation in and absorption of the material that the person is being exposed to. A good example of this would be attending a short themed conference as part of your continuous professional development (CPD) or a keynote speech at a leading industry trade show.

aEsthetics is immersive and passively enjoyed. Think of attending a gallery opening or an exhibition at the local museum.

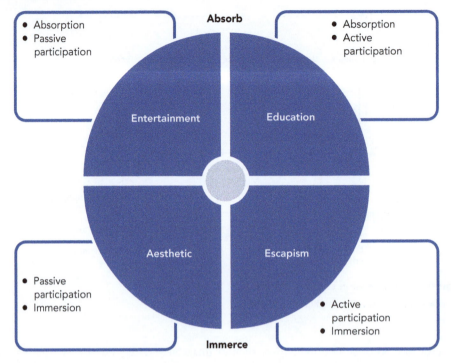

Figure 3.2 The 4E framework of the experience economy
Source: Adapted from Pine and Gilmore (1999)

Escapism is gained by being immersed in an activity in which the person actively participates and which takes him or her to 'another place'. Think of a 1920s-themed team-building session attended by a team of co-workers who take on the roles of detectives in solving a murder mystery.

Pine and Gilmore's (1999) notion of the meaningful experience is complemented well by the work of other notable authors recognising the shift in the concept of value. We've already mentioned Jensen's (2001) Dream Society, which argues the role of the emotional connection in creating six new markets:

1 The market for **adventure**.

2 The market for **love**, **belonging** and **togetherness**.

3 The **care** market.

4 The **who-am-I** market.

5 The market for **peace of mind**.

6 The market for **convictions**.

Each of these markets would be driven by stories and the emotional connections being created with their audiences. According to Jensen (2001), companies that fail to anticipate the creation of these six markets will fail to create a positive brand image, which will have a negative impact on their sales and, ultimately, their productivity. Fifteen years later and this is coming true: think of five of your favourite brands – chances are all of them will fit nicely into at least one of the markets mentioned above.

VIGNETTE 3.1 THE *DOCTOR WHO* EXPERIENCE

Doctor Who is a science-fiction drama produced by the UK's leading broadcaster, the BBC (British Broadcasting Corporation). The programme first aired in 1963, was put on hiatus in 1989 and was revived in 2005. Currently in the eighth season of its revival, the show has become an important part of British popular culture and has also earned a significant fan base outside of the UK. The programme revolves around the adventures experienced by the main character, named Doctor Who, who is a humanoid alien and travels through time in his time-machine called TARDIS in an effort to right wrongs, help people and save civilisations.

A spin-off from the original show, The Doctor Who Experience is an exhibition dedicated to the TV show, which launched at Olympia London in February 2011 and then moved to Cardiff Bay in 2013, where it is planned to remain until 2017. Although other seasonal and permanent exhibitions of the show's props, costumes and sets have been held fairly regularly ever since the first airing of the show in 1963, this most recent exhibition is the first interactive and fully immersive experience where the visitors actually get to interact with the Doctor himself. It was designed by the theme park design and installation veterans, Sarner Ltd, with the tried-and-tested key principles of visitor attractions incorporated in its design.

The exhibition begins with an immersive, timed episode within the Doctor's time machine – the TARDIS. This interactive area enables the visitors to experience their own episode of the show, being guided by the Doctor himself whilst they encounter some of the most famous and popular villains from the show's long history. This area boasts a smart use of walls, lights and video screens, as well as a moving floor simulator and a host of special effects to create a realistic feel to the activities. The 'experience' then ends with a short 3D movie in which Doctor Who takes the visitors through the Time Vortex and in the end thanks them for their participation and assistance. The exhibition then continues with a comprehensive freeflow walk-through exhibition of the show's artefacts and memorabilia gathered throughout the half century of the show.

The two aspects of the exhibition illustrate Pine and Gilmore's 4E framework in action: Entertainment, Education, aEsthetics and Escapism. However, the prominence of each of the four aspects of this experience is subject to every visitor's individual experience of the show.

For more information on the Doctor Who Experience, please visit the exhibition webpage at www.doctorwho.tv/events/doctor-who-experience/, the event's Facebook (Doctor Who Experience) and Twitter (@DW_Experience) pages.

For more information about the TV show, please visit the show webpage at www.doctorwhotv.co.uk, the show's Facebook (Doctor Who) and Twitter (@bbcdoctorwho) pages, or the show's YouTube channel (Doctor Who).

Other authors worth noting, whilst we're on the topic of experiences, are Michael J. Wolf (2003), whose work focuses on the role of entertainment in creating appealing products and services, and Davenport and Beck (2001), who somewhat oversimplify the new concept by arguing that it's all about getting attention, regardless of how it is obtained. Although less prominent than Pine and Gilmore or Jensen, the work of these authors is useful in framing the tectonic shift that is the 'experience economy'.

In 2003, Dutch academic Diane Nijs introduced the concept of imagineering, which is closely related to the creation of experiences. Dubbed 'Engineering for Imagination' (Nijs, 2003) and originally introduced by the Disney company, imagineering denotes a company-wide commitment to fantasy, exemplified in the following:

- Broader creative thought.
- Creation of values that the business shares with their target audiences.
- Creation of stories that are serialised, ongoing and continually refreshed.
- An open system in which the classic 'customer relationship management' (CRM) has evolved into active co-creation and interaction between the business/employees and consumers in the creation of a business's market offering.

Although the term 'Imagineer' is protected by the Disney company and denotes specialist staff devoted to designing experiences in Disney theme parks (and is thus not suitable for official use in a wider range of contexts), the notion of 'engineering for imagination' is very much applicable to any business in any industry and, particularly, to businesses in the tourism, hospitality and events sectors, which depend on memorability in order to create repeat business and positive word of mouth.

Similarly and around the same time as Nijs, another author noted the impact of Disney on contemporary human consumption. Bryman (2004), in his book *The Disneyization of Society*, argues that the key principles employed in Disney theme parks are increasingly infiltrating a growing number of areas of social, cultural and economic life in the twenty-first century. He identified *Disneyization* as a process with four key and distinct dimensions:

1 *Theming*, or the 'application of narrative to institutions or locations' (Bryman, 2004, p. 15), used to differentiate products, services and brands in an increasingly over-crowded marketplace, which infuses meaning into these market offerings and thus increases their appeal to consumers.

2 *Hybrid consumption*, or an amalgamation of different forms of consumption in a single location (e.g. shopping malls offering not just shops, but also restaurants, cafés and other aspects of entertainment), which is aimed at increasing the amount of money that is spent by consumers in that location and follows the 'stay longer' principle, which implies that the more services are offered, the more consumers will consume.

3 *Merchandising*, or the promotion of goods bearing copyright images and/or logos, the purpose of which is to extract further revenue from a brand image that has already attracted people. For example, think of the amount of merchandising on offer in Hard Rock Café and similarly franchised restaurant chains and similar establishments.

4 *Performative labour*, which ties into Pine and Gilmore's (1999) notion of the experience economy and which identifies work as a theatre performance, requiring workers to assume the role of an actor and display the behaviour and emotions conducive with the character of the brand they are representing. In itself, performative labour is composed of two key areas: emotional labour (i.e. workers feeling and projecting the emotions characterising the brand) and aesthetic labour (i.e. the physical appearance of employees in line with projected brand image).

VIGNETTE 3.2 ENGINEERING FOR IMAGINATION AT DISNEY

Walt Disney Imagineering is the creative and design division of the Walt Disney Company, in charge of developing and implementing new fantasies at Disney outlets, which include theme parks, resorts, hotels, attractions, cruise ships, real estate developments and regional entertainment venues worldwide. It brings together talented creative and technical professionals from all around the world whose skills help pioneer new entertainment storylines in the nearly century-old family entertainment and media enterprise. Disney Imagineers bridge the gap between science and fantasy in order to create unique and memorable experiences; they envision and then bring to life new attractions and park features on a regular basis. First introduced in 1962 and patent-protected since 1967, the coveted title is aspired to by many, but attained by only a few. Since the introduction of Imagineering, Disney has acquired 115 patents on the designs developed by Imagineers, which have been incorporated into Disney theme parks and other properties around the world. Today, Imagineers can hold a variety of roles, with a reported 140 unique role profiles ranging from illustrators, architects and engineers to writers, producers and graphic designers. As a leader in the field of fantasy fulfilment and the archetype of the Dream Society, Disney is well aware of the need to keep fresh ideas flowing. This is why in 1992 they introduced Imaginations – an annual competition open to university students aspiring to a career in imagineering, who work collaboratively on pitching their design projects to a team of judges from a variety of backgrounds. Over the years, contestants have provided interesting, fresh, out-of-the-box ideas for the development of the next chapter in the Disney story and many of them have secured and successfully completed internships and seen their work installed in Disney properties around the world.

For more information on Walt Disney Imagineering, please visit their webpages:

The Walt Disney Company – http://thewaltdisneycompany.com/.

Disney Imaginations – https://disneyimaginations.com.

Information compiled from a number of online sources.

Emotion economy and the role of co-creation

Having become more comfortable over the past decade with the notion of the consumer in the centre of the consumption experience and the need for this experience to be memorable, academics and practitioners alike are now turning to the exploration of what it is that impacts on the consumer's experience of a product, service and the event. Emotion is one of the key elements that defines us as human and, as such, is at the heart of creating a positive and memorable consumer experience. As early as the eighteenth century, philosophers of the Age of Enlightenment such as David Hume, Adam Smith and Thomas Reid believed emotions to be vital to individual and social existence. Contrary to today's popular view of the conflict between the emotional and the rational side of the individual, they perceived emotion complementary to reason (Evans, 2001) and, therefore, an integral part of the human decision-making process.

Evans (2001) identifies six basic emotions which are universal and innate: joy, distress, anger, fear, surprise and disgust. Whilst there is some debate amongst theorists about the number of basic emotions, these six, he argues, are present in every culture around the world and, therefore, the exploration of these basic emotions can help develop a broad understanding of their role in consumer decision making, which can then be generalised across age, gender, cultural and ethnic characteristics.

Jensen (2001) anticipated a time when consumers will make their purchases for emotional, non-materialistic reasons. That time is well and truly upon us. In the age when consumers buy to reflect their perceived image of self (Lindstrom, 2012), the notion of the cool, calm and rational Economic Man is but a distant memory. We discuss this in some more detail in Chapter 7. Ten years later, Layard (2011), one of the leading explorers of happiness as a method of measuring human success, foresees 'positive psychology' (i.e. psychological techniques focused on knowing and nourishing the inner self) as the obvious basis of twenty-first-century culture. It follows, then, that knowing the full range of human emotions, as well as how to evoke and manage them, will be the equivalent of hitting the jackpot for any brand and organisation in the third millennium. But how is a marketer to know what goes on inside consumers' minds (and hearts!)? The obvious answer is *co-creation*.

The idea of *co-creation* originated between 2000 and 2004 from Venkat Ramaswamy and C.K. Prahalad (Ramaswamy and Gouillart, 2010), two academics who foresaw (much like Toffler) the development of business and the future need for businesses to involve their consumers in creating value. As defined by Ramaswamy (2011, p. 195), co-creation is 'the process by which mutual value is expanded together, where value to the participating individuals is a function of their experiences, both their engagement experiences on the platform, and productive and meaningful human experiences that result'. If we recognise that events are rather limited in terms of creating impact during the event itself, it becomes a priority for most (if not all) events to extend their impact to the period in the lead up to and after the event. It is, therefore, the marketer's role to design the content that will engage event audiences throughout this process: before, during and after the event.

Events as experiences

Experience is increasingly recognised as an essential part of the leisure service delivery (Torkildsen, 2005). In that sense, the concept of experience is particularly pertinent to events. Jackson (2000, cited in Berridge, 2007) defined experience design as an integrative and inclusive activity, which should be done in co-operation with consumers. At roughly the same time, O'Sullivan and Spangler (1999, p. 120) identified the following key factors of an experience:

- The participation and involvement of the individual in the consumption.
- The state of being physically, mentally or emotionally derived through such participation.
- A change in knowledge, skill, memory or emotion derived through such experience.
- The conscious perception of having intentionally encountered, gone to or lived through an activity or event.
- An effort directed at addressing a psychological or internal need of the participant.

Figure 3.3 presents the process of experiencing, as defined by Boswijk *et al.* (2007).

The experience begins with the sensory perceptions (prompted by visual, auditory, olfactory and tactile stimuli) within a particular context (the event). These sensory perceptions evoke particular emotions, which create and colour the experience of the individual. The experience has meaning for the individual within that particular context (event) and entices the individual to create a wider meaning on the basis of it.

Getz (2007) recognises three levels of experience in the specific context of the events industry:

Basal experience, which creates an emotional reaction to a stimulus but is insufficient to be memorable.

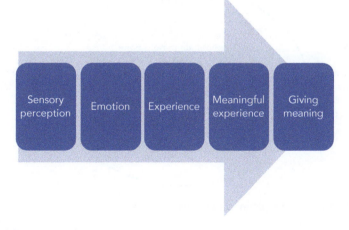

Figure 3.3 The process of experiencing
Source: Adapted from Boswijk *et al.* (2007)

Memorable experience, which creates strong emotions that can be recalled after the experience has ended.

Transformative experience, which results in attitude or behaviour changes.

If an event is to be a memorable and a transformative experience, it is vital that it is able to construct an optimal experience (Czikszentmihalyi, 1990) for its consumers (attendees). The notion of optimal experience is rooted in the Theory of Flow which posits that, in order to create the 'time out of time' (as recognised by Getz (2007) and outlined in Figure 3.4), an event must engage consumers in intense and intrinsically motivating activities. Without intrinsic motivation, a transformative experience is impossible to achieve. Whilst we discuss intrinsic motivation in much greater detail in Chapter 8, for now let us explore Czikszentmihalyi's (1990) six key elements of flow which combine challenge and skill in the creation of the experience. These are:

1 Merging of action and awareness: complete attention is on the activity in any given moment.

2 Goals are clearly defined and feedback is immediate, allowing the individual to become completely lost in the activity.

3 Complete concentration focused on the activity.

4 Paradox of control – the individual is completely in control of the environment, but not through explicit, physical control of time or space, but rather through lack of worry about the loss or lack of control.

5 Lack of self-consciousness: individual becomes one with the activity and stops worrying about themselves.

6 Time is perceived within the context and speed of the activity, rather than in the absolute terms of hours and minutes or specific times during the day (or night).

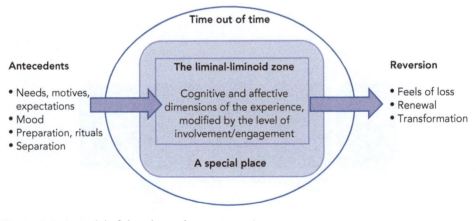

Figure 3.4 A model of the planned event experience
Source: Adapted from Getz (2007)

Whilst Czikszentmihalyi argued that people are much more likely to report having 'optimal experiences' on the job than during leisure (Pink, 2009), the notion of optimal experience is, slowly but surely, making its way into the academic literature related to leisure, tourism and events.

The value chain for events

In previous sections we've discussed the notion of events as value-adding properties. It is now time to explore how value is created in the process of the planning and delivery of events.

The supply chain is defined as a 'continuum of steps that occur in manufacturing and distribution of products that ranges from the original point of manufacture to the end user (customer)' (Tesone, 2010). The notion of the value (or supply) chain was first introduced in academic literature by Michael E. Porter in his 1985 book *Competitive Advantage: Creating and Sustaining Superior Performance*, in which he argued that value is created by the various activities in each stage of the supply chain. This value should, then, be expressed in the price of a particular good or service, consequently the final product that the consumer buys will cost considerably more than the raw materials with which the manufacturer started off the process. It is precisely this thinking that has led authors and industry practitioners to focus primarily on price when discussing the concept of value for the good part of the last twenty years. Events are a specific type of market offerings, as we've already discussed in Chapter 2, so it is important to identify how the supply chain differs in the 'production' of events, as opposed to regular products and/or services. Figure 3.5 helps us do just that.

As can be seen from Figure 3.5, the supply (value) chain for products makes a clear distinction between the various stages of adding value to a raw material. Take the example of selling bread. The production or, rather, manufacture of bread involves taking flour, yeast and water (raw materials), mixing them together at particular quantities, making dough and then baking it until bread loaves are golden brown. The baker (usually) then takes the bread to the retailers who will sell them to the general public. People will purchase bread in the store, take it home, consume it and, in that act, reap the value or 'benefits' (i.e. reducing their hunger). As Prahalad and Ramaswamy (2004) pointed out, this traditional view of the value chain means that value is largely created 'inside the firm', with the customer being outside

The supply chain for products

The supply chain for events

Figure 3.5 The value chain for events

of it, leading to very distinct roles of production and consumption. The value chain for events is somewhat simpler, yet (in a sense) more complex. The event itself is the manufacturer and the distributor of the experience and these two stages occur at the same time as the consumption of the event by the consumer. This amalgamation of production and consumption of products and services, as anticipated some time ago by du Gay (1995) and, more recently, Prahalad and Ramaswamy (2004), both simplifies and complicates things for the very same reason: the removal of the constraints that time puts on the production process, requiring each stage to be done sequentially. Whilst this can be beneficial because it creates immediacy in the interaction between the event organisers ('producers') and the attendees ('consumers'), it can also be very risky because in the event of one or more aspects of the event going wrong, there is very little that can be done to mitigate these, which can lead to the consumer having a negative experience and, subsequently, not perceiving adequate (or, indeed, any) value in the experience.

Helm and Jones (2010) provide an even more complex interpretation of co-creation as a cyclical system perpetuated by four key interlinked components: stakeholder expectations of a brand, successful brand delivery by the brand owner, customer satisfaction with this brand delivery and the level of loyalty that derives from it. The value-generating resources of the brand owner and value-seeking processes of the consumers both feed into this cycle to define a broader and more interactive approach to value creation in the twenty-first century.

Similarly to this, Ramaswamy (2011) eloquently recognises that value is not the function of service, but rather a function of the human experience. This implies that there is a limit to how the 'producer' can control the amount of value they create for the consumer and that consumer input is crucial in creating meaningful experiences that can affect consumers' brand perceptions and positive purchasing decisions. Therefore, brands and organisations should focus on the following key factors of effective co-creation (Prahalad and Ramaswamy, 2004; Frigo, 2010):

- Creating a dialogue through designing effective engagement platforms between the organisation/brand and its consumers.

- Facilitating access of consumers to products, services or brands, as well as the above-mentioned engagement platforms.

- Focusing on experiences of individuals and understanding how they evaluate the perceived risks and benefits associated with each option they are considering.

- Ensuring transparency in communicating the benefits and value of their own brand, products and services to consumers and making sure that there is an environment of trust and appreciation for the individual consumer.

Following these four key principles of co-creation will enable event organisers and, in particular, event marketers to be clear about consumer expectations of an event and to extend consumer engagement with the event from the pre- to the post-event stages. This, in turn, is likely to help create a positive and meaningful experience for the attendees, leading to greater attendee satisfaction and, more importantly, positive perceptions, increased word-of-mouth and (hopefully) increased repeat visitation. However, it is important to note that this is a rather simplistic overview of the importance of co-creation in events marketing. As we mentioned already in Chapter 2, every event is unique and, therefore, the role and importance of co-creation will be slightly different in every single case. There are a number of other factors that will need to be taken into consideration when incorporating co-creation into events marketing plans, such as the type and profile of the customer, the cultural and social setting within which the event takes place, as well as financial constraints within which the event is being organised. Still, the fact remains that co-creation should be an integral part of the event marketing campaign and, whenever possible, the event design itself, if the event is to really meet the needs and expectations of its key stakeholders.

CASE STUDY

Tough as Tough Mudder

Tough Mudder is a global series of endurance events which take place annually in 60 cities around the world, spanning North America, Europe, Australia and New Zealand. Originating in the USA in 2010, to date the event has hosted 2.5 million participants at over 200 events overall, which averages at around 10,000–15,000 attendees per event. The participants are predominantly male (around 70 per cent), with an average age of 29 years. Tough Mudder has participants tackling a 10–12 mile-long course of obstacles designed around the key human fears of fire, water, heights and electricity and are indeed so 'tough' that about 22 per cent of participants never actually get to complete the course, leading to the event being dubbed 'Probably the toughest event on the planet'. The event course mimics the ones originally designed by British Special Forces to test mental and physical strength of the soldiers and the event organisers honour this military origin of the event by supporting a variety of charities that care for and support the successful integration of wounded servicemen and women back into their communities: in America they help raise money for the Wounded Warrior Project, in Canada for Wounded Warriors Canada, in the UK for Help for Heroes and in Australia for Legacy. It is important to note, though, that these charities are not supported by direct donations from the event organisers, but rather by donations raised by individual participants.

Despite its tough name, the event is not a competitive one, but focuses on promoting team work and camaraderie: it is untimed and the main goal is for the participants to complete the course whichever way possible, making sure that all team members that started the course actually get to the finish line. For those that are not excited by the possibility of getting all muddy and conquering their deepest fears, there is always an option to volunteer at the event and help out either with the practical event delivery tasks or by simply cheering contestants on and helping raise their spirits and motivation to complete the course. In fact, Will Dean, CEO and co-founder of Tough Mudder, claims that part of the inspiration for coming up with the event concept was the need to provide people with shared experiences which will allow them to spend quality time and connect with the people that matter in their lives. The event's commitment to promoting team spirit (in whichever shape, way or form) is also evident from their pricing policy which offers a variety of rebates on attendance fees for people participating in teams, people applying to volunteer with the event, military personnel applying to attend, people raising money for the event's designated charity or people who want to attend more than one event in any given year.

Apart from the togetherness promoted within the teams participating in the events, the organisers are also committed to creating a sense of community within the event as a whole and inspiring participants to identify with the event's brand. All contestants who are registered to attend the event automatically become part of the event's community – Mudder Nation. The Mudder Nation area of the Tough Mudder website is a space for contestants who have already registered to attend one of the events and provides information on pre-event training and activities; it hosts the Mudder Nation forum and blog, as well as a photo and video gallery. The main purpose of this area is to build up excitement and anticipation in the lead-up to the event, as well as to extend the sense of achievement and community after the event has finished. Apart from offering one-way information from the organisers to the participants, the Mudder Nation forum also provides a space for contestants to share their experiences of events, obstacles, training and team journeys. Participants are also encouraged to share their own individual stories and are provided with the opportunity to look up and reconnect with people whom they had met at the event but perhaps did not have the time to exchange contact information with.

For those contestants who want to live a true Tough Mudder life and participate at events frequently, there is the even more exclusive Mudder Legion club. Mudder Legionnaires have completed at least two Tough Mudder events, have passed the Legionnaire's Loop – a special part of the obstacle course accessible only by Mudder Legionnaires, not regular contestants, and benefit from a series of other benefits. Like any other community, Mudder Nation and Mudder Legion are distinguishable with a variety of branded event gear, such as head bands and shirts.

In the 2013 event in Gerrardstown, West Virginia, the event suffered its first fatality when a contestant died conquering the Walk the Plank obstacle. Although the death was ruled accidental drowning by the coroner and no criminal charges were warranted, the organisers are currently facing a civil lawsuit brought by the mother of the deceased contestant. Despite this tragic incident, the organisers claim that every event is supported with more than 70 emergency personnel and that their events are about 20 times safer than regular triathlons. The risky obstacles and recent incidents seem to have not had a negative impact on attendance, as the event has been steadily growing and the organisers are on track to expand into Asia and the Middle East at the end of 2016. It seems that people indeed are in search for experiences, even if they are challenging, risky and unpredictable – or maybe precisely because of it.

More information about Tough Mudder events can be found on the event global webpage at www.toughmudder.com, on their Facebook (Tough Mudder) and Twitter (@ToughMudder) pages, as well as their YouTube channel (Tough Mudder).

Case study questions

1 Which of Jensen's (2001) six markets does Tough Mudder correspond to?

2 Examine the event within Pine and Gilmore's (1999) 4E framework: what are the 4Es of Tough Mudder?

3 Have a look at the event's webpage and social media pages. What kind of experience are the participants looking for when entering this challenge? How are they co-creating the experience together with the event organisers?

4 What would you say are the key elements of the Tough Mudder event brand?

5 Why do you think the popularity of this event is growing year on year, as evidenced by the number of new events launching and increasing number of participants?

SUMMARY

This chapter follows on from our discussion of the nature of events as market offerings which we presented in Chapter 2 and has looked at the notion of value in the context of event management from two key perspectives: how events help create value for consumers and how value is created within the event management process. We have provided a review of dominant theories of the new value creation over the past two decades and have presented the value creation chain for events and the importance of the amalgamation of the production and consumption stages within it. The chapter has also discussed the increasing importance of the concept of co-creation in many different aspects of consumption today and why it is particularly pertinent to events as leisure offerings. Further on in this book, in Chapters 7 and 8 we discuss the key aspects of demand for events which are shaped by attendee motivations, which are, in turn, shaped by the human nature of the individual. Co-creation, therefore, can be viewed as the proverbial bridge over troubled water, bringing together the needs of both the event audiences and event organisers, helping to create engaging experiences that successfully address these needs and create a win-win situation for all stakeholders involved.

REVIEW QUESTIONS

1 What are the key contributions of Pine and Gilmore's (1999) *The Experience Economy* and Jensen's (2001) *The Dream Society* to contemporary marketing thought?

2 What are the 4Es of experience? Think of five different events you've attended over the past couple of years and profile each of them according to this framework.

3 How does Jensen's (2001) Six Markets Model manifest itself in your life today? Think of yourself as the consumer and identify one event within each of the six markets that you have or would like to attend.

4 What are the four dimensions of Disneyisation and how do they manifest in your own immediate environment?

5 Define the term 'event experience' and discuss the key elements that would make up an optimal experience for you.

6 Provide examples of basal, memorable and transformative experience you have encountered so far.

7 What is the role of emotion in the design of event experience?

8 What is the role of co-creation in contemporary business and how does it manifest itself in the events industry?

EVENT MARKETING SCENARIO

You have been hand-picked by your city's mayor to design marketing activities for the city's brand new campaign aimed at rejuvenating the event sector within the city. The city council has approved the plans to launch three big events in the coming year: a motor show, a summer film festival and a medical congress. The city's leadership hopes that these three events can help boost tourism revenues. In order for that to happen, the events need to be well attended by tourists. As the newly appointed marketing manager for these events, explain what benefits (and potential drawbacks) a co-creation approach would have with these events. Furthermore, provide specific ideas about how these events could engage their audiences in co-creating their experience: think about co-creation of the event concept and content, as well as the co-creation of audience engagement through the marketing of the event.

Further reading

Books

Boswijk, A., Thijssen, T. and Peelen, E. 2007. *The Experience Economy: A new perspective*, Amsterdam: Pearson Education
This book provides a good overview of the evolution of the concept of the experience economy and is a good starting point for anyone wishing to explore the concept further.

Bryman, A. 2004. *The Disneyization of Society*, London: SAGE
This book provides a fascinating insight into the patterns of human consumption and discusses the impact that these patterns will have on the future of our society. It also acknowledges the role of theming and 'setting control' in influencing the customer experience and 'directing' consumption.

Evans, D. 2001. *Emotion: A very short introduction*, Oxford: Oxford University Press
This is a great introductory text to the nature and role of emotions. It provides a wealth of examples, which cement the author's arguments in a very convincing, almost irrefutable manner.

Porter, M.E. 1985. *Competitive Advantage: Creating and sustaining superior performance*, New York: Simon and Schuster
This is a seminal work by a leading author in the field and should be consulted at least once by any student on a business- and/or management-related degree programme. It provides an insight

into how value is created and helps to understand a broader range of business mechanisms, drivers and constraints, useful to marketers in all business fields.

Journals

Hirschman, E.C. and Holbrook, Morris B. 1982. Hedonic Consumption: Emerging concepts, methods and propositions, *Journal of Marketing*, 46, Summer, pp. 92–101
This seminal article has helped set the stage for current discussions of customer experience in the context of marketing.

Pine, J.B. and Gilmore, J.H. 1998. Welcome to the Experience Economy, *Harvard Business Review*, July–August 1998 Issue.
This is the seminal article that preceded Pine and Gilmore's book. It provides a concise introduction to the concept of experience and discusses briefly its four aspects – the 4Es. Students are, of course, encouraged to find the book and explore the concept more in depth.

Prahalad, C.K. and Ramaswamy, V. 2004. Co-creation experiences: The next practice in value creation, *Journal of Interactive Marketing*, 18(3), pp. 5–14
This is a good and easy-to-read article that introduces the concept of co-creation and its relevance in the twenty-first century. A good starting point for learning about co-creation.

Other resources

Imagineering Disney www.imagineeringdisney.com
This is the unofficial Disney blog maintained by people who had once worked at Disney theme parks. It provides an interesting overview of the evolution of Disney parks and the processes behind running these successful ventures.

Ellen O'Sullivan webpage www.ellenosullivan.com/index.html
Ellen O'Sullivan is a marketing author and practitioner, who co-authored the book *Experiential Marketing: Strategies for the new millennium*. Her personal page is a rich source of information about her approach to marketing and is a useful source of initial information needed to start on the journey of creating targeted and unique marketing campaigns.

Grönroos, C. 2014. Principles of Service Management 5: Value creation and co-creation, and their marketing implications. Available at www.youtube.com/watch?v=OiIYTX2tp6c
This is a great lecture by one of the leading thinkers in the field of marketing, who talks through the implications of co-creation and new ways of value creation for today's marketing practice.

References

Berridge, G. 2007. *Events Design and Experience*, Oxford: Butterworth-Heinemann.
Boswijk, A., Thijssen, T. and Peelen, E. 2007. *The Experience Economy: A new perspective*, Amsterdam: Pearson Education.
Bryman, A. (2004). *The Disneyization of Society*, London: SAGE.
Chaffey, D. and Ellis-Chadwick, F. 2012. *Digital Marketing: Strategy, implementation and practice*, 5th Edition, Harlow: Pearson Education Ltd.
Czikszentmihaly, M. 1990. *Flow: The psychology of optimal experience*, New York: Harper and Row.
Davenport, T.H. and Beck, J.C. 2001. *The Attention Economy: Understanding the new currency of business*, Accenture.
Evans, D. 2001. *Emotion: A very short introduction*, Oxford: Oxford University Press.

Frigo, M.L. 2010. How enterprises can drive new value creation, *Strategic Finance*, December 2010, pp. 17–18 and 69.

Gay, P. du 1995. *Consumption and Identity at Work*, London: SAGE.

Getz, D. 2007. *Event Studies: Theory, research and policy for planned events*, Oxford: Butterworth-Heinemann.

Grönroos, C. 2000. *Service Management and Marketing: A customer relationship management approach*, Chichester: John Wiley & Sons.

Helm, C. and Jones, R. 2010 Extending the value chain – A conceptual framework for managing the governance of co-created brand equity, *Brand Management*, 17(8), pp. 579–589.

Jensen, R. 2001 *The Dream Society: How the coming shift from information to imagination will transform your business*, New York: McGraw-Hill Education.

Kotler, P., Harris, L.C., Armstrong, G. and Piercy, N. 2013. *Principles of Marketing*, 6th European Edition, Harlow: Pearson Education Ltd.

Layard, R. 2011. *Happiness: Lessons from a new science*, 2nd Edition, London: Penguin Books.

Lindstrom, M. 2012. *Brandwashed: Tricks companies use to manipulate our minds and persuade us to buy*, London: Kogan Page.

Nijs, D. 2003. *Imagineering: Engineering for the imagination in the emotion economy*, NHTV Breda University.

O'Sullivan, E.L and Spangler, K.J. 1999. *Experience Marketing: Strategies for the new millennium*, Abingdon: Spon Press.

Pine, J.P. and Gilmore, J.H. 1999. *The Experience Economy: Work is theater & every business a stage*, Boston: Harvard Business School Press.

Pink, D.H. 2009. *Drive: The surprising truth about what motivates us*, Edinburgh: Canongate Books Ltd.

Porter, M.E. 1985. *Competitive Advantage: Creating and sustaining superior performance*, New York: Simon & Schuster.

Prahalad, C.K. and Ramaswamy, V. 2004. Co-creation experiences: The next practice in value creation, *Journal of Interactive Marketing*, 18(3), pp. 5–14.

Ramaswamy, V. 2011. It's about human experiences... and beyond: to co-creation, *Industrial Marketing Management*, 40, pp. 195–196.

Ramaswamy, V. and Gouillart, F. 2010. *The Power of Co-Creation: Build it with them to boost growth, productivity and profits*, London: Free Press.

Tesone, D.V. 2010. *Principles of Management for the Hospitality Industry*, Oxford: Elsevier Butterworth-Heinemann.

Toffler, A. 1970. *Future Shock*, New York: Amereon Ltd.

Torkildsen, G. 2005. *Leisure and Recreation Management*, 5th Edition, London: Routledge.

Wolf, M.J. 2003. *The Entertainment Economy: How mega-media forces are transforming our lives*, New York: Three Rivers Press.

Chapter

How many Ps are there?
The foundations for the Marketing Mix for events

LEARNING OUTCOMES

By the end of the chapter, students should be able to:

- Explain the various versions of the Marketing Mix concept

- Demonstrate the application of these concepts in an event context

- Appreciate the critiques of the Marketing Mix concept

- Critically evaluate why this concept is not, or is no longer, relevant to event marketing practice

> *The practice of classification, as means to reduce cognitive load, ends up more taxing when it fails to accurately reflect the underlying core.*
>
> *Siemens (2006)*

Introduction

The Marketing Mix concept has formed the foundation of every 'serious' marketing activity since the early 1960s. This chapter outlines how the concept has evolved over the past half century and discusses its role in twenty-first-century marketing. It also discusses the relevance (or lack thereof) of this concept for contemporary event marketing practice and lays the foundation for a completely new approach to event marketing which we discuss in detail in Chapter 14.

Dominant marketing philosophies

In Chapter 3 we discussed the evolution of society from the agrarian to the emotion economy. These developments were accompanied by a shift in how products and services were exchanged for money in the marketplace, in which different aspects of the process were emphasised. Table 4.1 outlines the dominant marketing philosophies that have shaped marketing over time.

Over the period of a couple of hundred years, the underlying drivers of marketing have changed considerably. At the turn of the twentieth century, companies had focused on increasing their efficiency in the production and distribution of their products (*production concept*). This meant that products were fairly uniform, but widely available, and the company that managed to place its product in the most outlets in the market enjoyed the biggest profits and the largest market share. This, however, left a gap in the market, as consumers were becoming increasingly bored with always seeing the same types of products on offer and so the *product concept* emerged. By emphasising product quality and features, companies brought variety to the market, which meant that they could define a slightly higher price and enjoy larger profits than those that utilised the production concept. With a large number of products satisfying similar consumer needs, but differing in quality and features, came the need to actively push the products to consumers in order to meet the sales targets that would create profits for the company. This led to the rise of the *selling concept*. Consumers were being increasingly bombarded with sales pitches, which led them to actively ignore aggressive sales efforts by companies' sales staff. Hence, the need arose for the creation of products that truly satisfied the needs, wants and desires of consumers. Companies started utilising a variety of market research methods to understand these needs, wants and desires, so that they could design products that will meet consumers' expectations. This is known as the *marketing concept*, which has dominated contemporary marketing practice for the large part of the past fifty years. However, at the beginning of the twenty-first century additional considerations are being put before the marketers. Consumers are becoming more and more conscious of the impact of production and consumption on the environment and society as a whole and these issues of sustainability have come to the forefront of business decision making. Today it is, thus, imperative that these are taken into consideration by companies and this forms the basis of *the societal marketing concept*. Companies are no longer just product or service providers, but are guardians of consumers and society and, as such, need to incorporate ethics and sustainability into both their production and their marketing practices.

With the rise of societal marketing the nature of the marketing game is changing: focus is shifting from the economic balance to the balance of wellbeing in consumption and marketing activities. Customers are no longer interested only in their individual benefits from using particular products or services but are very much viewing consumption of any sort in its societal context, which helps shape their buying decisions. Kotler *et al.* (2010) refer to this as 'the human spirit'. Any company that wants to survive in the twenty-first-century marketplace must develop a holistic understanding of how customers operate in their societal context and what triggers and influences their consumption patterns, as well as how they relate to each other and not just to the product/service or its providers. This implies a thorough understanding of a company's network of stakeholders and a strong emphasis on their effective management. The above is particularly important for events which depend on successful and effective relationships with a wide variety of stakeholders in their planning and delivery.

Table 4.1 Dominant marketing philosophies

	Production concept	Product concept	Selling concept	Marketing concept	Societal marketing concept
Basic assumptions	Consumers favour products that are widely available and highly affordable	Consumers value quality, performance and features of a product and these are primary purchase drivers	Consumers are reluctant to purchase and need encouragement	Consumers are not necessarily price driven, but are looking for products and services that best fit their individual needs	Consumer characteristics need to be recognised, but their welfare needs to be addressed as well
Management response/what creates the competitive edge	Increase production and distribution efficiency to make products widely available (increases likelihood that consumers will buy)	Continuous product improvements which add value to the product in the eyes of the consumer	Large-scale selling and promotion efforts ('sell what you make')	Creating products and services that satisfy the needs and wants of the target consumer segments and marketing these in a targeted way	Know consumer wants and needs better than they do themselves and deliver customer satisfaction more effectively and efficiently than the competitors, whilst protecting the overall wellbeing of the consumers and society as a whole

Source: Adapted from Brassington and Pettitt (2003) and Kotler *et al.* (2005)

The marketing mix

The marketing mix has formed the basis of marketing planning and decision making since it was first introduced in the 1960s by Borden (1964) and McCarthy (1964, cited in Bennett, 1997 and Rafiq and Ahmed, 1995). Stemming from the idea of the marketer as the 'mixer of ingredients' (Grönroos, 1997; Rosenbloom and Dimitrova, 2011; Rafiq and Ahmed, 1995), it defines the main elements required for the successful marketing of products to consumers. The main idea behind the concept is that the organisation (or, rather, the marketer) is able to manipulate a variety of elements in order to maximise the profits made from the sales of its products and/or services to its target customers. It focuses on identifying the 'ideal' combination of characteristics that will guarantee a product or service a lead position in the marketplace.

Below we explore in detail two of the most prominent Marketing Mix concepts that have dominated marketing literature in the past several decades – the famous 4Ps and 7Ps.

The 4Ps (Borden, 1964; McCarthy, 1964)

Although the discussion around successfully marketing products had emerged in the 1940s, it was Professor E.J. McCarthy who first coined the term 'marketing mix' in the 1960s. He defined the now proverbial 4Ps as a 'combination of all the factors at a marketing manager's command to satisfy the target market' (McCarthy, 1964). Originally, the concept was envisaged to facilitate the marketing of products in an increasingly competitive environment which evolved from the strong economic development post-World War II. The idea was that each particular product would have a unique combination of characteristics, which would make it distinctive in the marketplace and would, thus, support its sales by enabling marketing plans to be successfully executed in practice. The 4Ps, now also known as the 'original', the 'traditional' or the 'classic' marketing mix, encompass the following elements:

Product denotes the 'bundle' of benefits that the customer receives by buying the product. This includes product features, branding, packaging and the after-sales service.

Price is the total price a customer will pay for using the product. Apart from the actual financial cost of buying the product (i.e. actual product price), the element of price also includes:

- the cost of effort in buying the product and getting it home (time spent going to the shop, travel costs associated with it)
- the time needed to learn how to use the product
- the cost of disposing of predecessor product
- incentives
- competitiveness
- opportunity cost of using alternative products to satisfy customer needs.

Thus, the P for price actually represents the value a customer receives for the money they spend on purchasing the product.

Place represents the location in which the 'exchange' between the producer and the customer takes place. Back in the 1960s this would have been a retail store, although today this could be anything from placing an order by mail with a catalogue company to ordering items online (e.g. through Amazon, eBay and similar retail sites), or buying things in the Sunday market. Today, factors such as access to the target market, channel structure, retailer image and logistics need to be considered in order to adequately define the P for place for events.

Promotion encompasses the tools used for getting the message about the product to the target customers. Also known as the marketing communications mix (or promotions mix), this element of the marketing mix traditionally included a combination of advertising, sales promotion, sales management, public relations and direct marketing (Brassington and Pettitt, 2003). Today, however, this particular P includes a number of new marketing strategies and tactics, which are discussed more in detail in Chapters 9–12.

The 'traditional' marketing mix, as it is known in contemporary marketing literature, is a much contested concept. With the evolution of the economy, from products, towards services, then knowledge and, more recently, experiences and emotions, the old conceptual frameworks are struggling to fit with the new market propositions. So let's have a look at some of the more recent Marketing Mix concepts that have appeared over the past couple of decades.

The 7Ps (Booms and Bitner, 1982)

The concept of the 7Ps expands on the traditional 4Ps by adding the variables of people, process and physical evidence. It has been developed for use in the service economy, in which McCarthy's four Ps were not able to adequately describe the market propositions of services. Some authors (see: Berry, 1984, or Lovelock, 1979, both cited in Rafiq and Ahmed, 1995) highlight the inherent nature of services as being intangible, perishable, heterogeneous and inseparable. The additional three Ps are thus introduced so that marketers can overcome these inherent characteristics of services and make sure they are effectively and efficiently delivered to the target customers. So how do these additional Ps formalise in the marketing of services?

People are vital in delivering any type of service offering. The level of customer satisfaction with a service is normally dictated by the quality of the interaction between the service provider and the customer. As such, a company's employee is crucial in creating the company's brand image in the eyes of the customer. This is why it is vital that companies invest in their front-of-house employees to make sure they are reflecting the nature of the corporate brand and are demonstrating superior customer service.

Process refers to the actual 'production' and 'consumption' of a service, which happens 'live' (in real time). Services are unique in that the production and consumption happen simultaneously (Rafiq and Ahmed, 1995) – without the production of a service, there would be no consumption and vice versa. Both the service provider and the consumer need to be in the same space (although not necessarily a physical one) at the same point in time for the service to be delivered and consumed. Provision of products, on the other hand, is more sequential: they are made on a factory production line, then distributed via various wholesale and retail outlets to consumers who purchase, and subsequently use, those products at a different point in time and (most often) at a different location to where they were first purchased. Whilst with products consistency is fairly easy to accomplish in terms of achieving a certain standard of production or a uniform appearance through product packaging, streamlining the service process can be more of a challenge. It is crucial in this process that there are benchmarks against which the process can be evaluated to make sure that customers using the same service at different points in time and provided by different employees are able to experience a similar (if not the same) level and quality of customer service.

Physical Evidence denotes the 'lasting proof' that the service has happened. This might be a building in which the service took place, the staff uniforms of the people who have served the customer, or other physical representations of the service (e.g. purchasing contracts being signed, receipts given out, flyers or brochures with information about the service, various merchandising items purchased representing a lasting memory, etc.). The role of physical evidence is to physically frame the service interaction and thus provide evidence of service delivery at a particular point in time.

The additional three Ps outlined above were intended to frame the provision of services as inherently variable market offerings. Perceptions of service quality and overall customer satisfaction largely depend on these three components. It thus proves crucial to invest in training programmes and streamlining and standardisation of the service processes in order to ensure the consistency of outcome in each occasion in which the service is being delivered.

VIGNETTE 4.1

The 7Ps of the 2012 *Titanic* Memorial Cruise and *Titanic* Anniversary Cruise

On 10 April 1912, the RMS *Titanic* sailed from the port of Southampton, UK, on her maiden voyage towards New York City, USA. At the time, *Titanic* was the most opulent and luxurious ocean liner, leading the way in comfort and speed in overseas travel. Five days after setting sail, in the early morning of 15 April 1912, *Titanic* had sunk and taken the lives of over 1,500 of its passengers.

One hundred years later, on 8 April 2012, Miles Morgan Travel organised two cruises to commemorate one of the most famous maritime disasters of all time. The MS *Balmoral* set off to retrace *Titanic*'s original route to New York via Cherbourg (France) and Cobh (County Cork, Ireland) carrying 1,309 passengers, some of whom were family members of passengers who had lost their lives in the 1912 disaster. Two days afterwards, on the other side of the Atlantic, in New York, the Azarmara Journey set sail on a round-trip journey to Southampton, via Halifax (Nova Scotia) – the resting place of hundreds of victims who had died aboard the *Titanic* and whose bodies were discovered and brought back to land in the aftermath of the disaster.

Table 4.2 The 7Ps of the *Titanic* Memorial Cruises

Product	A 12-day cruise event commemorating the loss of 1,502 lives aboard the *Titanic* in April 1912. The cruise included the memorial service at the *Titanic* wreck site and a series of lectures and key note speeches delivered by historians and family members of the *Titanic* victims and survivors.

Price	Tickets for the cruise event reportedly cost between £2,799 and £5,995.
Place	Cruise started off in Southampton and roughly retraced *Titanic*'s original route to New York via Cobh (County Cork, Ireland) and Halifax (Nova Scotia).
Promotion	The cruise was promoted via a variety of channels: Printed press – news reports and paid adverts appeared in the leading UK media – The Times, The Telegraph and the Daily Mail to name only a few. Television – BBC crew was on board the Balmoral filming and reporting from the event and a short documentary was produced after the event, whilst Azarmara Journey hosted the crews of CNN and ITN. Social media – Facebook and Twitter were also used to engage the target audiences, namely the people taking the cruise.
People	The people comprised the ship crew, passengers and members of the press. The passengers included people related to the original *Titanic* victims and survivors, as well as historians and teachers.
Process	The process entails everything that happened aboard these ships – from the regular day-to-day operations of the ships, to the daily agenda of sessions and keynote speeches and evening meals with entertainment. A specific feature of the process for these two events included the memorial ceremony at Southampton dockside and an on-board memorial service above the *Titanic* wreck site.
Physical Evidence	The physical evidence includes the ships themselves and the authentic internal decoration of the cabins, the period costumes the majority of the passengers wore aboard the ships, the tickets and other memorabilia sold, as well as the news reports and the BBC documentary, which have captured the essence of the event for future generations.

Over the years a vast number of different authors have identified the elements of the marketing mix in different sectors and organisational contexts. Table 4.3 provides an overview of the dominant generic marketing mix paradigms of the past half century.

As can be seen from the table, the Marketing Mix concept has been adapted in a number of ways since it was first introduced, largely due to the fact that the original 4P concept was very inflexible and did not appropriately reflect the nature of marketing as a business function in various contexts (Rafiq and Ahmed, 1995). Marketing, as a dynamic and interactive element which requires a two-way communication between the product/service provider and its customers, was very difficult to frame within an overly simplistic and fragmented framework of the 4Ps. None of the 4Ps actually indicate any kind of process that would drive or even support this communication and so each author tweaked the original concept by introducing additional Ps that would (in their view) adequately frame the product/service offering in their

Table 4.3 Outline of generic Marketing Mix concepts

4Ps (McCarthy, 1964)	5Ps (Judd, 1987)	6Ps (Kotler, 1984)	7Ps (Booms and Bitner, 1981)	8Ps (Goldsmith, 1999)	15Ps (Baumgartner, 1991)
Product	Product	Product	Product	Product	Product/service
Price	Price	Price	Price	Price	Price
Place	Place	Place	Place	Place	Place
Promotion	Promotion	Promotion	Promotion	Promotion	Promotion
	People	Political power	People	Personnel	People
		Public opinion formation	Process	Physical Assets	Politics
			Physical evidence	Procedures	Public relations
				Personalisation	Probe
					Partition
					Prioritise
					Position
					Profit
					Plan
					Performance
					Positive implementations

Source: Adapted from Gummeson (1994), Goi (2009) and Rafiq and Ahmed (1995)

respective contexts. The result, as can be seen in Table 4.3, is an explosion of Ps which were introduced as each particular author saw fit. In an attempt to simplify things, Rafiq and Ahmed (1995) call for the use of the 7Ps as a generic marketing mix tool which would fit both products and services, arguing that with any product being offered in the market there are complementary services being offered with it and vice versa. Currently no unanimity exists amongst marketers as to what is the 'best' marketing mix and it is unlikely that any such thing will ever be defined. In a world of constant and rapid change, it is each marketer's individual decision to use one (or more) of the frameworks currently offered in the literature.

So we've covered products and services, but how does the marketing mix apply to events?

The marketing mix for events

Arguably, the marketing mix for events is closer to that of service marketing than that of the marketing of products, although it is not exactly the same as either of these. Events represent an amalgamation of products and services, and as such it is rather difficult to pigeonhole their marketing in the currently dominant frameworks of the 4Ps and the 7Ps. Moreover, events are largely defined by their experiential component, which further complicates things. The following section provides an outline of concepts presented by a variety of recognised event management authors and discusses their relevance and ease of application in practice.

9Ps (Getz, 2005)

Product refers to the event itself.

Place includes the location and setting of the event itself, the atmosphere and destination features. Additionally, this P refers to the distribution of event products.

Programming or 'creating targeted benefits'. Event programme should be unique and attractive, combining various 'elements of style' which appeal to the target audiences.

People include staff and volunteers as essential ingredients in making the event a success. The notion of event people as the event 'cast' which 'acts' the event gives rise to the need for internal marketing (further discussed in subsequent chapters). This P also refers to the customers (event participants) without which an event would not exist.

Partnerships include joint business and marketing initiatives between the event organisers and other entities, such as tourist organisations, government agencies and private companies. These partnerships can be utilised in facilitating event delivery (in view of providing much-needed financial resources or providing value in kind), or event promotion.

Promotion refers to the marketing communications mix (a combination of strategies and tactics utilised to promote the event and encourage target audiences to attend).

Packaging and distribution refers to defining (or framing) the event experience in such a way that the target customers will say 'yes' to the actual market proposition (i.e. participating in the event). It involves attractive pricing, maximising convenience and adding value, including a package of additional benefits where possible (e.g. event plus accommodation bundle, or transport being included in the price of the event ticket).

Much of this refers to the event's ticketing policy and ticket distribution, rather than to the delivery of the actual event or the remainder of its marketing activities.

Price includes cost of ticket, cost of space, cost of time, travel and lost opportunities (i.e. other activities that the customer could have been doing/paying for instead of participating in the event).

Positioning and branding involve establishing and maintaining the desired image relative to competitor events and other attractions that are competing for participant's free time and money.

10Ps (Allen *et al.*, 2010)

Product experience represents the core service the event offers. For example, with a music festival this would be entertainment and with a conference it could be education and/or networking.

Programming emphasises different components of the event programme, their quality and/or style. This element focuses on identifying what experiences the organisers are providing for participants. Programming for a small local community art fair attracting a couple of hundred people will be completely different (both in scale and scope) to the programming for a large music festival attracting hundreds of thousands of attendees.

Packaging refers to the mix of opportunities offered within the event itself, as well as how the value is leveraged with additional external offerings. For example, people attending a theatre performance in the West End can book the ticket only, but they may also have the option of buying a package deal which includes an evening meal in a local restaurant, an overnight stay in a local hotel or a weekend mini-break bundle of transport, accommodation and entry to some of the local attractions in addition to the event ticket price.

Place denotes not only the location of event delivery, but also the mix of channels used for the distribution of event tickets. In that sense, the element of place within this marketing mix model amalgamates the point of distribution and consumption of the event by its target audiences.

Physical setting refers to the venue at which the event is taking place, as well as its theming and decorations that help to shape the participant experience at the event.

Processes outline the relevance of a variety of ingrained activities that support the event planning, delivery and evaluation. The processes can be classified according to the time frame within which they take place into pre-event phase, event phase and post-event phase.

People involved with the event are many and varied. They will normally include 'the cast' – hosts, including event organisers, staff and volunteers – event attendees (guests) and suppliers of products and (particularly) services for the event.

Partnerships include a variety of stakeholder relationships such as those between the event and its sponsors, suppliers or the media.

Price encompasses the cost of attending the event, but also the value of experiencing the event.

Promotion refers to the integrated marketing communications that encompass a strategic choice of media channels and messages which will help build relationships with the event's target markets and audiences.

4Ps (Raj *et al.*, 2009)

Raj *et al.* (2009) return to the basics and reproduce McCarthy's 4Ps (product, price, place and promotion) in the context of events, with a very brief explanation of each. They argue that the 4Ps enable the marketers to control the characteristics of the event offering to fit with their chosen target audiences; however, they do not expand on this in great detail.

8Ps (Bowdin *et al.*, 2011)

Bowdin *et al.* (2011) talk about events as 'service experiences' (p. 368), echoing Pine and Gilmore's (1999) ideas of engaging and immersing experiences as the basis of event design. They refer to Getz's (2005) framework in their exploration of the marketing mix for events, which they adapted into yet another set of Ps – the 8Ps:

Product experience

Place

Programming

People

Partnerships

Packaging (including the distribution of event tickets)

Price

Promotion (marketing communications)

From the examples above, it is quite clear that, just like with the marketing mix for products and services, there is little unanimity on what constitutes the 'standard' marketing mix for events. Different authors approach the topic from different angles and prefer to use varying selections of Ps in order to frame the event market offering. It is thus needed to re-evaluate the relevance of the Marketing Mix concept in the context of events marketing and perhaps identify an alternative framework that would be better suited to the amorphous nature of events. Chapter 14 presents a model which, rather than move completely away from the concept of the Marketing Mix, reshapes its elements into (what feels like) a more natural, fluid and dynamic framework for events marketing.

Table 4.4 Marketing Mix concepts for (event) experience

4Ps (O'Sullivan and Spangler, 1998)	9Ps (Getz, 2005)	10Ps (Allen et al., 2010)	4Ps (Raj et al., 2009)	8Ps (Bowdin et al., 2011)
Parameters of the event experience	Product	Product experience	Product	Product experience
People	Price	Price	Price	Programming
Peripherals	Place	Place	Place	Packaging
Per-info-com	Promotions	Promotion	Promotion	Price
	People	People		Place
	Programming	Programming		Promotion
	Packaging and distribution	Packaging		People
	Partnerships	Partnerships		Partnerships
	Positioning and branding	Physical setting		
		Processes		

VIGNETTE 4.2

Levels of product – Yahoo! Wireless Festival

As we have seen so far, every model of the marketing mix we have mentioned so far includes the P for product. In the marketing literature a variety of authors refer to different levels of product in order to get around the intrinsic inflexibility of the Marketing Mix concept. This is particularly true for the marketing mix models that refer to services, rather than physical products. Figure 4.1 identifies the levels of product for the Yahoo! Wireless Festival 2013.

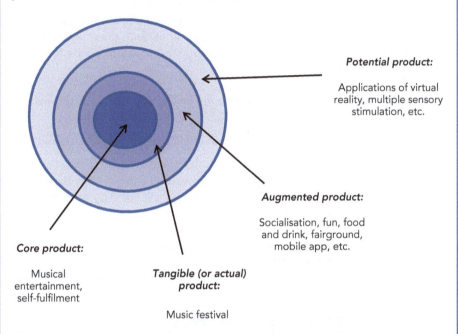

Potential product:

Applications of virtual reality, multiple sensory stimulation, etc.

Augmented product:

Socialisation, fun, food and drink, fairground, mobile app, etc.

Core product:

Musical entertainment, self-fulfilment

Tangible (or actual) product:

Music festival

Figure 4.1 Levels of product for the Yahoo! Wireless Festival 2013
Source: Adapted from the work of Brassington and Pettitt (2003)

The core product defines the underlying need that is being fulfilled by that particular product. For the attendees coming to listen to the festival line-up, the core product can be defined as musical entertainment. For the performers, on the other hand, the core product denotes self-fulfilment.

The tangible (or actual) product is what is actually being sold, the event itself, in its format and content. In this case, it is a music festival.

The augmented product outlines the added benefits that the event attendees and performers get from being present at the event. For attendees these include food and drink stalls, fairground with rides, souvenir and other merchandise outlets, lockers for storing valuable items, cash machines for easy access to money, VIP area for top-of-the-range ticket holders, brand areas (e.g. Red Bull, Tuborg,

Vodafone) and generally the ability to socialise and have fun with friends and meet new people. For performers, the augmented product includes the ability to network with other artists, producers and tour managers in the backstage area, as well as the PR and increased public profile that will be generated by their performance at the festival. Additional features that shape the augmented product in this case are also the location in which the event is taking place – the newly opened Queen Elizabeth Olympic Park, the location of the London 2012 Summer Olympic Games, as well as the mobile phone app which allows the attendees to always have the most up-to-date information about what is happening at the event and can follow the news from the event in real time.

The potential product indicates how this festival could be developed further in the future, by incorporating a variety of techniques to enhance the attendee and performer experience. For example, the organisers could incorporate the following features:

- Holograms on and off stage to create the feeling of a virtual reality (similar to what was done at the Coachella 2012 festival in the United States).

- Use of multiple sensory stimulation (not just audio and visual) to expand the attendee experience.

- Develop opportunities for members of the audience to get to meet their music idols in person or perform with them on stage – this could be done in the form of a pre-event competition, or similar.

More information about the Yahoo! Wireless Festival can be found on the festival website at www.wirelessfestival.co.uk.

Criticism of the Marketing Mix concept

Despite the fact that the marketing mix has dominated marketing research and literature since its inception, there have been a number of criticisms highlighted over the years. Unfortunately, these are severely under-represented in contemporary marketing literature and have struggled to gain foothold and build a strong following in mainstream marketing. As a result, the average student will most probably be largely unfamiliar with these critiques. It is worth, however, highlighting some of the main drawbacks that have so far been attributed to the Marketing Mix concept.

The following points have been raised by a number of different authors (see: Grönroos, 1997; Gummesson, 1994; Rafiq and Ahmed, 1995; and/or Bennett, 1997):

Restrictiveness and inflexibility – the model is not adaptable to all marketing situations and thus there are a number of industries and companies in which it cannot be used (Grönroos, 1997). This has influenced the appearance of a wide variety of extended marketing mix models that have been introduced over the past 30 to 40 years, some of which we have presented earlier in this chapter.

The model is static – it outlines four broad components of a marketing strategy, but it neither explains on what basis those components have been chosen, nor outlines how these components interact with each other. More specifically, there is no reference made by any of the authors to what kinds of results that interaction can produce for the organisation that uses the concept. Some authors have taken it upon themselves to elaborate on the dynamism of the model by linking it to the processes of market research, segmentation, targeting and positioning (see Brassington and Pettitt, 2003 and Gummesson, 1994), but these are not really integrated within the model as such. Gummesson (1994) thus sees scope for a shift in which the elements of the marketing mix stop being the founding parameters of marketing to becoming contributing parameters to relationships, networks and interactions – a new marketing paradigm that has dominated the marketing scene for the past decade (for a more detailed overview of relationship marketing see authors such as Christopher *et al.*, 2002, Gummeson, 2008, or Egan, 2011).

The model does not fit with the nature of the marketing concept – earlier in this chapter we've identified the marketing concept as one in which companies define the needs and wants of their target consumer groups and design products or services that best fit those needs. The marketing mix as a conceptual model focuses largely on the supply side and not the demand side of the market (Rosenbloom and Dimitrova, 2011), focusing on what companies can 'do' to consumers, rather than identifying consumer needs and being creative about how those needs can be fulfilled by the company's innovation in product or service delivery. This makes the model fit better with the production or product concepts (Grönroos, 1997), also mentioned earlier in the chapter. The current shift towards societal marketing and appealing to the human spirit (Kotler *et al.*, 2010) further emphasises the inadequacy of the Marketing Mix concept and opens up a whole new debate about how to frame the characteristics of an organisation's market offering in a way that is appealing and inspiring for consumers to action their purchase of a product or a service.

Trying to frame the ephemeral nature of events within the highly restrictive Marketing Mix concept is both challenging and unwise. It is challenging because there are very few elements of an event that will fit neatly into just one P and unwise because the concept itself does little to accurately capture the essence of what an event is in the eyes of the target customers. If marketing in the twenty-first century is all about consumers' needs and wants being met through societal marketing, then there is a pressing need for a model that is more flexible, adaptable and dynamic. In the age of increasing fragmentation of markets and constant innovation in terms of what companies can offer to the consumers, focus is shifting from defining products or services (or even events) to defining value propositions (Gummeson, 2008). Before embarking on any marketing activity whatsoever, it is essential that an event's value proposition accurately represents the benefits consumers will receive and is able to successfully meet their expectations. This notion of event value and other relevant elements of the new marketing framework for events is discussed in depth in Chapter 14 of this book.

2012 SUP 11-City Tour, The Netherlands

SUP 11-City Tour is a stand up paddle surfing competition that takes place annually at the beginning of September in the Dutch province of Friesland. The event is a five-day 136-mile challenge where competitors (both male and female) paddle the local waterways in an attempt to not only discover who is the best, the fastest and the fittest, but to also get familiar with the region from an unusual perspective – the water. The weather conditions, which can range from beautifully clear and sunny, to stormy, windy and freezing, add an unknown element to the overall event experience and can seriously test even the most prepared and most committed of competitors.

Stand up paddling as a sport was invented in Hawaii in the 1960s, but it hadn't become widely popular until the early 2000s, when a host of professional athletes and a number of celebrities helped it become the fastest growing water sport in the world. The SUP 11-City Tour event was initiated in 2009 by Anne-Marie Reichmann, a Dutch professional water sports athlete, who discovered the sport a year previously in Hawaii. The event's route follows the original route of the better-known 'Eleven City Tour' ice-skating competition, starting and finishing at Leeuwarden and passing through Sneek, Ijlst, Sloten, Stavoren, Hindeloopen, Workum, Bolsward, Harlingen, Franeker and Dokkum.

SUP 11-City Tour brings together both professional and amateur stand up paddlers from around the world. In its first year, 2009, only 23 national and international athletes were invited to compete in the event. In 2012, the event brought together over 100 participants, both professionals and amateurs. By this time the event had also expanded and now offers solo and team competitions for both men and women, senior and junior athletes, as well as special one-day challenges open to all competitors regardless of their level of fitness. Individual competitors and teams pay an entry fee in the range of €85 to €500, depending on the category they are enrolling into. However, the event is free for spectators who are there just to watch or support the competitors.

The event begins with competitor enrolment and a prologue through Leeuwarden in fancy dress on day zero and finishes with a trophy awards ceremony on day five. In between, the event is split into five consecutive stages lasting one day each, with resting points in Sneek and Stavoren, en route between Bolsward and Harlingen, before Bartlhiem and in the village of Gytsjerk. Event sites are organised in each of these locations around the waterways used on the route of the event and each site offers a variety of services, including food and drink, refreshments and power drinks, stamping points, house boats for participants' overnight accommodation, tents for general event logistics and evening entertainment, etc.

One of the traditions of the event is collecting stamps as proof of completion of each of the stages of the event. Once they complete a particular stage of the competition and reach the relevant rest location, the competitors need to collect a stamp from specifically dedicated spaces at the event sites where the event staff can confirm that they have indeed completed that particular stage of the challenge. 'Stamping', as it is known, entails ringing a bell and shouting out one's name and number for registration purposes. Once this has been done, the competitor is registered by the event staff as having completed the stage. Collecting all the five stamps enables the competitors to prove that they have completed the entire 136 miles of the route in order to be awarded their very own SUP 11-City cross: the medal and proof of completion. Winners of the challenge, both male and female, are awarded prize money and teams are awarded a team trophy which is treasured for a year and then passed on to the next winning team in the following year.

The event is sponsored by a number of high-profile organisations, which include (amongst others): the Friesland provincial administration, FrieseVloot (a cooperative of traditional sailing ships), Greenpeace, World Paddle Association, equipment producers such as Starboard, Naish, DaKine, Von Orange and Sensoboard, as well as the influential water sports media such as SUP Magazine, Paddle Surfmagazine and Stand Up Magazine. Some of these sponsors hold open workshops on the event site for people who wish to learn more about the sport or try out new equipment. This allows the companies to get directly in contact with their current and potential consumers and engage them in an interactive way, thus raising their brand awareness amongst their target market. Being a niche event, SUP 11-City Tour focuses its marketing efforts on specialised sports media, as well as the digital platforms of its own webpage, Facebook, Twitter and YouTube accounts for reaching its professional and amateur competitors. The fact that the founder, Anne-Marie Reichmann, was one of the leading female water sports athletes and champions for over a decade, certainly helps in giving credibility to the event brand and helps to reach those niche target audiences. The conversations on Facebook and Twitter indicate a tight-knit community of people who have met at the event and stay in touch in between different editions of the event. The engagement and communication on these platforms is strong throughout the year, not just in the immediate lead up to the event itself. The local TV and print media, as well as word of mouth, posters and flyers, are particularly important in raising awareness within the 11 cities that make up the competition route and attracting spectators from the local areas to attend the event and show their support for the competitors.

More information about this event can be found at http://sup11citytour.com/ and the event's Facebook (www.facebook.com/sup11citytour?fref=ts) and Twitter (@SUP11CityTour) pages.

Case study questions

1 Apply the various Marketing Mix concepts covered in this chapter on this case study. Which one do you think is best suited for this event and why?

2 Are there any alternative Marketing Mix concepts you would prefer to apply on this case study? If so, which ones? Why do you think they are appropriate?

3 Who are, in your opinion, the target market(s) for this event? Referring back to the marketing concept, what kinds of needs and wants of the target customers do you think this event satisfies?

4 What do you think are the key characteristics of this event that should be emphasised in its marketing campaign? What should be the basis of its marketing approach?

SUMMARY

The chapter has introduced the evolution of the dominant marketing philosophies and their role in business today. In the age of marketing (and particularly societal marketing) orientation, it has never been more important to truly understand an organisation's target audiences and their underlying needs, wants and desires. This chapter has also looked at the role and relevance of the currently dominant marketing mix paradigms that drive the marketing activities of products and services in the twenty-first century and concluded that a shift is needed in how marketing is viewed and executed. The current Marketing Mix concepts are too static and too fragmented to be able to accurately reflect the subtle (and sometimes not-so-subtle) relationships between product/service providers and their customers. The situation is even more complicated with events due to their ephemeral and amorphic nature. This is why it is essential that a new framework is developed that will more accurately reflect the nature of event market offerings and help define a blended approach to defining the elements of marketing strategy essential for business success. The new model is presented in detail in Chapter 14, but before we get there, we first need to explore the context for the management of marketing for events – in Chapter 5 we discuss the environment, positioning and differentiation for events.

REVIEW QUESTIONS

1 What is your understanding of the concept of the Marketing Mix? How would you define it?

2 Identify and explain the main components of a marketing mix.

3 Think of a product, a service and an event. Apply the Marketing Mix concepts discussed in the chapter on these examples. How do these concepts fit with the nature of the product/service/event you have chosen?

4 What alternatives to the concept of the Marketing Mix could you put forward for defining marketing strategy? Justify your answer.

***

EVENT MARKETING SCENARIO

You have been hired to plan a twenty-first birthday party for a rich heiress. The party is to take place in your town/city of residence and no expense should be spared. Come up with the concept and venue for the party and then compare and contrast the usefulness of the different marketing mix models presented in this chapter. Decide which marketing mix model would be most suitable to co-ordinate your marketing strategy and why. Discuss the ease of application of this marketing mix model for your signature event.

***

Further reading

Books

Christopher, M., Payne, A. and Ballantyne, D. 2002. *Relationship Marketing: Creating stakeholder value*, Revised Edition, Oxford: Butterworth-Heinemann
This is a revised edition of one of the early works on relationship marketing. It is particularly useful in terms of identifying the variety of stakeholder groups that marketers need to keep in mind in order to successfully implement a relationship marketing strategy.

Gummesson, E. 2008. *Total Relationship Marketing: Marketing management, relationship strategy, CRM, and a new dominant logic for the value-creating network economy*, 3rd Edition, London: Elsevier/Butterworth-Heinemann
A good book that advocates the shift away from the dominant concept of the Marketing Mix towards a more intuitive and comprehensive concept of relationship marketing. A particular strength of this text is a holistic view of relationship marketing, the introduction of the network theory and the effective linking of various marketing concepts in the pursuit of positive relationships with consumers.

Kotler, P., Kartajaya, H. and Setiawan, I. 2010. *Marketing 3.0: From products to customers to the human spirit*, Hoboken, NJ: John Wiley & Sons
This is an excellent text providing an introduction to the paradigm shift in twenty-first-century marketing, focusing on identifying the drivers behind why consumers buy and arguing the relevance of engaging consumers in *conversations*.

Kotler, P., Wong, V., Saunders, J. and Armstrong, G. 2005. *Principles of Marketing*, Harlow: Pearson Education Ltd
Clearly written, engaging and insightful with a European perspective, this is a must-have textbook for any marketing and business student, offering detailed explanations of all the relevant theoretical concepts in marketing.

Journals

Constantinides, E. 2006. The marketing mix revisited: Towards the 21st century marketing, *Journal of Marketing Management*, 22(3/4), pp. 407–438
This article provides an informed discussion of the concept of the Marketing Mix and contrasts it to the new proposition of relationship marketing. It draws on a variety of relevant sources and provides an excellent starting point to the exploration of the Marketing Mix concept.

Grönroos, C. 1997. Keynote paper: From marketing mix to relationship marketing – towards a paradigm shift in marketing, *Management Decision*, 35(4), pp. 322–339
This keynote paper presents an interesting debate around the relevance of the Marketing Mix concept for contemporary marketing strategy. It also stresses the role of consumers in marketing and, interestingly, emphasises the impact of internal marketing on overall marketing success.

Morgan, R.E. 1996. Conceptual foundations of marketing and marketing theory, *Management Decision*, 34(10), pp. 19–26
This article provides a review of classic marketing literature and outlines the historical development of a variety of marketing concepts. It is a good introductory reading to prepare for tackling the more fundamental debates outlined in this chapter.

Other resources

American Marketing Association www.marketingpower.com
This is the website of the American Marketing Association, the leading global industry body. It is a member association, but student memberships are reasonably priced and offer access to a variety of useful resources.

Chartered Institute of Marketing, UK www.cim.co.uk
This is the website of the official UK industry body for marketing. CIM offers a variety of membership options and qualifications, as well as well-structured career enhancement support for marketing professionals.

Marketing Magazine www.marketingmagazine.co.uk
This is the leading publication for marketing professionals and enthusiasts. It offers lots of good case studies and reports on a variety of current issues in the marketing industry.

REFERENCES

Allen, J., O'Toole, W., McDonnell, I. and Harris, R. 2010. *Festival and Special Event Management*, 5th Edition, Milton: John Wiley & Sons Australia.

Bennett, A.R. 1997. The five Vs – a buyer's perspective of the marketing mix, *Marketing Intelligence & Planning*, 15(3), pp. 151–156.

Berry, L.L. 1984. Services marketing is different, in Lovelock, C.H. (Ed.), *Services Marketing*, Englewood Cliffs, NJ: Prentice Hall.

Booms, B.H. and Bitner, M.J. 1982. Marketing services by managing the environment, *The Cornell Hotel and Restaurant Administration Quarterly*, 23 (May), pp. 35–39.

Borden, N.H. 1964. The concept of the Marketing Mix, in Schwartz, G. (Ed.), *Science in Marketing*, New York: John Wiley & Sons.

Bowdin, G., Allen, J., O'Toole, W., Harris, R. and McDonnell, I. 2011. *Event Management*, 3rd Edition, Oxford: Butterworth-Heinemann.

Brassington, F. and Pettitt, S. 2003. *Principles of Marketing*, 3rd Edition, Harlow: FT Prentice Hall.

Christopher, M., Payne, A. and Ballantyne, D. 2002. *Relationship Marketing: Creating stakeholder value*, Revised Edition, Oxford: Butterworth-Heinemann.

Egan, J. 2011. *Relationship Marketing: Exploring relational strategies in marketing*, New York: FT Prentice Hall.

Getz, D. 2005. *Event Management and Event Tourism*, 2nd Edition, Putnam Valley, NY: Cognizant Communication Corporation.

Goi, C.L. 2009. A review of marketing mix: 4Ps or more?, *International Journal of Marketing Studies*, 1(1), pp. 2–15.

Grönroos, C. 1997. Keynote paper: From marketing mix to relationship marketing – towards a paradigm shift in marketing, *Management Decision*, 35(4), pp. 322–339.

Gummesson, E. 1994. Making relationship marketing operational, *International Journal of Service Industry Management*, 5(5), pp. 5–20.

Gummesson, E. 2008. *Total Relationship Marketing: Marketing management, relationship strategy, CRM, and a new dominant logic for the value-creating network economy*, 3rd Edition, London: Elsevier/Butterworth-Heinemann.

Kotler, P., Kartajaya, H. and Setiawan, I. 2010. *Marketing 3.0: From products to customers to the human spirit*, Hoboken, NJ: John Wiley & Sons.

Kotler, P., Wong, V., Saunders, J. and Armstrong, G. 2005. *Principles of Marketing*, 4th Edition, London: Pearson Education Ltd.

McCarthy, E. J. 1964. *Basic Marketing*, Homewood, IL: Richard D. Irwin.

Pine, J.P. and Gilmore, J.H. 1999. *The Experience Economy: Work is theater & every business a stage*, Boston: Harvard Business School Press.

Rafiq, M. and Ahmed, P.K. 1995. Using the 7Ps as a generic marketing mix: An exploratory survey of UK and European marketing academics, *Marketing Intelligence and Planning*, 13(9), pp. 4–15.

Raj, R., Walters, P. and Rashid, T. 2009. *Events Management: An integrated and practical approach*, London: Sage.

Rosenbloom, B. and Dimitrova, B. 2011. The marketing mix paradigm and the Dixonian systems perspective of marketing, *Journal of Historical Research in Marketing*, 3(1), pp. 53–66.

Siemens, G. 2006. *Knowing Knowledge* [Online]. Available at: www.elearnspace.org/Knowing Knowledge_LowRes.pdf [Accessed 13 November 2012].

Chapter

5

Analysing the environment and the foundations of positioning and differentiation for events

LEARNING OUTCOMES

By the end of the chapter, students should be able to:

- Explain the significance of the competitive environment to the event experience and event marketing practice

- Explain and apply the various techniques appropriate to environmental analysis that event marketing can employ

- Discuss the various elements relevant to differentiation

- Identify different positioning strategies available to events

> *Understanding the market in which a good or service will be offered is a key ingredient in marketing success.*
>
> *Clow and Baack (2010)*

Introduction

As we've discussed already at the beginning of this book, events don't exist in a vacuum. They are very much defined by their context and this context depends on the nature of the environment in which the event operates. The event context will also influence the criteria for differentiation and positioning of the event in the market, which will in turn influence the type of media channels that will be used for marketing the event, as well as the frequency of the communication with the event's target audiences. In Chapter 4 we discussed the various models of the marketing mix and how they frame the key aspects of events. This chapter discusses the various types of environments that surround events and presents the most common tools for the analysis of these environments. Additionally, this chapter identifies the various criteria for differentiation that can be used by events in securing their place in the market they operate in as well as some of the common positioning strategies employed by events today. Chapter 6, which follows, explores the role of segmentation in marketing and links it back to some of the concepts discussed in this chapter.

Marketing environment for events

General marketing textbooks all stress the role of the marketing environment in the shaping of marketing decisions and delivery of the marketing activities. Event marketing is no different. In fact, one could argue that the role of the environment is even more important with events, as it can strongly influence not just the marketing activities planned for the event, but also the nature and concept of the event as a whole. Therefore, event marketers need to be experts in the art of market analysis (Clow and Baack, 2010), recognising and appraising the event's environment and the industry on a macro level, but also understanding the event's customers and competitors on a micro level.

Figure 5.1 outlines the general approach to the analysis of the marketing environment. Event environment can broadly be recognised as internal or external. *Internal environment* is integral to the event and is largely within the control of an event manager or event director. It refers to the internal organisation of the event organising team and the functions that need to be managed for the successful delivery of the event (for example, the human resource function, the finance function or the marketing function). The event context is determined by the forces within its *external environment*, namely the macro- and the microenvironment.

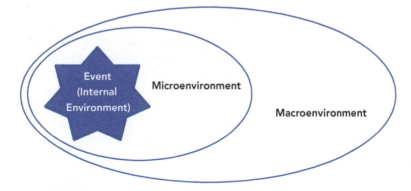

Figure 5.1 An outline of the event marketing environment

In the following sections we explore these environments more in detail.

Internal environment

The **internal environment** of the event encompasses the variety and mix of functions that exist within the event management team. These usually comprise the following:

- Finance
- Human Resource Management
- Procurement
- Marketing and Communications
- Operations/Logistics
- Risk Management
- Sponsorships/Partnerships Management
- IT support.

The scope and scale of the event will determine the structure and the hierarchical organisation of the event organising team which will coordinate each of the functions mentioned above.

Apart from the organisation of functions within the event management team, there are additional elements for consideration when analysing the internal environment. These include:

Human resources – the number and type of various staff, the nature of relationships between employees (formal vs informal) and particularly the role of volunteers in delivering events.

Physical and financial resources – the amount of each of these types of resources and their allocation across different business activities related to the planning and delivery of the event.

Corporate culture – the systems and processes that exist for executing the event management activities and which frame the interactions within the overall event management process.

It is important to stress that the internal environment does not refer just to the actual organisation of the internal event functions. Its dynamics are defined by the relationships between different functions and, more importantly, by the relationships between different people who are tasked with managing these functions. The corporate culture and the physical and financial resources available to the event create the frame in which these relationships can develop and thrive.

Microenvironment

The **microenvironment** encompasses the event's immediate surroundings which have a direct bearing on its delivery and success. Kotler *et al.* (2005) refer to the microenvironment as a 'value delivery network' which is shaped by the interactions of stakeholders that have a relevance in the delivery of an organisation's products or services to its consumers. In the context of events, the microenvironment can encompass the event itself, suppliers, media, competing market offerings, its target audiences and other relevant stakeholders within the industry. Below we explain each of these in more detail.

The event

The event itself consists of a variety of areas that need to be effectively managed for the event to be delivered successfully. These are known as the event's internal environment and have been presented in the section above.

Suppliers

The suppliers which service the event play a crucial role in an event's success or failure. Arguably, the entire event delivery process is one of co-ordinating the suppliers in delivering their products and services in the time frame in which the event is being delivered. Depending on the nature of the event, the suppliers may include:

- venue(s)
- caterers
- transport and logistics companies
- florists
- AV and technical equipment companies
- registration and ticketing solutions companies
- security agencies
- printing companies producing marketing materials
- merchandising companies
- stage design companies
- corporate entertainment providers
- event staffing providers.

The list above is by no means exhaustive. Depending on the type and scale of the event being organised, the complexities of co-ordinating different suppliers can vary and in some instances suppliers can have a great deal of power in negotiating the price of the products and services they provide. This can happen because they have a strong reputation for offering high quality products or services, or because they are specialised in offering a particular type of product or service, which means no other company can provide it. It is thus extremely important that the event manager is well-informed about the suppliers in the market and that they are able to negotiate mutually agreeable terms of service.

Media

The media is an important element of the event microenvironment. Although it is almost entirely out of the scope of control of the event manager, the media has a 'make or break' role in the marketing and delivery of events. Aside from the fact that media is crucial in conveying the information about the event to the event's target audiences, the tone of the media coverage, whether positive or negative, helps shape the image and perception of the target audiences towards an organisation (McCabe, 2009). This can seriously impact on the reputation of an event and help or hinder any future successes.

VIGNETTE 5.1

The rise and fall of the London Pleasure Gardens and the BLOC Festival 2012

Founded in 2011, London Pleasure Gardens (LPG) seemed to be one of the most revitalising and exciting projects of the London event and entertainment industry. Their mission was to turn a 60,000 square metre derelict area in Pontoon Dock into a multi-purpose site with capacity for up to 40,000 people. Directed by a team of people that had previously worked on a variety of large-scale events, the £5 million venture was backed with a £3 million loan from Newham council, not only to provide a spectacular venue nurturing a vibrant cultural scene, but also to offer jobs to residents and generate revenue to be reinvested into the community.

In the run-up to the London 2012 Olympics, LPG became the number one obsession of music promoters and the flood of booking enquiries was creating a very positive atmosphere. Amongst the interested was Baselogic Productions, organisers of Bloc Festival, which was looking for an outdoor space that could hold an increasing number of people interested in attending their events. The move saw them leave their initial event site at the family-oriented holiday park in Minehead, which they had been using since 2006.

Announced as the flagship festival of the year, the three-day Bloc Festival came up with one of the most amazing line-ups of the electronic music scene, featuring names such as Snoop Dogg, Ricardo Villalobos and Richie Hawtin. The interest in the event was so big that ticket sales went from the usual 5,000 people to an impressive 15,000 within days of tickets being released. It was supposed to be the beginning of a lucrative period, both for the LPG and for the Bloc Festival. However, the situation quickly took a turn for the worse. With the event site still unfinished on the event opening date, the official start time of the event had to be delayed by hours, leaving excited ticket holders waiting outside the venue entrance. Issues with ticket control and security caused by inadequate number of entry lanes and lack of functioning electronic ticket scanners created additional delays in allowing attendees to enter the site, leading to a change in spirits and visitors becoming frustrated. The pressure at the entrance was so severe that, in order to relieve it and prevent any health and safety issues, at one point in the evening all ticket controls were suspended and everyone waiting outside the entrance was allowed into the site. Once inside the venue, crowd flow was extremely limited due to the number of site locations for which the construction had not been completed. The construction issues meant that the variety of entertainment that had been advertised by the venue and the festival organisers was significantly reduced and on top of everything else the headliner for the night, Snoop Dogg, made a last-minute decision not to appear at the event at all. This all left the revellers with very little choice of entertainment and very little space to move freely around the event site. Ultimately, the situation got so bad that just before midnight the organisers, supported by the London Metropolitan Police, decided to cancel the event and evacuate the event site.

The disappointment and frustration of the festival goers, combined with the intervention of the emergency services, quickly found its way to the media, with a large number of attendees also sharing their photos, opinions and footage from the night via various social media. The backlash was so intense that within five days of the incident Baselogic Productions went into administration. Some days later most of LPG's Olympic and Paralympic programming had been cancelled and within a month of the incident LPG also went into voluntary administration, bringing a dark end to what was once a bright light in London's entertainment industry.

Competing market offerings

The core premise of this book is that every event is unique and, therefore, competition in its purest form does not really apply to events. However, in today's time of austerity, events are very much competing for the customer's pound with alternative leisure and entertainment opportunities, such as mini-breaks, days out and visits to galleries, museums, the theatre and the cinema. Therefore, it is the role of the actual event experience to create the competitive edge for the event as a whole and this edge can be further strengthened by the strategic choice of event timing or location. These issues of differentiation and positioning are further discussed later on in this chapter.

Target audiences

We will talk about event target audiences more in detail in Chapters 7 and 8 of this book, but broadly these can be split into two main categories:

- Business-to-Consumer (B2C) audiences.
- Business-to-Business (B2B) audiences.

The main difference between the two lies in the decision-making process by which each of these audiences decides whether or not to participate in an event. These are discussed at length in Chapter 6.

Sponsors

Sponsorship today can be viewed as almost an integral part of the event management process. Very few events can survive without any kind of support from sponsors. Whether it is financial support, or value in kind that is being given by the sponsor, the issue of sponsorship value is at the heart of any sponsor–event relationship. Sponsorship is no longer just about providing on-site hospitality and cross-promotion of logos in the marketing materials (Merrilees *et al.*, 2005). Today, companies are looking to sponsor events because they provide platforms for building strong brand awareness with particular target audiences, thus enabling companies to increase the *heart share* with these audiences. It has been argued that event sponsorship can help create *goodwill* towards the sponsoring brand amongst the event attendees (Bowdin *et al.*, 2011). It is thus important that a good 'fit' between an event and its sponsor is achieved (Masterman and Wood, 2006).

Other stakeholders

Other stakeholders related to events include:

- the local and national government

- special interest groups concerned with some of the impacts the event will have or some of the issues raised with the event

- industry associations and alliances that set guidelines which event managers must adhere to, and various other external organisations (e.g. EU organisations or international organisations operating in the global market).

Each of these will have varying degrees of power, depending on the context in which the event is being delivered. For example, the local and/or national government can have the power to stop the event from happening by withdrawing its financial support for the event, which nearly happened with the 2012 Notting Hill Carnival. Special interest groups, on the other hand, can damage the event by demonstrating outside the event venue (or even within the event venue) and obstructing the natural movement of people in and out of the venue, which can create a lot of negative publicity around the event and can negatively impact on the attractiveness of that event to potential sponsors.

Macroenvironment

The **macroenvironment** is the overall societ   that includes the political, economic, demographic, environmental, legal, social, cu   other factors that shape the society as a whole. The macroenvironment will, thus, determine the nature of the market in which the event operates and help shape the characteristics of different stakeholders within it, which have a direct bearing on the success or failure of the event. So let's have a look at some of the factors shaping the macroenvironment for events.

Political factors

Political factors primarily include the overall government strategic direction, as well as the general political climate and the government's relative power to pursue its agenda. For example, the UK government has recognised the importance of mega-events in driving economic development and decided to officially encourage and endorse different cities to bid for hosting large-scale events. These included the London 2012 Olympics, the Glasgow 2014 Commonwealth Games or the Grand Depart for the 2014 Tour de France, which was awarded to Yorkshire.

Additionally, governments' immigration, fiscal and taxation policies can also influence whether or not an environment is attractive for organising events (particularly large-scale ones) and it can also have a bearing on the type, scale and nature of the events being organised.

Legal factors

Legal factors refer to legal frameworks that are affecting the delivery of events and these are closely linked to the political factors. Event delivery is governed by a variety of legal acts which outline the obligations and duties of event organisers. These include regulations on licensing, health and safety issues, and aspects of commercial trading at events and dealing with event suppliers.

Apart from various legal acts, legal environment for events can also include official guidelines issued by relevant bodies, which seek to streamline the relevant processes related to event management and ensure that the important legal acts are followed. These include, for example, the CAP Code (UK code of non-broadcast advertising, sales promotion and direct marketing published by the Advertising Standards Authority) and the Event Safety Guide published by the HSE (Health and Safety Executive).

Economic factors

The economic downturn of 2008 has had more severe and far reaching effects than anyone could have predicted. These have important ramifications for the events industry. The global recession has increased unemployment levels and caused inflation, which has reduced the disposable income levels of ordinary people. With utilities, food and other expenses costing more (in relative terms) than in previous years, people have less money to spend on leisure activities. The additional challenge here is posed by the fact that events entail not just the cost of the actual ticket, but also the associated cost of travel to and from the event venue, as well as other expenses (such as food and drink or event merchandise) on top of that.

Apart from reducing the disposable income levels of individuals, the recession has also impacted on the amount of funds being offered by local and central government for the hosting and delivery of various events.

The third aspect of the impact of the recession on the events sector came through the shrinking of revenues and profits of companies operating in the private sector, which means that not only are commercial sponsorship opportunities severely reduced, but companies also reduced their investment in internal events (for example, training days, team building events and conferences).

In addition to the above, the focus on the delivery of the London 2012 Olympics (particularly in the final two years prior to the event happening) meant that in the UK financial support from the government for other events was reduced (if not completely cut) and sponsorships from corporates were extremely difficult to come by. It seems as if everyone was trying to get a small piece of the Olympic cake, which further exacerbated the direct negative impacts of the recession on the sector.

Social factors

Social factors refer to the make-up of a society (or part of it) in which events take place. These factors include demographic ones (proportion of the population in various age ranges), ethnic and religious backgrounds, income levels and income distribution, as well as lifestyle choices and preferences. All these factors will have an impact on the demand for different types of events. It is thus especially important to understand the structure and the characteristics of the population in a particular location in the planning stages of the event to make sure the event will resonate with target audiences and will inspire their support and engagement.

Technological factors

Events depend on technology. Regardless of the size or scope of the event, the likelihood is high that there will be some element of technology involved in the delivery of the event. Event staging, ticketing, data mining and database management are just some of the examples of areas that depend on technology. Creation of the event experience can also depend on technology. For example, at the 2006 Grammy Awards, the performance of Madonna and the Gorillaz was actually delivered through 3D holograms and this was successfully replicated at the 2012 Coachella festival when Snoop Dogg and Dr Dre were joined on stage by a walking and singing hologram of the late Tupac Shakur.

Other than affecting the delivery of the event itself, technological factors strongly impact on events marketing as well. With the current shift from traditional towards contemporary digital marketing platforms, the nature of event marketing is fundamentally challenged. Technology helps facilitate *conversations* with customers, rather than push for sales to be closed whatever it takes. These conversations are particularly effectively supported by the internet, which helps engage the target audiences in the run-up to the event, as well as post-event, thus extending the life of the event beyond the actual event delivery parameters.

Environmental factors

These factors relate to the natural environment and how it can impact events. The climate change has a significant twofold impact. In the first instance it has affected the reliability of the seasonal weather, occasionally causing disruption to the delivery of outdoor events, particularly during the summer festival season in the UK. In fact, the summer of 2012 reportedly saw a record number of event cancellations due to the weather (Britain for Events, 2012).

Additionally, climate change has influenced a shift in governmental policies, not just in the UK but throughout the world, which try to mitigate the negative environmental impacts of business activities. For example, governments are regulating the acceptable levels of CO_2 emissions from business activities, mainly through the use of taxation. This has a knock-on effect of increasing the costs of different modes of transport, which ultimately increases the overall costs of participating in a particular event. Entire governmental strategies have been formed around this concept of sustainability and the event industry is one of the pioneers in implementing sustainable management practices, which is accentuated by the development of the British and the international standards for sustainable event management (BS8901; ISO 20121). Event providers and suppliers are increasingly embracing these standards, which means that funds needed for the implementation of these are being reallocated from other aspects of the event planning and delivery process, which can ultimately influence the budget and the overall event design.

Analysing the event environment

Environmental analysis for events can be done through a variety of generic market analysis tools. These include the PESTLE, C-PEST, SWOT and Porter's 5 forces analyses.

PESTLE analysis

This type of analysis focuses on the macroenvironment and the identification of the political, economic, social, technological, legal and environmental factors that shape the society. It enables the event marketer to understand the context in which the event will be organised and marketed. These insights can be useful in understanding the structure of the potential customer base and in the design of the event concept. Table 5.1 offers an example of a PESTLE analysis of the macroenvironment.

Table 5.1 An example of a PESTLE analysis of the event macroenvironment

	PESTLE analysis of the event environment in the UK
Political factors	• Existence of the all-party parliamentary group for events to advocate the industry in Parliament • Tight UK immigration policy (particularly relating to visits from the emerging BRICS area which is an attractive market for the UK business events industry) • Increase of the VAT and other taxes that have a bearing on the costs of organising events (e.g. taxation on carbon emissions, in line with EU regulations)
Economic factors	• Triple dip recession in the UK, inflation and increased taxes reducing people's disposable income as well as reducing funds available from the public and corporate sector • Rising costs of fuel influencing an increase in travel costs related to events • Growing need to justify marketing costs and calculate return on investment (ROI) • Consumers are more cautious in terms of what they spend their money on – emphasising the 'event experience' may be the key to attracting audiences that would not normally spend money on leisure activities
Social factors	• The 'feelgood' factor of the London 2012 Olympics inspires people to take part in sporting and cultural activities • Changing customer demographics – increasing proportion of the over-50 age group in the overall population dictates an increase in products and services aimed at this particular audience • Increasing number of people with access to smartphones, laptops and netbooks (Mintel, 2012) • Although consumption is generally reduced as a result of the recession, the seeking of escapism in the form of 'experiences' is on the rise – people are prepared to spend money on events that make them forget about their daily hardships. • Continuing influx of migrant workers from different ethnic backgrounds is changing the structure of target audiences

	PESTLE analysis of the event environment in the UK
Technological factors	• Explosion of data available through technological channels, which complicates decision making • Growing number of channels offered to customers – particularly related to mobile marketing (apps and mobile advertising) • Rise of social media, listings and tools associated with it (e.g. Glean. in for monitoring, managing and measuring Twitter activity) • New sound management technologies (e.g. waveform integrity) creating new possibilities for large-scale events requiring sound enhancement facilities • Accessibility of technology within the country: 79% of households own a laptop/netbook, 64% own a desktop computer, whilst 62% of individuals aged 16+ own a smartphone (Mintel 2012) – highlights increased importance of digital marketing in the twenty-first century • Facial recognition software in use to support security at large-scale events
Legal factors	• BS8901 and ISO 20121 guiding sustainable event management practices – increasing numbers of event organisers and venues choose to get certified to demonstrate their commitment to sustainability • Event insurance requirements (public liability insurance required for certain types of events) • Licensing Act 2003 – regulating the sale and supply of alcohol, provision of regulated entertainment and late-night refreshment • Health & Safety at Work Act 1974 – outlining the requirements for creating safe environments to live and work in • Equality Act 2010 – establishing the framework for incorporating diversity in communities and the workplace • Climate Change Act 2008 – regulating the targets and limitations in terms of CO_2 emissions that have been linked to global warming
Environmental factors	• Global warming influencing the weather, which is an extremely important factor during the UK summer festival season (record cancellations of summer events due to the weather in 2012 (Britain for Events, 2012)) • Prospect of the global peak of conventional oil production will drive prices of transport up, which will impact on the entire value chain for the majority of products and services, many of which are connected to events • Environmental issues being advocated by various special interest groups may impact on the PR surrounding specific events (e.g. G20 summits are usually accompanied by protesters advocating a variety of causes, most prominent of which is the protection of the environment)

There are a number of limitations to the PESTLE analysis. First, it can be perceived as overly simplistic in that it provides a very broad list of factors that can (but don't necessarily have to) influence the organisation and marketing of an event. It does not really explore the interrelationships of various factors in the context of a particular event. Second, this is a tool that needs to be regularly reviewed and updated, meaning it can take a lot of time that could more effectively be used elsewhere in the event planning, marketing and delivery process. Third, sourcing the information which will be included in the analysis can in itself be a complicated, expensive and time-consuming process. And finally, the final product of the analysis (i.e. the insights it provides and the opportunities and threats it identifies for an event) is largely subjective in nature and dependent on the skill and commitment of the person who is conducting the analysis. It is not just about finding the hard facts, but about interpreting them in the context of the event's current situation. Despite all its drawbacks, however, PESTLE is still a dominant tool in analysing the external environment in business and as such is extremely relevant in the context of events marketing today.

C-PEST analysis

This type of analysis incorporates elements of the macro- and microenvironment. The macro aspects analysed are the political, economic, social and technological, and the micro aspect explored in detail are the company's competitors. C-PEST is slightly less comprehensive than PESTLE analysis and can sometimes provide an overly simplistic view of the macroenvironment. However, the added analysis of the competition within the industry in which the event operates adds some depth and helps determine the interactions of the main players in the market. As mentioned earlier, competition in its purest form does not exist with events and thus this type of analysis usually needs to be expanded to recognise alternative leisure and entertainment products and services that may be competing with a particular event in a particular geographic location and at a particular point in time.

SWOT analysis

The SWOT analysis combines the analysis of both the internal and the external environment. The S stands for strengths and the W stands for weaknesses, both of which stem from the event's internal environment. The O stands for opportunities and T for threats, and these are both largely defined by the various macro- and microenvironmental factors that are analysed through the PESTLE or C-PEST analyses. Thus, these different tools are not mutually exclusive, but rather complementary to each other. Table 5.2 highlights some of the points that could be raised in a SWOT analysis.

Table 5.2 A sample SWOT analysis for an annual small community youth art festival

S	W
• Strong attendee base from within the local community • Positive image in the community • Expertise of staff delivering the event this year • Own venue	• Lack of continuity in the organising team • Outdated attendee and artist database • Lack of specific marketing knowledge and experience • Limited internal funds available
O	**T**
• Local council is committed to supporting youth participation in art programmes • Large pool of existing and prospective talent in the local community • Cooperation with local schools and colleges could boost attendance	• Limited funds available from local government – competing with other types of activities in the local area • Limited interest from corporates in sponsoring youth-related activities • Local schools running similar youth art programmes – could create competition

Porter's 5 forces

This model was first introduced in the early 1980s and has since been applied in a variety of industries, from aviation to soft drinks. More recently it has been further developed by its originator, Michael E. Porter (2008), and presents an interesting tool which helps to identify the underlying dynamics of an industry as a whole. It is particularly applicable to events, as it recognises competition in its broader sense, not just focusing on other companies producing the same (or similar) product or service, but analysing other components that determine the nature of competition: buyers, suppliers, potential substitutes and potential new entrants into the market.

The model comprises the following five competitive forces:

- *Rivalry amongst existing competitors* – in the events industry this is a relatively benign factor, as every event is unique and thus direct competition (in its purest form) is not applicable to the sector. However, events as leisure and tourism offerings have to compete with a variety of other products and services being offered in this sector, such as nights out, day trips, cinema or theatre, which widens the pool of potential competition and rather complicates the situation.

- *Buyers* – 'buyers' of events (whether corporate or individuals) have significant power in affecting the survival of events. One characteristic that sets events apart from other leisure and tourism products and services is the 'event experience' – events offer something unique and inherently personal to their target audiences, which means that the demand for events will largely depend on the motivations of consumers to attend and their perceptions of the value and benefits they will get by attending. The 'buyers' ultimately decide what they will spend their money on, so it is vital that the event marketer knows how to effectively communicate its value and benefits to its 'buyers' in a way that inspires them to take action.

- *Suppliers* – successful delivery of events depends on various suppliers playing their part. The supply side of the industry is well developed and thus suppliers of basic products and services do not have a great deal of bargaining power. However, for events that are branded as 'high-end' and those that depend on technology for creating and delivering the event experience, suppliers of these more specialised solutions will have a higher bargaining power.

- *New entrants* – although there are rarely direct competitors within the events industry, new entrants in the sector (regardless of whether or not they are offering similar types of events) can severely impact on the survival of the current players in the market because they can diversify the market offering and widen the pool of opportunities for potential target audiences. This in turn brings down the overall industry profit potential and makes everyone in the market worse off. Some areas of the event industry have higher entry costs than others and the current players in these areas are safer than in others. For example, high costs related to organising exhibitions, particularly international ones, create quite a comfortable market for the current major players and deter new entrants from trying to penetrate the market. On the other hand, smaller-scale events, such as club nights or corporate parties, are more open to the possibility of new event providers entering the market.

- *Substitutes* – although, as we mentioned earlier, there is (arguably) no direct competition in the events industry, there is a high threat that various other leisure activities could potentially present substitutes to events. Consumers' purchasing decisions are largely determined by their personal preferences in relation to their personal perceptions and interests. In a sense, as already mentioned above, events should emphasise the element of 'experience' in order to differentiate themselves from potential substitutes and create a competitive edge.

Bases for differentiation in the events industry

It is generally accepted that in other industries products and services can be differentiated on the basis of price, location, distribution or promotional mix (Brassington and Pettitt, 2003) in order to gain competitive advantage and increase revenues and market shares.

The main source of differentiation within the events industry is the actual event experience, which depends on a unique mix of a variety of other elements, including:

- stakeholders
- pricing policy
- location
- timing
- entertainment
- education
- aesthetics
- escapism
- corporate tie-ins.

All of these elements represent integral characteristics of events as market offerings. There are no two events that utilise exactly the same mix of these elements, which makes differentiation an inherent characteristic of an event. Perhaps that is why it is difficult to identify pure competition within the industry as a whole – when every event has something different, something unique about it, it is difficult to actively pursue any particular direction for differentiation. In a sense, differentiation with events then becomes a non-concept.

Event positioning strategies

Positioning of an event depends on how the event is viewed and defined by its target audiences, i.e. the place it occupies in the minds of the consumers (McCabe, 2009). It will largely depend on the perception that these audiences have about the event – whether positive or negative.

There are two main avenues for positioning an event. It can be done:

1 Based on specific event (or experience) attributes.

2 Against an existing competitor.

The criteria for positioning an event with its target audiences include the following (Allen *et al.*, 2011):

Existing reputation
Long-running events, particularly hallmark and mega-events that are well known on a global scale (such as the Olympic Games or Rio Carnival) already enjoy a strong position in the market, which is maintained through the continued investment in the event and emphasising the unique experience it offers.

Charisma of the event director
Some events can position themselves on the basis of the reputation of their event director. For example, Duncan Reid, former portfolio director at UBM, has largely contributed to the growth and success of the International Confex, the UK's largest and most successful event for the event industry.

Brand/reputation of the event organising company
The Exhibition News Awards event is organised by the publishing company Mash Media and relies heavily on the strength of the Mash Media brand in the conference and meetings sector of the events industry.

Focus on event programming
One-off events can position themselves on the basis of the quality of programme they offer. One such event was the London 2012 Festival which marked the culmination of the Cultural Olympiad that ran alongside the planning and delivery of the sporting competitions of the London 2012 Olympics.

Focus on performers and 'theatre'
Showcase events, such as Cirque de Soleil or concerts by superstars such as Beyonce, Rihanna or Bon Jovi, position themselves on the basis of uniqueness of the performer(s) and the theatrical elements that accompany the core of the show.

Emphasis on location and/or facilities
Hallmark events, such as Wimbledon, create their position in the market by focusing on their location and the facilities they offer. Smaller community events may also use the location as an element for their positioning when trying to attract local audiences.

Price and/or quality
High-end events, such as The Three Tenors concerts or the New Year's Day Concert by the Vienna Philharmonic, position themselves on the basis of the quality of the experience they offer, which is partly also reflected in the price of the ticket.

Tradition and celebration
Many cultural events, such as the Diwali Festival of Lights, pride themselves in showcasing ethnic traditions. Others, such as the Notting Hill Carnival, have evolved over the years to include an opportunity to celebrate a broader range of cultures and traditions than those initially represented by the event at its inception and now enjoy a reputation as a 'street party'.

Multiple attributes

An event can, of course, use a combination of two or more of the attributes presented above, to create its unique market position.

Whilst events do emphasise different attributes in order to differentiate themselves from competing products and services, the actual positioning of an event largely depends on how that event is viewed by its target audiences. This means that, although an event can manipulate the basis of its differentiation and choose the criteria by which it hopes to create a position within the market, much of the actual positioning of the event will depend on how its target audiences perceive its communication messages and how they interpret the value that the event creates for them as individuals.

VIGNETTE 5.2

The positioning strategy of the Lake of Stars Project, Malawi

The Lake of Stars Project is the brainchild of Will Jameson and was conceived in 2004 as a vehicle to support the development of tourism and the cultural and arts scene in Malawi. Its flagship event, the Lake of Stars music festival, was awarded the Malawi Tourism Award in its first year and has since become a force to be reckoned with on the global music scene. The purpose of the event from the very beginning was to raise money for Malawi's developing economy and to help promote Malawi as a global tourist and cultural destination, thus changing the perception of global audiences of Malawi as a poor and famine-ridden developing country.

Traditionally, the festival was held on the shores of Lake Malawi, every year in a different location. The festival started off in 2004 with only 700 attendees from the UK, Malawi and the surrounding countries, but by 2011 had grown its audiences to over 3,000 enthusiasts from all around the world, a large number of who come back year after year. This has created some space for growth, expansion and repositioning.

From its inception, the event has had to work hard to secure funding for its delivery and often times there was serious doubt whether the event would take place at all. The event experienced a planned hiatus in 2012, announced by the organisers as their time to support local Malawi initiatives and reflect on the feedback from performers, festival goers and other stakeholders involved in order to refresh the event and bring it bigger and better in the following year.

Following the feedback from stakeholders, in 2013 the event moved to an urban location, the Sanctuary Lodge, a woodland area in the centre of the Malawi capital Lilongwe, making the event more accessible to both domestic and international visitors. Due to this change in location, the festival has been renamed the City of Stars Festival and is backed by a number of sponsors, such as the Royal Norwegian Embassy in Lilongwe, Malawi's Latitude 13 hotel and Scotland's David Livingstone 200 Fund, alongside a number of influential creative figures from Malawi's cultural scene. The event is now positioned as an 'exciting two-day, multi-venue arts festival and conference showcasing the best in emerging and acclaimed talent from Malawi and beyond'. The scope of content has expanded to include film, theatre and other forms of arts expression, broadening its audience base by catering for a variety of audiences that have so far been ignored. This helps strengthen the event brand and expand its customer base, both in terms of attendees and in terms of performers and exhibitors, thus creating a strong basis for its future long-term financial sustainability.

More information about the Lake of Stars can be found on the event webpage at: www.lakeofstars.org/, the event's Facebook page www.facebook.com/lakeofstars?fref=ts and Twitter account @LakeofStars.

CASE STUDY

UBM

UBM is a global live media, B2B communications, marketing service and data provider. The company operates on five continents with a presence in Europe, Australia and North America and a particularly strong presence in the emerging markets of Asia and Latin America (China, Brazil, India, Thailand, Singapore, Indonesia, Malaysia, Philippines, Mexico and UAE).

Its business is split into five distinct segments: events, PR newswire, data services, online marketing and print marketing. In the events segment, UBM runs over 400 events in more than 30 countries around the world, which comprises 1.9 per cent of the total world market for events and establishes the company as the fourth largest player in this market. In the UK, UBM organises flagship events, such as International Confex, Technology for Marketing and Advertising (TFMA), Internet World, The Big Data Show and eCommerce Expo amongst others.

For a global player, success depends on knowing the environment of each of its business segments in each of the locations where the company operates and on being able to adapt to the changing market conditions. During 2012, UBM made a number of business decisions in the UK which demonstrate how the business follows changes in the environment in order to stay on top of the game.

- *Live Experience* (formerly known as International Outdoor Expo – IOEX) is an industry exhibition co-locating at the London's ExCel with its better-known sister show International Confex. The show experienced strong growth in 2013 in terms of floor space and exhibitor numbers, as well as in terms of show features. This followed a record 'event year' 2012, which saw the Queen's Diamond Jubilee and the London 2012 Olympics boost visitor numbers and inject a considerable amount of income into the UK economy, as well as showcase the UK as a top global event destination.

- For 2013 the company scrapped three events due to take place in Olympia, London: the Building Services, Energy Solutions and FM Event shows. The reasons behind this decision included an attempt to streamline the event offering by focusing on adding value to existing strong shows, such as the Ecobuild and the Built Environment portfolio, but also cutting on costs which yield unsatisfactory returns. Additionally, it was announced that the Ecobuild show concept would be launched in Kuala Lumpur, Malaysia, in September 2013 and co-locate with Greenbuild Asia – the biggest event for the sustainable building community in Southeast Asia. Malaysia was chosen because of its openness to green building and the commitment of its government to promoting green technology, as well as its regional significance in terms of business development.

- UBM's leading UK trade exhibition for the property market, *RESI*, has built on its significance in the age of slow growth in the property market. It provides a platform for different stakeholders within the industry to come together and discuss the developments (or lack thereof) within the market and offers opportunities for networking, debates and coming up with ideas that can take the market forward. This is particularly relevant in a situation when the growth of the market is stalled and in need of a significant push.

- Towards the end of 2012 it was announced that UBM extended a contract with its supplier DB Systems to include the delivery of seven UK-based shows, in addition to four European events that the company had been servicing traditionally. The move signified a growing trust between the two companies and (reportedly) reflected the outstanding quality of service DB Systems had been providing for UBM events. It demonstrates the importance of having reliable partners who are able to cater to client's demands and consistently deliver high quality of service and outlines an approach to controlling the event's microenvironment.

- The above points illustrate how an event organising company can recognise the relevant macroenvironmental forces and adapt to the changing market conditions in order to not just maintain, but enhance its position in the market by adding value to the events it organises. Staying on top of the game will require close monitoring of the external environment, anticipating changes and capitalising on opportunities quickly whilst actively controlling elements within the microenvironment.

For more information on UBM, please visit their webpage at www.ubm.com.

Case study questions

1 Which macroenvironmental factors have affected UBM's operations in the events sector during 2012?

2 Explain in more detail the reasons that have driven the company to scrap three events and focus only on Ecobuild?

3 What do you think makes Asia an attractive market for global event organisers?

4   What are the benefits from hiring one supplier to cover a large number of events in a company's portfolio, as has been agreed between UBM and DB Systems? Think about these from the client's and from the supplier's perspectives.

5   If you were a portfolio director with UBM, what kind of global macroenvironmental factors would you be most vigilant about?

SUMMARY

In the twenty-first century the marketing environment for events is rapidly changing. The heterogeneous nature of events also embraces change as their core characteristic. Changes in the external environment, coupled with changes in the inherent nature of events, tend to create a rather volatile situation, which can compromise an event's ability to consistently improve and thrive in the long term. This chapter has identified the various elements that make up the environment for event marketing. It has explained the difference between the internal and external environment and elaborated on the structure and underlying forces shaping the micro- and macroenvironment for events. Knowing the environment in which an event operates is crucial in enabling the organisers to be able to anticipate changes and to respond to them quickly, so that the opportunities arising can be capitalised on and threats avoided.

The chapter has highlighted a number of tools which event marketers can use to analyse the external environment in which they operate. These include the PESTLE, C-PEST and SWOT analyses and the Porter's 5 forces model. It is important to understand how these different types of analyses can work together to create a rounded picture of the event's environment, which will enable effective decision making.

Based on the structure and characteristics of the event's internal and external environment, event managers and event marketers can decide on the most effective basis for event differentiation and the most suitable criteria for event positioning. It is worth noting, however, that event positioning will ultimately be determined by the perceptions its target audiences will have towards the event and, as such, this may not always be under the direct control of the event marketer. However, knowing the event's external environment will certainly help in making an 'educated guess' regarding the differentiation and positioning criteria. This will, in turn be crucial in attracting the key target markets identified by marketers – we discuss these in more detail in the following chapter.

REVIEW QUESTIONS

1   Define the nature of the event environment. How can it be classified?

2   What is the difference between internal and external environment?

3   What is the difference between macro- and microenvironment?

4   Identify and explain some of the tools that can be used to analyse the event environment.

5   Why is environmental analysis important to contemporary event marketing?

6 What is the difference between the PESTLE and SWOT analyses?

7 What are the key components of the Porter's 5 forces model? Elaborate its application on a practical example of your choosing.

8 What are the key factors for differentiation and positioning within the events industry? Find five practical examples and explore which of these can be applied to each one.

EVENT MARKETING SCENARIO

You are the owner of a small event production agency. You started off with only one employee ten years ago and have managed to grow your business to employ 50 people in two departments: corporate events and party planning. In the past year, your agency has successfully delivered 43 corporate events, comprising a variety of conferences, product launches, annual general meetings (AGMs) and team building events, as well as 150 parties and celebrations for private clients. Your clients value your work and you have a strong portfolio of clients who use your agency as their exclusive events provider, amounting to roughly 50 per cent of your overall annual turnover.

However, the global financial downturn has affected your existing clients' budgets and they are now reducing the number of events they hire you for, as well as the overall budget per event. This is particularly true for the corporate side of your business. You are now faced with a difficult choice of how to reduce your costs whilst keeping up the quality of your events.

Discuss how you would go about resolving this issue. Conduct an environmental analysis for your business and identify some options to:

a Reduce your overall agency running costs.
b Reduce the costs of organising specific events.
c Identify new opportunities to grow your business (you can think of new event concepts, new potential markets/clients or new product/service providers).

FURTHER READING

Books

Brassington, F. and Pettitt, S. 2003. *Principles of Marketing*, 3rd Edition, Harlow: FT Prentice Hall
One of the landmark introductory marketing textbooks, this edition offers a sound introduction to the basics of exploring the marketing environment and uses a wide variety of European examples to illustrate the main theoretical concepts.

Clow, K.E. and Baack, D. 2010. *Marketing Management: A customer-oriented approach*, London: SAGE
The book offers a very practical approach to marketing and provides a variety of industry examples which are useful for understanding the marketing theory behind them. It is useful for developing an understanding of the origins and underlying drivers of marketing decision making, such as the marketing environment. A particularly useful feature is the career guidance offered in each chapter.

McCabe, S. 2009. *Marketing Communications in Tourism and Hospitality*, Oxford: Elsevier Butterworth-Heinemann
A good textbook that provides insightful overview of the environmental context for marketing communications in the field of tourism and hospitality. Another particular strength is the chapter on segmentation, targeting and positioning.

Schmidt, M.J. and Hollensen, S. 2006. *Marketing Research: An international approach*, Harlow: FT Prentice Hall
The book offers a good practical foundation for conducting market research. It outlines a number of practical tools that can be used and is suitable both for marketing beginners and seasoned marketers. A particular strength is the international context to which the book refers, providing the reader with a variety of different perspectives.

Journals

Bhat, S. and Reddy, S.K. 1998. Symbolic and functional positioning of brands, *Journal of Consumer Marketing*, 15(1), pp. 32–43
This is a very good article that provides a clear overview of how positioning is influenced by customer motivations in the context of developing strong brands.

Saxby, C.L., Peterson, R.C. and Abercrombie, C.L. 1995. Selecting marketing strategy through environmental analysis, *Journal of Marketing Management*, 5(1), pp. 16–20
Although this is a fairly 'old' article, it provides an interesting overview of how the company environment helps shape its marketing strategy.

Other resources

Business Visits and Events Partnership www.businessvisitsandeventspartnership.com
This is the industry partnership which is currently working on having events recognised as an official industry within the UK, through lobbying at all levels of society. It is particularly interesting because this is the world's first initiative of this kind, leading the way for other global destinations to take action to have the events industry officially included in the government.

Euromonitor International www.euromonitor.com
Euromonitor International has been conducting strategy research for consumer markets since 1972. With a presence in 80 countries around the world, it is a good resource for fact finding on global level. Their website provides a wide range of reports and analyses helpful to identify the general economic and specific market trends.

Keynote www.keynote.co.uk
Keynote is the UK's leading provider of market intelligence. The data and reports it provides focus on the UK markets and provide a detailed insight into national, regional and local trends. Keynote reports are expensive, but students should be able to access them through their university library log in.

Mintel www.mintel.com
Mintel is one of the key global players in the area of consumer research and market analysis. It collects data, interprets it and compiles reports which help identify the current and coming trends in a variety of consumer markets. Mintel reports are paid for, but students should be able to access them through their university library log in.

People 1st www.people1st.co.uk
People 1st is the sector skills council for the hospitality, passenger transport, travel and tourism industries. The portal offers a variety of useful resources, including market reports and analyses, research outputs, national strategies and career development support.

References

Allen, J., O'Toole, W., Harris, R. and McDonnell, I. 2011. *Festival and Special Event Management*, 5th Edition, Milton: John Wiley & Sons Australia.

Bowdin, G., Allen, J., O'Toole, W., Harris, R. and McDonnell, I. 2011. *Events Management*, 3rd Edition, Oxford: Butterworth-Heinemann.

Brassington, F. and Pettitt, S. 2003. *Principles of Marketing*, 3rd Edition, Harlow: FT Prentice Hall.

Britain for Events. 2012. Supporter Update: Issue Six, AEME, 21 December [Online]. Available at: aeme@jiscmail.ac.uk.

Clow, K.E. and Baack, D. 2010. *Marketing Management: A customer-oriented approach*, London: SAGE.

Health and Safety Executive. 1999. *Event Safety Guide*, 2nd Edition, HSE Books.

Kotler, P., Wong, V., Saunders, J. and Armstrong, G. 2005. *Principles of Marketing* [Online]. Pearson Education Ltd. Available at: http://lib.myilibrary.com?ID=60133 [Accessed 1 February 2013].

Masterman, G. and Wood, E. 2006. *Innovative Marketing Communications*, Oxford: Butterworth-Heinemann.

McCabe, S. 2009. *Marketing Communications in Tourism and Hospitality: Concepts, strategies and cases*, Oxford: Butterworth-Heinemann.

Merrilees, B., Getz, D. and O'Brien, D. 2005. Marketing stakeholder analysis: Branding the Brisbane Goodwill Games, *European Journal of Marketing*, 39(9/10), pp. 1060–1077.

Mintel. 2012. Digital Trends Winter – UK – December 2012. [Online] Available at: Mintel Oxygen [Accessed 1 February 2013].

Porter, M.E. 2008. The five forces that shape competitive strategy, *Harvard Business Review*, January 2008, pp. 86–104.

Segmenting event markets

By the end of the chapter, students should be able to:

- Explain what is meant by the 2-plus customer rule and why it is unique to the event industry

- Explain the variety of generic segmentation strategies in contemporary marketing

- Argue which segmentation strategies are appropriate to event markets and the reasons why

- Define the criteria for an event marketing epidemic

Who is it that is segmenting the market – the marketer or the consumer?

Hill (2013, p. 75)

Introduction

This chapter tackles the challenging nature of the concept of segmentation and its application within the events industry and provides a background for the concepts of targeting and positioning discussed in Chapter 5. Aside from presenting the variety of consumer segmentation criteria dominant in contemporary marketing literature, this chapter also contextualises segmentation in the context of multiple audiences necessarily related to events. It further provides the basis for the exploration of the demand side of events which we discuss in Chapter 7.

What is market segmentation?

Market segmentation is one of the key concepts in marketing, which has been gaining popularity in academic research since the mid-1970s. It was first introduced by Smith (1956) as an alternative to the dominant mass marketing approach of the time, which used advertising as a means to promote marketing messages to a mass market. With the development of the markets and corresponding marketing philosophies (which we discussed in detail in Chapters 3 and 4), it was recognised that consumers are many and varied and, therefore, they would need to be approached in different ways, if the marketing messages are to be successful in driving the sales of products and services. This led to the introduction of segmentation as a process that enables marketers to understand their market by means of market research, which enables them to split the large market into smaller parts or segments (Hoek *et al.*, 1996). The concept is underpinned by the idea of dividing one large heterogeneous market into smaller, (arguably) more homogenous segments in which individuals share certain similar characteristics (Brassington and Pettitt, 2003; Kotler *et al.*, 2003) and have specific needs in common (Blythe, 2013).

According to Wright (1996), the usefulness of market segmentation hinges on two key assumptions. The first one is that consumer preferences are relatively homogenous within the segments identified, whilst consumer preferences amongst these segments are relatively heterogeneous, and it is these differences amongst segments that facilitate a marketer's decision as to which segment to focus on. The second assumption is that companies that match their products and marketing mixes to particular segments within a market will have greater financial payoffs, i.e. their sales volumes and resulting profits will be greater than those of companies who don't segment their markets.

Drawing on the work of Morgan (1996), Kotler *et al.* (2001, cited in Fuller *et al.*, 2005) and, more recently, Hill (2013), have argued that segments, in order for them to be effective, must be:

- *Measurable* – their size must be quantifiable, i.e. there needs to be a finite number of individuals within each particular segment.

- *Accessible* – they must be reachable with the existing marketing tools of the company and the media channels it most commonly uses.

- *Substantial* – they must be large enough and profitable enough (i.e. producing a reasonable return on investment) to be worth approaching.

- *Actionable* – effective marketing strategies can be designed for each of the segments within the limitations of the marketing budget and other potential constraints (e.g. legal requirements and professional codes).

- *Differentiable* or *uniquely responsive* – each segment must respond differently, but favourably, to different marketing stimuli.

Ever since its introduction as a marketing tool, there has been much debate around the benefits and drawbacks of segmentation. The benefits apportioned to segmentation, which are almost universally accepted in the marketing community, have been highlighted by Kotler (1988, cited in Hoek *et al.*, 1996) and include:

- a thorough understanding of the market

- ability to predict consumer behaviour with a great degree of accuracy

- higher chance of recognising and exploiting new market opportunities.

These are, however, still just theoretical assumptions and there is little empirical evidence that either supports or disproves these claims. The continued popularity of segmentation as a key marketing tool, both with marketing practitioners and academics in the field is, therefore, rather surprising and Wright (1996) has even gone so far as to say that the marketing community is somewhat uncritical in this respect.

Defining event marketing audiences and target markets – the 2-plus customer rule

The 2-plus customer rule simply emphasises that every event will necessarily have two or more types of customers it needs to attract. This is true for events of all sizes and profiles. Table 6.1 provides some examples of the variety of target audiences associated with events of different scope and complexity.

Certainly, this is not an exhaustive list of potential target markets and some of these categories will ultimately have to be broken down further for every single event. For example, the category of suppliers will need to be explored more in depth for each particular type of supplier, e.g. caterers, AV equipment suppliers, security providers, registration and ticketing providers and merchandising providers. This list also implicitly suggests that there are three key categories of audiences that could (or should) be segmented in relation to events: individuals, businesses and the media. Table 6.2 provides an overview of the three categories and the types of criteria that could be used to segment each of these into manageable segments. We discuss these more in depth in the following sections.

Consumer market segmentation criteria for events

Segmentation is widely believed to help in identifying the size of the company's potential market. Blythe (2013, p. 405) defines four levels of markets, depending on the type of segments chosen by the marketer: *mass markets*, *segmented markets*, *niche markets* and *micro markets*. The business-to-consumer (B2C) market segmentation criteria prevalent in the current marketing literature and outlined in Table 6.2 are discussed here in more detail.

Geographic segmentation

Geographic criteria are still one of the most commonly used criteria for events. These categorise event attendees according to where they come from in relation to the event. Thus, the segments identified could be local neighbourhoods, cities, counties, regions, states or nations (Kotler *et al.*, 2003). It is quite important for events to know which locations their attendees come from. For example, using the geographical location as a basis of segmentation has helped the London Organising Committee of the Olympic Games (LOCOG) co-ordinate marketing campaigns in a variety of countries encouraging people to visit London and the UK during August 2012. On the other hand, a local community event in a neighbourhood in

Table 6.1 An overview of event audiences

	Local community arts festival	Trade show on trends in digital marketing	Music festival	Global sporting competition
Types of stakeholders (i.e. potential target markets)	Venue	Venue	Venue	Venues
	Suppliers	Suppliers	Suppliers	Suppliers
	Event staff	Keynote speaker(s)	Acts/performers	Sportspeople or teams and their support networks (e.g. national sporting committees)
	Local residents and other attendees	Workshop/seminar leaders	Local government (licensing)	Local government (licensing)
	Local businesses (for sponsorship)	Exhibitors	Event staff and volunteers	National government (funding)
	Local schools	Event staff and volunteers	Independent food/drinks/merchandise providers	Event staff and volunteers
	Local artists	Local, regional, national and industry-specific media and (sometimes) international media	Attendees	International sporting bodies
	Artists from outside the local community		Local residents	Attendees
	Local government (licensing)		Local businesses	Local residents
	Local and regional media		Emergency services	Local businesses
			Local transport operators	Emergency services
			Local, regional, national and/or international media (depending on event scope)	Local transport operators
				Global media channels, broken down by location and focus

Table 6.2 Segmentation criteria for key categories of target audiences

	Consumer audiences	Business audiences	Media
Segmentation criteria	Geographic	Geographical location	Audience type
	Demographic	Industry sector and/ or sub-sector	Publication/channel profile
	Geo-demographic	Company size and/or scale of operations and/or annual turnover	Circulation figures
	Psychographic (lifestyle)	General attractiveness of products/services offered by the company	Profile of target audiences
	Behavioural	Reputation	Speed and frequency at which the message can reach the audiences

San Francisco probably would not have much need for geographic segmentation, as it is already focused on the smallest unit of segmentation.

Demographic segmentation

Demographic segmentation uses demographic variables such as gender, age, income, occupation, education, religion, race and nationality (Kotler *et al.*, 2003). Whilst still one of the most popular criteria for segmenting consumer markets, criticisms have been voiced about the fact that just because individuals can (fairly neatly) be categorised into groups according to the above-mentioned variables, that does not necessarily imply that they will be making the same purchasing decisions as a result of the same marketing stimuli (Bowen, 1998). This, then, directly challenges the assumption that all individuals within a segment will exhibit similar purchasing behaviour. Bowdin *et al.* (2011) have adapted Morgan's (1996) classification of socioeconomic market segments for events, which outlines the propensity of each of the segments for particular types of events. An adapted version of this overview is provided in Table 6.3.

Geo-demographic criteria

Geo-demographic classification systems were first developed in the UK in the 1970s and 1980s, from where they then spread across the world and are now a popular tool for segmenting markets. This type of segmentation combines the geographic and demographic criteria to identify segments within a particular location that exhibit similar characteristics in terms of demographic criteria. Table 6.4 outlines current geo-demographic classification systems most commonly used for marketing purposes today.

Table 6.3 A generic classification of socioeconomic segments for events

Segment	Social status	Social grade	Head of household's occupation	Types of events segment members are likely to attend
A	Upper middle class	Higher managerial, administrative or professional	Professional people, very senior managers in businesses or commerce or top-level civil servants, retired people (previously grade A) and their widows	Cultural events such as fundraisers for the opera, classical music festivals
B	Middle class	Intermediate managerial, administrative or professional	Middle management executives in large organisations (with appropriate qualifications), principal officers in local government and civil service, top management or owners of small businesses, educational and service establishments, retired people (previously grade B) and their widows	Cultural events (but purchasing cheaper seats), food and beverage festivals, historical festivals, arts and crafts festivals, community festivals, music festivals and other music events
C1	Lower middle class	Supervisory or clerical and junior managerial, administrative or professional	Junior management, owners of small establishments, all others in non-manual positions. Jobs in this group have very varied responsibilities and educational requirements. It also includes retired people (previously grade C1) and their widows	Most popular cultural events, some sporting events, community festivals, music festivals and other music events
C2	Skilled working class	Skilled manual workers	Skilled manual workers and those manual workers with responsibility for other people, retired people (previously grade C2) with pensions from their job and widows (if receiving pensions from their late husband's job)	Motor vehicle festivals/shows, sporting events, community festivals, music festivals and other music events
D	Working class	Semi-skilled and unskilled manual workers	Semi-skilled and unskilled manual workers, and apprentices and trainees to skilled workers, retired people (previously grade D) with pensions from their job and their widows (if receiving a pension from their late husband's job)	Some sporting events, ethnic festivals, local entertainment events (e.g. pub quiz, local band night, etc.)
E	Those at lowest levels of subsistence	State pensioners, widows (no other earner), on benefit/unemployed, casual or lowest grade workers	Those entirely dependent on the state long term, through sickness, unemployment, old age or other reasons, those unemployed for a period exceeding six months (otherwise classify on previous occupation), casual workers, those without a regular income. Only households without a chief income earner will be coded in this group	Very little, except occasionally free events

Source: Adapted from Bowdin et al. (2011)

Table 6.4 Types of geo-demographic classification systems

	Nielsen Prizm (formerly Claritas Prizm)	Cameo	Mosaic	ACORN	Output Area Classification (OAC)	geoSmart
Originated in	US	UK	UK	UK	UK	Australia
Developed by	Claritas Inc. later acquired by Nielsen Company	Callcredit Marketing Solutions	Experian	CACI	Office for National Statistics (ONS)	RDA Research
Segments identified	14 groups and 66 segments	57 neighbourhood types and 10 marketing segments	15 socioeconomic groups and 67 different types	6 categories, 18 groups and 62 types	3 tiers of 7, 21 and 52 groups	
Currently used in	USA	UK and overseas	Western Europe, USA, Far East and Australia	UK	UK	Australia

Psychographic segmentation

Psychographic segmentation splits consumers based on social class, lifestyle and personality characteristics. Social class is said to have a strong influence on the choice between basic, standard and luxury goods. Similar reasoning could be applied to events, as is visible from Table 6.3. Profiling consumers according to their lifestyle may also be useful for events. For example, speed dating events target individuals who are single and unattached, with less emphasis being put on their age and other demographic criteria, such as ethnicity, level of income or level of education. Using personality characteristics as the basis of segmentation can help event marketers to appeal to particular traits within individuals, again bypassing the usual demographic criteria. For example, the Telegraph Ski and Snowboard show, which is a B2C exhibition held annually in London's Earl's Court, focuses on attracting people with a keen interest in snow sports, regardless of their age, gender, ethnicity or employment status and profile. However, skiing and snowboarding are inherently social activities, so this event focuses on people who are (predominantly) extroverts with a (reasonably) wide social network who like to spend time with likeminded people and have an active vacation with family and/or friends.

Behavioural segmentation

Behavioural segmentation identifies segments of people who: seek similar benefits from a particular product or service, exhibit similar purchase behaviour, have similar usage patterns for a particular product or service, share similar attitudes towards the product or service, use similar types of media channels to find out about their interests or share personal preferences to particular types of products or services. Whilst behavioural segmentation might make the most sense, it is also one that is nearly impossible to complete, due to the intangible and non-quantifiable nature of the segmentation criteria used. Jackson (2013) has adapted the behavioural criteria presented by Kotler *et al.* (2008) and these include:

Occasions – at which point do people attend events. Two key aspects – work and play.

Benefit – what benefits are consumers looking to get from an event?

User status – in what way do the target segments 'use' the event? These usually include non-attendees, former attendees, potential attendees, first-time attendees and regular attendees.

Usage rate – how often or how frequently do the target segments use the event? Do they exhibit light attendance, medium attendance or heavy attendance?

Attitude – what do target segments think about the event? This would require a more structured form of primary research to be conducted with each segment to explore attitudes and opinions related to the event.

For events, two more criteria introduced by Kotler *et al.* (2003) may prove useful:

Loyalty – this is particularly relevant to recurring events and helps to establish whether particular members of a target segment are loyal, somewhat loyal or completely non-loyal towards the event.

Buyer readiness stage – this criterion identifies target segments based on awareness and determination in relation to a particular product or service. They can be completely unaware of the product; aware but not interested; aware and informed, but not ready to buy; aware, informed and wanting the product but constrained by other circumstances or aware, ready and have an intent to buy. This range of options and the relative number of people within each of these categories can have a profound impact on the overall direction of a marketing plan for an event, key messaging and the choice of particular communications strategies and tactics to reach the chosen market segment(s).

VIGNETTE 6.1

The Great New England Air Show

The Great New England Air Show (GNEAS) is traditionally held at the Westover Air Reserve Base in Chicopee, Massachusetts. It is jointly sponsored and delivered by three key stakeholders: the Galaxy Council, the Westover Air Base of the US Air Force and the Greater Springfield Convention and Visitors Bureau. Air shows have been defined as sporting events which showcase flying performances and which usually include some element of acrobatics, competitions and other displays of aerial feats, as well as on-the-ground exhibition of static aircraft and other aviation-related exhibits. With attendance numbers in the region of 300,000–400,000 annually, the GNEAS is one of the largest special events in New England and has special economic significance for the area. A recent study by Warnick *et al.* (2011) conducted a post-hoc analysis of the geographical segments of visitors at the 2008 edition of the event. They used a cluster segmentation technique which accounted for three key factors: travel distance, purchase decision involvement and frequency of attendance of current visitors. The authors identified four core clusters of events attendees visiting the event:

1 Locals.

2 Heavily involved enthusiasts.

3 First-timers/Non-loyals.

4 Fringe visitors.

Table 6.5 profiles each of the segments with regards to specific criteria.

The four clusters identified can be useful to help understand how invested different segments are in the event and how loyal they may be expected to be. The information about income levels and average spend is useful to help design and price the products and services that these visitors could buy and the information about the average age and who these visitors are bringing along is useful for anticipating the types of services and entertainment they may be interested in. On the whole, detailed profiling of event audiences is crucial in identifying whether or not the event is fit for purpose and in helping to determine the future direction of the event and its marketing activities.

Table 6.5 Visitor segment profiles for the Great New England Air Show

Segment	Proportion of sample	Distance travelled	No. of visits	Level of involvement	Average spend (pppn)	Average length of stay	Likelihood to return	Average age	Attend with	Average income
Locals	19.6%	<15 miles	1–2	4.73	$15.38	1.31 nights	6.34	42	2–3 friends/relatives	$50,000–$75,000
Heavily involved enthusiasts	20.9%	50 miles	3–4	6.45	$33.98	2.15 nights	6.34	49	2–3 friends/relatives	$50,000–$100,000
First-timers/Non-loyals	32.2%	70–75 miles	1	5.21	$37.56	1.68 nights	5.76	43	2–3 friends/relatives	$50,000–$100,000+
Fringe visitors	27.3%	35 miles	3–5	4.99	$26.54	1.36 nights	6.09	46	2–3 friends/relatives	$50,000–$100,000

Segmenting business markets

The need for B2B segmentation (segmentation of business markets) arises from the fact that organisational (or business) buyers have a slightly different purchasing behaviour than individual consumers. More specifically, any purchasing decision made by an organisation will, in most cases, need to be agreed amongst a number of individuals within that organisation (Abratt, 1993, cited in Brassington and Pettitt, 2003). For example, for a destination management company (DMC) to decide to buy exhibition space at a leading international tourism and events trade exhibition that decision will usually need to be agreed by the head of finance, head of marketing and the CEO. Below we outline briefly the variety of criteria suitable for segmenting business audiences, which we introduced in Table 6.2.

Geographical location

Segmenting business markets according to geographical location may be more relevant to some events than others. For example, an exhibition of local artists in a local gallery will probably target a sponsor from within that same city, thus this criterion will not apply. Similarly, mega-events such as the Olympics will target companies with a strong global presence (such as Visa, Coca-Cola or McDonald's) for their top-tier sponsors, whilst lower-level tiers will attract companies from the city and country in which the event is being staged. Again, this criterion is less relevant. However, trade exhibitions which operate on a global level will heavily rely on segmenting their business markets by geographical location and this will usually reflect the geographical spread of the industry which the event is serving.

Industry sector and/or subsector

Segmentation of business markets according to sector and/or subsector will probably be of more use for most events than segmentation according to geographical location. This is because businesses from a particular industry sector or subsector will be more relevant in terms of the types of products or services they offer, which link in with the profile of the individuals attending a particular event.

VIGNETTE 6.2

World Medical Tourism & Global Healthcare Congress

The World Medical Tourism & Global Healthcare Congress is the annual international conference of the Medical Tourism Association. The MTA is the first membership-based international non-profit trade association which brings together top international hospitals, healthcare providers, medical travel facilitators, insurance companies and other players within this industry. The organisation is committed to promoting the highest-quality healthcare in a global environment. It does this by raising awareness of international healthcare opportunities amongst its members and educating consumers about opportunities for healthcare abroad. The World Medical Tourism & Global Healthcare Congress 2014, held in Washington DC, USA, was sponsored by companies ranging from medical organisations (hospitals, university hospitals and private clinics), companies offering immediate supporting services (outpatient care, medical hardware and software producers), other support stakeholders (staff training and development companies, legal firms and insurance brokers specialising in healthcare, design and architectural companies with a portfolio of medical construction projects), as well as tourist bureaus of countries focusing on health tourism and some prominent international airlines. The agenda for the event included a variety of keynote speeches, as well as a range of smaller networking events, summits and forums, designed to appeal to specific subsectors of the global healthcare industry. For example, the delegates could have opted to learn more about medical tourism research, wellness tourism, business development or new trends in medical tourism. Additionally, the participants had the opportunities to set up one-to-one meetings with persons of interest, thus enabling them to establish and nurture relationships to grow and develop their business. These tailored networking opportunities were praised as one of the most important and useful features of the event, which brought out the value of the event for the participants.

Company size and/or scale of operations and/or annual turnover

Another criterion that might be relevant for segmenting business markets is that of company size, scale of operations and/or annual turnover. This is particularly relevant to large-scale events that will have sizeable sponsorship appetites and will, understandably, need to approach companies that are able to expend sizeable amounts for the purposes of sponsorship or other form of participation in an event (e.g. exhibiting at a global trade show).

General attractiveness of products/services offered by the company

This segmentation criterion is usually driven by the profile of the core attendee audiences for an event. It means that companies will be targeted based on how attractive their products or services are to the audience segments. It is important to note that there is no black-and-white approach to this type of segmentation as the attractiveness will be determined by consumer preferences of the intended event attendees. It is not implicit that, just because a company delivers luxury products or services it will immediately be perceived as 'more attractive'. For example, a jobs fair trying to combat high levels of unemployment in a particular geographical area would have no benefit in attracting companies producing high-end clothes or shoes, as its intended consumer audiences would not be able to afford these types of products. What would make more sense is to target high-street retailers who offer good deals and generally provide good value for money when it comes to these particular items.

Reputation

Companies can also be segmented according to their reputation. How this reputation is assessed and graded will depend on each individual event that decides to utilise this particular segmentation criterion. Here are some suggested segments of reputation:

Prestige players – companies which have a strong reputation in the market with a wide range of their target audiences. They proactively engage with their stakeholders, excel at customer service and employee satisfaction and their media presence is consistently positive.

Middle-of-the-road players – these companies have a reasonably good reputation and their engagement with their audiences is strong. However, these companies also leave their customers and employees with a variety of experiences ranging from negative to positive and fairly regularly experience issues that affect their customer satisfaction and the image reported in the media.

Flakeys – these companies serve their markets, although not very well. Customer and employee satisfaction is consistently low and their media image is consistently negative.

Segmenting media markets

The third and final type of markets or audiences that an event might have are the media. Regardless of whether they are broadcast, print or digital, the segmentation criteria suggested in Table 6.2 will necessarily apply.

B2B or B2C

One of the key factors in choosing a particular media channel should be whether or not that channel focuses on business or consumer markets. Trade shows or conferences would necessarily need to advertise in industry specific print or digital media, whilst music festivals would focus mainly on consumer-focused media.

Channel profile

Media channels can also be segmented by their profile. Thus, media segmentation will differentiate between broadcast, print, outdoor and digital media.

Circulation numbers

Segmentation of media according to circulation numbers may prove useful in providing an overview of the potential reach of a particular channel. For most events it will make more sense to pay for advertising space in a publication that reaches 20,000 individuals with each edition than to get some free PR in a publication that reaches only 1,000 individuals. Although this principle can be argued either way with the ever-present marketing conundrum of quantity vs quality of exposure, current event marketing practice still reflects a preference for as wide an exposure as possible.

Channel's target audience profile

This particular criterion will be particularly relevant with events that segment their consumer audiences according to lifestyle or personality. In the twenty-first century there is an overwhelming range of media options for every single type of lifestyle or personality, which significantly complicates the choice for an event marketer. For example, fashion-focused events may choose to advertise in any of the following magazines: *Vogue, Marie Claire, Elle, Grazia, InStyle, Cosmopolitan* or many others. Whilst *Vogue* is more upmarket and targets high earners and high spenders, *Cosmopolitan* focuses on attracting the 'fun, fearless female' with an overwhelmingly strong presence in the college market (The Hearst Corporation, 2014).

Speed and frequency of message

Media channels can also be segmented according to how quickly they can spread the marketing message of an event. Thus, these can be categorised as dailies, weeklies, bi-weeklies, monthlies, etc.

Criticisms of the market segmentation concept

Now that we have presented this great variety of segmentation criteria and discussed their applicability within the events industry, we also need to touch upon some of the criticisms of the concept and its validity.

Hoek *et al.* (1996) stress that segmentation is only useful if it enables the marketer to choose the most appropriate option that will serve the core purpose of marketing: initiating, reinforcing or changing behaviour patterns (Nord and Peter, 1980). This will, reportedly, lead to increased sales of a particular product or service and ultimately to increased revenues. Dibb (1998), on the other hand, highlights the gap between the needs of marketing practitioners in relation to implementing segmentation effectively within their businesses and the usefulness (or lack thereof) of the academic literature, which focuses on the choice of base variables and the range of statistical analysis tools that are suitable for defining segments.

Whilst a lot has been written about segmentation and a variety of approaches to segmentation have been introduced over the decades, there is a clear lack of empirical evidence that the two key assumptions about segmentation, which we discussed at the beginning of this chapter, really are valid (Wright, 1996). Hence, much of the validity and, therefore, relevance of the concept in actual marketing practice is debatable. Without hard empirical evidence (Wright, 1996), how can event marketers really be able to identify which segments will be most profitable and make an informed choice of which segments to target?

CASE STUDY

International Confex

International Confex is a two-day trade exhibition for the events industry that has been running in excess of 30 years. Currently positioning itself as 'the UK's leading exhibition for the events industry' the event is a landmark in the business calendar of a variety of industries, ranging from experiential marketing to travel and destination management. Although it is based in the UK, the event is attractive both at home and internationally and this is reflected in the number and profile of visitors and exhibitors that participate in the event year on year. In 2013 the event reportedly attracted over 900 exhibitors in the following core exhibitor segments:

• UK venues and destinations.

- International venues and destinations.

- Logistics companies.

- Event suppliers who provide products and services to create that WOW factor.

These segments are clearly identifiable both on the event webpage, with colour coding and a dedicated web area developed for each. The segmentation is also reflected in the event site via the colour coding, so that the layout is clear and exhibitors are co-located according to their profile to allow for better visitor orientation and to provide good quality networking opportunities.

Apart from the core exhibitor segments, segmentation can also be noticed in the event's educational programme. This is reflected through the variety of themed theatres in which guest speakers deliver seminars, workshops and keynote speeches during the event. For 2013 the educational programme was split into seven themed theatres, each of which had their own individual sponsor:

- *How To & Corporate Theatre* – sponsored by SO Group (www.thesogroup. co.uk/).

- *Keynote & Agency Theatre* – sponsored by GES Global Network Services (www.globalexperiencespecialists.co.uk/index.php/pages/ges.html).

- *Specialist Programmes Theatre* – sponsored by GES Global Network Services (www.globalexperiencespecialists.co.uk/index.php/pages/ges.html).

- *Brand Activation Arena* – sponsored by Arena Group (www.arenagroup.com/).

- *Loyalty Lounge* – sponsored by Solutions2 (www.solutions2uk.co.uk/).

- *Confex Central* – sponsored by GES Global Network Services (www. globalexperiencespecialists.co.uk/index.php/pages/ges.html).

- *Status Update* – sponsored by Mobile Promotions.

For the purposes of marketing, the event regularly uses a range of media, including:

- Print advertising and PR in industry publications (e.g. *Conference News, Exhibition News, Conference & Meetings World, Exhibition World, Access All Areas, Facetime Magazine, M&IT, Stand Out, Prestige Events, Hospitality & Events North* and *Executive PA*).

- Social media, including Facebook, Twitter, LinkedIn and the Confex Blog.

- Direct mail (online and hard copy).

- Telemarketing.

- Exhibitor promotions (affinity marketing).

Having been acquired by Mash Media towards the end of 2013, the event plans to incorporate a stronger focus on the event production segment to drive the growth of the event. Additional pressure to 'refresh' the event comes from the rival Event Production Show (www.eventproductionshow.co.uk) which happens a month earlier and attracts a big chunk of the target markets traditionally related to International Confex, thus posing an increasing threat to the brand equity and financial survival of the event. The threat is so tangible that, following the change of ownership of the event, a steering group was formed to help guide strategy and content for the show. The group is composed of leading figures within the UK events industry, including Michael Hirst, chairman of the Business Visits and Events Partnership – an industry initiative advocating the official formation of the events industry as part of the UK economy, with its designated government department and policy.

More information on International Confex can be found on www.international-confex.com.

Case study questions

1 Identify the range of target audiences that are attracted to International Confex.

2 Which segmentation criteria do you think have been used to segment the variety of markets for International Confex?

3 Which criteria would you suggest to be used to segment the event visitors and why?

4 Conduct your own research around International Confex and identify at least two potential new segments that the event could target in the future.

SUMMARY

This chapter has contextualised the concept of market segmentation in the events industry. Having recognised that events will necessarily attract at least two or more types of audiences, segmentation is considered a crucial tool in classifying and managing these audiences for the effective implementation of marketing strategies. The variety of event audiences identified in this chapter includes individual consumers, companies or organisations and media. The range of criteria for the segmentation of each of these categories into smaller, more manageable segments has also been presented and their pros and cons discussed. There is no right or wrong approach to segmenting event target markets: the beauty and the challenge of segmentation lie in the fact that, ultimately, the event marketer is the one creating the profile of the event's target audiences. Whilst this entitles him or her to considerable freedom in choosing the segmentation criteria in each of the aforementioned categories, it should still be recognised that an event's target segments should stem from the design of the event experience and vice versa; the event experience needs to be tailored to the needs and wants of the event's potential target markets. In the following chapter, we explore what drives the demand for events.

1 What is the essence of the 2-plus customer rule defined in this chapter?

2 What is your understanding of the term segmentation and how is it relevant FT the context of the 2-plus customer rule?

3 Which generic segmentation criteria do you think are relevant to the following types of events:

- A national graduate recruitment fair.

- A fundraising run for a local hospice.

- A global tourism trade show.

- A classical music festival.

- An 'oldies' film festival.

4 What are the drawbacks of segmentation and how can they affect the success of an event's marketing plan?

EVENT MARKETING SCENARIO

You have just been hired in an events graduate role in a large events production agency based in your home town. The agency's portfolio of events includes 250 Europe-wide consumer and trade shows spanning the following sectors: fashion, pharmaceuticals, oil and gas and pregnancy/baby. You have been assigned to the fashion events team and have been tasked with researching the market and establishing new market segments in which the events could develop. The key events for this team include consumer exhibitions by leading brands in Berlin, Amsterdam, Prague and Warsaw, as well as trade exhibitions in Paris, Milan and Frankfurt. Choose the appropriate criteria to conduct market segmentation for these types of events and elaborate on the targeting and positioning strategy you would use to access these market segments.

FURTHER READING

Books

Brassington, F. and Pettitt, S. 2003. *Principles of Marketing*, 3rd Edition. Harlow: FT Prentice Hall This is one of the core marketing text books which clearly presents a variety of marketing concepts. Sections on segmentation of business and consumer markets are particularly useful to create a solid reference point from which to build a deeper understanding of segmentation within the events industry.

Jackson, N. 2013. *Promoting and Marketing Events*, 1st Edition, Abingdon: Routledge

One of the most recent events marketing texts provides a useful contextualisation of events consumers in Chapter 6.

Masterman, G. and Wood, E.H. 2006. *Innovative Marketing Communications: Strategies for the events industry*, Oxford: Butterworth-Heinemann
This text focusing specifically on marketing communications for events provides an overview of segmentation and targeting from a communications perspective (Chapter 3).

Journals

Smith, W. 1956. Product differentiation and market segmentation as alternative marketing strategies, *Journal of Marketing*, 20, pp. 3–8
This landmark paper, which introduces the concept of segmentation, is a useful read for anyone wishing to begin to understand the concept of segmentation.

Warnick, R.B., Bojanic, D.C., Mathur, A. and Ninan, D. 2011. Segmenting event attendees based on travel distance, frequency of attendance, and involvement measures: A cluster segmentation technique, *Event Management*, 15, pp. 77–90
This is a good case study of an alternative approach to segmentation post-event. It demonstrates the logic behind the approach and discusses its usefulness in the practical context.

Wright, M. 1996. The dubious assumptions of segmentation and targeting, *Management Decision*, 34(1), pp. 18–24
This is a very useful article that discusses the underlying issues of the concept of segmentation and helps the reader develop a critical attitude towards the concept.

Other resources

Geodemographics Knowledge Base www.geodemographics.org.uk/
This is a very useful directory with a wealth of information about geodemographics and its usability for a variety of purposes.

References

Blythe, J. 2013. *Consumer Behaviour*, 2nd Edition, London: SAGE.
Bowdin, G., Allen, J., O'Toole, W., Harris, R. and McDonnell, I. 2011. *Events Management*, 3rd Edition, Oxford: Butterworth-Heinemann.
Bowen, J.T. 1998. Market segmentation in hospitality research: No longer a sequential process, *International Journal of Contemporary Hospitality Management*, 10(7), pp. 289–296.
Brassington, F. and Pettitt, S. 2003. *Principles of Marketing*, 3rd Edition, Harlow: FT Prentice Hall.
Dibb, S. 1998. Market segmentation: Strategies for success, *Marketing Intelligence and Planning*, 16(7), pp. 394–406.
Fuller, D., Hanlan, J. and Wilde, S.J. 2005. Market segmentation approaches: Do they benefit destination marketers?, Center for Enterprise Development and Research Occasional Paper, No. 4, Southern Cross University, Coffs Harbour, NSW.
The Hearst Corporation. 2014. Count on Cosmo. The Hearst Corporation [Online]. Available at: www.cosmomediakit.com/hotdata/publishers/cosmopoli2521681/categories/COSMO_Readership_Section.pdf [Accessed 1 February 2014].
Hill, M.E. 2013. *Marketing Strategy: The thinking involved*, London: SAGE.
Hoek, J., Gendall, P. and Esslemont, D. 1996. Market segmentation: A search for the Holy Grail?, *Journal of Marketing Practice: Applied Marketing Science*, 2(1), pp. 25–34.
Jackson, N. 2013. *Promoting and Marketing Events*, 1st Edition, Abingdon: Routledge.

Kotler, P., Bowen, J. and Makens, J. 2003. *Marketing for Hospitality and Tourism*, 3rd Edition, Harlow: Pearson Education Ltd.

Kotler, P., Wong, V., Saunders, J. and Armstrong, G. 2008. *Principles of Marketing*, 5th Edition, Harlow: Pearson Education Ltd.

Morgan, M. 1996. *Marketing for Leisure and Tourism*, London: Prentice Hall.

Nord, W. and Peter, J. 1980. A behaviour modification perspective on marketing, *Journal of Marketing*, 44, pp. 36–47.

Smith, W. 1956. Product differentiation and market segmentation as alternative marketing strategies, *Journal of Marketing*, 20, pp. 3–8.

Warnick, R.B., Bojanic, D.C., Mathur, A. and Ninan, D. 2011. Segmenting event attendees based on travel distance, frequency of attendance and involvement measures: A cluster segmentation technique, *Event Management*, 15, pp. 77–90.

Wright, M. 1996. The dubious assumptions of segmentation and targeting, *Management Decision*, 34(1), pp. 18–24.

Chapter **7**

The demand for events and their consumers

By the end of the chapter, students should be able to:

- Explain the range of event customer needs and wants
- Explain the relationship between need, events and event marketing
- Critically define the relationships between event supply and demand
- Explain the three laws of marketing epidemics and apply these to events

Dissatisfaction is the beginning of all behaviour

Jim Blythe (2013)

Introduction

Marketing, as any other business function, adheres to the economic laws that govern the business within which it occurs. The fundamentals of supply and demand make up one such economic law. In Chapters 2–4 we explored the identity of events as market offerings, i.e. the supply side of the industry. We now turn our attention to the event consumers whose behaviour defines the demand for events.

Jobber and Fahy (2009) and Jobber (2010) identified the five key dimensions of consumer behaviour as the following:

1 *Who* is important in the buying decision?

2 *How* do they buy?

3 *What* are their choice criteria?

4 *Where* do they buy?

5 *When* do they buy?

It is these five key dimensions that are crucial to event marketers if they are to design effective and efficient marketing campaigns to drive the popularity of and demand for the events they are marketing. The 'who' dimension was explored in Chapter 6 when we talked about market segmentation for events. The 'how', 'where' and 'when' dimensions are discussed towards the end of this chapter when we present the consumer decision-making processes in relation to event consumption. The 'what' dimension is then explored in depth in Chapter 8, where we talk about the variety of motivations of different stakeholders for being involved with events.

Defining needs and wants within the 2-plus customer rule

Any and all discussions of human needs and wants in a business context almost always start with Maslow's (1954) hierarchy of needs. Figure 7.1 outlines the five levels of needs, as identified by Maslow. His key argument is that all human behaviour is driven by needs which can be categorised in five hierarchical levels. This implies that, as soon as the lower-level needs (e.g. physiological needs) have been fulfilled, the higher-level needs come into focus and drive a person's behaviour towards their fulfilment. This, Maslow argued, continues until all of the levels of needs have been fulfilled or until something happens to put the focus back onto the lower-level needs. Whilst this theory still has merits in the wider business context, it is difficult to imagine that any one person would be able to compartmentalise their needs in such a manner. Maslow himself (as cited in Mullins, 2008) argues that higher-level needs, such as love, esteem and self-actualisation, will be valued differently by different people, therefore, any of these needs may come into level three, four or five at any one point in time. Indeed, Blythe (2013) also points out that in the developed countries of Western Europe and North America the first two levels of needs are taken care of, so individuals usually balance somewhere between levels three and five. It is also possible that there will be people who may not really move beyond lower-level needs (physiological and safety) and for them the pyramid may, effectively, have only these two levels. It would be reasonable to assume that these people would, therefore, not really be interested in much else other than satisfying these two key sets of needs.

Brassington and Pettitt (2003) highlight the need to identify who the customer is and what they want as one of the fundamental responsibilities of a marketing manager. Aside from knowing what the customers want now, the continued success of a product or service in the market depends on the marketer's ability to anticipate future needs and wants of existing consumers, as well as potential target markets that may be of interest in the future. This is particularly important for events, which serve multiple audiences at the same time and operate in a dynamic environment of changing consumer tastes and personal circumstances.

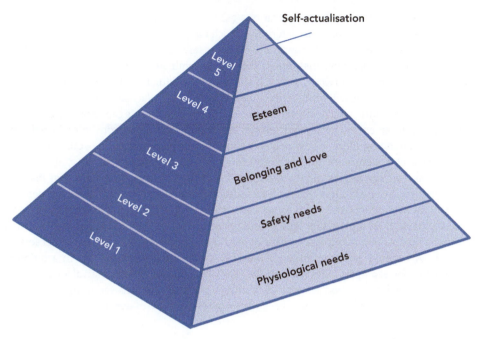

Figure 7.1 Maslow's hierarchy of human needs

Source: Adapted from Maslow (1954), Mullins (2008), Page and Connell (2010), Blythe (2013) and Tribe (2005)

The satisfaction of consumer needs and wants – foundation of consumer behaviour

We mentioned in Chapter 4 that the marketing orientation towards the consumer has had a big impact in how brands promote their products and services to their target audiences. Putting the consumer in the centre of the marketing function requires marketers to understand how these individuals make decisions about which products, services and brands to consume, in order to be able to ensure that the consumers pick the products, services and brands they are promoting. A particular field of marketing thought deals with these types of issues – it is called consumer behaviour. Bennett (1995, cited in Blythe, 2013) defines consumer behaviour as 'the dynamic interaction of affect and cognition, behaviour, and environmental events by which human beings conduct the exchange aspects of their lives'. This implies that what consumers actually *do* when it comes to buying products or services depends on three key internal processes: what they *think* (cognition), what they *feel* (affect) and their initial intended behaviour (conation). The interaction of these three processes is further shaped by the environment in which the consumer operates and other personal factors that determine their disposition. Jackson (2013) goes even further to identify that, apart from the factors mentioned previously, which depend on a variety of personal, psychological and social variables of any individual consumer, the 'why' component of the consumer buying behaviour also depends on the amount and type of marketing activity that marketers are gearing towards consumers. In Chapter 6 we talked about the various criteria for the segmentation of target markets – these criteria are closely linked to consumer behaviour factors. Most of them use various aspects of the consumers' environment and personal characteristics in order to determine which types or clusters of consumers would be most likely to behave favourably towards a product, service or organisation (Blythe, 2013). It is important to understand that one of the key determinants that is likely to induce the purchase of any product, service or event, is the perceived value that the consumption of that product, service or event will bring to the individual consumer. Jackson (2013) defines value as a 'bundle of benefits' which will satisfy the individual consumer's range of functional and emotional requirements. These requirements are, indeed, driven by consumers' needs and wants. Understanding these is only one step towards really understanding your consumers. These needs and wants are further complemented by the notions of *drive, involvement, motivation* and *decision making*. Blythe (2013, p. 29) defines drive as 'the force that makes a person respond to a need'. It is this drive to satisfy our needs and wants that creates demand for a variety of products and services we consume, including events. However, drive only vocalises the need for a particular type of product or service. It is then pertinent to ask: what is it that actually makes consumers want to attend one type of event over any other leisure activity? Why would a person attend a music festival over a weekend trip in a different context? Or, for example, participate in the JORVIK Viking heritage festival in Yorkshire rather than the Robin Hood festival in Nottinghamshire? The answer is in the level of involvement that a consumer experiences with a particular type of event.

The notion of involvement has become more prominent in academic literature since the mid-1980s. Rothschild (1984, cited in Benckendorff and Pearce, 2012) defined involvement as a state of 'motivation, arousal or interest' in relation to a product, an activity or an object. Similarly, Zaichowsky (1985) defines involvement as the level or relevance an object (product or service) holds in relation to the individual's inherent needs, values and interests and proposes a *Personal Involvement Inventory* scale for measuring consumer involvement. Chen and Wu (2010) state that involvement in the context of leisure denotes how consumers' needs, values and interests shape their thinking about leisure and their subsequent consumption choices. Although a number of theoretical models of involvement have developed over the past couple of decades, the most widely accepted model of involvement antecedents (and the one most pertinent to leisure) is Laurent and Kapferer's (1985) *Consumer Involvement Profile Scale*, which identifies five key components to leisure involvement:

- Personal interest in/perceived importance of an activity (i.e. consuming a product or service).

- Perceived hedonic or pleasure value of a product or service.

- Perceived symbolic (sign) value of a product or service, i.e. its emotional appeal and ability to provide pleasure and/or affection.

- Perceived importance of negative consequences in case of poor choice, i.e. the importance of risk related to the consumption of a product or service.

- Perceived probability of the risk materialising, i.e. making the poor choice.

More recently, Kyle and Chick (2002), have narrowed these down to three key areas:

- Attraction of a product/activity, or its perceived importance and hedonic (pleasure) value derived from use/participation.

- Sign, i.e. implied statements that usage/participation conveys about the person (image building).

- Centrality to the consumer's lifestyle, i.e. whether or not the leisure activity provides an avenue for interacting and relating to friends and family or impacts on their sense of self.

The level of involvement a consumer has with a particular brand, product, service or event has a direct bearing on how much time and effort the person will spend in searching for and evaluating alternative solutions to their perceived need. Jackson (2013) identifies three types of decision-making processes that consumers will utilise:

- *Routinised response behaviour* implies little to no information search, fast decision making and is usually related to low-value products, such as groceries or fast-moving consumer goods (e.g. shower gels, toothpaste, soap, etc.).

- *Limited problem solving* implies some consideration of alternatives and some information search to find the best option in any given situation. This is usually the case with consumer durables, fashion clothing and entertainment.

- *Extensive problem solving* implies the consumer moves through all the stages of the decision-making process and spends considerable time identifying and evaluating alternatives. This type of decision making is usually related to expensive or important occasional purchases (e.g. going to university, buying a car or a house, etc.).

Jackson (2013) argues that most consumer decisions related to attendance at events will fall into the second category – limited problem solving, however, it could be argued that for attendance at high-profile mega-events, such as the Olympics or the World Cup, as well as for attendance at business conferences or trade shows, it is more likely that the consumer will be careful about how much money is spent and what direct benefits this will create, and so is much more likely to devote a considerable amount of time and effort to weighing up options before making the final decision.

Ultimately, as Blythe (2013) argues, consumers express their level of involvement through the level of attachment and loyalty they feel in relation to a particular product or brand. The notion of involvement is, therefore, useful in all stages of the event–consumer relationship, from understanding a consumer's pre-visit behaviour, to understanding how they experience events and how they perceive post-event outcomes, such as satisfaction and loyalty, which are the key drivers in repeat attendance and positive word of mouth.

Defining event consumer demand and its relationship to supply

In the academic literature events are recognised as a type of leisure activity (Page and Connell, 2010; Page and Connell, 2012; Bowdin *et al.*, 2011) and as such they are constrained by the following set of issues (Page and Connell, 2010):

- Limited amount of time available to individuals.

- Freedom from constraints or obligations.

- An individual's state of mind and perception of the event as a leisure activity.

- The significance of work and non-work activities.

- An individual's lifestyle.

Thus, there are three key determinants of demand for events as leisure activities (Page and Connell, 2010):

- An individual's discretionary time.

- Attitude towards participation.

- Behaviour and experience of leisure.

Page and Connell (2010, p. 130) recognise the multiplicity of forms of demand in the context of leisure consumption. Table 7.1 outlines the key forms of demand in the leisure context, with specific examples of how these may occur within the events industry.

Demand is a key economic driver in any industry – in order for businesses to be able to sell their products, services and 'experiences' there need to exist people who would be buying and using these products, services and experiences. The dynamics of demand and the way in which it shifts from one form to another are specific to each particular industry, but the occurrences of demand outlined in Table 7.1 provide some food for thought as to how the different types of demand can be recognised and managed by an event manager and event marketer in order to sustain the financial success of their business.

Demand for events as leisure activities depends on three key types of determinants: economic, geographical and social-psychological (Page and Connell, 2010). We discuss these further in the sections below.

Economic determinants of demand for events

Demand for and participation in events as leisure activities will depend on a variety of economic determinants. First, one of the key factors is an individual's disposable income, which will dictate whether or not a person will even consider attending paid events or focus only on those with free entry. Second, the price of the ticket is not the only cost that is associated with attending an event: event participation will also (usually) include the cost of travel to and from the event site, the cost of food and drink for the duration of participation in the event and, occasionally, the cost of buying merchandising and souvenirs as mementos of the event and the cost of accommodation. These are usually referred to as the *average cost of participation* (Page and Connell, 2010, p. 134). Aside from all of these actual costs, another important aspect is also the *opportunity cost* (Tribe, 2005) of attending an event, i.e. a consideration of what the individual could have done with the time and money that was spent on event participation and whether or not that would have brought the individual an equal, smaller or greater degree of satisfaction in comparison to event attendance.

Table 7.1 Forms of leisure demand that exist within the events industry

Form of demand	Definition	Examples from the events industry
Effective demand	Demand that exists and is sometimes referred to as 'participation'	Evidenced by ticket purchases, attendance figures and attendee profiles for various types of events.
Latent demand	Demand that is constrained by various reasons and could be realised if the constraints are removed	A local community youth arts festival which does not include performing arts elements may be missing out on reaching youths that are interested in this type of artistic expression.
Future demand	Demand that may occur if resources to support it become available in the future	A trade show that makes a strategic decision to move to a larger venue to increase future attendee numbers is addressing the issue of future demand.
Induced demand	Latent demand promoted to effective demand due to usage of existing or new facilities which cater for it	The aforementioned local community youth arts festival which adds a selection of performing arts workshops/classes to its schedule is turning latent demand into induced demand.
Diverted demand	Demand shifted from one type of leisure activity to another due to the provision of new facilities	For example, a person who has been a regular music festival attendee and used to attend three to four music festivals every year may decide to pause a year in order to attend another special event (e.g. the FIFA World Cup or the Olympic Games) which doesn't happen as regularly.
Substitute demand	Demand for leisure products or services that meet the same original need, but which could either cost less, or provide more value to an individual	An avid festival goer might decide to switch attendance from one type of festival to another, due to a change in music genre preferences or a difference in ticket price.
Deferred demand	Demand unfulfilled due to lack of opportunities	A particular city may have a high proportion of young professionals aged 21–35, who enjoy music concerts by high-profile artists, but the city may not have a venue of appropriate size to organise these on a regular basis. If a purpose-built venue were built, this would turn the deferred demand into effective demand.
Potential demand	Demand constrained by issues of money or mobility, but which could be turned into effective demand if these constraints are removed	Senior citizens are usually described as having a lack of interest in attending events due to their cost and the need to travel to and from the event site. An event that is aiming to attract these audiences may be able to turn potential demand into effective demand by offering discounted or free tickets to senior citizens, as well as organising some form of subsidised or shared transport initiatives.

Source: Adapted from Page and Connell (2010, p. 131) and Tribe (2005)

From an economic standpoint, the demand for an event will most often (and at least partly) be a function of the price of attendance (i.e. ticket). *Ceteris paribus,* it is safe to assume that any decrease in ticket price will lead to an increase in the demand for tickets for a particular event. Figure 7.2 provides an example of the demand curve for an eight-week run of a theatre play, as derived from the information provided in Table 7.2.

It is visible from Table 7.2 that the demand for tickets for the theatre play increases as the ticket price decreases. At the top price of £75, only 40 people are looking to buy the tickets to the show. However, if the price of the ticket is reduced to £25, there will be 140 people interested in buying the ticket and attending the show. Figure 7.2 presents these numbers visually and depicts the demand curve for this particular event.

Demand, of course, does not happen in a vacuum. Indeed, the actual market performance of any product or service depends on the relationship between demand and supply. Figure 7.3 depicts the interplay of demand and supply for our theatre tickets and how it helps define the equilibrium price and quantity.

Table 7.2 The demand for tickets for an eight-week run of a theatre play

Ticket price (£)	75	65	55	45	35	25
Demand (per day)	40	60	80	100	120	140

Source: Adapted from Tribe (2005)

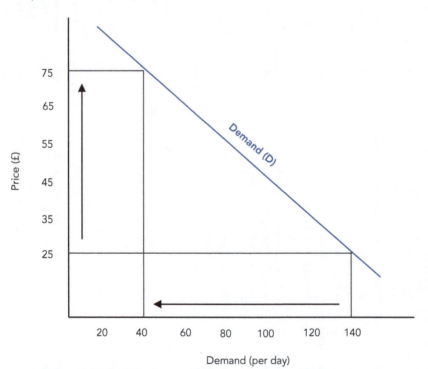

Figure 7.2 The demand curve for an eight-week run of a theatre play
Source: Adapted from Tribe (2005)

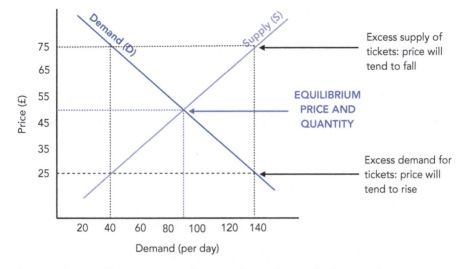

Figure 7.3 The equilibrium scenario for an eight-week run of a theatre play

Table 7.3 The supply of tickets for an eight-week run of a theatre play

Ticket price (£)	75	65	55	45	35	25
Demand (per day)	140	120	100	80	60	40

Source: Adapted from Tribe (2005)

Figure 7.3 has been designed based on the information from Table 7.2 and Table 7.3. It is visible from both tables that the demand for tickets will rise as the ticket price falls. On the other hand, with the falling ticket price, there will be less willingness by the organisers to sell tickets – they would prefer to sell a larger quantity of tickets with a higher unit price, in order to make more money. The equilibrium point in the relationship between the demand and supply for this particular item is at the ticket price of £50 where the quantity demanded is (roughly) 90 tickets. Economists would argue that the economic forces will always work to bring the price and quantity of each particular good to the equilibrium level. However, where would that leave us in this particular scenario? If the organisers have roughly 140 seats in the theatre, selling only 90 tickets at the equilibrium price would leave them with 50 empty seats – that is more than a third of their everyday capacity and not a great indicator of profitability. Thus, performing arts events, such as theatre plays, will often have some sort of ticket scaling scheme in place: offering various types of tickets at different prices. Prices may be determined based on the profile of the target audiences (e.g. concessions for students or senior citizens, ticket bundles for families) or based on other factors affecting the delivery of the event which are outside of the event manager/marketer's control (e.g. discounted ticket prices for shows on days of the week identified as 'slow days' or discounted prices for seats which have a restricted view of the stage or some form of sound impairment).

Shifts in the demand and supply curves

In the sections above we've recognised how price can affect the demand and supply of a type of event. In real life, however, both the demand for and the supply of products and services will be influenced by an interplay of their price as well as a variety of other factors. Tribe (2005) outlines level of income, other prices, comparative quality, fashion and tastes, advertising, opportunities for consumption and population as just some of the factors that can have an impact on the demand for and supply of a product or service. These factors will not influence the angle of the demand curve on the graph (which is determined by the level of elasticity of demand, not discussed in this book), but will influence the positioning of the curve more to the left or to the right of the diagram. Sources of movement of the demand curve more to the left or to the right of the diagram are presented in Table 7.4 and have been plotted on the diagram in Figure 7.4.

Figure 7.4 depicts the shifts in the demand curve for our theatre play we've analysed above. In a situation of a national recession, such as the one experienced globally in the period from 2008–2013, people's disposable income is almost completely wiped out. Thus, the demand for leisure goods and services diminishes rapidly in such a context. Demand curve D1 depicts a situation of reduced demand for theatre tickets, which will ultimately lead to a further reduction in ticket prices, in order to attract audiences. In our case, even at the minimum ticket price of £25, only 120 tickets would be wanted, as opposed to the previous 140 tickets. This would, most probably, lead to reduced turnover and reduced profits for the event organisers, which may put them in the unfavourable position of (perhaps) not being able to cover the costs incurred by putting this event on the theatre schedule.

On the other hand, demand curve D2 depicts a situation of increased demand for theatre tickets. As can be seen from Table 7.3, this might be caused by the theme of the play, which may be of particular interest to the target audiences or a heavy promotional campaign put together by the play producers. The increased demand will ultimately push up the price of tickets, so that the minimum ticket price rises to £35 (as opposed to the previous £25) and the maximum may potentially be around £85. This would lead to a healthy extra profit for the theatre, which would ensure their continued financial success.

Table 7.4 Sources of shifts in the event demand curve

Event demand curve shifts to the left	Event demand curve shifts to the right
Fall in an individual's disposable income	Rise in an individual's disposable income
Rise in price of complementary goods • e.g. rise in the price of gas (or travel fare) for events to which an individual must travel for a significant amount of time	Fall in price of complementary goods
Fall in price of substitute activities • these do not necessarily need to be other events, but can be a variety of other types of leisure activities	Rise in price of substitute activities
Unfashionable event theme	Fashionable event theme
Less promotion	More promotion
Less available leisure time	More available leisure time

Source: Adapted from Tribe (2005)

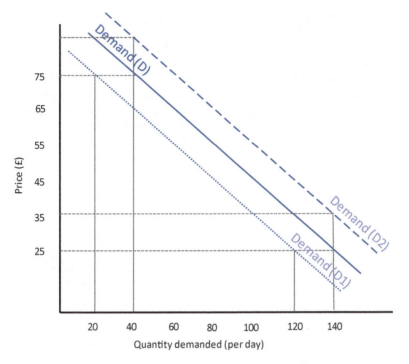

Figure 7.4 The shifts in the demand curve for an eight-week run of a theatre play

As with the demand curve, the supply curve can also shift to the left or to the right, depending on a variety of factors within the market. An outline of factors which may cause these shifts of the supply curve is provided in Table 7.5 and a practical example is plotted on the diagram in Figure 7.5.

It is visible in Figure 7.5 that a decreased supply (S1) of tickets is proportionate to the rise in ticket price. For example, whilst in the 'original' situation the ticket price of £25 would have had a guaranteed supply of 40 tickets, the same quantity of tickets would be realised at an increased price of (roughly) £36. This could be caused by increased fixed costs of running the theatre (e.g. increased staff costs or increased rent of premises). The curve S2 demonstrates an increased supply of tickets: at the price of £25 roughly 60 tickets would be on sale. The reasons for this could be the fall in the overall costs in the staging of the event, or perhaps a sponsorship, donation or grant that has helped offset a good chunk of the costs, thus enabling theatre management to reduce the prices of tickets to attract a larger number of people to see the play.

The examples above, of course, are hypothetical and 'controlled' examples designed to present the general *neoliberal* economic principles of *aggregate* supply and demand in the event context. In real life, the interplay between the supply and demand is dynamic and situation changes from day to day, the environment in which this happens is a lot less 'sterile' than presented in this chapter. It is, therefore, difficult to record continuously the changes in the prices of event tickets and quantities demanded and supplied. Additionally, as Ariely (2008) points out, the discussion of aggregate demand and supply usually assumes the notion of the Economic Man. This implies that humans make completely rational decisions

Table 7.5 Sources of shifts in the event supply curve

Event supply curve shifts to the left	Event supply curve shifts to the right
Rise in ticket price of other events/activities the organiser could be delivering	Fall in ticket price of other events/activities the organiser could be delivering
Rise in the costs of staging the event	Fall in the costs of staging the event
Effects of taxes payable by the event organisers	Effects of grants or sponsorships obtained by the event organisers
Lack of qualified staff available	Abundance of qualified staff available
Lack of resources provided by suppliers due to market saturation (e.g. lack of security personnel available for other events during the London 2012 Olympics)	Abundance of resources provided by suppliers

Source: Adapted from Tribe (2005)

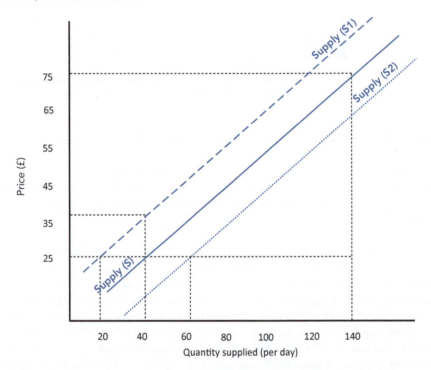

Figure 7.5 The shifts in the supply curve for an eight-week run of a theatre play

all of the time, that we are 'rational calculators of our own economic self-interest' (Pink, 2009). It has been argued, however, that humans can be very irrational in their decision making and, even more so, that there is a degree of certainty in this irrationality. People may tend to evaluate their options in economic terms some of the time, but there is a strong case to be made for marketers to take into account the inherently unpredictable and irrational side of the human nature. Indeed, in 2002 Israeli psychologist Daniel Kahneman was awarded the Nobel Prize for Economics for his seminal paper in behavioural economics: 'Prospect theory: an analysis of decision-making under risk', co-authored with another leading Israeli intellectual, Amos Tversky. Behavioural economist Bruno Frey (1997) has presented a compromise between the two which he titled *Mature Economic Man* (Homo Oeconomicus Maturus), arguing that intrinsic motivation needs to be taken into account in addition to the extrinsic motivation of maximising one's economic wealth in any given 'transaction'.

Regardless of the intensity of the debates mentioned above, it is important for every event marketer to be aware of the underlying forces of supply and demand, and how these can affect (and be affected by) factors such as ticket price, sponsorship, general business context, stakeholders and resources available. Issues of demand with events are even more complex, as events are unique market offerings and, therefore, the pure notion of scarcity may influence consumers to more flexible on the price they would be willing to pay in order to attend/ participate in an event. This is particularly true for mega- and hallmark events, whose reputation alone creates a strong draw for a variety of audiences.

VIGNETTE 7.1

Opportunity cost: summer festival fever in Croatia

Croatia is a small country on the Adriatic coast with a population of roughly 4.5 million people. Rich in cultural heritage and traditions, it is a country that relies heavily on tourism as part of its national economy. Part of the summer tourism offer is a host of music festivals taking place between early July and late August. These festivals often attract top-level artists and performers and create a strong pull for the young tourist, both domestic and foreign. Table 7.6 outlines the key summer music festivals in Croatia and their brief profile and ticket prices.

Table 7.6 An overview of summer music festivals in Croatia

Festival title	Dates in 2014	Location	Profile	Ticket price
FOR Festival	19–22 June	Island of Hvar	Clubbing festival	£182 w/e pass
INmusic Festival	23–25 June	Zagreb	Pop-rock	£50 per day (inc. camping)
Hideout Festival	30 June–3 July	Novalja, Pag	Electronic	£129 4-day pass
Garden Festival	2–9 July	Tisno	Electronic	£120
Electric Elephant	10–14 July	Tisno	Electronic	£126
Ultra Europe	11–13 July	Split	Electronic	£107
Seasplash Festival	17–21 July	Pula	Dance, reggae, ska, drum'n'base	£32.50
Soundwave Croatia	17–21 July	Tisno	Summer dance	£125 w/e pass
Fresh Island Festival	23–25 July	Novalja, Pag	Hip-hop	£67

Festival title	Dates in 2014	Location	Profile	Ticket price
SuncéBeat	23–30 July	Tisno	Electronic	£125
Stop Making Sense	31 Jul–3 Aug	Tisno	Electronic	£100 early bird
Barrakud	9–16 Aug	Pag	Electronic	£125
Sonus Festival	21–25 Aug	Novalja, Pag	Electronic	£129
Dimensions	27–31 Aug	Pula	Electronic	£166 5-day pass
Outlook Festival	3–7 Sept	Pula	Electronic	£151 5-day pass
Unknown Festival	8–12 Sept	Rovinj	Electronic	£109 early bird

As can be seen from the table, the music festival season in Croatia begins in mid-June and lasts all the way till mid-September. Although there are a large number of festivals on offer, there is less variety in terms of music type and festival location, with the majority of events showcasing electronic music and most of them taking place in three most prominent locations: the town of Tisno, near Zadar; the island of Pag, also known as the party destination in Croatia; and the Istrian peninsula in the northern part of the Croatian Adriatic coast. As such, it can be argued that there is a lot of competition between these events. Assuming consumers are faced with limited financial resources (and these are particularly tight for domestic, as opposed to foreign tourists), the question of which event to choose to attend comes to the fore. Ticket price will be the initial screening factor in the evaluation of alternatives. Next, the type of music being played and, in particular, the specific artists that will be playing at the event will be considered, followed by the type of participation (full festival attendance, possibly including camping, versus single day ticket). Following this, the consumers will also take into consideration the cost of travel to and from the event venue, cost of accommodation (either camping on festival site, or in local accommodation nearby) as well as the opportunity cost of participation in the event. This can include anything from the cost and benefits from participating in one of the competing festivals, cost of visiting the location at another point during the season, cost of going to a completely different location and focusing on a different type of tourist activity or event participation. But, more importantly, the value that is placed on the event experience expected to be lived, should the consumer decide to attend the event, needs to exceed the value that could be gained from any alternative activities and experiences that the person might do or undergo instead.

Geographical determinants of demand for events

The geographical aspect of leisure participation has been explored in leisure and tourism literature for a long while now (Hall and Page, 2006, cited in Page and Connell, 2010). Ultimately, leisure participation will depend on an individual's mobility and ability to reach various geographical locations. Page and Connell (2010) highlight the role the popularisation of cars has had on participation in leisure activities 'further away' from home and a similar conclusion can be drawn for events as leisure activities. Whilst we've argued that each event is different and unique (see Chapter 2 for more details), the fact remains that geographical distance from an event location will play a part in the actualisation of demand for it. It is also feasible to assume that the barrier posed by the geographical distance a person might be willing to travel in order to participate in an event may be reversely proportionate to the uniqueness, size, scope and duration of the event. For example, people from all corners of the Earth travelled to London in August 2012 to experience the uniqueness of the Summer Olympic Games and Brazil in July 2014 to support their national teams competing in the FIFA World Cup. The sheer size, scale and reputation of these events have been strong *pull* factors which dwarfed the barriers posed by airline ticket fares, accommodation expenses and other miscellaneous expenses related to the consumption of this event experience, which formed the average cost of participati... vent we mentioned in the previous section.

Social-psychological determinant... and for events

Ultimately, the choice of whether to... e or not in a leisure activity will depend on every individual's discretion – 'the fr... :hoose and the exercise of choice' as defined by Pigram (2003, cited in Page and... 2010). Dumazedir (1967, cited in Page and Connell, 2010) argued that leisure... is a condition of a person's daily experience and, as such, is guided by the need to... ax, be entertained or pursue the development of one's personality. It is this notion... ice that Pine and Gilmore (1999) later argued companies design to engage custom... morable way.

Following Swarbrooke and Horner's (2007) two broad types of determinants for participation in tourist activities, we can argue that these can also apply to events:

- Factors which determine whether or not someone will be able to participate in an event.
- Factors shaping decisions about the type of event to attend, if the first set of determinants allow this to happen.

These two categories can further be broken down into external and internal factors, which are outlined in Table 7.7.

Table 7.8 outlines the differences in the characteristics between business and leisure event consumers, which have an impact on determining the demand for a variety of events. As can be seen from the table, business event consumers will normally have higher expectations of event quality and service standards, as opposed to leisure event consumers. Additionally, they will normally be more flexible on cost and distance to travel, whereas leisure event consumers will normally be more price sensitive and usually less willing to travel long distances. This is partly because attendance for business event consumers is related to personal and professional development and advancement, and partly because the cost of participation in the event is usually covered (at least partly) by the person's employer. Leisure attendees, on the other hand, pay for event attendance themselves and will be more cost conscious and probably less willing to travel very far. It is, of course, important to note, that these are generalisations and that there will be instances where the behaviour of both business and leisure event attendees falls outside of the parameters outlined here.

Table 7.7 Factors determining the type of event to be attended

External determinants	Internal determinants
Global political, economic, social and technological factors	Circumstances, including: • health • available disposable income • available leisure time • work commitments • family commitments • car ownership
National, society-wide political, economic, social and technological factors	Knowledge of: • destinations • availability of different types of events • price differences between events and competing leisure offerings
The influences of the media	Attitudes and perceptions, including: • perceptions of localities in which events take place • political views (precluding certain types of events, or making certain types of events particularly interesting to attend) • preferences for particular cultures • fear of certain modes of travel (limiting the locations to which the consumer is able to get to, thus eliminating particular events based on their location) • propensity to plan attendance in advance • ideas on what constitutes value for money in an event/leisure context • attitudes to standards of behaviour at particular types of events
The marketing activities within the events industry	Experience of: • types of events • different venues and localities • particular event organisers • participation in events with particular individuals or groups (how good of an experience can it be?) • attempting to spend as little as possible (getting discounts on tickets, or freebies)
Views of friends and relatives	

Source: Adapted from Swarbrooke and Horner (2007)

Table 7.8 The characteristics of business and leisure event consumers

Business event consumers	Leisure event consumers
Little decision-making power: usually the employer decides which event to attend	Sole decision-making power about event(s) to be attended
Fairly frequent attendance at business-related events	Attends relatively infrequently
Purposive attendance, usually because participation is related to professional and/or personal development	Casual attendance more prominent than purposive – convenience!

Table 7.8 *continued*

Business event consumers	Leisure event consumers
Event-related trips are generally shorter in duration	Event-related trips are usually longer in duration and combine a variety of other leisure activities
Either short-term or long-term planning of the event-related trip required	Usually planned in the medium term
Less budget-conscious (employer pays)	Very budget-conscious, particularly families
Flexible on distance to travel	Less flexible on distance to travel, particularly if travelling alone
Usually more experienced and more demanding from events	Generally less experienced and less demanding (although not always!)

Source: Adapted from Swarbrooke and Horner (2007)

VIGNETTE 7.2

Demand for events: the Six Markets model

In Chapter 3 we presented Rolf Jensen's (2001) Six Markets model. Jensen argued that his concept of the Dream Society would have significant consequences for 'the workplace, the marketplace and leisure'. Since the introduction of his Six Markets model and the evolution of the experience paradigm in modern business, the events industry seems to be best positioned to really capitalise on the change. Events are – essentially – experiences. Table 7.9 shows some examples of how the demand for events reflects the Six Markets model.

Table 7.9 The Six Markets in the events industry

Market	Event type
Adventure	Racing events, challenge events (e.g. Red Bull Flugtag, Tough Mudder, etc.)
Love, belonging, togetherness	Personal celebrations (weddings, birthday parties, baptisms, bar and bat mitzvahs, etc.) Festivals (music, community) Fetes
Care	Consumer shows and other events focusing on health and wellbeing (care for self and others), family, pets, home decoration, etc.
Who-am-I	Personal development events, professional conferences and conventions (CPD)
Peace of mind	Consumer shows and other events focusing on health and wellbeing, as well as home ownership, insurance, etc.
Convictions	Political party conventions, protests and demonstrations, fundraising and other events in the third sector, etc.

Source: Adapted from Jensen (2001)

Since the mid-1990s experiences have been 'introduced, integrated and infused' into all aspects of consumption and existence' (O'Sullivan and Spangler, 1999). Events have followed suit and have permeated every aspect of society: today there are events for every type of consumer, designed to meet every need and fit any budget. For any ordinary person it is virtually impossible to avoid them. Like general products and services, event participation is about expressing the uniqueness of one's character, their individuality. Hence, the event experience becomes a big part of a person's expression of self, which makes event experience design hugely important in ensuring consumers feel a sense of belonging within an event, prompting repeat visitation and positive word of mouth.

Consumer buying process with events

The consumer decision-making process in relation to attending events is illustrated in Figure 7.6 and loosely follows Engel, Kollat and Blackwell's 7-step consumer decision process (Blackwell *et al.*, 2005; Blythe, 2013).

The seven stages include the following:

- *Need recognition* – for example, a university graduate may very well want to have some fun during the summer following their graduation, before entering the job market. They will, therefore, be experiencing a need for entertainment and fun.

- *Information search* – the graduate may then take some time to explore what kinds of fun and interesting things they might be able to do; they will also need to look at what budget they will have available, so they may try and find out if their parents or other relatives may be willing to help out financially.

- *Evaluation of alternatives* – the graduate will then look at the key viable options and evaluate what would appeal to them most and bring them the most enjoyment and fun. The choice may include, for example, staying fairly local to their place of residence but then travelling to events which are within easy reach (depending on transport availability), or it may involve going further away on vacation – this may be more expensive, but if the person can afford it, it could potentially generate a higher level of enjoyment and satisfaction. The evaluation of alternatives happens in what Funk (2008, p. 33) calls the 'mental box'. This 'mental box' processes the environmental, psychological and personal inputs, which help the individual reach the final decision about what alternative to take. The level of energy and time spent on the evaluation of different alternatives will depend on the level of *involvement* the person has with the consumption of a particular product or service (Jobber and Fahy, 2009). For relatively expensive purchases, the level of involvement tends to be higher, whilst for cheaper alternatives, the level of involvement tends to be lower. Therefore, if the graduate is planning to spend a large amount of money on going abroad on a holiday, they will spend considerably more time on researching different destinations and air carriers than they would on finding out a lot of detailed information about local events and attractions if they decided to spend their summer fairly local and attending local events.

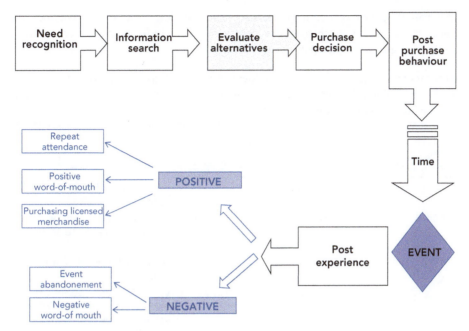

Figure 7.6 The buying decision-making process for events

Source: Adapted from Brassington and Pettitt (2003), Masterman and Wood (2006), Blythe (2013) and Kim *et al.* (2013)

- *Purchasing decision* – based on the budget available and other factors (e.g. whether family and friends will be participating in these activities) the graduate will then make their final decision.

- *Post-purchase behaviour* – this stage involves the 'waiting time' which is a big part of most leisure activities and particularly events: the consumer will buy a ticket and confirm their attendance at an event, but will then have to wait for a period of time between the actual ticket purchase and the event itself. During this time, a phenomenon called *cognitive dissonance* is likely to occur – this is when the consumer starts rethinking their purchase and wondering whether or not they have made the right decision. The notion of the opportunity cost we discussed earlier in this chapter: with a finite budget available, consumption of a particular product or service usually means that any other alternatives need to be rejected. Therefore, cognitive dissonance is a post-purchase re-evaluation of alternatives which aims to reaffirm to the consumer that they have made the right choice and the alternative they've chosen will bring them the maximum amount of enjoyment and satisfaction.

- *Post-experience* – this is the period following the attendance at the event. At this point, the consumer has experienced the event and is able to compare the experience with their initial expectations and the amount of money it has cost them. This analysis then helps the consumer decide whether they have received value for money, which influences their final level of satisfaction (or dissatisfaction) with the event. If the consumer has had an overall positive experience, they are likely to have a favourable predisposition towards attending future editions of the same event or other events of this type, promoting the event via positive word of mouth to their extended networks and/or purchasing licensed merchandising that acts as memorabilia. If the consumer feels their experience was a negative one, they are likely to spread negative word of mouth about the event and are not likely to be attending the event in the future.

The process presented above is highly influenced by the criteria consumers adopt to govern their choices. Table 7.10 outlines some of the key choice criteria and how they are relevant to the consumption of event experiences.

Table 7.10 Choice criteria for the consumption of event experiences

Type of criteria	Examples	Relevance to events
Technical	Comfort	Which amenities are available at the event site?
	Ease of access (convenience)	How easy/convenient is it to get to the event site and back home?
Economic	Price	How much does it cost to attend?
	Value for money	What different options of attendance are there? What value do they represent for what the customer needs?
Social	Status	Does the attendance at the event reinforce a particular status the individual wants to project externally?
	Social belonging	Does the attendance at the event provide an opportunity to express affiliation with a particular social group?
	Socialising	Does the attendance at the event provide an opportunity to socialise with family and/or friends? Does it enable networking and meeting new people?
	Fashion	Is the event theme fashionable?
Personal	Self-image	Does the attendance at the event enable the individual to express and reinforce their self-image?
	Emotions	Does the attendance at the event evoke particular emotions within the individual?
	Happiness	Does the attendance at the event contribute to the individual's sense of happiness?
	Accomplishment	Does the attendance at the event contribute to the individual's sense of accomplishment?

Source: Adapted from Jobber and Fahy (2009)

Organisational buying process with events

Earlier in this chapter we discussed the notion of the Economic Man and how neoliberal economics assumes that people are completely rational when making choices about the products and services they consume. In the previous section we also talked about the needs and drives that shape consumer behaviour and steer it away from being entirely rational. We discuss other emotional factors that shape consumer decision making in Chapter 8 where we explore consumer motivations and their link to a person's sense of self. The final section of this chapter, however, focuses on the key factors in organisational buying behaviour. It is often assumed that organisational buyers' choices are guided more by rational and less by emotional factors. However, it is important to recognise that organisational buying behaviour is always governed by human beings and, therefore, will never be 100 per cent rational, although it is reasonable to assume that it will be more rational than general consumer-focused buying behaviour.

Organisational buying behaviour is much more complex than the behaviour exhibited by individuals. Whilst an individual consumer will make purchasing decisions relatively quickly and always in their own personal interest, these types of decisions within an organisation will always be a result of fairly lengthy processes and subject to input from a variety of people with the ultimate goal of improving the 'bottom line', i.e. profits for the organisation. The group of people that helps shape buying decisions within an organisation is often referred to as a *decision-making unit* (DMU) or a *buying centre* (Blythe, 2013). It is important to note that the structure of the DMU is decided on an ad hoc basis, meaning that the people involved in the buying process will be different depending on the nature of product or service (or event attendance) that is being considered for purchase. The concept of a DMU is fairly old in marketing: Webster and Wind (1972, cited in Blythe, 2013) had identified six key categories of members within the unit:

- *Initiators* – recognise a particular organisation problem or need and draw the attention of others towards it.

- *Gatekeepers* – collect and/or filter information gathered in order to address the recognised problem or need.

- *Buyers* – conduct the actions of buying products or services to address organisational problems or fulfil organisational needs.

- *Deciders* – authorise purchasing decisions for the organisation; usually senior managers or specialists.

- *Users* – employees who will be using the purchased product or service.

- *Influentials* – those who are in direct contact with deciders and are often relied on to provide input on purchasing decisions.

In the context of events, organisational buying behaviour is just as important (if not more) than consumer buying behaviour. In Chapter 6 we presented the 2-plus customer rule – a large proportion of events will require at least one organisational buyer in addition to needing to appeal to individual consumers. This is particularly true in the sector of business events (consumer and trade shows, conferences, meetings, etc.) in which a bulk of sales is done with organisations, rather than individual consumers. Additionally, the principles of organisational buying behaviour are also important to understand in order to effectively sell sponsorships for events. Event marketers should know who the members of the decision-making unit are within potential sponsor organisations, so that they are able to effectively communicate all the benefits of potential involvement with the event to these individuals. We've mentioned already that the members of the decision-making unit will vary depending on particular organisational problems and/or needs. In addition to this transiency, the relative importance of each particular member of the DMU in making the final purchasing decision will also be different. This is why it is very difficult for people external to the organisation (for example, event marketers selling event participation to potential organisational buyers) to be clear on who is making the final decision and who has the highest degree of influence in swaying the decision away from or towards the final purchase. This makes event marketers' work considerably more difficult and uncertain – they can do their very best in preparing the marketing materials and conducting the sales pitch, but a good proportion of the decision is entirely out of their scope of responsibility and influence.

Just like individual consumers making purchasing decisions, organisational buyers are also influenced by **personal** and **environmental factors** when making their decisions. However, it can be argued that in the context of organisational buying behaviour environmental factors will have a higher degree of influence over the purchasing decision, in comparison to personal factors. Environmental factors include a variety of different influences that need to be taken into consideration; the key ones relevant to events are highlighted below (adapted from Blythe, 2013):

- *Physical (or location) influences* – for example, the location of the event will need to be taken into consideration.

- *Economic influences* – direct (price of attendance) and indirect (cost of staff attending the event versus the amount of work they would be able to complete if they were not attending the event) costs of the event will have budgetary implications at the micro level, whilst the macro-level implications include the state of the industry, as well as the general economic situation within the location within which the organisation operates.

- *Political influences* – national, regional and local legal frameworks and guidelines governing business within a particular location. For example, in the UK there is currently a rising political debate about the constitution of events as a distinct industry within the UK economy, which, if approved by Parliament, would have a designated government department.

- *Legal influences* – specific standards can be required by law of product or service providers and this is particularly true within the events industry: from health and safety legislation governing risk assessments and contingency planning with events, to legal frameworks governing marketing, such as the Code of Advertising Practice (CAP) or the Direct Marketing Code of Practice (DMCP), which regulate what is acceptable in the promotion of products and services, to local licensing regulations governing the provision of categories of products and services on event sites and public liability insurance requirements, events are a highly regulated industry.

- *Ethical influences* – ethical considerations are (or at least should be) at the forefront of all business decisions. Organisational buyers must at all times be conscious of the fact that they are buying products and services for the benefit of the organisation they represent. In that sense, they must be governed by the organisational mission, vision and values and invest in products and services that will strengthen the organisational brand image. For example, Body Shop, which prides itself on being an ethical producer of beauty and grooming products and runs the Body Shop Foundation, which advocates animal and environmental protection and human rights, is likely to be very selective in terms of the types of events it organises and participates in, as well as critical of the types of organisations with which it is linked via these events.

- *Cultural influences* – organisations related to events need to also be aware of the cultural implications of their connection with these events. This applies both to ethnic culture, as well as societal cultures and subcultures. For example, the global beverage brand Coca-Cola's sponsorship of the Sochi 2014 Olympic Games caused it to be dropped from the running for a gay magazine's awards ceremony. Out in the City and G3's annual awards are given to individuals and organisations championing LGBT rights and Coca-Cola's initial shortlisting in the 'Brand of the Year' category was rescinded as a consequence of its sponsorship of a mega-event in a country which outlawed the promotion of 'gay propaganda'.

In addition to the above discussed environmental influences, organisational buying behaviour is also subject to internal **organisational influences**. These are shaped by the corporate culture within the organisation, its vision, mission and values, which all govern top-level decision making within the organisation. They are further influenced by the formal and informal organisational structure, policies and communications systems, which define how employees of the organisation relate to each other and to external stakeholders, particularly customers and clients.

Creating demand – foundations of event marketing epidemics

One fairly new concept which is particularly pertinent to the marketing of events is Malcolm Gladwell's (2009) notion of the *tipping point*. In his book of the same title, Gladwell explores the life of epidemics and the applicability of the concept in the wider business context. He has defined the tipping point as 'that one dramatic moment in an epidemic when everything can change all at once...the moment of critical mass...the boiling point'. If we relate this back to the Product Life Cycle (PLC) model we presented in Chapter 2, we can identify the tipping point at the transition from the Introduction to Growth stage when the demand for an event really starts to take off. According to Gladwell, there are three key components to any epidemic: the people who transmit the infectious agent, the infectious agent itself and the environment in which the infectious agent operates. These components are contextualised within the three rules of epidemics:

The Law of the Few
Gladwell identifies three key groups of individuals that are relevant to spreading the epidemic: *mavens* who provide the message, *connectors* who spread the message and *salesmen* who persuade others into action.

The Stickiness Factor

The stickiness factor refers to the memorability of the marketing message – it requires the message to be practical and personal to the intended recipient. Only if these two conditions have been met will the message actually be actioned by the intended consumers.

The Power of Context

As with everything else in life, context is key to the success of a marketing campaign. Environmental conditions have the power to determine the success or failure of the message being transmitted because it has an impact on the way people behave. Gladwell argues that epidemics can be sustained through groups the size of up to 150 people, any more than that and communication will inevitably break down.

Although it is not yet a recognised academic framework, the concept of epidemics in marketing is exciting to explore in the context of events for two reasons. First, the variety and numerousness of stakeholders related to events makes the concept relevant and, second, the exciting new channels of e-marketing provide endless possibilities in exploring how marketing epidemics gain momentum and what it is that really makes them 'tick'. The three rules of marketing epidemics enable event marketers to shift their way of thinking and create contexts conducive to delivering impactful marketing campaigns by fully utilising the unique traits of key consumers (mavens and connectors) to drive word of mouth, the 'gold star' of event marketing.

CASE STUDY

A tale of two approaches: Bibliotekspop at Rotundan, Stockholm Public Library

The Bibliotekspop was a series of free music concerts organised in 2008/2009 at the Stockholm Public Library. It was organised by a husband and wife team, Henrik and Sara Linden, who had (for a good while) aspirations to organise something special at the Stockholm Public Library, which stemmed from their idealism and a love of music as well as books and libraries. The series of events was to, first, help them realise their personal artistic and creative goals, but also help raise the profile of the library and attract a new audience to it. Particularly for Henrik, who at the time was a musician as well as a librarian, the event grew out of a romantic idea of performing at the library – and it could not be anywhere but the Gunnar Asplund's rotunda at the Stockholm Public Library. For anyone who knows Stockholm, the 1920s building forms a notable part of the cityscape, and the Stockholm Public Library is particularly famous for its rotunda and architecture with elements of both classicism and functionalism.

Initial enquiries to host a concert there had been made by Henrik more than a year prior to the first event, although nothing came of it. However, the idea stayed with the organisers, and when Twig (Henrik's pop group) took part in SVT's (Swedish Public Television) series *PSL* – where artists get to choose an unconventional location to perform an acoustic song live – the two arranged for permission to record the video in the library rotunda. The band was allowed to come in on a weekday evening just before the 9 o'clock closing time and it was all done and over with very quickly. Whether it was through the attention the video received or whether it was because of a change in the library policy, when the team approached the library again in the autumn of 2008 they got the permission to stage a series of concerts there – one Saturday afternoon per month – and this time they were not going to be acoustic.

What the library had in mind, as evidenced in their apparent astonishment over the attention the event received, was something very small scale, attracting a tiny audience. It appears, however, that they underestimated both the idealism prevalent in the Stockholm indie pop scene (and Twig being a significant part of it), Sara's marketing nous and the audience's urge for 'something different' in the Stockholm event landscape. From the word go, however, plans were made for a series of themed concerts under the name Bibliotekspop (Library Pop), which were also financially supported by Henrik's employer at the time, the Nobel Museum. This later turned out to be another aspect that would cause suspicion on the part of the library and lead to the eventual termination of the event series. The music themes became an integral part of the promotional plan and to start on a high the organisers decided that the first concert should consist of librarians performing. The event did not, however, target just any librarians: performances were given by artists who already had records out and were part of the music scene either locally or, as was the case with Peter Morén from Peter Bjorn and John, internationally.

With Sara's background in copywriting and advertising the organisers thoroughly understood the importance of having a great story: one that would not be too complicated for news editors to run with, but which also, at the same time, was intriguing to a wider audience. Thus certain elements were emphasised, such as the organisers being a husband and wife team, the library as a magical and creative space, and the questioning of the myth of the quiet and ordered library (and librarians). The story was successful in attracting a wide range of media: the pre-event press conference at the library rotunda was attended by the biggest Stockholm morning newspapers present, as well as local television and some local papers, in addition to all the artists, and Sara's name appeared in the biggest morning paper of all, *DN*. At this point, it became clear to the library's management and marketing teams (who had been quite hands-off throughout this process) that this event had succeeded where their own previous attempts had failed: it had generated publicity, and lots of it, and only positive, which led to their interest in claiming some ownership of the event.

At this point, rather than at the start of the planning process and during the organisers' initial meetings with the library management team, it became evident that there was a clear divide between the two parties. There were no clear objectives set out by the organisers, other than those mentioned above – and they were certainly not SMART. Similarly, the library management team had not suggested any particular objectives themselves and were happy with the organisers doing things their way. Thus, the organisers saw the library management team as providers of the venue, and the library management team saw the organisers as a convenient and cost-effective way of bringing more events into the library. However, with the increasing external interest in Bibliotekspop (even before the first concert took place) the library seemed to realise the event's potential as a platform for conveying messages to their target audiences. What they did not realise, however, was that the attention received was down to the amount of work the organisers put in and their unique previous experience and existing network of contacts, which helped the message get across. The event was a platform to express the organisers' talent, values, dreams and aspirations and much less focus was put on promoting the excellence of the library, although it did manage to position itself as a positive force in society.

The event got a lot of media coverage, both in official media channels and in music-related blogs. The event's Myspace page (with Sara's interviews with all artists – reprinted on the library website as well) was frequently visited, as was its Facebook page (this was before the proliferation of Twitter). Henrik appeared on local television (also broadcast nationally) and on the radio. Due to the amount of coverage received before the start of the event, the organisers anticipated a big audience to the event, and this was definitely achieved by the first Bibliotekspop. Although no actual headcount was done and the numbers reported in the media varied from source to source, the venue was packed with people of all ages and profiles, including children who came with their parents.

The event concept focused on a synergy between the music and the library and so the organisers took care that the qualities of the venue were reflected in the event experience. First, the organisers incorporated in the venue a book table with the performers' favourite books: this aimed to create a deeper level of connection between the audiences, the performers and the library. The sound was, of course, a challenge with acoustics reminiscent of a church, but this was skilfully managed by the event's sound technician (a friend of the organisers) and so the haunting sound contributed to the uniqueness of the event. As it was close to Christmas, the library served coffee and ginger snaps to its audiences and backstage the artists ate smorgastarta. The atmosphere was playful and welcoming. The initial idea that the event line-up be presented by the librarians on the day posed several challenges. First, the librarians were not allocated many hours by their employer to prepare for the event, and they could not be expected to put in the extra hours like the organisers. The library management team, however, expected them to deliver on command, and had given them instructions to emphasise the importance of reading and the role of the library in society. These explicit messages, although well intentioned, were not what the event needed and impacted on the overall atmosphere. Therefore, for the following concert (with an Ingmar Bergman/Nordic Noir theme) the organisers decided to bring in Peter Zander from the Nobel Museum to host the event instead.

Overall, the event itself was a success, and generated further online activity. As the theme for the second concert was announced it was evident that the media and audience demand for this type of event was long term. The organisers had booked three exciting artists with a relationship to Bergman and the dark side of humanity – and more interviews with the artists were published in the major newspapers in the lead-up to the second event in the series. The organisers also started being approached by a range of artists and organisations that wanted to become more involved and other libraries approached them for advice on how to host their own 'Bibliotekspops'. However, during this time the rift between the organisers and the library management team continued to grow. It was evident that the library had developed its own agenda, and it also became clear that it was rather inexperienced in planning, managing and marketing events such as this. Despite the second event taking place on 7 January, the lack of support from library staff over the Christmas and New Year period resulted in some of the organisers' more ambitious plans having to be cancelled. Again, the lack of overall objectives posed a problem, as the organisers were unsure of what would be regarded as a success in the eyes of the library management team. They wanted more control, but they did not understand the mechanisms behind the event's popularity. For the second event the library management team decided, without consulting the organisers, to bring in a professional (and expensive) sound technician – a questionable decision considering the peculiar natural sound in the rotunda and little influence a sound system would actually have. Despite this, the event itself went well again, with another big audience and with an exhibition in the rotunda presented by the Nobel Museum on the plays written by Nobel laureates that Ingmar Bergman had directed. By this point the event series was already well established, and the second Bibliotekspop spawned a number of positive reviews both online and in the print media. However, although the organisers went into this process enthusiastically and had initially planned for one event per month throughout the spring of 2009, they decided shortly before the second event that it would be the last. With most of the work being done after hours and on a voluntary basis, the lack of positive communication and understanding with the library management team had a negative impact on the organisers' motivation to proceed, as they felt the amount of work they put in to get the project off the ground (such as getting the right artists to perform for free, producing promotional material and contacting the right editors and journalists and getting them to write about the event) was not being valued accordingly. An additional issue was also the pressure exerted by the library management team with regards to the organisers relinquishing their artistic control of the event, which (in the organisers' view) would compromise the original event concept.

In the end, despite everybody's good intentions, it seems that the organisers' and the library management team's approaches towards the event were too different to successfully address this clear gap in the Stockholm event calendar, despite the clear demand demonstrated by the media and audiences of all ages.

Case study questions

1 What can you identify to be the main reasons for
   a the event's success, and
   b its failure?

2 Do you think the event itself 'created' the demand, or was the demand already present within Stockholm for this type of event? Justify your answer.

3 Which determinants of demand, in your opinion, played the key role in getting people to attend this event?

4 What do you think was the role of the event concept and its marketing activities in eliciting attendance at the event?

5 Identify and discuss the types of opportunity costs audiences of this event could have potentially faced in making their decision to attend.

6 In your opinion, if this event were to be ticketed (i.e. charging admission), would this impact on attendance levels and/or change the profile of audiences? Why/why not?

7 How would you suggest this type of event to be evaluated, if it were to be revived in the future? What difference (if any) would having SMART overall objectives have made to
   a the management of the event itself, and
   b to the control and evaluation of the event?

Case study courtesy of Sara and Henrik Linden, London Metropolitan University

SUMMARY

This chapter has introduced the key economic principles of supply and demand in the context of events. It has explained the neoliberal economic notion of the Economic Man who makes rational decisions in terms of the products and services he or she consumes. However, it is important to understand that the degree of 'rationality' will differ between different types of consumers: individual consumers' purchasing decisions are likely to be more driven by 'irrational' personal factors (such as emotions), whilst organisational purchasing decisions are likely to me more rational and geared towards achieving strategic organisational objectives and increasing profits. One key concept event marketers need to understand if they are to design effective marketing campaigns is the level of involvement their target customers are likely to have with their events – this can help them decide on the type of marketing messages, amount of marketing material to be produced and type of marketing channels to be used to promote their events. Furthermore, if event marketers were to adopt the thinking behind Gladwell's concept of marketing epidemics it is likely they would be able to increase the efficiency and effectiveness of their marketing campaigns. We discuss the different strategies and tactics available to event marketers in detail in Chapters 9 to 12, but for now we turn our attention to Chapter 8, which explores more in detail the personal factors driving consumer decisions to attend events and their link to a person's identity and sense of self.

REVIEW QUESTIONS

1 What are the key dimensions of consumer buying behaviour and how do they differ between consumer and business markets?

2 Explain the concept of consumer involvement and how it is relevant to consumer decision making in relation to event attendance. Think about it in the context of events as leisure (e.g. festivals), events as education (e.g. conferences and seminars) and events as business platforms (e.g. consumer and trade shows).

3 What are the key economic factors influencing buying behaviour of event attendees?

4 What are the key geographical factors influencing buying behaviour of event attendees?

5 What are the key social-cultural factors influencing buying behaviour of event attendees?

6 Explain how and why the concept of marketing epidemics is important to event marketing. Think of two events you've visited in the past and outline how the concept of a marketing epidemic could be applied in the context of these two events.

EVENT MARKETING SCENARIO

You have been working for your current employer for the past 12 years. Your daily work routine has become rather dull and uninspiring and you are currently thinking of changing careers. You have managed to save up quite a bit of money over the past decade and would like to take some time off work to decide what is next. Having given notice to your employer, you will be finishing your employment with them at the beginning of summer and have decided to indulge your passion for events and are looking to attend some events over the summer. There are quite a few options available, from large-scale hallmark and mega-events in your region, to a variety of other smaller local events you would be interested to attend. You have allocated yourself an 'events budget' of £4,000 for the whole of summer: this is to cover the cost of tickets, as well as any travel and subsistence expenses you may incur for the duration of the event. Therefore, you now need to make a firm plan. To that end, think of the following:

a Make a list of all the events you would consider attending.
b Draw up the total budget for your 'wish list' of events.
c Decide which events will make your final shortlist.
d Recognise the steps you've gone through whilst conducting this exercise, where you searched for information and how much time it took you to reach your final decision.
e Discuss the implications of what you've discovered for designing and delivering successful marketing campaigns for events.

FURTHER READING

Books

Funk, D.C. 2008. *Consumer Behaviour in Sport and Events: Marketing action*, Oxford: Elsevier Butterworth-Heinemann
This book provides a good overview of aspects of consumer behaviour within the sport and event sectors. A great strength of the book is a detailed account of the personal, psychological and environmental factors that influence consumer decision making in this context, as well as the implications of these for an event marketer's decision making.

Gladwell, M. 2009. *The Tipping Point: How little things can make a big difference*, London: Abacus
Written by one of the leading social commentators of our time, this is an insightful approach to the analysis of social interactions and how these can sustain the spread of marketing messages in

a variety of contexts. Innovative arguments of 'message contagiousness' and the role and impact of epidemics provide a new framework for thinking about event marketing and, indeed, marketing in general.

Page, S.J. and Connell, J. 2010. *Leisure: An introduction*, Harlow: Pearson Education Ltd
Written by one of the leading figures in the field of tourism, Professor Stephen Page, this book introduces the leisure industry and its various facets. The breadth of topics ranges from the historical development of the sector through to a detailed analysis of the contemporary and 'trendy' subsectors of urban, rural and coastal leisure, whilst the text also explores the key economic and social determinants of the industry.

Tribe, J. 2005. *Economics of Recreation, Leisure and Tourism*, 3rd Edition, Oxford: Butterworth-Heinemann
This is an excellent resource that contextualises core economic concepts within the sector of recreation, leisure and tourism. Key text for any leisure, tourism and events students embarking on the study of their respective sectors – without these foundations, any discussion of marketing can be nothing more but a superficial and generic overview.

Journals

Chen, A.H. and Wu, R.Y. 2010. Understanding visitors' involvement profile and information search: The case of Neimen Song Jiang Battle Array Festival, *Event Management*, 13, pp. 205–222
This article provides a good overview of the concept of involvement within leisure and tourism studies. It also exemplifies its application on an individual event.

Laurent, G. and Kapferer, J. 1985. Measuring Consumer Involvement Profiles, *Journal of Marketing Research*, 22(1), pp. 41–53
This seminal work is crucial in developing an understanding of the concept of involvement in consumer decision making. It is the starting point for any and all discussions of involvement, particularly in the context of leisure and tourism, and as such is a resource that any event marketer should be familiar with.

Other resources

Business in the Community www.bitc.org.uk
This is a website for the business-led charity that focuses on supporting the involvement of businesses in their communities in order to build a fairer, more sustainable world. Whilst it is not strictly related to marketing, there are a number of topics presented and discussed on the website that are relevant to understanding how individuals relate to businesses, as well as how organisational character (namely: the vision, mission, values and practices) helps shape the interaction between businesses and its consumers.

Consumer Psychologist www.consumerpsychologist.com
This is a website launched and maintained by Lars Perner, PhD, Assistant Professor of Clinical Marketing at the University of Southern California. The site specialises in discussing issues relating to consumer behaviour and its implications for marketing practice

HBS: Working Knowledge http://hbswk.hbs.edu/
This forum is an excellent resource of contemporary business thinking maintained by the Harvard Business School, one of the leading business schools in the world. It contains contributions from the world's leading academics and practitioners and covers a variety of topics, with particularly valuable insights in the areas of marketing and consumer behaviour.

References

Ariely, D. 2008. *Predictably Irrational*, New York: HarperCollins.

Benckendorff, P. and Pearce, P.L. 2012. The psychology of events, in Page, S.J. and Connell, J. (Eds), *The Routledge Handbook of Events*, London: Routledge.

Blackwell, R.D., Engel, J.F. and Miniard, P.W. 2005. *Consumer Behaviour*, 10th Edition, International Student Edition, Mason, OH: South-Western.

Blythe, J. 2013. *Consumer Behaviour*, 2nd Edition, London: SAGE.

Bowdin, G., Allen, J., O'Toole, W., Harris, R. and McDonnell, I. 2011. *Events Management*, 3rd Edition, Oxford: Butterworth-Heinemann.

Brassington, F. and Pettitt, S. 2003. *Principles of Marketing*, 3rd Edition, Harlow: FT Prentice Hall.

Chen, A.H. and Wu, R.Y. 2010. Understanding visitors' involvement profile and information search: the case of Neimen Song Jiang Battle Array Festival, *Event Management*, 13, pp. 205–222.

Frey, B. 1997. *Not Just for the Money: An economic theory of personal motivation*, Cheltenham: Edward Elgar Publishing Ltd.

Funk, D.C. 2008. *Consumer Behaviour in Sport and Events: Marketing action*, Oxford: Elsevier Butterworth-Heinemann.

Gladwell, M. 2009. *The Tipping Point: How little things can make a big difference*, London: Abacus.

Jackson, N. 2013. *Promoting and Marketing Events*, 1st Edition, Abingdon: Routledge.

Jensen, R. 2001. *The Dream Society: How the coming shift from information to imagination will transform your business*, New York: McGraw-Hill Education.

Jobber, D. 2010. *Principles and Practice of Marketing*, 6th Edition, Maidenhead: McGraw-Hill.

Jobber, D. and Fahy, J. 2009. *Foundations of Marketing*, Maidenhead: McGraw-Hill.

Kim, S.K., Byon, K.K., Yu, J.G., Zhang, J.J. and Kim, C. 2013. Social motivations and consumption behavior of spectators attending a Formula One motor-racing event, *Social Behaviour and Personality*, 41(8), pp. 1359–1378.

Kyle, G. and Chick, G. 2002. The social nature of leisure involvement, *Journal of Leisure Research*, 34(4), pp. 426–429.

Laurent, G. and Kapferer, J. 1985. Measuring consumer involvement profiles, *Journal of Marketing Research*, 22(1), pp. 41–53.

Maslow, A. 1954. *Motivation and Personality*, New York: Harper & Row.

Masterman, G. and Wood, E. 2006. *Innovative Marketing Communications*, Oxford: Butterworth-Heinemann.

Mullins, L.J. 2008. *Essentials of Organisational Behaviour*, 2nd Edition, Harlow: Pearson Education Ltd.

O'Sullivan, E.L and Spangler, K.J. 1999. *Experience Marketing: Strategies for the new millennium*, Abingdon: Spon Press.

Page, S.J. and Connell, J. 2010. *Leisure: An Introduction*, Harlow: Pearson Education Ltd.

Page, S.J. and Connell, J. 2012. *The Routledge Handbook of Events*, London: Routledge.

Pine, J.P. and Gilmore, J.H. 1999. *The Experience Economy: Work is theater & every business a stage*, Boston: Harvard Business School Press.

Pink, D.H. 2009. *Drive: The surprising truth about what motivates us*, Edinburgh: Canongate Books Ltd.

Swarbrooke, J. and Horner, S. 2007. *Consumer Behaviour in Tourism*, Oxford: Butterworth-Heinemann.

Tribe, J. 2005. *The Economics of Recreation, Leisure and Tourism*, 3rd Edition, Oxford: Butterworth-Heinemann.

Zaichowsky, J.L. 1985. Measuring the involvement construct, *Journal of Consumer Research*, 12(3), pp. 341–352.

Chapter

Customer motivations for attending events
The search for identity, authenticity and hedonic experiences

LEARNING OUTCOMES

By the end of the chapter, students should be able to:

- Understand the key facets of what it means to 'be human' in the context of event consumption and consumer decision making

- Explore the building blocks of consumer decision making: consumer personality, perception, motivation and attitude formation

- Identify and explain a range of specific customer motivations for attending events

- Compare and contrast the variety of motivations according to event type

- Critically explain the relationship between identity, authenticity and motivations, their impact on consumer decision making and the implications of this for event marketing practice

Consumers are not so much rational as rationalising.

Jim Blythe (2013)

Introduction

In Chapter 7 we discussed consumer decision making in the realm of economics and have presented the notion of a rational consumer. We have, however, also recognised that consumers rarely make their decisions completely rationally. This chapter discusses the 'flip' side of the consumer decision-making coin and explores consumers as human beings, looking at how their individual identities impact on their purchasing decisions. In Chapter 7 we also mentioned the notion of consumer involvement and its relevance to their decision making. It is now time to further explore this concept in the context of the human nature. We, therefore, frame event consumer behaviour in the context of two key psychological concepts: the theory of human identity and 'being human' and the individual's constant search for authenticity. The chapter also explores the concept of motivation more in depth, explaining how it manifests itself in the context of events and how it influences consumer preferences and purchasing decisions.

'Being human' – in search of authenticity, happiness and hedonism

The exploration of consumerism and the impacts of overconsumption started back in the 1980s and since then consumption has increasingly been explored through the lens of hedonism. Jansson-Boyd (2011) remarked how materialism and consumption are increasingly being used to 'fill a hole' in people's lives, caused by overemphasis on individualism versus community, uniqueness, increased speed of life, business and commercial trends and the rise of celebrity (Rojek, 2001). Individuals are using their purchasing behaviour to emphasise who they are and/or aspire to be, as well as to evoke positive feelings through consumption of products and services. Blythe (2013, p. 46) further notes that consumption today is intrinsically linked to socialisation and it is 'impossible to have a social life without at the same time being a consumer'. Consumption has moved from a merely utilitarian concept to a more hedonic one: it is no longer just about consumption of goods and services to ensure one's own existence and survival, but consumption is increasingly being viewed as an 'experience' and as 'play' (Holt, 1995). With the rise of disposable incomes over the past several decades, the consumption of leisure activities has also increased. Winlow and Hall (2006, cited in Page and Connell, 2010) identify leisure as a dominant feature of our lives. It is central to an individual's 'sense of self', permeated with meanings, hopes and fantasies (Page and Connell, 2010) and facilitates what Guignon (2004) calls 'moral perfectionism' – an individual being true to, cultivating and developing him(her)self. This *'moral perfectionism'* can be seen as generating authentic, joyous and happy individuals (Guignon, 2004 and Thaler and Sunstein, 2008). Consumers today crave *authenticity* (Derbaix and Derbaix, 2010).

In Chapters 2 and 3 we discussed in detail the nature of events as leisure market offerings and have stressed the concept of experience as one of the key elements that distinguish events from other types of products and services (Morgan and Watson, 2007; Morgan *et al.*, 2010). A number of authors in the field agree with Hosany and Gilbert (2010) that consumption in the sphere of leisure is primarily driven by *hedonic motives* (e.g. Higgins, 2006; Blythe, 2013; de Geus *et al.*, 2013). Indeed, leisure (and related event) experiences are largely viewed as settings for generating positive emotions (see de Geus *et al.*, 2013 for a list of authors expressing these views), which are recognised as mediators of consumer satisfaction with leisure activities and subsequent loyalty in the consumption of these (White, 2010; de Geus *et al.*, 2013). Previous work by Jensen (2001), O'Sullivan and Spangler (1999) and Pine and Gilmore (1999), which we explored in detail in Chapter 3, suggests that emotional responses within these experiences can (and should) be generated through the focus on fantasies, feelings, emotion, social interaction and fun. These, however, seem to often be overlooked by the producers of such experiences (Ayob *et al.*, 2013), i.e. event organisers, either because of lack of time or physical resources, or because the consumer's perspective is not usually taken into consideration when designing the event features which should support the delivery of the event experience. It is, therefore, time to switch from a supply-side to a demand-side perspective when defining and designing consumer experiences related to events (Peperkamp *et al.*, 2014).

Profiling event consumers

Understanding the way consumers will behave plays a big part in the management of marketing activities for any type of market offering. It is, however, particularly important in the context of events, where a range of customers can be equally important at any given point in time and the actions of the marketer need to satisfy sometimes conflicting agendas. Consumer behaviour is most often defined as 'the study of the processes involved when individuals or groups select, purchase, use or dispose of products, services, ideas or experiences to satisfy needs and desires' (Solomon *et al.*, 2013). In the context of events, this highlights the need to consider a customer's *journey* before, during and after the event itself. Event marketers should, therefore, expand the focus of their marketing activities from focusing just on marketing in the lead up to the event with the purpose of getting as many people as possible to attend. Instead, they should be mindful of creating a complete 'customer journey' to encompass interaction between the event and its audiences before, during and after the event has taken place, thus extending the life of the event and maximising its media exposure, as well as improving the quality and effectiveness of the event audiences' engagement.

Blythe (2013) defines consumer behaviour as an interplay of internal and external factors which impact on consumer decision making. A model of this interplay can be seen in Figure 8.1. Consumer behaviour in general is moderated by two types of factors: internal factors and external factors.

Internal factors are mediated by three key driving forces:

- Cognition, or thought processes, which reflect the thinking through and rationalising of decisions.

- Affect, or the emotional part, which justifies decisions based on emotional responses within the consumer.

- Conation, or intended behaviour, which initiates the purchasing process.

In Chapter 7 we discussed the notion of the Economic Man and its drawbacks in the context of consumer behaviour. The notion of the Economic Man relates primarily to cognition and its impact on conation, as presented in the model in Figure 8.1. However, consumers as human beings are also driven by the unpredictable affective (emotional) component and this is what results in sometimes very irrational and inexplicable decision making. These internal factors are also complemented by a range of external factors, depending on the context and the environment that forms the consumer's frame of reference. These can refer to their personal circumstances, such as the size, type and make-up of their family, relationships with immediate and extended family members, type of groups the person belongs to outside of their immediate and extended family (e.g. memberships in clubs and social circles), and ways in which the person relates to their friends, acquaintances and strangers, their level and type of education received, etc. Additionally, external factors also include factors in the consumer's immediate environment and the economic, social, cultural, political and other forces that shape it.

It is, therefore, essential for event marketers to be able to profile their target consumers, in order to understand the range of internal and external factors that might be influencing their decision making. We spoke in Chapter 6 about the range of strategies for segmenting events customers. Whilst geo-demographic segmentation criteria clearly define the location frame for marketing activities, in the context of events as leisure market offerings, psychographic and behavioural segmentation can be argued to be much more important. If the motivation is strong, the distance a person has to travel to attend an event will be only a secondary factor in making the decision to attend. Understanding the consumer's key characteristics of 'being human' can facilitate the profiling of event consumers and can help event marketers appeal to the affective part of the consumer psyche.

Profiling consumers is never an easy task, regardless of what industry the marketer operates in. Whilst the currently widely adopted segmentation criteria are a step in the right direction, actual profiling of consumers means taking these a step further and attempting to draw inferences about consumers' intended purchasing behaviours based on a selection of personality traits. The key question that concerns profiling event consumers is this: 'What are our customers *really* like?' In order to answer it, the marketer needs to take into consideration four key variables: the consumers' **drive and motivation**, their **personality**,

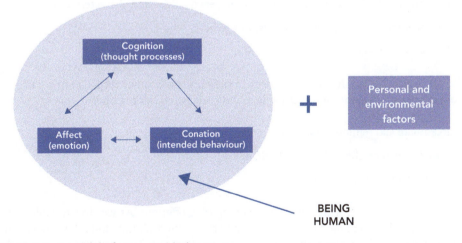

Figure 8.1 A model of consumer behaviour
Source: Adapted from Blythe (2013)

the **way they may perceive** an event and the way they will **form their attitude** about attending (or not attending) it. We discuss these four key concepts in greater detail in the following sections.

Event consumer personality

Blythe (2013, p. 79) defines consumer personality as 'the collection of individual characteristics that make a person unique, and which control an individual's responses and relationships with the external environment'. A consumer's personality is therefore unique to the individual and influences their concept of 'self'. Solomon *et al.* (2013) have identified that a person's self-concept is based on their physical appearance, mental aptitude and self-esteem. They have also found, similar to Blythe (2013), that a person's self-concept is:

- Learned, not innate – it develops over time based on the intensity of feelings and opinions a person has regarding their physical appearance and mental aptitude, which influences their self-esteem.

- Stable and consistent over time – it is not likely to be changed easily and can, therefore, be a good indicator of the person's decision-making patterns.

- Purposeful – it is there to protect and enhance a person's ego.

The exploration of personality was further popularised by popular psychologists, such as Dr Phillip C. McGraw (the popular 'Dr Phil', Oprah's resident psychologist), who has highlighted the notion of 'authentic self', which defines a person as 'a composite of unique gifts, skills, abilities, insights, wisdom, strengths and values'. Simply put, the self-concept is the person's own idea of and feelings about themselves.

Banister and Hogg (2003, cited in Blythe, 2013) have distinguished between three levels of self:

- The actual self – i.e. who the person is, their real qualities and characteristics.

- The ideal self – i.e. who the person aspires to be.

- The worst self – i.e. the worst version of the self.

The self-concept is an important element in defining a consumer response to a particular product or service, as the person is likely to use their purchases to either:

- accentuate and reinforce their actual self

- work towards reaching their ideal self, or

- avoid their worst self.

This is particularly true with events as leisure market offerings. As we already explained in Chapters 2 and 3, these are not essential to a person's survival, therefore, the person is not required to buy and 'consume' them to stay alive or to feel safe. They are seen as vehicles that help us express our identity and enable us to gather knowledge and experience. In today's world that supports individualism, events we attend can, therefore, be seen as an extension of our personalities. Thus, identifying consumer personality types that would be attracted by the key features and ideas of the event that is being organised is a key step in determining the profile of the event's target audiences. This information can then be used in establishing an overall marketing strategy and specific tactics which will emphasise the pull factors of the event and help draw out the drive that will push the individual to attend.

Event consumer perception

The second concept influencing event consumer behaviour is consumer perception: a social-psychological phenomenon of converting sensory input into an understanding of how the world works (Blythe, 2013). Essentially, perception is the way that an individual will select and consider a range of cues related to buying (and using) a product or service and evaluate how suitable different options are to meeting their specific need. Figure 8.2 outlines a model of consumer perception, adapted from Blythe (2013) and Solomon *et al.* (2013).

Essentially, what this model demonstrates is that consumer perception is a result of a range of activities. First, the consumer is stimulated through a combination of the five senses, which create sensations that might arouse the individual's attention. The individual will then either actively engage with a particular stimulus or they might choose to ignore it. If the individual engages with the stimulus, they will proceed to interpret the cues and allocate meaning to them, which will then elicit a particular response. This response will, then, lead to the forming of the individual's perception. It is clear, then, that not all stimuli will elicit a response and lead to perception and this has important implications for events (or indeed any other) marketing practice. Just because the marketer has created a piece of advertising or PR and has put this information out through a range of different channels does not automatically imply that the consumer will actually perceive them. As we will see later in Chapter 10, consumers are becoming more and more immune to the traditional marketing initiatives to the point where they are actually actively blocking their perception of brand marketing efforts. It is, therefore, important for marketers to choose the marketing stimuli (and marketing channels) wisely and strategically in order to capture consumers' attention and create a positive perception. This positive perception is a crucial element in the effective positioning of a product or service in the marketplace in comparison to its direct (and indirect) competitors (Foxall *et al.*, 1998).

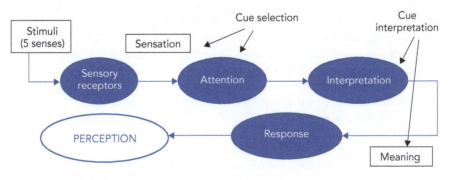

Figure 8.2 A model of consumer perception
Source: Adapted from Blythe (2013) and Solomon *et al.* (2013)

Consumer perception is affected by a range of personal factors, such as gender, personality, social class, age, educational level and overall intelligence. There are also external factors that can be manipulated to elicit positive perception and marketers have made use of approaches such as colourology, atmospherics and brand image to make the products and services they are selling more attractive to their target audiences. One of the most widely used approaches in determining the positioning strategy for any market offering is the use of *perceptual mapping* to highlight the source of its diversification and positioning.

Perceptual mapping is a practical exercise which enables marketers to understand how their market offering (product, service or event) does or can position itself against its competitors considering a range of criteria. The criteria is normally split into two separate categories: *important* and *determinant* attributes. *Important attributes* are the characteristics that a market offering absolutely **must** possess in order to even be considered by the consumer as a suitable choice to their purchasing decision. *Determinant attributes* are desirable attributes that help the consumer narrow down and make the final choice between various options that contain the same important attributes. Most marketing experts will advise caution with regards to the choice of determinant attributes. Whilst it would be easy to create perceptual maps relating the price and quality of a particular market offering, this is not the best approach to take, because price and quality are highly correlated and the evaluation of quality is very subjective. Therefore, using price and quality in a single perceptual map will not create results that are usable. A perceptual map should either use price OR quality as one of the dimensions (axis) and another specific feature of the market offering, which is comparable to a range of its competitors. It is advisable for marketers to develop determinant attribute sets which outline the brand's personality and can be used for comparing the brand to a range of its direct and indirect competitors. This will then be useful to make judgements about the strength of the brand in relation to its competitors and for using these judgements to define and execute marketing strategy and tactics.

An example of perceptual mapping is provided in Vignette 8.1.

VIGNETTE 8.1

Perceptual mapping of the UK summer music festivals

Jodie is a final-year student at a top UK university. Originally from London, she has lived away from home and worked hard for the past three years and this year she will be graduating with a First Class Honours degree in BA Marketing. She wants to take some time off to relax and party over the summer and she has already started planning what she might do. She is into music and will definitely want to attend at least one music festival in the UK, as she loves the idea of camping with her friends and enjoying the freshest beats. Jodie likes children, but NOT when she's trying to have some fun. She is proficient in mainstream pop music, but she wants to expand her horizons this summer and try out some new things. She is planning to spend a month abroad in June, come back home in July and then spend another month abroad in August. She has done some research and Table 8.1 shows what she has found about the summer music festivals in the UK.

Table 8.1 The list of festivals Jodie was considering to attend

Festival name	Dates/location/distance from London	Festival type
Latitude Festival	16–19 July, Suffolk (c.90 miles)	Pop-culture festival (inc. art, theatre, comedy, cabaret, politics, dance & literature)
T in the Park	10–12 July, Strathallan Castle, Scotland (c.460 miles)	Music festival, incorporating 'undiscovered talent' stages
Glas-Denbury Festival	10–11 July, South Devon (c.230 miles)	Family-friendly music festival
Lovebox Festival	17–18 July, Victoria Park, London (c.6 miles)	Dance, indie, rock, world and pop music festival; no camping
Monmouth Festival	24 July–1 Aug, South East Wales (c.215 miles)	Free festival encompassing a range of music genres and includes an annual carnival day, festival site is in the town and performances utilise a range of local venues
OutCider Festival	31 July–1 Aug, Somerset (c.150 miles)	Eclectic music, local cider, ale and food – simple!
V Festival	22–23 Aug, Chelmsford/Birmingham (c.40 miles/120 miles)	2 venues, commercial pop music
Leeds Festival	28–30 Aug, Leeds (c.200 miles)	Twin festivals, rock, indie, alternative rock, heavy metal and punk rock music; unattractive bands bottled off the stage by audience
Reading Festival	28–30 Aug, Reading (c.50 miles)	
Creamfields Festival	28–30 Aug, Cheshire (c.185 miles)	Dance music

In order to make her decision, Jodie will have a couple of important and determinant attributes that she will use to frame her perception. The key important attribute for Jodie will be the timing of the festival: as she is abroad in June and August, the only time she has available to attend a UK music festival is during July. Therefore, based on this important criterion, Jodie will immediately eliminate Leeds, Reading, Creamfields and V Festival. She will then proceed to decide what her determinant attributes for this decision might be. Let's say that she wants to base her decision on the distance of the event from her home in London, as well as the profile of the festival (i.e. she wants to attend a festival that is versatile and incorporates more than just music). The perceptual map in Figure 8.3 can help us identify which particular festivals might appeal to Jodie.

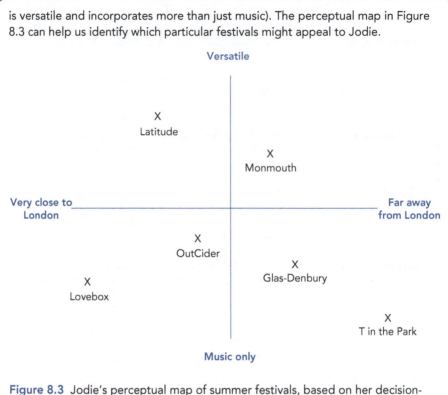

Figure 8.3 Jodie's perceptual map of summer festivals, based on her decision-making criteria

Based on the two determinant attributes, Jodie can now make her decision. She is likely to eliminate Glas-Denbury from further consideration, as this is a family friendly festival and she does not want to be surrounded by children whilst she is having fun. Lovebox is likely to be too close to her home and does not have camping facilities, therefore this would not allow her to really relax and have a sense of freedom. T in the Park is likely to be too far away from London and focuses on music only, therefore not meeting her need/desire for expanding her horizons and experiencing new things. The three remaining options of Latitude, Monmouth and OutCider are the likely contenders to get Jodie to spend her money on attending and having fun with her friends.

Event consumer attitudes

The next aspect of consumer behaviour that has a bearing on purchasing decisions relates to the consumer's formation of attitudes towards a product, service or an event. Consumer attitudes complement the perceptual processing by providing meaning, or the context for the interpretation of cues from the external environment. Katz (1960, cited in Foxall *et al.*, 1998) has identified four key functions of attitudes. They can be used to:

- Assess the utility of a product or service to the attainment of their personal goals (*adjustment function*).

- Help emphasise the individual's ego and their position within their specific social context (*ego-defensive function*).

- Aid the expression of deeply held values and beliefs (*value expressive function*).

- Facilitate meaning formation in relation to a range of phenomena (*knowledge function*).

In Chapter 7 (Figure 7.6) we presented a model of consumer decision making in relation to event participation. Figure 8.4 outlines the influence of consumer attitudes and which stages of the consumer decision-making process they come into play in.

As can be seen from Figure 8.4, consumer attitudes permeate the whole of the consumer decision-making process. Indeed, there is consensus amongst a number of marketing and consumer psychology authors that the relationship between attitudes and actual consumer behaviour is a reciprocal relationship (e.g. Foxall *et al.*, 1998; Blythe, 2013; Solomon *et al.*, 2013) which has no defined starting point. There are instances where consumers will form their behaviour before making an actual purchase, but there are also cases where consumers will purchase first and then form their attitudes based on their immediate experience of a product or service. The relationship is, however, ongoing and a consumer's experience of a

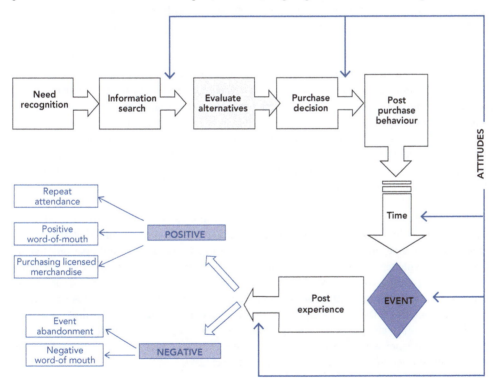

Figure 8.4 The influence of consumer attitudes in event consumer decision making

Source: Adapted from Brassington and Pettitt (2003), Masterman and Wood (2006), Blythe (2013) and Kim *et al.* (2013)

product or service will inform their attitude, which (if positive) will encourage re-purchase. This is particularly important for event marketers, as it is the strength of the attitudes that consumers hold towards the event brand that will play a key role in ensuring consumers take time out of their busy schedules to actually attend an event. Also, it is the event experience itself that will inform the formation, change or reinforcement of attitudes, which will influence future purchasing behaviour. The strength of these attitudes will influence the amount of persuasion the marketer will need to employ within their marketing campaigns to influence these consumers to attend the event.

The relationship between consumer needs, wants and motivations

The topic of motivation has been extensively researched, both in general management study and in the context of marketing. We've mentioned earlier in this chapter that events are leisure market offerings which aim to satisfy consumers' hedonic motives. Higgins (2006) argued the role of hedonic experiences which are pleasurable and fun and satisfy consumers' emotional and aesthetic needs. Therefore, attending events would correspond to levels 3–5 on Maslow's hierarchy of needs, which we discussed in Chapter 7 (Figure 7.1).

Building on the work of Iso-Ahola (1980) who defined motive as 'an internal factor that arouses, directs and integrates a person's behaviour', Nicholson and Pearce (2001) define motivation as a state of need that leads an individual towards satisfaction. Similarly, Pearce, Morrison and Rutledge (1998, cited in Benckendorff and Pearce, 2012) define motivation as the totality of biological and cultural forces which guide consumer choice, behaviour and experience. Adair (2006) identifies a want as a need that has become conscious and argues that a person is motivated when he or she *wants* to do something. Ryan and Deci (2000) define motivation as *being moved* to do something and stress that people will have a varying *level* (i.e. how much) as well as varying *orientation* (i.e. the type) of motivation. It is this orientation, or type, of motivation that demonstrates why people take certain actions and reveals their underlying needs and wants. Mitchell (1982, in Mullins, 2008) define motivation as a multifaceted phenomenon pertaining to an individual, which is usually intentional and is used to predict human behaviour.

Generally, we can recognise two key types of motivation: extrinsic and intrinsic motivation (Walker and Miller, 2007). *Extrinsic motivation* leads to actions that are aimed at achieving a desired outcome separable from the activity itself and are executed in anticipation of some form of consequence – usually an attainment of something perceived as 'good' or avoidance of something perceived as 'bad'. An example of this would be a monetary reward to an employee for completing all their administrative tasks well before the office closing time, or imposing penalties if they take longer than the advertised opening hours. *Intrinsic motivation*, on the other hand, refers to actions done because they are inherently interesting or enjoyable, they emanate from a person's sense of self, are volitional and are accompanied by the experience of freedom and autonomy (Ryan and Deci, 2000).

Although it is not effective to label intrinsic and extrinsic motivation along the spectrum of good versus bad, it has been recognised in the growing body of literature that extrinsic motivation can at times be counter-productive (i.e. not achieve the desired outcome), whilst intrinsic motivation tends to result in high-quality learning, creativity and achievement (Ryan and Deci, 2000).

Ryan and Deci (2000) additionally recognised that intrinsic motivation is not necessarily always internal to the individual, it usually exists in the nexus between a person and a task and can be heavily influenced by the individual's perception of that task. Deci and Ryan's (1985) Self-Determination Theory focuses primarily on identifying intrinsic motivation in the satisfaction of the three innate psychological needs for competence, autonomy and relatedness and does not encompass the discussion of motivations for the fulfilment of basic human needs. In this sense, it can be argued that – in the context of events and other leisure activities, at least – intrinsic motivation should be considered and discussed at levels 3–5 of Maslow's hierarchy of needs.

Drive is defined as an internal stimulus caused by the gap between the actual and the desired state: it is the force that makes a person respond to a need (a perceived lack of something) (Blythe, 2013). In Daniel Pink's 2009 book *Drive: The surprising truth about what motivates us* he explores the differences between extrinsic and intrinsic motivation with some surprising results. He identified that, whilst still the most commonly used tool, extrinsic motivators (also known as the 'carrot and stick' method) are only effective in a small number of situations, in which the nature of work is largely routine and requires mechanical skill and very little creativity and deep thinking. Building on the foundations laid by Deci and Ryan's (1985) Self-Determination Theory, Pink (2009) highlights three key human drives: *being autonomous, self-determined* and *connected to one another*.

Consumer motivations to engage with events

Visitor motivations to attend events have been a strong focus of event management research from the very early days of the event industry development (Getz, 2007). A range of theories of motivation are applicable to the study of event consumers. Li and Petrick's (2006) review of festival and event motivation research has found that the event motivation studies have more often than not adapted relevant theoretical frameworks already used in the fields of tourism, leisure and recreation research (see Crompton, 1979; Iso-Ahola, 1980, 1982; Dann, 1981; Crompton and McKay, 1997; Uysal *et al.*, 2006; Park *et al.*, 2009).

More recently, Benckendorff and Pearce (2012) posit that three key theories of motivation which dominate most studies of leisure, sport and tourism motivation are:

1 Murray's (1938) Needs Theory of Personality.

2 Maslow's (1943) Hierarchy of Needs.

3 Berlyne's (1960) Concept of Optimal Level of Stimulation.

Funk *et al.* (2012, cited in Kim *et al.*, 2013), on the other hand, have used Deci and Ryan's (1985) Self-Determination Theory to explore the intrinsic and extrinsic motivations of sport spectators, whilst Zuckerman's Arousal Theory (2000) outlined in Figure 8.5 comes closest to relating motivation to the hedonic nature of experiences. It argues that people need to be aroused in order to be motivated and that a person will aim to maintain an optimum level or arousal, thus enabling him (her) to move along the continuum depending on the specific context.

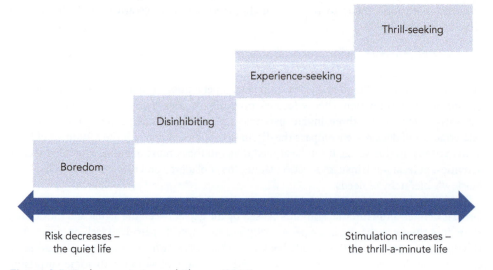

Figure 8.5 Zuckerman's Arousal Theory (2000)
Source: Adapted from Blythe (2013)

When discussing antecedents of event attendee motivation, Getz (2007) argues that motivations are influenced by individual factors, such as personality, values, attitudes and lifestyle, as well as interpersonal factors, such as cultural background and social norms that shape a person's perception. An interaction of these factors, he believes, shapes a person's desire to experience certain events. These desires (or *wants*) clash with a number of constraints that limit a person's choice. The constraints are defined as structural, personal or interpersonal (Crawford *et al.*, 1991, cited in Getz, 2007). What makes a difference between attending or not attending an event is the level of motivation that drives the decision-making process.

Swarbrooke and Horner (2007) recognise the importance of six broad types of tourist motivators in driving consumer behaviour in the context of tourism. These are presented in Table 8.2. As the table indicates, all of these broad factors are applicable to the events sector. There is some consensus amongst researchers that emotions play a dominant role in tourism motivation research (Gnoth, 1997, cited in Hosany, 2012, and Goossens, 2000), which is in line with the hedonic nature of tourism activities, as well as events. Following Crompton's (1979) findings, most current studies of motivation in the context of tourism and events explore motivations within the *push–pull* dichotomy: consumers are *pushed* by their internal needs and drives, dependent on their individual situation, and are *pulled* by specific characteristics of events (or tourism destinations). Iso-Ahola (1980) had similar findings, indicating that individuals are motivated by either *seeking* specific pleasurable experiences, or *escaping* specific negative ones. These are illustrated in Figure 8.6.

Table 8.2 Types of tourist motivators

Motivator group	Types of motivators	Applicable to events?
Personal	Visiting friends and relatives, making new friends, need to satisfy others, cost-consciousness if on very limited income	Personal events, such as birthdays, weddings or religious celebrations
Emotional	Nostalgia, romance, adventure, escapism, fantasy, spiritual fulfilment	Wellbeing retreats, nostalgia-driven music or cultural events, team building events, etc.
Physical	Relaxation, suntan, exercise and health, sex	Parties in tourism destinations such as e.g. Ibiza, bootcamp events, etc.
Cultural	Sightseeing, experiencing new cultures	Heritage- and culture-oriented events, often tied to a particular destination
Status	Exclusivity, fashionability, obtaining a good deal, ostentatious spending opportunities	Premium, top-tier events such as the London Boat Show, or exclusive hospitality packages at mega-events such as the Olympics, the World Cup or the F1 Grand Prix
Personal development	Increasing knowledge, mastering a new skill	Conferences, conventions, trade shows, workshops, trainings, etc.

Source: Swarbrooke and Horner (2007)

Figure 8.6 The push-pull/seeking-escaping dichotomy

Consumer motivation and event type

The area of research relating to consumer motivations for attending events has grown in popularity in recent years. There are now a considerable number of resources that enable us to explore this area in greater detail and draw conclusions based on event type. A broad overview of event-related literature focusing on motivation to attend a range of specific event types is presented in Figures 8.7–8.10.

Motivations for attending festivals are amongst the most researched areas in the study of event motivations. As can be seen from Table 8.2, the motives for attending these types of events are broadly in line with the seeking and escaping dichotomy discussed in the previous section. In all instances consumers are seeking some form of socialisation, whether that's spending time with family and friends (i.e. known-group socialisation) or attending these events to socialise with new people. Aside from socialisation, festival attendees are in all instances seeking novelty – something that will take them out of their everyday routine and allow them to have a completely different experience.

Motivations for attending sporting events also broadly fit within the seeking–escaping dichotomy. Attendees are generally seeking excitement, achievement and salubrious effects, whilst escaping from their everyday routine.

Formica and Uysal (1996)	Crompton and McKay (1997)	Faulkner et al. (1999)	Nicholson and Pearce (2001)
Excitement and thrills	Cultural exploration	Local culture/identity	External interaction/soc.
Socialisation	Novelty/regression	Excitement/novelty seeking	Novelty/uniqueness
Entertainment	Recover equilibrium	Party	Variety
Event novelty	Known-group socialisation	Local attractions	Entertainment/excitement
Family togetherness	External interaction/socialisation	Socialisation	Escape
	Gregariousness	Known-group soc.	Family
		Ancillary activities	
		Seeing artists perform	

Figure 8.7 Consumer motivations for attending music festivals

Source: Adapted from Gelder and Robinson (2009) and Schofield and Thompson (2009)

Sloan (1989, in Kshetri et al., 2009)	Kim et al. (2013) – F1 Event	Wann (1995, in Kshetri et al., 2009) – Sport Fan Motivation Scale (SFMS)
Entertainment	Entertainment	Eustress (positive stress)
Achievement seeking	Achievement seeking	Escape from everyday life
Catharsis and aggression	Catharsis	Entertainment
Stress and stimulation seeking	Salubrious effects	Economic factors
Salubrious effects		Aesthetics
		Group affiliation
		Family needs

Figure 8.8 Consumer motivations for attending sporting events

Source: Kshetri et al. (2009) and Kim et al. (2013)

Although they are not as popular (in academic terms) as festivals and mega-events, there is a range of research published relating to motivations to attend food and wine events. These can be broadly attributed to the seeking of enjoyment in the taste of specific food and wine, as well as socialisation and learning more about specific types of each. It is interesting to note that with these types of events no specific element of motivation corresponds to the need for escaping.

The body of literature explored in relation to motivation to attend business events encompasses a range of different examples. It is widely accepted that the key motivator for attending these types of events is the search for information/education, as well as networking. This is true for conferences, trade shows and exhibitions. Interestingly, though, this set included the Shanghai EXPO, which, although a mega trade show, attracts a wide range of audiences, both B2B and B2C. It is, therefore, unsurprising that this event included

Park *et al.* (2008) – Food and wine festival	Smith and Costello (2009) – Culinary event	Tanford *et al.* (2012) – Wine festival
Taste	Food (quality, uniqueness and experience)	Social recognition (inc. interaction at the event and recognition for attending)
Enjoyment	Event novelty	The wine experience
Social status	Socialisation	Enjoyment
Change		Diversion (attending just to pass time)
Meeting people		
Family		
Meeting experts		

Figure 8.9 Consumer motivations for attending food and wine events
Source: Adapted from Park *et al.* (2008), Smith and Costello (2009) and Tanford *et al.* (2012)

Severt *et al.* (2007) – Convention (conference)	Park *et al.* (2009) – Boat Show	Lee *et al.* (2010) – Hong Kong exhibitions	Lee *et al.* (2012) – Shanghai EXPO 2010
Activities and opportunities	Boat purchasing information	Fulfilment of business needs	Cultural exploration
Networking	Boat and boating-related products	Networking opportunity	Family togetherness
Convenience	Boat financing and slip information	Information search	Event attractions (inc. atmosphere)
Education benefits		Reward (incentive) travel	Socialisation
Products and deals		Market investigation	Novelty
			Escape

Figure 8.10 Consumer motivations for attending business events
Source: Adapted from Severt *et al.* (2007), Park *et al.* (2009), Lee *et al.* (2010) and Lee *et al.* (2012)

motivations such as 'family togetherness' and 'cultural exploration' rather than the more business-oriented ones of seeking information and networking in a professional context.

Consumer motivation and event marketing

So what is the role of motivation in event marketing? As the growing body of motivation research indicates, motivations are an extremely pertinent concept in the study of consumer behaviour. The inherent ephemeral nature of events, discussed earlier in Chapter 2, adds to the complexity of identifying what motivates people to attend events.

Wolfheil and Whelan (2006) emphasise the importance of understanding consumer motivations and experiential needs in designing effective marketing strategies. They talk about this in the context of marketing events (for further information on these please refer to Chapter 13), but this is equally crucial for all other types of events: from small local fetes or celebrations to mega- and hallmark events which require years of planning. Similarly, Miller and Layton (2000, cited in Allen *et al.*, 2011) refer to marketing as a tool that facilitates the satisfaction of human needs and wants and Crompton and McKay (1997) stress the usefulness of understanding event motives in designing offerings for event attendees, monitoring attendee satisfaction and trying to understand attendees' decision-making processes.

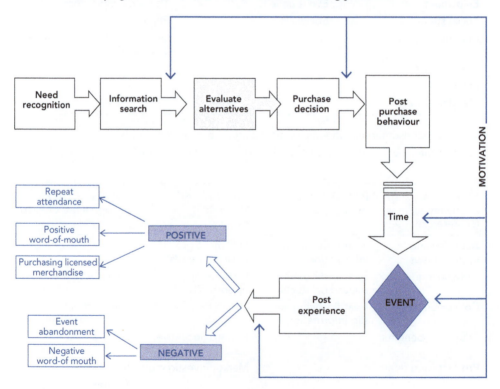

Figure 8.11 The role of motivation in event consumer decision making

Source: Adapted from Brassington and Pettitt (2003), Masterman and Wood (2006), Blythe (2013) and Kim *et al.* (2013)

Figure 8.11 highlights the role of motivation in the process of consumer decision making. It is clear to see that motivation is important in every step of the consumer decision-making process: it will sustain the consumer's interest in attending and learning more about the event or its specific features or participants. Without motivation, event attendance would be seriously negatively affected and the financial and other success of the event would be jeopardised.

CASE STUDY

The Harley-Davidson Experience – 'Because you don't just fit in. You belong.'

Bikers have a reputation for being 'renegades', 'outlaws' and 'troublemakers' of a mostly dubious integrity and questionable relationship with the law. These perceptions have long been reinforced through mainstream media, particularly popular Hollywood films, such as the 1953 *The Wild One* starring Marlon Brando, the 1955 *Rebel Without a Cause* starring James Dean or the 1969 *Easy Rider* starring Peter Fonda, Dennis Hopper and Jack Nicholson. One resilient brand changed it all – the Harley-Davidson.

Harley-Davidson: the brand

Since its inception as an endeavour of a group of close friends from two families in 1903, the Milwaukee-based motorcycle producer Harley-Davidson has gone through cycles of ups and downs, but has managed to survive as the ultimate all-American brand. This is only partly due to the image their bikes have for being big, rugged, bold and 'different'. The other ingredient is their ability to successfully adapt to the changing market conditions, particularly their ageing target audience – the Baby Boomers – and engaging them in what the brand calls the Harley-Davidson 'way of life'. In the mid- to late 1980s and early 1990s, faced with their primary target audience reaching their middle age, as well as increasing competition from Japanese motorcycle manufacturers entering the US market, the company was at a crossroads. It needed to attract a different profile of customers: from its loyal and reliable blue-collar, regular working-class 'Joes' to a more affluent type of riders who would (a) spend more money in any given purchase and (b) make more purchases over a longer period of time. The company's answer to its predicament was twofold:

- They improved the quality of their product by improving the engine reliability, reducing vibration on its top-of-the-line touring bikes and even introducing sophisticated stereo systems and intercoms built into the helmets.

- They introduced the feeling of exclusivity delivered via its newly formed Harley Owners Group (HOG) club, which gives those new owners of a Harley-Davidson motorcycle access to an alternative lifestyle so different from their day-to-day lives.

By the second half of the first decade of the twenty-first century, half of Harley's sales came from new customers, with the other half comprised repeat purchases by loyal seasoned Harley riders (Weber, 2006).

Harley-Davidson: the culture

Over the past two decades, Harley-Davidson has successfully repositioned itself and built up a strong following of affluent ageing Baby Boomers, who in their ordinary lives occupy mundane, mainstream white-collar jobs, such as dentists, doctors, accountants, financial advisors, advertising executives, real estate managers and government administrators. There are even anecdotal reports that the new generation of American bikers actually believes in conservative values, which is in stark contrast to the image of outlaws and troublemakers so deeply ingrained in society's mind and reinforced in the media since the 1950s. It might, therefore, be more accurate to describe them as biker enthusiasts (Schembri, 2009). So why do so many of these professionals flock to Harley-Davidson? The answer is: the Harley-Davidson culture.

The culture Harley-Davidson has built up through its products appeals to its target market's need for having a release from the daily stresses and worries they experience in their work and home lives. They long for a sense of freedom, being able to just take off, ride their Harley and feel the sun on their face and the wind in their hair. They seek a sense of belonging to something bigger than themselves and for connecting with like-minded individuals in search for an escape from their everyday lives. Despite the differences in their profiles, gender and career aspirations, the Harley riders predominantly (but not 100 per cent of the time):

- Are white, middle-aged, middle class.

- Sport tattoos, even if they are temporary ones.

- Prefer riding their bikes in a group, or at least with a passenger, rather than alone.

- Would ride almost twice as often in a group.

- Prefer Harley-Davidson to other motorcycles, not because of the quality of its products, but because of the brand's personality, what it stands for and how it can reflect their own aspirations.

- Intend to and do commit to the brand long term, purchasing both bike-related and other Harley-Davidson branded items: aside from owning a Harley-Davidson bike, they also wear Harley-Davidson branded clothing, boots and personal accessories and spend fortunes on bike gear and accessories.

- Harley-Davidson answers these needs with strongly incorporating an experiential component to its brand through a range of events that cater to these types of audiences.

Harley-Davidson: events

The Harley-Davidson's HOG club provides new Harley owners with exclusive access to various events and exclusive discounts on a range of products via their local dealers. Aside from participating in the local HOG chapter club rides, riders also form informal clubs of their own and gather for rallies, rides and runs on a regular basis. At these events, there are largely three groups of attendees (Corey and Millage, 2014):

- HOGs – the Harley-Davidson owners who proudly rev their engines and make a lot of noise.

- Riders who own and ride another make of motorcycle, but openly aspire to owning a Harley in the future – these are usually actively nagged at by the HOGs as not riding a 'true bike' and feel somewhat embarrassed because of it.

- Those who can't afford to buy a Harley-Davidson but are so enamoured with the brand that they aren't willing to settle for an 'inferior' make of motorcycle, and therefore ride pillion with the HOGs.

Events give HOGs the opportunity to immerse themselves in the Harley-Davidson culture: the focus is never on the functional value of the product itself, but on how it (and its image) contributes to the individual's self-concept. Through their participation, the HOGs co-construct their own experience of the Harley-Davidson brand, as well as explore, build and/or reinforce their own sense of identity. Therefore, these events help the consumers define the brand, whilst at the same time the brand defines the consumer (Schembri, 2009).

The HOGs themselves refer to their culture as ageless and classless, where the only thing that matters is that riding a Harley-Davidson gives you the freedom to go wherever, whenever. Their values revolve around respecting the bike, time on the road and respecting others, including authorities (Schembri, 2009). Whilst they don't dwell on differences in terms of their backgrounds, age, gender or other characteristics marketers would normally use to segment their target markets, the HOGs do have a form of internal hierarchy, which is reflected in the way they ride, and rituals which strengthen their sense of community and belonging. For example, the HOG chapter rides are led by the elected Director and Road Captain, followed by other chapter committee members and established members with no formal chapter roles. New members ride in the back of the formation, supervised by the Safety Officer and the nominated Tail-End Charlie (the very last bike). Before each ride, the Director addresses the group, the route is announced by the Ride Captain, and the Safety Officer assesses the risk and briefs the participants on the rules for a safe ride in a staggered formation. While riding, the HOGs watch out for each other's safety and for the safety of the general public they are passing along the way.

In addition to internalising the symbolism of the Harley-Davidson brand as one of freedom and full self-expression, the HOGs also view their individual bikes as extensions of their own personalities and no two Harleys, therefore, are the same. Before each group ride, the HOGs wash and polish their bikes and kit them out with a range of accessories. With each ride, the HOGs earn their 'stripes', i.e. pins, which they proudly add to their leather jackets, to demonstrate their history, belonging to the community and to have physical reminders of the experiences they have gathered along the way. Although it may appear to outsiders that HOG events are open only to individuals or couples, there are surprisingly many families participating in them each year and the members endeavour to make them as child friendly as possible, again breaking the preconceptions others may have of who they are as people and the values they uphold.

A thundering group of contemporary outlaws rolling down the street is a postmodern spectacle worth relishing, because, ultimately, they don't just fit in. They belong.

More information about the brand and the Harley Owners Group (HOG) can be found on their website at www.harley-davidson.com, and their social media sites on Facebook: 'Harley-Davidson', Twitter: @harleydavidson, and YouTube channel 'Harley-Davidson'.

Case study compiled from a range of sources, including:

Agnihotri, A. 2013. Turnaround of Harley Davidson – cult brand or strategic fit approach?, *Journal of Strategic Marketing*, 21(3), pp. 292–230.

Corey, J. and Millage, P. 2014. Ethnographic study on the Harley Davidson culture and community, *Journal of Technology Management in China*, 9(1), pp. 67–74.

Schembri, S. 2009. Reframing brand experience: The experiential meaning of Harley-Davidson, *Journal of Business Research*, 62, pp. 1299–1310.

Schembri, S. and Boyle, M.V. 2013. Visual ethnography: Achieving rigorous and authentic interpretations, *Journal of Business Research*, 66, pp. 1251–1254.

Weber, J. 2006. Harley just keeps on cruisin'; aging customers? Sure. Nostalgia brand? Definitely. So why is its stock at a record high? (Harley-Davidson Inc.), *Business Week*, Issue 4008, p. 71.

Case study questions

1 What is the profile of Harley-Davidson's target audiences? What distinguishes them from consumers who buy Hondas, Kawasakis and other types of motorcycles?

2 How does the Harley-Davidson brand engage with their consumers?

3 How could Harley-Davidson marketing and product development executives capitalise on the HOG culture and develop new products to fit the target market?

4 What emerging markets/audiences do you see for Harley-Davidson in the next 10–20 years and how would you suggest they engage these effectively?

SUMMARY

This chapter has explored in detail the key components of the consumer decision-making process in relation to events: consumer personality, perception, attitudes and motivations. We have demonstrated how each of these components impacts on consumer decision making. Consumer personality influences event consumption to satisfy consumer's self-concept. Perception is crucial in establishing which strategies, tactics and specific marketing channels the marketer will use to promote the event. Consumer attitude can change at any given point in the decision-making process, so the management of perception is crucial for maintaining a positive attitude of consumers towards the event. And finally, whilst there is a range of motivations related to specific types of events, these largely fall within Crompton's push–pull and Iso-Ahola's (1982) seeking–escaping dichotomies, which are in line with the notion of events as hedonic leisure experiences.

REVIEW QUESTIONS

1 What are the crucial human characteristics that may impact on consumer decision-making processes in relation to events?

2 Elaborate on what the role of personality is in consumer choice.

3 How can consumer perception be useful in the process of planning marketing activities for events?

4 How do event consumers form their attitudes towards the event and what implications does this have for the marketing?

5 Identify the range of motivations that have been recognised in the academic literature as relevant to attending events. How do these fit within Crompton's (1979) push-pull dichotomy?

6 What are the key components of consumer profiling and how can these be used effectively in planning and managing event marketing activities?

EVENT MARKETING SCENARIO

You have been working in your local government's head office as an Events Coordinator for the past two years. Your boss has been happy with your performance so far and has indicated that she would like to put you forward for a promotion to an Events Manager within the next 12 months. However, in order for her to do this, you will need to up your game and produce some tangible results within that period. In particular, your boss would like you to come up with specific ideas to increase participation of the local families in the range of community-oriented events the local government regularly hold. These include mum and baby clubs, family fun days and children's arts and crafts workshops held every other Saturday. Using your knowledge of consumer profiling, identify who your target audiences are and produce a profile of these, to include some reference to their personality, perception, attitude and likely motivations to attend. Once you've completed the profiles, discuss what approaches you would take with marketing these events in order to drive attendance.

FURTHER READING

Books

Blythe, J. 2013. *Consumer Behaviour*, 2nd Edition, London: SAGE
This is an excellent textbook that offers a good insight into the key aspects of consumer behaviour. It is written as a generic marketing text, but there are some references to the context of leisure and tourism, which would be useful for events students.

Foxall, G.R., Goldsmith, R.E. and Brown, S. 1998. *Consumer Psychology for Marketing*, 2nd Edition, Andover: Cengage Learning
This textbook looks at consumer behaviour from a psychological perspective and is a good introduction to the psychology of consumption. The concepts are explained in a clear and concise manner and thus should be accessible for both undergraduate and postgraduate level students.

Pink, D.H. 2009. *Drive: The surprising truth about what motivates us*, Edinburgh: Canongate Books Ltd
This book, written by the leading author in the field, provides an excellent overview of the differences between extrinsic and intrinsic motivation and gives ample examples for the reader to understand how both work in practice.

Thaler, R.H. and Sunstein, C.R. 2008. *Nudge: Improving decisions about health, wealth and happiness*, New Haven, CT: Yale University Press
This is a good resource that discusses some of the core themes of needs, drives and motivations in a wider context of life, rather than business. It is helpful to develop an understanding of consumers as human beings and the key aspects of basic human decision making.

Journals

Holt, D. 1995. How consumers consume: A typology of consumption practices, *Journal of Consumer Research*, 22, pp. 1–16
This article deals with the basics of human consumption and is one of the key articles used by a number of researchers when conducting projects related to consumer behaviour in a range of contexts. It is a good resource to develop an initial understanding of consumption, from which one can then build one's own understanding in the specific context of events.
Ryan, R.M. and Deci, E.L. 2000. Intrinsic and Extrinsic Motivations: Classic Definitions and New Directions, *Contemporary Educational Psychology*, 25, pp. 54-67
This article provides a good general overview of the theories of intrinsic and extrinsic motivation, with some discussion of potential future applications – a very good resource for developing a broad understanding of motivational factors in the context of consumption.
Schofield, P. and Thompson, K. 2009. Segmenting and profiling visitors to the Ulaanbaatar Naadam Festival by motivation, *Event Management*, 13, pp. 1-15
This article is a good starting point for any discussion on event visitor motivations. It provides a detailed overview of some of the key research projects dealing with the topic of visitor motivations for attending events and offers a range of further literature that might be of use.

Other resources

Psychology Today www.psychologytoday.com
Psychology Today is a website bringing together insights from a range of people involved with different aspects of psychology which is an extension of the hard copy magazine of the same title. Whilst not all of the website will be interesting to events marketers, the section focusing on consumer behaviour is useful for keeping abreast of the current developments and trends within this area and most resources have been written up in language that is accessible to a wide range of audiences.
Society for Consumer Psychology www.myscp.org/
The Society for Consumer Psychology is a network of scholars and practitioners dedicated to the growth and advancement of consumer psychology. The website is very helpful in identifying the leading resources and key authors within this subject area. As such it is a valuable resource for academics and students interested in this area of study.

REFERENCES

Adair, J. 2006. *Leadership and Motivation: The fifty-fifty rule and the eight key principles of motivating others*, London: Kogan Page.

Allen, J., O'Toole, W., Harris, R. and McDonnell, I. 2011. *Festival and Special Event Management*, 5th Edition, Milton: John Wiley & Sons Australia.

Ayob, N., Wahid, N.A. and Omar, A. 2013. Mediating effect of visitors' event experiences in relation to event features and post-consumption behaviors, *Journal of Convention and Event Tourism*, 14, pp. 177–192.

Benckendorff, P. and Pearce, P.L. 2012. The psychology of events, in Page, S.J. and Connell, J. (Eds), *The Routledge Handbook of Events*, London: Routledge.

Berlyne, D. 1960. *Conflict, Arousal and Curiosity*, New York: McGraw–Hill.

Blythe, J. 2013. *Consumer Behaviour*, 2nd Edition, London: SAGE.

Brassington, F. and Pettitt, S. 2003. *Principles of Marketing*, 3rd Edition, Harlow: FT Prentice Hall.

Crompton, J.L. 1979. Motivations for pleasure vacation, *Annals of Tourism Research*, 6, pp. 408–424.

Crompton, J.L. and McKay, S.L. 1997. Motives of visitors attending festival events, *Annals of Tourism Research*, 24, pp. 425–439.

Dann, G. 1981. Tourist motivations: an appraisal, *Annals of Tourism Research*, 8, pp. 189–219.

Deci, E.L. and Ryan, R.M. 1985. *Intrinsic Motivation and Self-Determination in Human Behaviour*, New York: Plenum.

Derbaix, M. and Derbaix, C. 2010. Generational concerts: In quest of authenticity?, *Recherche et Applications en Marketing* (English Edition), 25(3), pp. 57–84.

Faulkner, W., Fredline, E., Larson, M. and Tomljenovic, R. 1999. A marketing analysis of Sweden's Storsjoyran musical festival, *Tourism Analysis*, 4(4), pp. 157–171.

Formica, S. and Uysal, M. 1996. A market segmentation of festival visitors: Umbria Jazz Festival in Italy, *Festival Management and Event Tourism*, 3, pp. 175–182.

Foxall, G.R., Goldsmith, R.E. and Brown, S. 1998. *Consumer Psychology for Marketing*, 2nd Edition, Andover: Cengage Learning.

Gelder, G. and Robinson, P. 2009. A critical comparative study of visitor motivations for attending music festivals: a case study of Glastonbury and V Festival, *Event Management*, 13, pp. 181–196.

Getz, D. 2007. *Event studies: Theory, research and policy for planned events*, Oxford: Butterworth-Heinemann.

Geus, S. de, Richards, G. and Toepoel, V. 2013. The Dutch Queen's Day Event, *International Journal of Event and Festival Management*, 4(2), pp. 156–172.

Goosens, C. 2000. Tourism information and pleasure motivation, *Annals of Tourism Research*, 27(2), pp. 301–321.

Guignon, C. 2004. *On Being Authentic (Thinking in Action)*, Abingdon: Routledge.

Higgins, E.T. 2006. Value from hedonic experience and engagement, *Psychological Review*, 113(3), pp. 439–460.

Holt, D. 1995. How consumers consume: a typology of consumption practices, *Journal of Consumer Research*, 22, pp. 1–16.

Hosany, S. 2012. Appraisal determinants of tourist emotional responses, *Journal of Travel Research*, 51(3), pp. 303–314.

Hosany, S. and Gilbert, D. 2010. Measuring tourists' emotional experiences toward hedonic holiday destinations, *Journal of Travel Research*, 49(4), pp. 513–526.

Iso-Ahola, S.E. 1980. *The Social Psychology of Leisure and Recreation*, Dubuque: Wmc Brown.

Iso-Ahola, S.E. (1982) Toward a social psychology theory of tourism motivation: A rejoinder, *Annals of Tourism Research*, 9, pp. 256–262.

Jansson-Boyd, C. 2011. *Consumption Matters: A psychological perspective*, Basingstoke: Palgrave Macmillan.

Jensen, R. (2001) *The Dream Society: How the coming shift from information to imagination will transform your business*, New York: McGraw-Hill Education

Kim, S.K., Byon, K.K., Yu, J.G., Zhang, J.J. and Kim, C. 2013. Social motivations and consumption behavior of spectators attending a Formula One motor-racing event, *Social Behaviour and Personality*, 41(8), 1359–1378.

Kshetri, N., Queen, B., Schiopu, A. and Elmore, C. 2009. The profile and motivation of golf tournament attendees: An empirical study, *Journal of Interdisciplinary Mathematics*, 12(2), pp. 225–241.

Lee, C-K., Kang, S.K. and Lee, Y-K. 2013. Segmentation of mega event motivation: The case of EXPO 2010 Shanghai China, *Asia Pacific Journal of Tourism Research*, DOI:10.1080/10941665 .2012.695287.

Lee, M.J., Yeung, S. and Dewald, B. 2010. An exploratory study examining the determinants of attendance motivations as perceived by attendees at Hong Kong exhibitions, *Journal of Convention and Event Tourism*, 11(3), pp. 195–208.

Li, X. and Petrick, J.F. 2006. A review of festival and motivation studies, *Event Management*, 9(4), pp. 239–245.

Maslow, A. 1943 A theory of human motivation, *Psychological Review*, 50, pp. 370–396.

Masterman, G. and Wood, E. 2006. *Innovative Marketing Communications*, Oxford: Butterworth-Heinemann.

Morgan, M. and Watson, P. 2007. Resource guide in extraordinary experiences, HLST network of the UK Higher Education Academy. Available at: www.hlst.heacademy.ac.uk/assets/hlst/ documents/resource_guides/extraordinary_experiences.pdf.

Morgan, M., Lugosi, P. and Ritchie, B.J.R. 2010. Introduction, in Morgan, M., Lugosi, P. and Ritchie, J.R.B. (Eds) *The Tourism and Leisure Experience: Consumer and managerial perspective*, Bristol: Channel View Publications.

Mullins, L.J. 2008. *Essentials of Organisational Behaviour*, 2nd Edition, Harlow: Pearson Education Ltd.

Murray, H. 1938. *Exploration and Personality*, New York: Oxford University Press.

Nicholson, R.E. and Pearce, D.G. 2001. Why do people attend events: a comparative analysis of visitor motivations at four south island events, *Journal of Travel Research*, 39, pp. 449–460.

O'Sullivan, E.L and Spangler, K.J. 1999. *Experience Marketing: Strategies for the new millennium*, Abingdon: Spon Press.

Page, S.J. and Connell, J. 2010. *Leisure: An introduction*, Harlow: Prentice Hall.

Park, K., Reisinger, Y. and Kang, H. 2008. Visitors' motivation for attending the South Beach Wine and Food Festival, Miami Beach, Florida, *Journal of Travel and Tourism Marketing*, 25, pp. 161–181.

Park, K., Reisinger, Y. and Park, C. 2009. Visitors' motivation for attending theme parks in Orlando, Florida, *Event Management*, 13, pp. 83–101.

Peperkamp, E., Rooijackers, M. and Remmers, G.J. 2014. Evaluating and designing for experiential value: the use of visitor journeys, *Journal of Policy Research in Tourism, Leisure and Events*, 7(2) pp. 134–149.

Pine, J.P. and Gilmore, J.H. 1999. *The Experience Economy: Work is theater & every business a stage*, Boston: Harvard Business School Press.

Pink, D.H. 2009. *Drive: The surprising truth about what motivates us*, Edinburgh: Canongate Books Ltd.

Rojek, C. 2001. *Celebrity*, London: Reaktion.

Ryan, R.M. and Deci, E.L. 2000. Intrinsic and extrinsic motivations: classic definitions and new directions, *Contemporary Educational Psychology*, 25, pp. 54–67.

Schofield, P. and Thompson, K. 2009. Segmenting and profiling visitors to the Ulaanbaatar Naadam Festival by motivation, *Event Management*, 13, pp. 1–15.

Severt, D., Wang, Y. Chen, P-J. and Breiter, D. 2007. Examining the motivation, perceived performance, and behavioural intentions of conference attendees: Evidence from a regional conference, *Tourism Management*, 28(2), pp. 399–408.

Smith, S. and Costello, C. 2009. Segmenting visitors to a culinary event: Motivations, travel behavior and expenditures, *Journal of Hospitality Marketing and Management*, 18(1), pp. 44–67.

Solomon, M.R., Bamossy, G.J., Askegaard, S. and Hogg, M.K. 2013. *Consumer Behaviour: A European perspective*, 5th Edition, Harlow: Pearson Education Ltd.

Swarbrooke, J. and Horner, S. 2007. *Consumer Behaviour in Tourism*, Oxford: Butterworth-Heinemann.

Tanford, S., Montgomery, R. and Hertzman, J. 2012. Towards a model of wine event loyalty, *Journal of Convention and Event Tourism*, 13(2), pp. 77–99.

Thaler, R.H. and Sunstein, C.R. 2008. *Nudge: Improving decisions about health, wealth and happiness*, New Haven, CT: Yale University Press.

Uysal, M., Marshall, E., King, J. and Snepenger, D. 2006. Modelling Iso-Ahola's motivation theory in the tourism context, *Journal of Travel Research*, 45, pp.140–149.

Walker, J.R. and Miller, J.E. 2007. *Supervision in the Hospitality Industry: Leading human resources,* 6th Edition, Chichester: John Wiley & Sons.

WamWara-Mbugua, L. and Cornwell, T. 2010. Visitor motivation to attend international festivals, *Event Management*, 13, pp. 277–286.

White, C.J. 2010. The impact of emotions on service quality, satisfaction, and positive word-of-mouth intentions over time, *Journal of Marketing Management*, 26(5–6), pp. 381–394.

Wolfheil, M. and Whelan, S. 2006. Consumer motivations to participate in event-marketing strategies, *Journal of Marketing Management*, 22(5–6), pp. 643–669.

Zuckerman, M. 2000. Are you a risk-taker?, *Psychology Today*, November/December, pp. 54–87.

Chapter

An introduction to generic marketing communications strategies for events

LEARNING OUTCOMES

By the end of this chapter, students should be able to:

- Describe the various Push and Pull marketing communications strategies and explain the difference between them

- Distinguish between the strategies that interrupt the customer and those that seek permission, and be able to recognise which ones are suitable in particular situations

- Identify a number of marketing communications tactics which can support these marketing strategies

- Explain the implications of using an integrated event marketing approach in the delivery of marketing objectives

Reality is complex – it is not a sound bite or a one-liner – and marketing complexity has to be addressed with an open and daring mind.

Gummeson (2008)

Introduction

At the beginning of the twenty-first century, there was a strategic shift in how companies market their products and services to customers. In Chapter 4 we briefly outlined the evolution of marketing philosophies over the past hundred years or so. With the focus of marketing moving away from products and more towards consumers themselves (the shift from the production to the societal marketing concept), the nature of marketing has fundamentally changed. Marketing tools have followed suit and the differences between the traditional and contemporary marketing tactics are becoming increasingly obvious. In Chapters 7 and 8 we presented the key characteristics of event consumers. We now turn our attention to the how of marketing. This short introductory chapter seeks to establish a frame of reference for this change of tack, explain why the shift is occurring and provide an outline of the main marketing communications strategies that are available to event marketers today. A variety of marketing tactics that support these strategies are discussed in greater detail in Chapters 10, 11 and 12. Then in Chapter 14, as a conclusion to this book, we present a new conceptual model which puts the consumer to the centre of all marketing decisions.

Generic marketing communications strategies – from push to pull

The discussion of push and pull marketing communications strategies is not new. In fact, it emerged back in the late 1980s when it was recognised that there are two ways of going about increasing product sales. The push strategies imply that products are 'pushed' to consumers down the distribution chain of wholesalers and retailers, who communicate the marketing messages and try and close the sale. The pull strategies focus more on building the image of the product that customers will be able to relate to and will want to buy. Arguably, this would then help create demand and, effectively, pull the customers to buy the product or use the service (Oliver and Farris, 1989, cited in Brassington and Pettitt, 2006).

Fill (2011) takes a slightly different approach and identifies three distinctive communications strategies:

- The *pull-positioning strategy* – implies direct communication with product or service customers, whether in a business-to-business or business-to-consumer scenario.

- The *push-positioning strategy* – is concerned with marketing a product or service through its standard distribution channels through which different customers are reached.

- The *profile-positioning strategy* – is not necessarily concerned with directly increasing the sales of particular products or services, but rather building a strong profile for the company brand, as it is believed that this is what gives credibility to the products and/or services the company provides.

At the heart of each of these concepts is the notion of positioning – creating an image of the product or service in the mind of the customer that will be relevant enough to drive, or at least influence, the buying decision. The younger generation of marketing and change management experts (see some work published by Seth Godin, Martin Lindstrom, David

Meerman Scott and Malcolm Gladwell) have developed these conversations of *push* vs *pull* to focus on the shift between interrupting consumers with marketing messages and engaging with consumers to get their permission to be contacted with a variety of communications. It is important to note, however, that permission marketing does not revolve around explicitly asking consumers for their permission to be contacted. Rather, it emphasises the role of smart positioning and the use of more subtle marketing communication strategies and tactics that help create a positive perception of the brand in the mind of the consumer. This makes the consumers more open to receiving marketing messages from that particular brand as opposed to actively blocking them out. So what are the main interruption and permission marketing communications strategies? The following sections explore these in detail.

Strategies that interrupt

In today's world, ordinary people are bombarded with thousands of marketing messages each day (Meerman Scott, 2011; Godin, 2007; Lindstrom, 2008). Just think of how many advertisements and other marketing materials you usually see on your way to work or school each day. In an increasingly saturated marketing arena, companies often feel that they need to shout louder than everyone else in order to be heard. Consequently, more and more aggressive forms of marketing are increasingly being used to help capture the customers' attention. The idea is that the louder and more distinctive your message, the more likely it is that consumers will buy your product or service. Godin (2007) calls this *interruption marketing*. In a world where a person's attention is their greatest and most treasured possession (Meerman Scott, 2011) marketers try and use the traditional marketing channels of TV, radio, newspapers and magazines to deliver messages that interrupt a prospect's regular train of thought whilst watching or listening to their favourite broadcast programme or reading about an area of interest. Interruption marketing takes little notice of the fact that consumers today are getting better and better at actively blocking out any message that interrupts their attention, and in the situations where they don't block it out they are getting increasingly annoyed at being interrupted, which can only lead to negative brand perception. Adding to this the fact that the general effectiveness of mass media is very difficult to calculate, the game of interruption marketing becomes increasingly risky to play. Below we explore some of the most commonly used interruption strategies.

Guerrilla marketing

Levinson (1984, cited in Godin, 2007) coined the term *guerrilla marketing* in his seminal book of the same title. He had correctly recognised that the marketplace is becoming increasingly saturated with traditional advertising and PR efforts, so he led the way in identifying a new and (arguably) more effective approach to communicating with consumers. The idea behind guerrilla marketing is that it uses the element of surprise in catching the target audience's attention. There is still no official definition of what guerrilla marketing actually is, so its nature is very open to interpretation, which can lead to some extraordinary creative concepts in delivering these types of campaigns. It is largely recognised as an innovative, low-cost/high-impact solution to dealing with the usual marketing clutter, which produces a memorable experience. This experience usually involves some form of entertainment and creates a buzz that helps increase the positive perception of and feelings towards a particular brand or product. Guerrilla marketing activities are mini-events in themselves and some of the most commonly mentioned ones were delivered as part of the T-Mobile campaign 'Life's

For Sharing'. These included a dance spectacular at London's Liverpool Street rail station, a large-scale karaoke-style show in Trafalgar Square and the 'welcome back' show for passengers arriving at Heathrow airport's Terminal 5. The T-Mobile guerrilla campaign, however, was extremely high budget and was used as a creative solution for their standard advertising campaign, as well as the viral aspect, which saw videos posted on YouTube and shared via email and social media.

Another view of guerrilla marketing links the military origins of its name to the aggressive approach it can sometimes take. There have been instances where guerrilla marketing has been used by companies to deliver their marketing messages at the expense of their direct competitors. A particularly fruitful area for this type of marketing is large-scale mega-events, which bring vast amounts of PR to their sponsors and present an attractive playground to their sponsors' competitors. Companies that are not officially sponsoring the event can sometimes use ethically dubious approaches in order to associate themselves with the event without paying the sponsorship fee and overshadow the event's official sponsors. For example, during the Denmark vs Netherlands match at the 2010 FIFA World Cup in South Africa, 36 Dutch female spectators took off their top layers of clothing to reveal bright orange dresses with the Bavaria logo. This was interpreted as a co-ordinated attack on the official sponsor of the FIFA 2010 World Cup – Budweiser and FIFA quickly launched legal proceedings against the two women who were identified as leaders of the group. The charges, however, were ultimately dismissed when the case was settled out of court as nothing could be proven beyond reasonable doubt. This type of aggressive and offensive guerrilla marketing is also known as *ambush marketing*.

VIGNETTE 9.1

T-Mobile 'Dance' guerrilla campaign

T-Mobile's 'Dance' guerrilla campaign kicked off the era of high-profile guerrilla marketing campaigns for a variety of brands. Conceptualised and delivered in early 2009 by one of the leading marketing agencies, Saatchi and Saatchi, it took the world by storm when a series of T-Mobile adverts featuring the campaign aired globally.

'The Dance' was filmed in real time by hidden professional TV cameras, in order to capture the initial uninhibited reactions of the public at the location, which added a dimension of surprise, wonderment and delight to the campaign. The general 'feel' of the guerrilla campaign and the subsequent series of adverts was one of recognising that there are some things in life individuals want to share with their family and friends. The campaign is in line with the brand's tagline 'Life's For Sharing' and positions T-Mobile as a brand that is dedicated to supporting its customers in sharing life's important moments with their loved ones. The advert implicitly reflected the profile of the brand's target audiences through the use of professional dancers dressed as individuals from particular walks of life: young urban professionals, students, working-class people and the elderly. Additionally, the types of music that were chosen to accompany the dance routine also helped frame the profile of the brand's audiences, including a medley of musical pieces from different genres and historical eras, spanning Strauss's 'Blue Danube', 'My Boy Lollipop' by Millie, 'Do You Love Me' by The Contours, 'The Only Way Is Up' by Yazz and 'Don't Cha' by The Pussycat Dolls.

Apart from the professional dancers hired for the campaign, who were doing the official routine, the campaign also relied on members of the public caught in the middle of the 350-strong dance formation to get involved. And most people did get caught up in the moment and just started swaying with the groove. After the music had finished, the dancers dispersed in a matter of seconds, leaving the members of the public wondering what just happened and whether it was all a dream.

When asked about their experience after 'The Dance' had finished, people who had witnessed it and those participating in it were noticeably in good spirits, smiling and talking about how it made them smile and feel happy, with one particular interviewee emphasising that the campaign had helped put her in a good mood for the day. This highlights the true value of a guerrilla campaign: when designed thoughtfully and with a gripping concept, this marketing strategy can have a profound impact on the target audiences, leading to a more positive perception of the brand itself. The 'Dance' campaign was so successful that it was later followed up with a variety of variations, creating a strong platform for the integration of traditional and contemporary marketing strategies, helping T-Mobile build and position itself as a leading brand in the telecommunications market.

The advert featuring the dance can be viewed on the T-Mobile YouTube channel 'lifesforsharing'.

Viral marketing

Viral marketing is relatively new as it is inherent to electronic and mobile communication channels. It is designed to spark word-of-mouth (or, rather, word-of-mouse) marketing by using interesting, catchy, funny or sometimes even outrageous material in order to capture a prospect's attention and elicit them to forward that material onto the contacts in their immediate network. The staple of a viral campaign is usually a video that has since posting found its way to a large number of email inboxes or social media sites. These direct the traffic back to the original place of posting, usually a YouTube page, and thus help improve the online rankings of the video, which makes it feature more prominently in online search results. However, viral campaigns have also been known to incorporate less popular chain emails that encourage people to forward the message by promising good fortune or particular favourable outcomes. Some of the more well-known examples of viral campaigns include the Glass Half Full Productions' viral campaigns for Cadbury's, such as the 'Drum-playing Gorilla' or the 'Eyebrow' videos, and the rocketing success of the South Korean pop artist Psy's promotional video of his hit single 'Gangnam Style', which saw over a billion YouTube hits in the very short span of just five months from July to December 2012.

In the event industry, viral marketing is usually used for extending the life of a particular event or an experiential campaign. For example, the Peugeot 208 launch campaign in 2012 titled 'Let Your Body Drive' centred on a promotional video of the well-known dancer Marquese Scott dancing to the Rudimental track 'Feel the Love', which was supplemented with dance showcases incorporated into the national roadshow for the launch. Another great example is the 20th Century Fox European roadshow aimed at showcasing the Blu-ray editions of the company's leading titles in the lead up to Christmas 2010. The viral element included a personalised video clip of the roadshow attendees on a movie trailer of their choice, which they could then share on their social media sites and promote the event and the product to their extended networks.

Direct marketing

Direct marketing focuses on reaching customers and future prospects directly, often with personalised material designed to promote a particular product or service. Whilst 15 years ago it was still fairly common to receive hard copies of specifically targeted marketing material in the post (e.g. catalogues, newsletters and promotional flyers), the rise of the digital media is making direct marketing even simpler and more prevalent than ever, with all sorts of digital promotional materials (e-newsletters, sales promotion discounts, etc.) being delivered straight to a person's inbox. Another form of direct marketing is street flyering, where teams of people (usually called street teams) hand out flyers and other promotional materials in the street to anyone who is passing by, thus encapsulating the essence of interruption marketing.

Direct marketing usually presents a specific 'call for action' requiring a response to the marketing message, which – if it is acknowledged and completed by the target individual – presents the starting point to building a long-term relationship with that individual. The response is normally facilitated by the use of sales promotions (discount codes, vouchers, etc.) which tempt the prospect to purchase the product or service being promoted by emphasising the value of the deal.

Ambient or stealth marketing

Whilst no common definition of stealth marketing exists, the notion is far from new. First introduced in Vance Packard's (1957) seminal work *The Hidden Persuaders*, it highlighted the use of deep psychological and subliminal techniques which were designed to manipulate consumers into desiring particular products and services. Today, stealth marketing has moved away from its negative connotations of the past and denotes techniques that are subtly and seamlessly woven into consumers' everyday lifestyle and culture. Kaikati and Kaikati (2004, cited in Roy and Chattopadhyay, 2010) have identified six key facets of stealth marketing: viral marketing, brand pushing, celebrity marketing, bait and tease marketing, marketing in video games and marketing in pop and rap music. Ambient or stealth marketing today refers to the usage of consumers' everyday surroundings in order to push the company's marketing messages. It is slightly different from traditional advertising in the sense that bespoke marketing materials are being made to fit into the natural and built, physical and virtual environment, rather than being displayed at purpose-built advertising spaces, such as billboards and other outdoor media, media screens and poster boards. Some interesting examples can be seen in Figures 9.1–9.4.

Figure 9.1 Stealth marketing for Lloyds TSB at Stratford tube station in August 2012 – brand focused

Source: Author's own

Figure 9.2 Stealth marketing for Lloyds TSB at Stratford tube station in August 2012 – sponsorship focused

Source: Author's own

Figure 9.3 Stealth marketing for VISA at Westfield Stratford City in August 2012 – brand focused

Source: Author's own

Figure 9.4 Stealth marketing for VISA at Westfield Stratford City in August 2012 –
sponsorship focused

Source: Author's own

E-marketing and m-marketing

Contemporary marketing has gone digital. Companies are using the new channels of the internet and mobile phones to target customers more directly than ever before. However, a large proportion of marketers are still applying the 'old rules' (Meerman Scott, 2011) to these new media, cluttering the space with one-way marketing messages rather than using the environment to inspire consumers to engage with their brands. For a lot of companies, e-marketing and mobile marketing are nothing more than traditional advertising and PR in a new environment – interruption marketing at its worst. Think of all the banner ads you see when you're browsing the internet on your laptop, netbook or PC. Or the ads that rudely pop up whilst you're using free versions of mobile apps. Or the floating ads with music or sound on a transparent background that take you ages to figure out how to close them down. As we discuss further on in Chapters 12 and 13, these old rules are no longer applicable. What is needed now is a complete shift in how companies view their consumers, which will impact on how they interact with them in the digital world over the long run.

E-marketing

Over the past several years with the rise of search engine optimisation and other tools for strengthening a company's presence in online search results, e-marketing has become a more sophisticated tool with endless possibilities for optimal marketing in the digisphere. It has created a completely new set of rules that lead the way in permission marketing by seamlessly weaving a net around the customer who is both aware of it and willing to participate in the communication.

Strategies that seek permission

Whilst there will always be companies that think loudest is best, arguably those that are more subtle and create the right pull are more successful in converting initial consumer interest into an actual purchasing action. *Permission marketing* (Godin, 2007) focuses on engaging consumers and prospects over the long run, in order to make them more open to receiving messages from a particular brand when the call to action is issued. So what are the strategies that seek permission?

Branding

Branding is concerned with identifying the position that the event wishes to occupy in the market and working heavily on aligning all the elements of the brand with its business aspirations. A successful brand has at its core a compelling idea (Frampton, 2009) and a set of brand values which define what the brand stands for. These are supported by the brand language and brand image, both visual and sonic, as well as the brand experience (Smith, 2009) that is offered in the interactions between the brand and its consumers. It is imperative that all the elements of the brand are carefully co-ordinated, so that each of them supports the brand story and there are no inconsistencies or ambiguities that could negatively impact on the brand by weakening its image, overall presence in the market or, ultimately, financial value. Whilst branding of products and services is a mature art of marketing, branding with events is still in its infancy. This is not only because events in themselves are a relatively young industry, but also because of the inherent amorphous nature of events where every instance of an event is a completely separate and unique entity, even if it is an event that has been running for a considerable amount of time. Additional constraints are posed for one-off events, which do not have the time or the space to really focus on branding. Regardless of these challenges, branding in events is an increasingly important aspect of the event planning and management process which is evidenced by the fact that 1.8 per cent of the Coolbrands survey list is made up of event-related brands (King, 2012), with Glastonbury Festival firmly leading the way at number five (Superbrands, 2014). Event branding is set to become more defined as the industry develops and strengthens its position in the global economy.

Affinity marketing

Affinity marketing focuses on targeting audiences who have an affinity with a company's product or service, but may not currently be using it. It relies heavily on building relationships with other companies or individuals who appeal to these audiences and presents a safe option to expand the existing target market. Affinity marketing with events is usually delivered through the strategic use of sponsorship or celebrity endorsement. Big companies often use events to raise own brand awareness with their target markets and to implement their positioning strategy. For example, Petronas, the national oil company of Malaysia, is the title sponsor for the Formula 1™ Petronas Malaysia Grand Prix, where its brand is showcased to a variety of participating teams who fall into its primary target audiences. Celebrities, on the other hand, are used by events to raise their profile and tap into new target audiences. For example, the smoothie brand Innocent Drinks is currently launching a series of one-off events aimed at sharing their business values, for which it is using the support of Olympian James Cracknell, TV GP Dr Pixie McKenna and world-renowned model Erin O'Connor. On a somewhat smaller scale, celebrities are often used to promote particular clubs or club nights in party capitals all around the world. Spotting celebrities in these venues is likely to bring on an increase in target demographics' interest in visiting these clubs on particular days of the week when these events take place.

Aspirational or lifestyle marketing

Aspirational or lifestyle marketing relies on the inherent human desire to own products, use services or associate with individuals that are deemed as offering a particular level of prestige. This does not necessarily have to mean using luxury products and services, or rubbing shoulders with A-list celebrities, but it does need to support an individual's aspirations of the kind of life they want to lead. From reputation for lavish and luxurious lifestyle, to exuding peace, calmness and confidence, or championing sustainable living, aspirational marketing helps build strong brands and reach audiences that share similar interests and aspirations. As with affinity marketing, the tactics most commonly used with aspirational marketing are sponsorships and celebrity endorsement. For example, the choice of Danny Boyle as the director of the opening ceremony for the London 2012 Olympics aimed to exude Britishness every step of the way. Similarly, The World Hunger Day charity concert, held on May 2012 at the Royal Albert Hall in London, was aimed at raising money and awareness for The Hunger Project UK, a charity focusing on eradicating poverty and hunger faced by countries in sub-Saharan Africa, Asia and Latin America. The event was supported by a host of stars including Dionne Warwick, Sir Cliff Richard, Boy George, Katie Melua and others who helped raise the profile of the event itself and, by association, the cause being championed. The unique combination of the worthwhile cause and the stars performing at the event created a strong pull for the audiences and the event ended up selling out the entire capacity of the venue of 5,500 seats.

VIGNETTE 9.2

Ian Somerhalder Foundation fundraising events

The Ian Somerhalder Foundation (ISF) was founded in 2010 by the American actor Ian Somerhalder, who made his name in a hugely popular TV show *The Vampire Diaries*. The great success of the show and his increasingly strong public profile enabled Ian to start working on promoting the environmental issues he is passionate about through the establishment of the Foundation, which focuses on environmental and animal protection. The Foundation operates on the principle of connecting some 200 groups worldwide into a network focused on promoting the core issues they are committed to resolving.

Considering its non-profit nature and the need to drive costs down and income up whenever possible, the ISF wisely uses affinity and aspirational marketing at a variety of levels in achieving its business goals. Both affinity and aspirational aspects are firstly reflected in the core structure of the organisation, which is heavily supported by a number of volunteers who promote its message across the globe. These volunteers are people passionate about the issues of environmental and animal protection who are happy to donate their time, energy and expertise to work with other like-minded individuals on tackling these – it reflects their aspiration to live in a world that is sustainable and mindful of each person's impact. The Foundation is also open to inviting people with an interest in and passion for environmental issues to contribute their views and opinions by guest blogging on the Foundation's official blog. The Foundation also uses principles of crowd-sourcing in raising money for its programmes through online platforms such as Crowdrise and in raising money on a local level by inspiring, encouraging and supporting individuals across the world to organise themselves and lead their own initiatives to tackle issues of environmental and animal protection. In this way, the ISF widens its reach and successfully implements the principles of co-creation in its core business.

In terms of broader marketing efforts, the Foundation benefits from the tie-ins that its founder creates with a number of organisations and individuals in a variety of spheres. First, the Foundation got exposure at the 'Think, Eat, Save' World Environment Day organised by the United Nations Environment Programme (UNEP) in June 2013, where Ian participated as the 'Expert of the Day' and helped champion the issues of environmental sustainability alongside a host of other celebrities including model Gisele Bündchen, actor Don Cheadle, musicians Eric Wainaina and Suzanna Owíyo and actress Li Bingbing. In addition to such high-profile connections, Ian also works more locally to promote the Foundation by connecting with companies and individuals on a local and national level. For example, in the USA the Foundation was represented at the Vampire Diaries Fan Convention in New Jersey in July 2013, where its volunteers were collecting donations for a local animal shelter. Similarly, in Australia, Ian has been working closely with Josie Maran Cosmetics and Barefoot Wines. The Josie Maran Cosmetics have chosen Ian as their Model Citizen for 2013. The appointment was marked with the launch of a limited edition of cosmetics by the brand and a proportion of the sale price of each item sold is planned to be donated to the ISF to help with the costs of building an animal sanctuary. With Barefoot Wines Ian is collaborating on their new initiative 'Soles of the Year' programme, which aims to celebrate and reward individuals who make the effort to leave their impression on the world by having a positive impact in their local communities.

Aside from this, the Foundation also uses fundraising events to promote its causes and raise money for its programmes. One such event was the ISF Influence Affair and Afterparty, held in April 2012. The event was a high-end networking event promoting the work of the Foundation and, particularly, their 'Let's Get Dirty' campaign that saw the involvement of 2,000 schools across California in an effort to clean up the state in one day, promoting environmental awareness amongst its youth.

It can thus be seen that affinity and aspirational marketing are often interconnected and where there is one, there is often the other. The underlying principle for the successful implementation of both is to correctly identify what internal needs and aspirations your brand caters to and then create an effective combination of marketing tactics that will allow you to reach your target audiences directly.

Peer-to-Peer (P2P) marketing

Peer-to-Peer (P2P) marketing is arguably the only marketing worth having. The bottom line with P2P marketing is that the quality of the product or service will drive the word of mouth amongst its target audiences and beyond, almost as if it has a life of its own. The trouble is that even P2P marketing needs to start somewhere. Companies often use guerrilla marketing, sales promotions, sponsorships and celebrity endorsements in order to drive word of mouth. However, the only thing that can guarantee a strong P2P campaign is the quality of the product and the service being offered to the customers and the value being created. Word of mouth is firmly behind the longevity of success for Glastonbury Festival, for which each year the 140,000 allocated tickets are sold out in a matter of hours after being released on sale.

Cause marketing

Cause marketing centres on choosing a particular cause to support in driving a company's marketing efforts, whether it's supporting a particular charity or just raising awareness about a particular issue. Events are often tied in with charitable organisations. Sometimes events are staged specifically to raise funds and support for a particular charity, as we've seen above in the example of the World Hunger Day charity concert (or a variety of charities, as is the case with the London Marathon, for example). Other times events themselves decide to support a particular cause by donating funds or by simply embedding the cause throughout the event planning and delivery, as was the case with the London 2012 Olympic Games, which put a strong emphasis on embedding sustainability in all aspects of the event planning and delivery process. Ultimately, however, cause marketing is as much about affinity marketing and expanding target audiences as it is about awareness and fund raising.

Social marketing

Social marketing is somewhat similar to cause marketing, only it is targeted on a much smaller scale. Whilst cause marketing is about raising awareness of particular issues facing society and humanity as a whole, social marketing is more about promoting the overall health, wellbeing and other areas of personal development that can help create positive impacts in an individual's life (for example, learning new languages and gaining new skills through community work). A rise in stress-related illnesses over the past ten to fifteen years has led to an increase in health and wellbeing initiatives and projects focusing on putting the individual's needs first. The event industry has followed suit, with a host of workshops, training sessions and personal development seminars, as well as a number of large-scale events aimed at increasing the overall health, wellbeing and happiness of people. For example, the UK's Vitality Show showcases a wide range of products and services aimed at this market. On a much smaller scale (but not less important), the Bali Spirit Festival offers a more immersive environment of a retreat in which a person is able to experience a variety of different styles of yoga and dance. Another good example is also the IMEX America, America's Worldwide Exhibition for Incentive Travel, Meetings and Events – the American version of the much more popular IMEX in Frankfurt, Germany. Although not a wellbeing-oriented event in itself, it embraces the fast pace of the events and travel industries and offers features within the event site which focus on helping attendees relax and unwind during their busy schedules at the show. In 2010 the two main features were the IMEX Relax Lounge Concept sponsored by the German company Home Health Products and the stress management feature (consisting of yoga, relaxation and energiser sessions) sponsored by Inner Sense, a Spanish wellbeing company which specialises in designing bespoke creative wellbeing solutions for all types of events, and MCI, a global event management company. This nurturing approach to defining additional event features helps position the event as recognising the levels of stress existing in the industry and supporting the individual health and wellbeing of its attendees.

Loyalty marketing

Loyalty marketing is a technique focusing on fostering long-term relationships between a company and its customers. Arguably, in the context of events, this is one of the most important techniques to get right, as loyal event audiences can mean the difference between a successful and sustained event or a one-off event that never took off. Loyalty marketing should permeate every aspect of event planning and delivery.

Interactive marketing

Interactive marketing focuses on creating a two-way communication between the brand and its audiences. It can range from sponsorship activation via third-party events or own brand activation programmes via bespoke events (e.g. Virgin's V Festival) to any other field marketing activity (e.g. trials and taster sessions such as cooking demonstrations in large shopping centres with celebrity chefs). The purpose of interactive marketing is to bring a brand to life and establish a conversation with the consumers in the hope that the memorable experience will increase their brand recognition and awareness, as well as predisposition to purchase that brand's range of products or services.

Towards integrated event marketing

Since the introduction of the concept in the mid-1980s (Reinold and Tropp, 2010) there has been much talk of the relevance of integration in the planning and execution of marketing campaigns. According to Kitchen *et al.* (2004), the term 'integrated marketing communications has now become the dominant replacement for the terms 'marketing communications' and 'promotion'. Whilst the concept of 'integration' is still rather 'fuzzy' in marketing literature, i.e. there is little clarity as to what the constructs of the concept are, there do exist several definitions. Shultz (1991, cited in Reinold and Tropp, 2010) defines integrated marketing communications (IMC) as 'the process of managing all sources of information about a product/ service to which a customer or prospect is exposed which behaviourally moves the consumer toward a sale and maintains customer loyalty'. Kliatchko (2008) provides a more condensed definition which identifies the four pillars of IMC: stakeholders, content, channels and results. Moving away from trying to provide a definition of the concept and trying to provide a critical overview of its merits, Cornelissen (2010) recognised the dual purpose of the concept. On the one hand, integration concerns the alignment of messages and media that a company uses to communicate with its external audiences, whilst on the other, it also concerns the alignment and co-ordination of disciplines within a particular company which deal with its marketing activities. This broadly follows Duncan and Everett's (1993) holistic view of IMC as both a concept and a process which argues the complementary nature of marketing tactics utilised to achieve the strategic objectives in relation to identified customer needs and within the constraints of the factors in the existing internal and external environments.

With the decreasing effectiveness of mass media, such as TV or radio, there is a strong need for concentrated marketing efforts that will yield results and turn prospects into loyal customers. This means that marketers of today need to recognise the multiplicity of markets, marketplaces, customers, channels and media (Schultz and Kitchen, 2000), which we've already discussed in Chapter 6. The focus is put not only on the creative solution(s) of a particular campaign, but also on the seamless integration of a variety of different channels in order to maximise the impact on target audiences. Rather than spending large amounts of money on expensive mass media which are in most cases ineffective, integrated campaigns emphasise both effectiveness and efficiency. An integrated campaign starts with identifying the relevant characteristics of the target audience, which will inform the design of the creative campaign idea. It also identifies the patterns of information search for the target audience, outlining the most frequently used channels as well as the type and quantity of information normally requested/analysed. This helps in designing a mix of channels to be used and the frequency with which these will be promoting the marketing messages specific to each particular campaign. Once the channels have been chosen, it is imperative that consistent messages are communicated via these channels, so that they can reinforce each other and deliver a coherent and targeted approach.

It is important to note that, although mass media is notoriously ineffective in reaching the majority of smaller scale or niche audiences, there is still a place for it in an integrated marketing campaign, although it may not feature in it as heavily as it did some 20 or 30 years ago. A successful integration of marketing communications activities is crucial in strengthening a brand's position in the market and creating strong relationships between the brand and its target audiences based on trust, exceeded customer expectations and customer delight.

CASE STUDY

Acer Aspire Touch-And-Type European launch

In 2012, experiential agency Mother London was tasked with creating and executing the European launch campaign for Acer Aspire Touch-And-Type products featuring the Windows 8 operating system, which was to run in the lead up to Christmas. The range of products being promoted included Aspire S7 Ultrabook, Aspire M3 Ultrabook, Aspire M5 Ultrabook, Aspire V5 Notebook, Aspire 7600U 27" All-in-one Desktop, Aspire 5600U 23" All-in-one Desktop, ICONIA W700 11.6" Tablet and ICONIA W500 10" Tablet. The campaign kicked off with a UK press event in London at the end of October, where the company's chief executive, Jim Wong, presented the 'touch-and-type' functionality of the products as 'a more natural and beneficial way' for their customers to experience their products, as well as a point of differentiation for the Taiwanese company in a highly competitive computing market.

The launch encompassed experiential stands in shopping centres in 25 different locations across ten countries in Europe. The creative solution for the experiential campaign stemmed from a previous 'VoxFox' advertising campaign for the range's flagship product Acer Aspire S7 Ultrabook featuring the well-known actress and model Megan Fox. The ad used Megan's hidden passion for marine biology, which led her to use the Acer Aspire S7 to develop software that would enable her to communicate with dolphins. The creative idea emphasised Acer's brand positioning, 'Explore beyond Limits', which aimed to inspire people to explore their passions and live up to their full potential. The advertising campaign utilised multiple channels including TV, cinema and print, as well as outdoor media in France, Germany, Russia and the UK. The campaign itself was also being promoted online and via the social media in the whole of EMEA (Europe, Middle East and Africa). The experiential concept for the launch revolved around creating 'experience centres' where target audiences could enjoy 30-minute sessions where Acer staff can introduce them to the products' new defining features.

The visual design of the stands was based on the dolphin tank featured in the VoxFox advert. The front of the stand was covered in screens across which a photorealistic animation of the dolphin from the TV ad, Zenya, came to life, showed off and chatted to consumers through the Acer Aspire S7 and Megan's software and encouraged customers to explore more. The back of the stand hosted the space for showcasing the entire range of Touch-and-Type products, with a team of experts dressed as scientists from the ad campaign on hand to offer advice and product demonstrations. The campaign aimed at bringing the Acer brand to life for consumers and was further supported with a touch enabled website to showcase the dual functionality of the promoted devices.

More information about the Acer Roadshow can be found on the Acer Facebook page at www.facebook.com/Acer/posts/100137026827456.

A quick preview of the event can be seen on the Acer YouTube channel at www.youtube.com/watch?v=86SOsPoUyYA.

The original Acer TV commercial with Megan Fox can also be found on YouTube at www.youtube.com/watch?v=A2DB7f-n1ow.

Case study questions

1 What types of marketing communications strategies can you identify in the case study? Support your answer with relevant examples.

2 Explain how the various marketing communications strategies and tactics have been integrated into a coherent campaign.

3 Why did, in your opinion, Acer decide to go with an experiential campaign?

SUMMARY

This chapter has introduced a variety of strategic marketing communications techniques available to event marketers and discussed the shift between push and pull marketing communications strategies, as well as the differences between interruption and permission marketing. In the following three chapters (Chapters 10–12) we present more in depth the variety of marketing communications tactics that can operationalise the strategies discussed in this chapter. In the twenty-first century a person's attention is a scarce commodity and the onus is on marketers to design new ways of inspiring their target audiences to engage with the brands they are promoting and really help co-create those experiences. Only brands that are successful in keeping the channels of communication open between themselves and their customers and those that create engaging and interactive experiences for the consumers will enjoy success in an extremely crowded and loud marketplace.

REVIEW QUESTIONS

1 What is the difference between the push and pull marketing communications tactics?

2 What is the difference between interruption and permission marketing?

3 Provide some examples of permission marketing you have identified in your environment.

4 What is meant by the term 'integrated marketing communications' and what is its relevance in twenty-first-century marketing?

EVENT MARKETING SCENARIO

You are the marketing manager for your city's leading cultural festival, taking place over two weeks in July and showcasing a variety of cultural and artistic endeavours, spanning arts and craft exhibitions, poetry readings, theatre and dance performances. This year, for the first time, the event is offering educational workshops in all areas showcased in the event's main agenda. Your task this year is to create a tailored marketing campaign to attract youths aged 12–18 to attend the workshops. Design an effective campaign concept and discuss which of the marketing strategies covered in this chapter would be most suitable to use and how could they be used for maximum impact.

FURTHER READING

Books

Godin, S. 2007. *Permission Marketing*, London: Pocket
This is an excellent book providing a clear and detailed overview of the current marketing context. It argues a strong case for the shift from push towards pull marketing strategies and tactics.

Levinson, J.C. 2007. *Guerrilla Marketing: Cutting edge strategies for the 21st century*, London: Hachette Digital
This is the revised and updated edition of Levinson's seminar work, first published in 1984. It provides some context for the change in approach to marketing and enables the reader to understand the need to find new ways of reaching their target audiences. It also offers a wealth of ideas for low-cost marketing for the practising marketer, with a focus on SMEs.

Levinson, J.C. and Horowitz, S. 2010. *Guerrilla Marketing Goes Green: Winning strategies to improve your profits and your planet*, Hoboken, NJ: John Wiley & Sons
Building on Levinson's original work *Guerrilla Marketing*, this book contextualises the creative low-cost marketing ideas in the context of sustainability, which is becoming increasingly important in twenty-first-century marketing.

Journals

Cornelissen, J. 2010. 'Integration' in communication management: Conceptual and methodological considerations, *Journal of Marketing Management*, 16(6), pp. 597–606
This article represents a good introduction to the concept of integrated marketing and discusses some of the issues surrounding it, thus providing a good foundation for any aspiring marketer.

Kitchen, P.J. 2005. New paradigm – IMC – under fire, *Competitiveness Review*, 15(1), pp. 72–80
This article provides some theoretical background to the concept of integrated marketing communications and presents the importance of integration of marketing initiatives from tactical to strategic level.

Solomon, M.R. 2005. Transfer of Power: The hunter gets captured by the game, *Marketing Research*, Spring, pp. 26–31
This is an excellent article by one of the leading global figures in the field of marketing and consumer behaviour. It discusses systematically the marketing paradigm shift and outlines the relevance of new marketing strategies and tactics in promoting participatory marketing.

Other resources

Marketing Magazine www.marketingmagazine.com
This is the leading publication for the marketing industry in the UK, which is published weekly and offers a wealth of information about the marketing environment, brands and leading current issues in marketing.

Seth's Blog http://sethgodin.typepad.com
This is the blog of Seth Godin. It is an excellent resource which offers daily bite-size chunks of contemporary marketing wisdom. It builds on the work published previously by the author and often refers to recent industry examples, providing an excellent resource for any twenty-first-century marketer.

The Marketing Blog www.themarketingblog.co.uk
This is an outstanding online resource which brings together news from a wide range of marketing areas, from the 'traditional' advertising, PR and retailing to entertainment, technology, digital and social media. It offers a variety of information from market statistics to creative campaign solutions.

REFERENCES

Brassington, F. and Pettitt, S. 2003. *Principles of Marketing*, 3rd Edition, Harlow: FT Prentice Hall.

Cornelissen, J. 2010. 'Integration' in communication management: Conceptual and methodological considerations, *Journal of Marketing Management*, 16(6), pp. 597–606.

Duncan, T. and Everett, S.E. 1993. Client perceptions of integrated marketing communications, *Journal of Advertising Research*, 33(3), p. 30.

Fill, C. 2011. *Essentials of Marketing Communications: A practical guide to structures, products, formulas, pricing and calculations*, Harlow: Pearson Education Ltd.

Frampton, J. 2009. What makes brands great, in Clifton, R. with Ahmad, S., Allen, T., Anholt, S., Barwise, P., Blackett, T., Bowker, D., Chajet, J., Doane, D., Ellwood, I., Feldwick, P., Frampton, J., Gibbons, G., Hobsbawm, A., Lindemann, J., Poulter, A., Raison, M., Simmons, J. and Smith, S. (Eds) *Brands and Branding*, 2nd Edition, London: The Economist in association with Profile Books Ltd.

Godin, S. 2007. *Permission Marketing*, London: Pocket.

Gummesson, E. 2008. *Total Relationship Marketing: Marketing management, relationship strategy, CRM, and a new dominant logic for the value-creating network economy*, 3rd Edition, London: Elsevier/Butterworth-Heinemann.

King, J. 2012. Event industry brands make up 1.8% of Coolbrands Survey, *Event Magazine*, 24 September [Online]. Available at: www.eventmagazine.co.uk/news/1151364/Event-industry-brands-18-Coolbrands-survey/?DCMP=ILC-SEARCH [Accessed 20 March 2013].

Kitchen, P.J., Schultz, D.E., Kim, I., Han, D. and Li, T. 2004. Will agencies ever 'get' (or understand) IMC?, *European Journal of Marketing*, 38(11/12), pp. 1417–1436.

Kitchen, P.J. 2005. New paradigm – IMC – under fire, *Competitiveness Review*, 15(1), pp. 72–80.

Kliatchko, J.G. 2008. Revisiting the IMC construct, *International Journal of Advertising*, 27(1), pp. 133–160.

Lindstrom, M. 2008. *Buyology: How everything we believe about why we buy is wrong*, London: Random House Business Books.

Meerman Scott, D. 2011. *The New Rules of Marketing & PR: How to use social media, online video, mobile applications, blogs, news releases & viral marketing to reach buyers directly*, Hoboken, NJ: John Wiley & Sons.

Reinold, T. and Tropp, J. 2010. Integrated marketing communications: How can we measure its effectiveness?, *Journal of Marketing Communications*, 18(2), pp. 113–132.

Roy, A. and Chattopadhyay, S.P. 2010. Stealth marketing as a strategy, *Business Horizons*, 53, pp. 69–79.

Schultz, D.E. and Kitchen, P.J. 2000. *Communicating Globally: An integrated marketing approach*, Basingstoke: Macmillan.

Smith, S. 2009. Brand experience, in Clifton, R. with Ahmad, S., Allen, T., Anholt, S., Barwise, P., Blackett, T., Bowker, D., Chajet, J., Doane, D., Ellwood, I., Feldwick, P., Frampton, J., Gibbons, G., Hobsbawm, A., Lindemann, J., Poulter, A., Raison, M., Simmons, J. and Smith, S. (Eds) *Brands and Branding*, 2nd Edition, London: The Economist in association with Profile Books Ltd.

Superbrands UK Ltd. 2014. *Coolbrands Official Results 2014/15*. Superbrands [Online] Available from: http://s3.coolbrands.uk.com/files/2014/09/CB-2014-15-Official-Results-53f39h.pdf [Accessed 1 December 2014].

Chapter **10**

Traditional marketing tactics for events

LEARNING OUTCOMES

By the end of this chapter, students should be able to:

- Identify and describe the nature of five key traditional marketing tactics: advertising, public relations, personal selling, sales promotion and direct marketing

- Understand the contexts in which the various traditional marketing tactics can be applied

- Make critical choices over the use of traditional tactics in constructing marketing plans

> *A key marketing decision is the choice of promotional blend needed to communicate to the target audience.*
>
> *David Jobber (2010)*

Introduction

In Chapter 4 we presented the evolution of marketing philosophies from production orientation towards societal marketing orientation. This shift has, understandably, been accompanied by a change in the type and profile of media channels and the nature of promotional tactics used to market products and services. In Chapter 9 we discussed the variety of strategic initiatives open to marketers which define their overarching approach to the marketing of products and services. In this chapter we now focus on identifying the so-called *traditional marketing tactics* that have been the primary avenue for communicating with consumers until the early 1980s. The chapter describes in detail each of the five staples of traditional marketing, identifies their purpose and main characteristics and provides practical examples that illustrate the key points. Chapters 11 and 12 which follow then elaborate on the contemporary tactics which have become more prominent over the past two decades: live brand experiences, sponsorship and e-marketing.

Above or below the line?

Marketing theorists and practitioners often engage in a debate around the usefulness of mass media versus more low-key approaches that speak directly to the consumer. Whilst 'the line' in most business conversations denotes a sort of moral or ethical threshold which separates the acceptable from the unacceptable business practices, in marketing 'the line' refers to the divide between the mass media and the direct, more personalised channels. *Above-the-line* (also known as ATL) marketing focuses on using mass media to communicate with as wide a range of consumers as possible and normally refers to the use of advertising and public relations tactics. *Below-the-line* (also known as BTL) marketing uses channels that can reach each particular consumer individually and offer a personalised encounter. ATL marketing was particularly relevant during the production and product orientation periods in marketing history, mentioned in Chapter 4, when the most important thing was getting the product into the market and making sure everyone was aware of it. This was done mainly by advertising on broadcast and print media, or being mentioned in a newspaper article or editorial. BTL marketing rose to prominence during the selling and marketing orientation period, as it allowed companies to create more personalised and meaningful relationships with consumers. It did this by using tactics such as personal selling, sales promotion and direct marketing in order to reach consumers individually and engage them in conversations about the brand, product or service. Below we assess the merits of each of these tactics in contemporary event marketing.

Advertising

Advertising is the most well-known traditional tactic and still represents the staple of most integrated marketing campaigns. It is often defined as 'any form of non-personal promotion transmitted through a mass medium' (Brassington and Pettitt, 2003, p. 604). The definition highlights the broad approach advertising takes, trying to reach large audience numbers through media that are most widely used. Jobber (2010) distinguishes between two key media decisions: *media class decisions* and *media vehicle decisions*. Media class decisions involve the definition of the overall approach to advertising, i.e. which type of channel will be used. These can include broadcast media such as TV, radio or (more recently) cinema screens, print media such as newspapers and magazines, outdoor media such as giant promotional screens, cityscapes, billboards or city lights, as well as the internet. A recent example of outdoor advertising can be seen in Figure 10.1. Media vehicle decisions focus on narrowing down specific outlets within a particular media type – for example, specific newspaper or magazine titles to be used or specific locations of cinemas or outdoor advertising.

Another defining characteristic of advertising is that it is paid-for marketing. All of the outlets mentioned above charge companies money in exchange for the media space used. Depending on what is financially viable, advertising campaigns can be designed in-house (by employees within the organisation which is in need of advertising) or be outsourced to specialised advertising agencies which offer the services of creative campaign design, media planning and media buying to their clients. Outsourcing the campaign to an agency is almost always a more costly solution, as the agency will charge a fee for their services on top of the costs associated with media buying and production of advertising materials (e.g. posters and TV commercials). This fee can either be a fixed fee, or can be defined as a percentage of the overall value of the campaign. A comparison of benefits and drawbacks of using an agency can be seen in Figure 10.1.

In-house	Agency
One person (usually the Marketing Manager of Director of Marketing) has strong control of the entire campaign management process	A company's Marketing Manager needs to be in constant communication with the agency Account Manager, who manages the creative process within the agency
Any changes necessary can usually be implemented relatively quickly	Changes may require more time to be implemented, as communication goes through a chain of people before it comes to the agency creative department and then the solution back to the Marketing Manager of the company who requested it
If the creative solution is done in-house by the Marketing Manager or other members of the Marketing department, no particular charge is incurred	Advertising agencies make money on fees they charge for their 'creative solutions' to a client's brief, and these fees can either be a fixed amount or a percentage of the overall value of the campaign (i.e. media space booked)
Production of marketing materials can be costly, particularly if the company has no preferred provider for these types of services (e.g. a production studio for broadcast materials, photographer for images, print company for printing materials, etc.)	Agencies usually have a list of preferred providers who charge them discounted agency prices for their services and majority of agencies transfer these discounts directly to their clients. This means that production of materials can actually cost less if a company is using an advertising agency. This discount is, however, usually offset by the fee the agency charges for their creative solution (see point above)
In-house campaign design usually means more control over the creative solution, but it can often mean more stress in the creative process, particularly when faced with the deadlines	Hiring an agency to manage the campaign takes the stress away from the Marketing Manager, but also relieves them of some control of the final outcome. If the Marketing Manager does not like the initial solution(s) presented by the agency, the process of actually agreeing to a creative solution can take more time and delay the production of materials and the execution of the campaign, which can be a hindrance if the timeline for the campaign is fixed and deadlines are looming.

Figure 10.1 A comparison of benefits and drawbacks of in-house vs agency advertising campaign design

Forms of advertising

Depending on the approach taken by the creators of ad campaigns, advertising can take a number of forms. Berkowitz *et al.* (1992, cited in Brassington and Pettitt, 2003) distinguish between two main types, depending on what is the object of the advertising campaign (i.e. what is being advertised):

Product advertising

Product advertising focuses on promoting a particular product (or service or, in our case, event). Depending on the approach taken with the promotion, product advertising can fall into one of three categories: pioneering advertising (advertising a completely new product), competitive advertising (aimed at boosting sales at the expense of competitors, it usually focuses on promoting unique features of the product or brand) or reminder and reinforcement advertising (post-purchase advertising aimed at ensuring repeat sales by customers who had already used the product or service in the past). Adverts for specific individual events would fall under this category; an example can be seen in Figure 10.2.

Institutional advertising

Institutional advertising focuses on promoting particular organisations and helping to build a strong image in the marketplace which will enable the organisation to successfully achieve its objectives in relation to a variety of stakeholders. As with product advertising, institutional advertising can also take one of three forms: pioneering advertising (announcing new developments within the organisation), image building advertising (build up and maintain the image of the organisation) or advocacy advertising (focusing on a specific issue and communicating the organisation's point of view regarding it). Institutional advertising in the events industry is usually seen on the supply-side of the industry, for example print adverts in industry magazines advertising companies providing products and services relevant to event delivery.

What makes an advert?

Having introduced the different forms of advertising, it is also important to identify what elements an advert is composed of. Whether one is dealing with a broadcast or a print advert, the main components of an advert are usually the same, as outlined below.

Message

Identifying the appropriate message and phrasing it in such a way that it is eloquent, catchy and speaks to the right target audiences can be a somewhat daunting process. It is a process that requires a thorough knowledge of the event and its features, a good overview of the external environment in which the event is being marketed and an in-depth understanding of the variety of the event's target audiences and their backgrounds, characteristics, lifestyles and, most importantly, interests and motivations to buy. Regardless of whether the aim of the message is to inform or encourage to buy, the message must be clear, understandable and relevant to the audience. The use of language is very important here, as adverts for a music festival aiming at 18- to 25-year-olds should use a different type of language than adverts for a high-profile charity gala concert aiming at a slightly older and more affluent audience.

Figure 10.2 Product advertising

Source: Advert courtesy of the University of Northampton

Copy

The way the message is phrased and presented on the ad is called *copy*, and the person producing it is called the *copywriter*. Copy for TV, cinema and print adverts will normally be considerably shorter than copy for radio adverts. The reason for this is that print adverts usually (though not always) incorporate a visual solution which can communicate various elements of the marketing message, and TV and cinema adverts include both video and audio components, making them a more rounded, or holistic, solution. Radio adverts, on the other hand, are limited to words and sounds, so more emphasis is put on these and the quality of the copy needs to be well thought out. Regardless of the length of the copy for TV, cinema and print adverts, consideration needs to be given to how the copy is organised on screen or on the print format. Depending on the amount and relevance of the information being conveyed, the copy may be split into a heading, a subheading and the body of the advert, with the accompanying disclaimer, where applicable (for more information about what a disclaimer is and its purpose, see the 'Other important elements' section below).

Visuals

The images that are used for print adverts and the sequences used for TV adverts are usually referred to as 'visuals'. The visual solution for an advertising campaign will depend on the purpose of the advertising campaign. If the campaign is focusing on strengthening the brand of an event or an organisation, there will be limited copy on the ad and the visual will be carefully chosen to convey as much of the message as possible. With sales-driven advertising, which is aimed at boosting short-term sales, the visual will be simpler but supplemented with relevant copy that provides important details about the purpose of the campaign and other relevant information.

Other important elements

In addition to the message, copy and visuals, there are several other components that can be part of an advert. These may include the following:

- *Logos* that are being used on the advertising materials, whether it is the logo of the event itself, or logos of event sponsors or supporters.
- *Disclaimers*, particularly if the advert is promoting, for example, early-bird discounts that are valid until a particular date, or via a particular ticket outlet.
- *QR codes* are increasingly being used on adverts today to provide consumers with a quick link to more detailed information about the company, brand, product, service or event. These codes can be read by applications on a variety of smartphones and directly take the customer to the company, product or event webpage, social media page, ticket outlet, etc. to facilitate the conversion of those who view the advert into actual paying customers.
- *Promotional codes.*
- *Endorsements*, for example industry approval stamps or similar.
- *Contact information.*

Most of the elements identified above can be distinguished on a print advert for a supplier in the UK events industry in Figure 10.3.

Figure 10.3 Elements of print advertising material

Source: Poster courtesy of Daniela Chialoufas and Kevin Lane (http://kevinlane.graphics/)

Regardless of which form of advertising and which media channel are being used, two elements are of paramount importance for the success of an advertising campaign: the creativity of the approach and the content fit (Perrey and Spillecke, 2011). Creativity ensures that the advert is compelling, will stand out from the crowd and trigger brand recall, whilst content fit succinctly captures the nature of the marketing message and paints a clear picture about the brand without overloading the target audience with irrelevant information.

VIGNETTE 10.1

Made with IBM

IBM is one of the world's leading business solutions providers. With its origins dating as far back as the 1880s, IBM has helped shape the evolution of global business for over a hundred years. Over the past couple of decades, IBM has invested heavily in sponsoring a small number of core event properties, which include the four Grand Slam tennis tournaments, the American NFL and the Augusta National Masters' Golf Tournament, amongst others.

Whilst there are a variety of exciting sponsorship activation initiatives running alongside each of these events, IBM still relies on good old TV advertising for most of them. The new above-the-line campaign in 2014, 'Made with IBM', emphasized the role that data management and analytics play in everyday life from the perspective of IBM clients ranging from hospitals to music production companies and retailers to an astronomical research group. The campaign was set to coincide with the 2014 Augusta Masters Tournament and consisted of 62 individual 30-second TV ads, each of which aired only once during the televised coverage of the event. The Masters was chosen because of the specificity of its audiences: top-level executives and other high net-worth individuals, who are also on IBM's target list.

Rather than following the same approach as everyone else in creating one or two ad mutations and then airing these a large number of times, IBM decided to use TV advertising to tell their story: the ads may all be different, but the underlying message is the same throughout: IBM's innovative solutions that help build a smarter planet. The notion ties in well with IBM's global communications tagline 'Smarter planet'.

Devised by the creative team at one of the leading global creative advertising agencies, Ogilvy and Mather, the campaign saw three directors teaming up with IBM employees to simultaneously film and edit case studies across twenty countries on five continents in the very lead up to the event itself. In a bid to complete the campaign in less than a month, the crews were supported by IBM's own Aspera software, which allowed for a reduction in the time between the filming, editing and post-production, enabling the campaign to launch with the kick-off of the event on 7 April 2014. The campaign reportedly cost $25 million, over 20 per cent of the company's entire annual advertising spend in 2013.

More information about the campaign can be found here:

www.adweek.com/news/advertising-branding/ad-day-ibm-ran-62-different-spots-masters-so-how-did-go-157018.

The playlist of all the video spots used for the campaign can be viewed on the dedicated YouTube channel at www.youtube.com/watch?v=4CltCeHIMSc&list=PLaFe0BJiho2qz2KOUVLdl1DLBA__P1K5Y.

More information about 'Made with IBM' projects can be found on the IBM microsite at www.ibm.com/smarterplanet/us/en/madewithibm/?cmp=usbrb&cm=j&csr=agus_madewith_140407&ct=usbrb301&cn=vanity.

Advertising decision making

Managing an advertising campaign involves making a lot of decisions, either as part of the regular campaign planning and management process or, quite often, troubleshooting 'on the hoof' when challenges arise. Some of the most important decisions in an advertising campaign, aside from the ones relating to phrasing the advertising message and choosing the creative solution for the campaign, are those decisions relating to the scope of the campaign and the mix of media being used. These decisions normally take into account the qualities of the media channels being considered and the potential engagement target audiences might have with these channels. These qualities are often identified as *reach, ratings, frequency* and *opportunity to see* (Brassington and Pettitt, 2003).

Reach refers to the percentage of target market that is exposed to the marketing message at least once during the relevant period – usually four weeks (Brassington and Pettitt, 2003).

Ratings are an important indicator of the popularity of a particular media channel. For TV and radio programmes, these include the number of viewers or listeners who tune in at particular periods of time during the day. For print media, these include the circulation figures that determine the readership of the publication and thus the potential pool of audiences. Ratings will normally influence the fee being charged for advertising at particular time slots – the higher the ratings, the higher the fee being charged.

Frequency refers to the average number of times a consumer – a member of the target audience – will be exposed to a media channel during a specific time period of the campaign.

Opportunity to see identifies how many times a member of the target audience will have an opportunity to see a particular advert.

Other decisions include making choices between whether the campaign is delivered in-house or outsourced to an advertising agency, as well as decisions relating to budgets and how they influence the creative process and the media planning.

Advertising evaluation

There are several parameters usually associated with advertising effectiveness. Most commonly evaluated is the impact of advertising on the sales of a particular product or service, but advertising evaluation also includes intangible effects, such as brand recall (aided or unaided), attitudes towards the product/service, enquiries generated, etc. With events, sales evaluations usually involve the tracking of ticket sales (on the B2C side) and sales of exhibitor space (on the B2B side), both physically at the event and in the event's promotional literature. In order to really ascertain the impact of an advertising campaign on sales, it is important to establish a benchmark period against which sales following the start of the advertising campaign will be assessed. This is usually an equivalent period (e.g. a month or two) prior to the campaign starting, or the equivalent period in the previous year. For example, if an advertising campaign is running between May and June 2015, the benchmark period can be April–May 2015 *or* May–June 2014 for a year-on-year comparison (this is particularly useful for long-standing events which happen every year). Some will argue that one month is quite a short period to make reliable conclusions about the effectiveness of an advertising campaign, so these can be evaluated over a longer term as well, depending on the type and scope of the event and the needs of the senior management team.

Of the non-financial indicators of success, the key ones related to advertising include:

- brand (or event) recall
- consumer attitudes towards the event, and
- enquiries generated about the event as a result of a specific advertising campaign.

Brand (or event) recall is usually tested in a sample audience in one of two ways: aided or unaided (Brassington and Pettitt, 2003). With *aided recall* a campaign advertisement is shown to the sample audience and they are then asked when and where they had seen that advertisement, as well as what their understanding of the advert is (i.e. have they grasped the key message(s) that were intended by the brand marketers). With *unaided recall* the sample audience is simply asked which adverts they have noticed recently and remember. A campaign would be deemed a success if the sample audience members are able to recall the advert without being prompted or asked about the specific advert.

Consumer attitudes towards the event are tested via a set of questions designed to uncover what consumers think and feel about the event. These can be explored via questionnaires, mini interviews or focus groups. For better accuracy, these types of tests are often conducted right before and right after the campaign is live, so that it is possible to identify the change in attitudes as a direct result of the campaign.

Tracking **enquiries generated** by a campaign is relatively straightforward as it involves monitoring the number of requests made by customers for information about the event. These enquiries can come through either via phone to the event's designated customer service representative, or – more commonly – via the event website. In order for these to be tracked correctly, it is important that information is captured as to where the customer heard about the event in the first place, which is a standard question asked by customer service representatives, or included in the online enquiry forms that customers can fill in with their queries.

Public relations

The Chartered Institute of Public Relations offers the following definition of public relations:

> *Public relations is the discipline which looks after reputation, with the aim of earning understanding and support and influencing opinion and behaviour. It is the planned and sustained effort to establish and maintain goodwill and mutual understanding between an organisation and its publics.*

The definition emphasises the importance of a two-way communication in ensuring that all the stakeholders' perceptions of an organisation are in line with the image that the organisation wants to portray. Creating this match between the two can be very hard work indeed. Aside from a strong understanding of the event itself and its features, this requires an in-depth understanding of a variety of primary and secondary stakeholders related to an event, the nature of these relationships, their current perceptions of the event and their preferred methods of communication.

Events, publics and communication

The term 'publics' is much wider than the term 'target audience'. Event publics encompass the variety of stakeholders that are in some way or another connected to the event and can affect its success or failure. Jackson (2013, p. 122) defines event publics as 'those individuals and groups who share some interest, perception or beliefs about that event, which can be positive or negative'. This definition is very much in line with the original definition of stakeholder by Freeman (1984) as being 'any group or individual who can affect, or is affected by, the achievement of a corporation's purpose'. The stakeholder approach is particularly relevant to events and adds to the complexity of designing and executing successful public relations strategies in managing an event's overall image. Due to their ephemeral nature, events depend on a careful orchestration of activities with a variety of stakeholders at particular points in the event management process, which is further constrained by the deadline posed by the event's timing. Although there is a variety of interpretations of the stakeholder theory in relation to events, the main event stakeholders include the following:

- event organisers
- event attendees (spectators)
- event participants (e.g. performers, key note speakers, workshop/seminar leaders, etc.)
- event suppliers
- event volunteers and/or temporary staff
- sponsors
- the local community (residents and businesses)
- local and/or national government bodies
- the media

- various special interest groups (e.g. anti-globalisation movement, environmentalist movement, etc.)

- the general public.

One of the most important things that influence the design of communication programmes for event stakeholders is the nature of the relationship that exists between the event and a particular stakeholder. Depending on this, the nature of the communication will either be reactive or proactive (Smudde and Courtright, 2011) and it will be done either directly or indirectly. Clarkson (1995) identifies two main types of stakeholders: primary stakeholders, who have a direct transactional relationship with an organisation, and secondary stakeholders, who do not have a direct transactional relationship with an organisation, but can still be affected by its day-to-day business operations. This view is very much applicable to events, but it is important to note that the notion of primary and secondary stakeholders is somewhat fluid with events. This is largely due to the fact that during the event planning and delivery process different stakeholder groups will switch from being primary to being secondary stakeholders and vice versa. For example, peaceful protests coinciding with the G20 summit may not directly influence the event itself and these special interest groups are thus seen as a secondary stakeholder. However, if the protesters decide to obstruct the security forces in doing their work, or if their actions cause major disruptions to the flow of people in and out of the event venues, as was the case with the G20 Summit in Pittsburgh in 2009, then they may well become primary stakeholders that need to be communicated with and managed directly. Similarly, event volunteers or temporary staff are considered primary stakeholders for a limited period of time during which their input is of extreme importance to the successful delivery of the event (namely, immediately before the event starts and up until the event finishes). Outside of this timeframe (for example, in the lead up to the event or after the event has finished) this stakeholder group would be classified as a secondary stakeholder.

The challenge with depending on so many different stakeholder groups is that it is very easy to give out confusing messages, which may dilute the image of the event. PR theory defines a variety of strands of public relations, including publicity, investor relations, corporate communication, media relations, employee relations, etc. Whilst this does help define the focus of communication to particular stakeholder groups (e.g. employee relations would address event management organisation's permanent, temporary and volunteer staff), this division can sometimes lead to a somewhat disjointed communication that fragments the event's image and ultimately creates a variety of different pictures about the event in the eyes of different stakeholders. Contemporary PR theorists and practitioners alike agree that what is required is a 'one voice' approach (Society for Human Resource Management, 2006; Seitel, 2004), which means that there needs to be consistency in how the key messages are communicated to a variety of different stakeholders. This requires careful co-ordination of PR messages across all media channels and towards all the different stakeholder groups, which can be very challenging, particularly with large events that depend on the involvement of a lot of different people in the event execution. Another important point to note is the role of staff in delivering good PR, which is of particular importance to events as 'experiences'. In order to create a good experience for event participants and attendees, the event staff need to be well trained and really take on the role of brand ambassadors for the event. No amount of external PR can rectify a negative image that has been created by rude, uninformed or shabby looking staff. It is, therefore, important to make sure all event staff, whether permanent, temporary or volunteer, understand the essence of the event and are able to transmit that essence to the event attendees and participants in an effective way. This makes internal PR a crucial element in defining and communicating the event brand to all the various publics that are related to it.

How do you 'do' traditional public relations?

The 'old school' style of public relations which emerged in the mid-twentieth century, is still very much the dominant approach, even in the events industry. This approach emphasises the role of a press release as the staple of any PR campaign and creating close personal relationships with the media (journalists and editors) so that they will be more inclined to write stories or features about a particular organisation, product, service or event, or mention these in their editorials. Back in the early days, these personal relationships were developed over time as PR managers, journalists and editors got to know each other and socialised in various social settings, which enabled them to have a more informal relationship that facilitated a company's name or product getting into press. However, today's staff turnaround, which is considerably faster than 50 years ago, complicates the possibility of creating long-term relationships with members of the press. This now remains the prerogative of seasoned 'PR people', mostly agency-based, whilst those that operate in-house have a much more challenging task of always being on top of the changes in the media sector and constantly refreshing their existing and building new connections within it. Whilst this may have been very effective in the early days of PR, the game has changed with the advent of the digital media and a new approach is required, as discussed in Chapter 12.

The PR toolkit

The process of getting press coverage normally starts with identifying the relevant contact people (journalists or editors) in the media channels where press coverage is being sought. The next step is to get in touch with the relevant person and briefly pitch the event in order to create interest. After getting a favourable response from the journalist or editor, indicating that they are interested to know more about the event, the phone call is followed up by sending a press release which provides the main details of the event, along with any other relevant supporting materials. A sample press release can be seen in Figure 10.4. The process will often involve following up on whether the material has been received by the media and trying to push the story through and persuade them to write about the event. It is important to note that there is a limit to what a PR person can do to determine the quality and tone of the press coverage their client, organisation, product or an event will receive. The best they can do is send out PR material with as much relevant information as possible, but once that material is received by a journalist or editor the power is transferred to them and they decide whether or not to write about the event and which angle to take with the story.

One of the things that helps PR professionals consolidate all the relevant information so that they are readily available is the event's media kit. The media kit should include the following:

- Press release containing all the relevant information about the event.
- Backgrounder – providing more background information on the event or the event organising company.

FOR IMMEDIATE RELEASE:

CONTACT:
Contact Name
Company/Organisation
Phone Number
Email address
Website Link

HEADLINE GOES HERE
Your headline must be attention-grabbing and concise. Thus, it should be formatted in larger font than the rest of the press release and should not exceed 130 characters.

Location, Date – Your press release should clearly and concisely outline the Who, What, When, Where, Why and How of your event. This includes information on:

- when and where the event is happening
- who is organising it and on whose behalf (if applicable)
- what is the purpose of the event (i.e. why it is being organised)
- what the event will include, such as the format and content of the event, any particular significant people or other entities connected to the event (e.g. celebrities, performers, keynote speakers, sponsors, etc.)
- when and where the tickets can be obtained (if it is a paid for event)
- which digital platforms your audiences can use to get more information about the event (e.g. the event's official website, your social media platforms, etc.)

For additional information about the <event title>, please contact <Contact Name> or visit <Website Link>.

BEAR IN MIND:

Your press release should be written in word-processing software.

You should choose a font which is widely accepted, such as Arial, Tahoma, Verdana, or Times New Roman.

Make sure you spell-check what you have written to eliminate any spelling, grammatical or sentence structure errors.

Use formal, factual language, rather than informal colloquial expressions.

If you can, include a quote from a credible source, someone who is in some way related to the event and who has some 'weight' when it comes to the theme of the event – this could be a celebrity, a keynote speaker, or other dignitary connected to your event.

Write concisely and try to make your press release as short as possible, but don't be too bothered with the actual word count – just make sure all the relevant information is expressed as concisely as possible.

Make sure you structure your press release in short, readable paragraphs and do not repeat content in different paragraphs.

Include further information about the parent company organising the event, or the organisation on whose behalf the event is being organised in a separate section and title it: ABOUT <COMPANY/ORGANISATION NAME>. This section should come after the 'additional information' section.

Any further relevant information, which does not specifically relate to the event or to the parent company/ beneficiary organisation should be presented concisely, in a separate section following the above, with an appropriate sub-heading.

You must clearly mark the end of your press release: this is usually done by including the mark:

- END -

If a press release covers more than one page, type '- **MORE** -' at the end of the first page and any subsequent pages on which the press release continues.

Figure 10.4 Press release guidelines for events

- Biographies of relevant key people, whether they are the event organisers or high-profile participants or attendees.

- Profiles of companies related to the event (e.g. event sponsors, high-profile suppliers, etc.).

- Photos or interactive/multimedia supporting materials on a memory stick or CD-ROM.

- Q&A sheets that answer the most commonly asked questions about the event.

- Any other item that may help the journalist or editor get a fuller picture of what the event is about.

It is important to find a good balance between words and visuals to create an appealing piece that will be easily read and understood.

Evaluating public relations

Public relations deals with an event's reputation and public perception. As a recognised marketing communications tool, public relations will (like advertising) have an impact on event sales, consumer awareness and attitudes towards the event, as well as interest generated in the event. The metrics used to measure this are, therefore, the same ones used with advertising. However, as a much more intangible form of marketing communications, it is often challenging to pinpoint exactly how much a specific item of PR (e.g. an editorial, newspaper article, or similar) has contributed to the generation of an event's image in the eyes of the target audience. Most of public relations evaluation, then, is a roughly estimated best guess by the event marketer and/or the senior management team. Despite this challenge, though, public relations is an important component of the marketing communications mix, particularly for large-scale recurring events, whose future performance depends on the strength of the event's brand and the reputation it enjoys with the public.

Advertising or public relations?

Public relations and advertising use exactly the same media channels: TV, radio, print and outdoor, which is why they are often compared and contrasted. The effectiveness of both tactics is subject to a fierce debate and Figure 10.5 outlines the main points of comparison for the two.

Although a lot can be said for championing one or the other, the fact remains that both advertising and public relations are legitimate marketing communications tools and the relevance of each will depend on each individual case. It is ultimately down to the event's marketing and/or PR manager to decide which one to use and when.

Advertising	Public relations
Paid-for media space – anyone can get it if they're willing to pay the asking price	Media space that cannot be bought, it is awarded on the basis of the newsworthiness of the material
Advertising is usually targeted specifically at target audiences, depending on the nature of the channel used	PR has a wider approach and aims at a variety of stakeholders relevant to the organisation
Consumers tend to block out advertising messages, thus reducing the effectiveness of this tactic	PR is more visible than advertising, as it is a story told in the form of an article or an editorial
Marketing message and the exposure of the target audiences to it is fairly easily controlled with advertising	The message communicated through PR may not be the one intended by the company – journalists and editors have considerable freedom to decide how they want to portray an issue, regardless of what the company is trying to communicate
The number of times an advertising message is placed in a particular medium is under complete control of the Marketing Manager of the company running the campaign and it can be repeated as many times as desired	The PR message will normally only appear in the press once (unless it is a particularly high-profile issue) and sometimes even that is not guaranteed
Advertising is recognised as paid-for media space, so target audiences tend to take the messages in adverts with a degree of caution	PR is more believable than advertising: it is viewed as a 'third party' account often believed to present an objective view of the issue

Figure 10.5 A comparison between advertising and public relations

Personal selling

Personal selling refers to interpersonal communication between an organisation's representatives (often called the 'sales force') and individual consumers. Jobber (2010) highlights personal selling as the 'embodiment' of the marketing orientation, which allows the seller to identify and respond to individual customer needs (Jobber and Fahy, 2009), creating a dialogue which goes beyond the pure provision of generic information usually done through advertising or public relations. The purpose of personal selling is not necessarily making the sale (although that is its ultimate objective), but also enabling the organisation to identify viable prospects, provide crucial information to consumers in order to generate initial or repeat sales, as well as identify particular consumers' needs that may be met by developing new products or services, thus filling a gap in the market. Personal selling can also help in delivering the required aftersales service, making the customer feel appreciated and valued. Over time, this marketing communications tactic has found a purpose in both business-to-business and business-to-consumer markets and whilst it is, arguably, most effectively delivered in a face-to-face scenario, a large number of organisations use also the voice-to-ear approach or telephone communication with potential customers.

In the context of events, personal selling is very much an integral part of the event management and marketing process and can manifest itself in the following ways:

- On-site ticket sales (B2C) – although this is becoming more and more obsolete with the rise of the digital media, early bird registration and paperless ticketing.

- Event hosts and hostesses ensuring event attendees are taken care of and comfortable at the event (B2C).

- Selling conference participation or exhibition space (B2B) – these are products and services that require direct communication between the event organisers and potential event participants.

- Pitching events for sponsorship (B2B).

- Pitching events for getting relevant permits or financial support from the local government or other relevant bodies (B2B).

- Pitching events for celebrity endorsement (B2C).

The personal selling process

Whilst there is no one-size-fits-all approach that can be used to organise the work of an event's sales force, there is a sequence of (very) broad stages that need to be completed for the effective implementation of the personal selling process. These stages are outlined in Figure 10.6.

As can be seen from the five stages described in Figure 10.6, personal selling requires quite a lot of planning. Whilst the quality of the information obtained in the first stage of the process is paramount to designing an effective approach, the success of personal selling also largely depends on the quality of people executing the pitch. The characteristics of a successful sales person are explored in the following section. The final ingredient of success is the structured approach to after-sales customer care and the value that is created in that domain by giving customers a voice and an input into creating their future experiences. Approached correctly, the after-sales customer care can have a big impact on the positive perceptions of event participants and attendees, even if their initial experiences with the event were negative. Giving them the chance to express their dissatisfaction and then addressing it directly encourages positive perceptions of the event and can help encourage repeat visits by those who maybe had not even considered coming back.

What makes a successful sales person?

Personal selling is a front-of-house role which requires excellent communication skills. An ideal candidate will be someone who is open-minded, personable, IT literate, a good listener with an eye for detail, confident and a good negotiator. Whilst some of these skills come to certain people more naturally than to others, all of them can be developed. This is why event management companies put a lot of emphasis on on-the-job training, particularly for roles that deal with business-to-business (B2B) customers.

As this is a performance-evaluated role, a successful sales person should also be goal-oriented, self-driven and persistent. In a world where people are being inundated with marketing messages everywhere they go, they have become good at blocking most of them out and cutting off any attempts at communication. In order to meet their sales goals, sales people will inevitably need to know how to capture a prospect's attention quickly and how to pre-empt any objections that may hinder the sale.

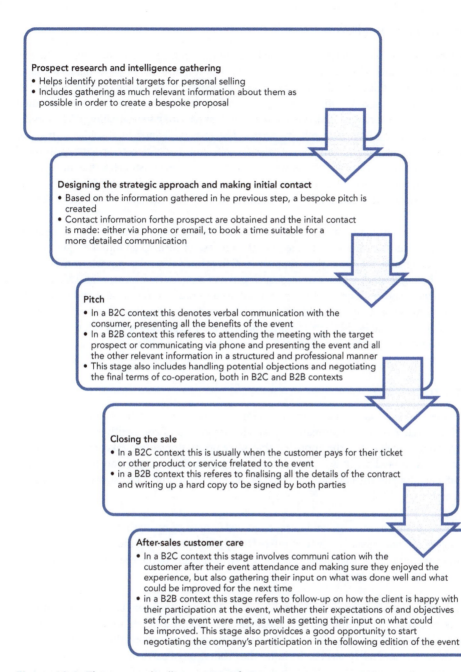

Prospect research and intelligence gathering
- Helps identify potential targets for personal selling
- Includes gathering as much relevant information about them as possible in order to create a bespoke proposal

Designing the strategic approach and making initial contact
- Based on the information gathered in he previous step, a bespoke pitch is created
- Contact information forthe prospect are obtained and the inital contact is made: either via phone or email, to book a time suitable for a more detailed communication

Pitch
- In a B2C context this denotes verbal communication with the consumer, presenting all the benefits of the event
- In a B2B context this referes to attending the meeting with the target prospect or communicating via phone and presenting the event and all the other relevant information in a structured and professional manner
- This stage also includes handling potential objections and negotiating the final terms of co-operation, both in B2C and B2B contexts

Closing the sale
- In a B2C context this is usually when the customer pays for their ticket or other product or service frelated to the event
- in a B2B context this referes to finalising all the details of the contract and writing up a hard copy to be signed by both parties

After-sales customer care
- In a B2C context this stage involves communi cation wih the customer after their event attendance and making sure they enjoyed the experience, but also gathering their input on what was done well and what could be improved for the next time
- in a B2B context this stage refers to follow-up on how the client is happy with their participation at the event, whether their expectations of and objectives set for the event were met, as well as getting their input on what could be improved. This stage also providces a good opportunity to start negotiating the company's partiticipation in the following edition of the event

Figure 10.6 The personal selling process for events

Source: Adapted from Brassington and Pettitt (2003)

Evaluating personal selling

Personal selling is a very performance-focused marketing communications technique which is fairly easy to evaluate. The key indicator of success is the amount of sales made within a particular business period, which are defined both as general sales targets (objectives) for the business as a whole and specific sales targets – often called sales quotas – for individual members of the sales force (i.e. individual employees tasked with personal selling). The targets can be defined in absolute or in relative terms. The targets defined in absolute terms will involve items such as a specific number of sales (specific number of tickets, specific quantity of event space sold, etc.) or a specific amount of income or new customers that need to be generated by sales. When defined in relative terms, the targets will include items such as conversion rates, i.e. the percentage of new enquiries that were turned into prospects or buyers.

In addition to evaluating the sales performance of the staff, another form of evaluation entails evaluating the fitness of the sales funnel, i.e. the process of turning an initial enquiry into a paying customer and the tools that support it. Oftentimes the sales funnels can be quite lengthy and complicated, which can impact negatively on conversion rates, in which case a complete review and redesign of the funnel is advised in order to optimise it and make it fit for purpose. An important aspect in this process is understanding the profile of the target audiences and what it is they are looking for and then designing a process that is fairly straightforward and enables the sales staff to close the deals quickly.

Sales promotion

Sales promotion is a tactical marketing tool aimed at boosting short-term sales of a product or service. It relies on the two innate human characteristics of competitiveness and fear of scarcity, which is evident in the approach that sales promotions often take: competing for a prize, or for a limited stock available at reduced prices. Sales promotion is, thus, action-oriented, encouraging the consumer to buy, or at least try, a product or service immediately (Smith and Zook, 2011).

Depending on which level it's taking place at, sales promotion with events can take two forms: *supply-side sales promotion* (which refers to suppliers promoting their products/services to event organisers) or *demand-side sales promotion* (which refers to the event's sales promotion efforts towards their customers, whether B2B or B2C).

Demand-side sales promotion in both B2B and B2C contexts can be based on money, products or gifts. *Money-based sales promotion* involves reduced prices for event attendance (e.g. early bird booking discounts, or discounts for buying tickets through a particular retailer). *Product-based sales promotion* includes the promotion of particular products at reduced prices. This can, for example, include 'buy one get one free', 'three for the price of two' or similar offers on tickets or event merchandising, or it can include sampling materials from companies participating at the event included in the event welcome packages (also known as 'goodie bags'). *Gifts and prizes* are also a popular type of sales promotion. Gifts can be given out to returning customers, or members of an event's loyalty scheme, whilst prizes are usually related to contests and sweepstakes which can be used to promote a particular element of the event, or to gather data about event attendees which can later be used for the purposes of personal selling campaigns.

Sales promotions are designed for fast, short-term results and their evaluation usually focuses on the volume of sales generated during the promotional period, the proportion of redemption (if done via coupons) or via sales force feedback for a more qualitative approach to understanding what the customers think about the promotion and how it is impacting their buying decision making.

Whichever type of sales promotion activity is chosen, it is important that its nature fits with the brand of the event that is being promoted and that due attention to detail is given so that any problems may be avoided (e.g. fulfilment) (Smith and Zook, 2011). A strategic approach to designing sales promotions and thinking them through in relation to the rest of the integrated marketing communications mix is essential for finding a good fit, whereas thorough research and planning the operational side of sales promotion can help anticipate take-up of the promotion by target audiences and avoid any major problems.

Direct marketing

Although present in various forms since the late nineteenth century, direct marketing was officially titled 'direct marketing' in the late 1960s (Brassington and Pettitt, 2003). Jobber (2010, p. 547) defines direct marketing as 'the distribution of products, information and promotional benefits to target consumers through interactive communication in a way that allows response to be measured'. It represents a cheaper and more focused alternative to the previously mentioned mass communication tactics of advertising and public relations, which enables companies to address the consumers directly and (in some instances) personalise the materials they give out. Fill (2011) argues that, combined with sales promotion, direct marketing builds on the basis created through mass media with advertising and public relations, and enables brands to create and sustain mutually rewarding relationships with their target audiences.

The main channels of direct marketing have been identified by the Direct Marketing Commission as follows:

- direct mail
- emails
- telemarketing
- leaflets, circulars and free publications
- catalogue or e-commerce
- inserts
- field marketing/demonstrations
- customer magazines – offering information and advice about company's products or services
- TV and radio advertising that promotes a particular call to action (e.g. 'see website for details')

- newspapers and magazine display advertising (not inserts, but adverts with website address or 'see website for details')

- mobile messaging

- interactive TV

- ambient/place-based media – which includes a clear call to action.

It is interesting to note that some tactics which would normally be classed as advertising are also channels for delivering direct marketing campaigns (Bauer and Miglautsch, 1992). Indeed, if an advert (broadcast or print) includes a direct call to action (phrased, for example, as: 'see our website for more details' or 'call our hotline for more information') it is automatically classed as direct marketing as it is soliciting a response from the consumer aimed at initiating a conversation. It follows that the division between above-the-line and below-the-line marketing communications mentioned earlier in this chapter lies not in the type of channel that is being used for communicating with consumers, but in the nature of the message being conveyed via the marketing materials.

One of the essential components of a direct marketing campaign is a database of potential customers (Jobber and Fahy, 2009; Jobber, 2010). The database includes names, contact details and demographic, psychographic and other information about people who meet the criteria to become a brand's current and potential customers. The database can be created by the company itself or it can be bought from a specialist provider. For example, an event that has been running for a number of years, which gathers profiling information during the registration process is likely to be able to create a database of previous attendees with whom it wants to maintain close relationships. However, should it wish to widen its pool of audiences it may need to buy a syndicated database created by a market research agency, from which it will then extract the details of the consumers who meet their new target audience criteria (age, background, lifestyle choices, etc.).

Evaluating direct marketing

The impact of direct marketing campaigns is fairly easy to evaluate, due to the fact that they are usually a short-term affair which requires a direct response from the interested consumers. Rather than looking just at the overall amount of sales that have occurred during the campaign, the effectiveness of direct marketing is usually evaluated through the use of ratios, to enable comparisons across audience profiles and across different campaigns. These ratios can include (Brassington and Pettitt, 2003):

- cost per enquiry

- cost per order

- response rate

- conversion rate from enquiry to order

- average order value

- renewal or repeat order rate.

All this data is stored in the customer database, which then enables marketers to identify the most profitable repeat customers, track emerging customer profiles and predict customers' future purchasing behaviour. This information is then used to design future incentives to be included in direct and other marketing communications campaigns which will appeal to the existing consumer profiles.

VIGNETTE 10.2

Jägermeister festival promotions

Jägermeister is an herbal liqueur which originated in Germany in 1935. The recipe was developed by a vinegar and wine producer, Curt Mast, and incorporates 56 different herbs, blossoms, roots and fruits, reflecting the traditions of the locality in which it was developed. By the 1960s, the brand had expanded internationally and was exporting to Scandinavia, Austria, the Benelux region and the US, after which it branched further out to South America, Africa, Australia and Asia. Today roughly 80 per cent of total sales of Jägermeister come from outside its native country, with biggest markets being the US, the UK, Italy and Hungary. More recently, the brand started developing associations with rock music, sponsoring a variety of festivals and launching its own Jägermeister Music Tour in the US in 2002 and the Jägermeister Independent Music Awards in Australia in 2006.

Personal selling and direct marketing have played a key part in the brand's promotional mix since the mid-1970s, following the brand's penetration of the US market. Back then, the core approach to capturing the market share included sending bottles of Jägermeister to key trendy bars and accompanying them with the Jägerettes, scantily clad brand ambassadors whose purpose was to engage people in bars in conversation and promote the drink face-to-face.

The brand's sponsorship strategy, which developed later on, incorporated and still heavily relies on these two traditional marketing tactics. In 2009 the brand toured the German Outdoor Festival Summer with its flying liqueur bar, which allowed the festival visitors to have their Jägermeister 50 metres above the festival ground, chatting to the brand ambassadors and living a unique and memorable experience. In 2012 the brand toured 25 UK festivals in a bid to align itself more closely with the UK's rock music scene, targeting its core audience of 20- to 30-year-olds and aiming to attract new drinkers who were unfamiliar with the brand. The on-site promotions focused around 'educating' festival goers on the 'perfect ice cold shot', which included product sampling and interaction with Jägermeister sales staff who spoke to each customer individually and personified the brand.

More information about Jägermeister's event promotions can be found online on the brand webpage at www.jager.com and the brand's social media sites:

Facebook: Jägermeister Music UK

Twitter: @JagerUK and @JagermeisterUSA

Whilst we have distinguished here between five different marketing and public relations tactics, in reality there is seldom (if ever!) a clear distinction between marketing and public relations (Kitchen, 1993). This debate has been ongoing since the late 1970s and over the past 30-odd years three key positions have proliferated in relation to this question:

1 The notion that the two functions are inextricably linked (as first advocated by Kotler and Mindak, 1978).

2 The notion that the two functions are completely separate (as first championed by Hart, 1991, cited in Kitchen, 1993).

3 The notion of PR as a corrective element to marketing (as posited by White, 1991).

The debate is still growing strong and no definite definition of marketing or public relations can be said to exist. Recent calls for distinguishing between the two disciplines (e.g. Hutton, 2010) seem to be slightly more vocal than those trying to put both under the same common denominator, although a new, complexity-based perspective seems to be emerging (McKie and Willis, 2012), arguing that both marketing and public relations are evolving disciplines, whose development should take into account not just one or the other, but also the external context within which this evolution is happening. The growth of events and other 'experiential' tactics tends to cause even more confusion. In reality, the key to the successful promotion of events lies in the understanding of the event's key target audiences and their interests and preferences, which can help marketers decide which tactics to use to reach them. Successful promotion is more about knowing 'which shoe fits' rather than stating firmly whether a particular tactic is classified as marketing or public relations.

CASE STUDY

Australian Open ATL campaigns

The Australian Open is the first of the four Grand Slam Tennis events held around the world each year and it takes place in Melbourne each January. Alongside the other three Grand Slams (the French Open, Wimbledon and the US Open), the Australian Open is one of the most popular tennis competitions, both with the players because of its significance in world tennis rankings, and with tennis fans, who attend to enjoy the beauty of the game and the performance of the world's top players. The event is considered somewhat of a traditional international fixture, which will celebrate its 105th staging in 2017.

As a major event in the Asia-Pacific region and the only Grand Slam event in the southern hemisphere, the Australian Open relies heavily not only on attendance at the event itself, but also on viewership across the world for the two weeks of the tournament. The relationships of the event and its key sponsors are emphasised heavily in the media, primarily through traditional advertising. However, in recent years the advertising campaigns which focus on the event are increasingly linked to a host of alternative marketing communications methods, such as social media and field marketing, in order to have a stronger overall impact on the target audiences.

Australian Open and KIA Motors

Kia Motors is the major sponsor of the Australian Open and has supported the event since 2002, providing over a hundred vehicles to ensure the safe and comfortable transport of the event's players and other key figures. In January 2013, KIA extended its sponsorship of the event for a further five years in a deal that is thought to be worth over $50 million. In 2014, Innocean Australia, a creative communications agency, delivered an interactive TV advertising campaign for KIA which created a unique experience of playing tennis for a professional athlete in the comfort of the TV viewer's own home. The campaign consisted of six TV commercials in which Australian tennis player Sam Groth serves six different serves, keeping the viewers guessing where each ball will go. Sam Groth's 'The Bomb' serve, running at 263 kilometres per hour, is listed as the world's fastest serve. The TV ad campaign was complemented by the 'KIA Game On' mobile app, developed by mobile solutions agency Mnet and media agency Initiative. The app allowed the viewers to use their phone as a racquet to return Sam Groth's serve in real time and all contestants were entered into a prize draw to win the newly launched KIA Cerato Coupe, which served as a pull to increase target audience participation.

Australian Open and Mount Franklin Water

Mount Franklin Water is Australia's premium spring water. The brand, owned by Coca-Cola Amatil, one of the largest non-alcoholic drinks bottlers in the Asia-Pacific region and one of the global top five Coca-Cola bottlers, is dubbed 'Australia's first and favourite bottled water'. In 2012 the brand became the official sponsor of the Australian Open for a period of three years, with the contract up for renewal towards the end of 2015. The sponsorship activation in 2014 included an above-the-line TV advertising campaign which ran for the duration of the Australian Open in the second half of January. Devised by the Australian arm of the global full-service creative advertising agency McCann, the campaign aimed to bring to life the refreshing feeling of drinking Mount Franklin water on a hot summer's day via a set of 15-, 30- and 45-second TV spots. The spots present a cloud following a group of young people who are having fun in the sun along the picturesque nature of northern New South Wales. The nature element of the TV ad is very much in line with the 'pure' and 'natural' qualities of the Mount Franklin brand itself. Alongside the TV ad, the campaign was also supported via YouTube clips, cinema and print advertising, as well as social media and field marketing consumer engagement, including the 'Mount Franklin Waterfall Dome' feature at the Australian Open event site.

For more information and some examples of the KIA Game On campaign, please visit the KIA Australia YouTube channel at www.youtube.com/channel/UCA9kcRbcaZ97vktbGHbiyxQ.

For more information on Mount Franklin Water sponsorship of the Australian Open, visit www.campaignbrief.com/2014/01/mount-franklin-brings-pure-fee.html.

To see the Franklin Water TV ad for 2014, visit their YouTube channel at www. youtube.com/watch?v=zereMcc06zk.

Case study questions

1 Why do you think the sponsors of the Australian Open decided to use an above-the-line advertising campaign as the staple of their sponsorship activation?

2 What other strategies, discussed in Chapter 9, can you identify in the above case study? Support your answer with specific examples.

3 What is, in your opinion, the role of broadcast advertising in twenty-first-century marketing?

SUMMARY

This chapter has sought to introduce the traditional marketing tactics. It has presented and contrasted the mass media tactics of advertising and public relations and identified some factors that might influence the choice of one over the other in particular situations. The section on public relations introduced the notion of stakeholders and identified the variety of publics events need to communicate with in order to build their brand image. The discussion of below-the-line tactics, namely sales promotion, personal selling and direct marketing, has attempted to identify the difference in approach these techniques use in contrast to mass media channels and has provided some food for thought on how these tactics fit in contemporary marketing practices in the events sector. In the following chapter, we turn our attention to contemporary marketing tactics of sponsorship, live brand experiences and celebrity endorsement.

REVIEW QUESTIONS

1 Identify the positive and negative characteristics of both above-the-line and below-the-line marketing communications.

2 Find three examples of adverts (broadcast or print). Identify specific elements of these ads (as presented in the chapter) and argue their fit with the brand they are promoting.

3 What is the difference between personal selling and direct marketing? Which one do you think is more effective and why? Think of some examples of each within the events industry.

4 Identify specific examples of sales promotion with three events you attended in the past. Do you think they were effective? Justify your answer.

5 What are, in your view, the similarities and differences between marketing and public relations?

EVENT MARKETING SCENARIO

You've just been hired as a brand strategist for the mobile communications network EE. EE is one of the fastest growing 4G providers in the UK and encompasses three mobile brands: EE, Orange and T-Mobile. The company is dedicated to improving telecommunications infrastructure in the rural areas of the UK and providing high-quality telecommunications services to its customers. The company's responsibility approach, 'Better Britain', focuses on working with people to improve their digital skills and using the scale of the company to boost youth employment. The company is planning to support a series of small local events in rural areas of the UK. It is your responsibility to design the direct marketing and personal selling strategy for these events. You need to develop the following:

- Promotional flyers – think of visuals, key messaging and copy.

- Brand ambassadors strategy – how will you organise your brand ambassadors at these events: what activities will they deliver, how should they be dressed, how should they behave?

- Sales promotion strategy – what kinds of packages of products/services could the brand be offering as incentives at these events?

FURTHER READING

Books

Fennis, B.M. and Stroebe, W. 2010. *Psychology of Advertising*, Hove: Psychology Press
This book provides a detailed examination of advertising as a marketing tactic, both from the 'supply' side (i.e. the perspective of the marketing/advertising professional and the 'demand' side (i.e. the perspective of the consumers exposed to advertising campaigns).

Fill, C. 2011. *Essentials of Marketing Communications: A practical guide to structures, products, formulas, pricing and calculations*, Harlow: Pearson Education UK
Excellent textbook written by one of the leading figures in the area of marketing communications education. It provides a good overview of a number of areas in marketing communications, including stakeholders, strategy, HR, branding and many more. This book is also included in reading lists of the UK's Chartered Institute of Marketing.

Jackson, N. 2013. *Promoting and Marketing Events: Theory and practice*, Abingdon: Routledge
This book contains some valuable information about the similarities and differences in contemporary marketing and public relations for events. Of particular interest are Chapters 7–10.

Potter. W.J. 2012. *Media Effects*, Thousand Oaks, CA: SAGE
This text is an excellent introduction to the broad area of media research and presents in reasonable detail the various effects media can have on consumers. The book is also particularly useful to students as it encourages them to explore the presented theories and concepts in their own, local context.

Journals

Bauer, C.L. and Miglautsch, J. 1992. A conceptual definition of direct marketing, *Journal of Direct Marketing*, 6(2), pp. 7–17
This insightful article provides an interesting discussion of the conceptual definition of direct marketing and is an excellent starting point for students to begin to develop a critical understanding of the concept.

Copp, V.F. 1997. Reinventing direct marketing, *Journal of Direct Marketing*, 11(4), pp. 14–25
This article provides a good overview of the issues faced by direct marketing at the end of the twentieth century and discusses the similarities between direct marketing and advertising. It offers some food for thought in comparing the practice of direct marketing then and now.

McKie, D. and Willis, P. 2012. Renegotiating the terms of engagement: Public relations, marketing and contemporary challenges, *Public Relations Review*, 38, pp. 846–852
This article seeks to renegotiate traditional turf wars between public relations and marketing through a review of significant marketing books. It argues that evolving disciplines need to respond not only to each other but also the wider environment, which requires cooperation as well as competition.

Other resources

The Direct Marketing Association (DMA) www.dma.org
The Direct Marketing Association is the trade association for direct marketing professionals. The website is membership-oriented, however, it also provides access to some interesting free reports and whitepapers outlining key trends and developments and networking events within the industry, as well as a useful blog.

The Direct Marketing Commission (DMC) www.dmcommission.com
The Direct Marketing Commission is the independent industry self-regulatory body, which oversees the Direct Marketing Association's DM Code of Practice. It provides an avenue for consumers to learn more about the legal requirements and constraints of direct marketing and a place for them to voice any concerns they may have about the tactic.

PR Week www.prweek.com
This is a useful source of information about the current industry trends in PR. It covers USA, UK and Asia and provides a good overview of global PR performance for a host of big brands, countries (destinations) and PR agencies.

Thinkbox www.thinkbox.tv
This is a great online resource which caters to TV advertisers. It offers a variety of content which brings the TV medium closer to its target audience, as well as other practitioners in the industry and the general public.

Think TV www.thinktv.com.au
Think TV is a resource created and maintained by Free TV Australia – the Australian broadcast industry body representing free-to-air channels. This is a good source of information about the effectiveness of promotion for a variety of free-to-air TV channels and, although the information is geographically focused only on Australia, it will aid the understanding of how broadcast advertising can be most effectively planned and evaluated.

References

Bauer, C.L. and Miglautsch, J. 1992. A conceptual definition of direct marketing, *Journal of Direct Marketing*, 6(2), pp. 7–17.

Brassington, F. and Pettitt, S. 2003. *Principles of Marketing*, 3rd Edition, Harlow: FT Prentice Hall.

Clarkson, M.E. 1995. A stakeholder framework for analysing and evaluating corporate social performance, *Academy of Management Review*, 20(1), pp. 92–117.

Fill, C. 2011. *Essentials of Marketing Communications: A practical guide to structures, products, formulas, pricing and calculations*, Harlow: Pearson Education Ltd.

Freeman, R.E. 1984. *Strategic Management: A stakeholder approach*, London: Pitman.

Hutton, J. 2010. Defining the relationship between public relations and marketing: Public relation's most important challenge, in Heath, R.L. (Ed.) *SAGE Handbook of Public Relations*, Thousand Oaks, CA: SAGE.

Jackson, N. 2013. *Promoting and Marketing Events: Theory and practice*, Abingdon: Routledge.

Jobber, D. 2010. *Principles and Practice of Marketing*, 6th Edition, Maidenhead: McGraw-Hill.

Jobber, D. and Fahy, J. 2009. *Foundations of Marketing*, Maidenhead: McGraw-Hill.

Kitchen, P.J. 1993. Towards the integration of marketing and public relations, *Marketing Intelligence and Planning*, 11(11), pp. 15–21.

Kotler, P. and Mindak, W. 1978. Marketing and Public Relations, *Journal of Marketing*, 42(4), pp. 13–20.

McKie, D. and Willis, P. 2012. Renegotiating the terms of engagement: Public relations, marketing and contemporary challenges, *Public Relations Review*, 38, pp. 846–852.

Perrey, J. and Spillecke, D. 2011. *Retail Marketing and Branding: A definitive guide to maximising ROI*, Chichester: John Wiley & Sons.

Seitel, F.P. 2004. *The practice of public relations*, 9th Edition, Harlow: Pearson Prentice Hall.

Smith, P.R. and Zook, Z. 2011. *Marketing Communications: Integrating offline and online with social media*, 5th Edition, London: Kogan Page.

Smudde, P.M. and Courtright, J.L. 2011. A holistic approach to stakeholder management: a rhetorical foundation, *Public Relations Review*, 37, pp. 137–144.

Society for Human Resource Management. 2006. *The Essentials of Corporate Communications and Public Relations*, Boston: Harvard Business School Press.

White, J. 1991. *How to Understand and Manage Public Relations*, London: Business Books.

Chapter 11

The new role of public relations in the promotion of events

Learning outcomes

By the end of this chapter, students should be able to:

- Understand how the role of public relations has changed in the 'experience economy'

- Appreciate the differences between 'traditional' and 'contemporary' PR approaches

- Explore the role of storytelling as a staple of contemporary PR activities

- Critically evaluate the role of sponsorship, live experiences and guerrilla marketing in gaining publicity for events

- Explore the pros and cons of celebrity endorsement in the marketing of events

> *If you do a good job of telling your story directly, the media will find out. And then they will write about you!*
>
> *David Meerman-Scott (2011)*

Introduction

In Chapter 9 we started our discussion of the range of strategies and tactics useful in the marketing of events. Chapter 10 introduced public relations as one of the 'traditional' marketing tactics, where we explored the 'old school' approach in getting the media to write about events. This chapter now explores the role of engaging content and, particularly, *stories* in creating the 'pull' for the event's target audiences. We discuss in detail how sponsorship, live experiences and celebrity endorsement represent the staple of the contemporary approaches to PR. Chapter 12 then focuses on examining the role of the internet and (particularly) social media in the marketing of events. Chapter 13 which follows then looks at the role of the planning function and compares and contrasts two approaches to marketing planning: one supported by the Marketing Mix concept (discussed at length in Chapter 4) and one supported by the VITER model (presented in Chapter 14).

Reframing public relations for events

In Chapter 10 we offered the definition of public relations as it is viewed by its leading industry body – the Chartered Institute of Public Relations (CIPR). We mentioned that PR is about managing reputation and establishing *goodwill* between the organisation and its publics and that this is done through two-way communication with stakeholders, understanding their needs and influencing their opinion and behaviour. The understanding of stakeholders and their demands for transparency (Wilcox and Cameron, 2007) in managing an organisation's public relations is critical and this is particularly important with events, which (as we have seen with the 2-plus customer rule mentioned in Chapters 6, 7 and 10) have a wide range of stakeholders whose decisions can have a direct impact on the success of an event at any given point in time.

Whilst we do recognise that the dominant approach to PR is still the traditional, 'old school' approach of writing press releases, schmoozing PR agents and hoping for coverage in the mainstream media, the events industry is slowly waking up to the idea that PR includes a whole lot more than this, often rather hit-and-miss, approach focused on media relations and publicity (Wilcox and Cameron, 2007). The spread of the internet has made all sorts of information more widely available to a range of publics than ever before and the shifts in consumer behaviour discussed in Chapters 7 and 8 have demonstrated that consumers are now much more proactive in finding just the right products and services to meet their unique needs (Meerman-Scott, 2011). In fact, academics and practitioners seem to agree that there is now a new type of consumer to reckon with: the *prosumer* (Toffler, 1980; Kotler, 1986; Ritzer and Jurgenson, 2010). Although the term is not new (indeed, it's been around for over thirty years since being introduced by the futurologist Alvin Toffler), its relevance has increased with the emergence of the notions of *experience economy* (Pine and Gilmore, 1999), *'dream society'* (Jensen, 2001) and *Imagineering* (Nijs, 2003), which we discussed at length in Chapter 3. The role of the experience in the consumption of products and services has transformed the way consumers search for and interact with products and services, thus amplifying Hirschman's (1980) view of consumers as innovative and creative novelty-seekers. The *prosumer* is, therefore, a proactive consumer: an individual who is (more or less) self-aware, understands his or her unique needs and wants and is willing to spend time and money to find alternatives that best meet these. Furthermore, the prosumer is in part consumer and in part producer of the products and services he or she consumes (Ritzer *et al.*, 2012; du Gay, 1995; Prahalad and Ramaswamy, 2004) – we briefly discussed this back in Chapter 3, when we talked about the role of co-creation in the event value chain.

Aside from being producers and consumers at the same time, prosumers also play the vital role of 'product and brand advocates' (Gunelius, 2010), which implies that if they are happy with the product or service they bought they are likely to be loyal to that particular brand and, thus, likely to promote it to their family, friends, colleagues and acquaintances. As discussed in Chapter 8, consumers' search for authentic and joyous experiences (Derbaix and Derbaix, 2010; de Geus *et al.*, 2013) requires a change in thinking on the part of the event marketers, from a *supply-side*-focused view of what can be delivered (within existing resource constraints) to a *demand-side*-oriented view of what the potential event attendees are looking for and expecting to get from an event. Therefore, understanding prosumers and incorporating effective opportunities for them to co-create their own experience is crucial in order to design and deliver events that really create an impact. In a world where the internet dominates as a source of information in the buying process, it is important for events to offer the right information on a range of platforms, enabling potential attendees to quickly and easily find the information that will help them make a decision. The internet also offers a convenient space for prosumers to share their opinions and experiences with others, thus helping the event create and maintain positive PR. Hence, event marketers need to move from the traditional, 'old school' press release and media relations programmes built on what the organisation wants to say, to a more engaging, interactive and co-creationist approach which offers the information the buyer wants to hear (Meerman-Scott, 2011) at the right time and through the appropriate channels. This new approach relies heavily on *storytelling*, which we present in greater detail in the following section.

Contemporary PR strategy: the role of storytelling

In Chapter 8 we presented the view of consumption of products and services as being infused with a person's sense of self – individuals purchase products and services that help them express aspects of their personalities. When talking about consumer motivations for attending events, we argued that events as leisure market offerings are attended by consumers who are in search of one, or a combination, of three things: *authenticity*, *happiness* and *hedonism*. Therefore, the totality of the event experience is crucial in ensuring that people's expectations are met and that these three key motivators are lived up to in the eyes of the target audience. That said, it is important to also note that the event experience can transcend the actual physical engagement of an individual during the event itself – through marketing, the event experience can be extended both to the period before and after the event has taken place. The role of the marketer is thus, according to Bagozzi and Nataraajan (2000), one of facilitator – marketers *help* people find products and services (and events) that make them *happy*.

In an age where consumers are looking at products and services they consume as extensions of themselves, and where there are almost infinite purchasing options for any given buying 'problem', market offerings can no longer be differentiated merely by their inherent characteristics, nor by the benefits they bestow upon their users. In the twenty-first century, consumers are looking for brands with compelling and credible stories, ones that they can relate to, live and share (Smith and Wintrob, 2013). Successful storytelling, therefore, is what helps brands move on from being just visual representations (logos, colour schemes, words and pictures) to become masters in creating engaging experiences that help deliver the total brand promise (Papadatos, 2006; Pringle, 2004). The role of contemporary PR, then, is to successfully communicate a brand through the use of stories (Prindle, 2011).

Although branding in the events industry has not yet evolved as much as it has in other industries, such as sports, automotive or hospitality, storytelling has an increasingly important role in helping to deliver compelling event experiences – before, during and after the event itself.

Smith and Wintrob (2013) have identified four types of brand stories:

1 *Heritage stories* – emphasising the origins of a particular brand.

2 *Contemporary stories* – narrating a brand's general purpose, their connection to today, and what they are doing to stay relevant and connected with their target audiences.

3 *Folklore stories* – created, driven and spread by consumers themselves, which reduces the amount of control a brand has over this type of stories.

4 *Vision stories* – presenting the direction a particular brand is planning to take in the future, where it wants to go.

Figure 11.1 exemplifies these four types of brand stories as they can be found within the events industry.

The consumers' demand for stories as a way of establishing an emotional connection to a particular brand is slowly transforming the way organisations manage their PR efforts. In the context of the 'push-pull' dichotomy (Crompton, 1979) we discussed in Chapter 8, stories help brands move from being aggressive and interrupting, i.e. 'pushing' their marketing messages to their target audiences, to becoming more engaging and interesting, thus creating a 'pull' for consumers to more actively seek out information about these brands and visualise how they exemplify aspects of their personalities and how they fit in their day-to-day life, gently nudging them towards the actual purchase. It could be argued that events, as leisure market offerings, can particularly benefit from using stories as part of their marketing efforts. Aside from these being useful in constructing and delivering on-the-day event experience, there is definitely also a place for them in the pre- and post-event marketing campaigns. This is particularly relevant to the folklore-type stories, which are essentially constructed by the consumers themselves and are imbued with their own meanings related to the event (Chen, 2012b). These folklore-type stories could (and should) form the staple of the consumers' sharing in a range of media, thus helping the event earn a significant place in the realm of digital and word-of-mouth space.

Type of brand story	Brands that use it well	Events that use it well
Heritage	NIKE, HP, Dell, Papa John's Pizza	Robin Hood Festival, UK
Contemporary	Harley-Davidson, Taylor's Guitars	Glastonbury Festival, UK
Folklore	TOMS shoes, Tiffany & Co.	Burning Man, USA
Vision	Corning ('A Day Made of Glass' campaign)	Lake of Stars, Malawi

Figure 11.1 Brand stories

Source: Adapted from Smith and Wintrob (2013)

VIGNETTE 11.1

Burning Man's storytelling strategy

The Burning Man festival is an annual arts event gathering over 60,000 people in the Nevada Black Rock Desert. The event is widely known as a beacon of *prosumption*: all participants in the event are in some way, shape or form producing the event, alongside consuming it. The event has developed an *inclusive community logic* (Chen, 2012a) which seeks to challenge the 'traditional' notions of what kind of art should be produced, who can produce it and how, in order to bring the art to the masses. Originating in 1986 as a small community event with only 20 people attending, the organisation of the event today has been professionalised: the now week-long event is produced by the Black Rock City LLC, which works all year round to prepare for the event and is supported by about 2,000 volunteers during the event itself. All of this is done on a no-longer-so-tiny budget in excess of $17 million per event (Chen, 2012a).

The event itself, however, is merely a vehicle to promote the Burning Man culture, which is defined as 'the sum of the experiences of the people who take part in it' (Burning Man, 2015) and which comprises six interconnected programme areas: Arts, Civic Involvement, Culture, Education, Philosophical Centre and Social Enterprise. It is, therefore, not surprising that much of the Burning Man's efforts is focused on bringing people together and the organisers actively encourage and support a range of audiences in sharing their stories of the event, particularly via the event website. The event's website, hence, includes the following forms of storytelling:

1 'Voices of Burning Man' is a collection of posts relating to the culture of the Burning Man, contributed by a range of stakeholders.

2 The 'Jack the Rabbit Speaks' is the event's official newsletter aimed at preparing event goers for their experience in Black Rock City.

3 'Tales from the Playa' is the section that collects contributions by event attendees about their individual experiences, perceptions and stories of the event.

4 The event's YouTube channel contains a collection of video material which aims to educate audiences about what the event is all about and what is expected of participants, including the event etiquette, as well as some video evidence of the participant experiences from previous events.

5 Media coverage section includes a comprehensive archive of all media coverage the event has received since 1996.

6 Community blogs section provides links to blogs focusing on the Burning Man event written by people who have attended the event.

7 The website also includes a comprehensive list of all the written materials scholars and other authors have published about the event, including books, monographs, academic articles and research papers in a range of disciplines from photography, organisational management, sociology, politics, and others.

With the Burning Man festival, the participants are both the observers and the creators of their own experiences and they use these to enhance and enrich the purpose and nature of the event itself. The Burning Man event brand relies heavily on storytelling, not just in the run-up and aftermath of the event, but also in the delivery of a unique and compelling event experience.

For more information about the Burning Man festival, please visit the website at http://burningman.org or the event's YouTube channel 'Burning Man'.

We said at the beginning of this chapter that PR is moving from the traditional, 'old school' approach to a more engaging and relational one. This contemporary approach to PR is delivered by utilising four key tactics: the internet, sponsorship, live experiences and celebrity endorsement. We present the power of Web 2.0 in Chapter 12, so in the following sections we turn our attention to the cross-promotional potential of sponsorship, live experiences and celebrity endorsement.

Sponsorship

Sponsorship is usually defined as a formalised, reciprocal and mutually beneficial relationship between two parties: the sponsoring brand (or sponsor) and the sponsored property. This relationship involves an exchange of money, goods, services or know-how offered by the sponsor and the rights to be associated with a particular individual, event or organisation, which are offered by the sponsored property (Lagae, 2005). Sponsorship is considered an effective tool for achieving an organisation's commercial corporate, marketing or media objectives (Meenaghan, 1983; Meenaghan, 2001) and it is, thus, not surprising that sponsorship has grown in value exponentially. Whilst events of various types have been supported with some form of private investment of various stakeholders since their emergence centuries ago, commercial sponsorship started developing rapidly since the establishment of the modern Olympic Games in 1896, where companies funded the delivery of the Athens Olympics in exchange for the opportunity to advertise their products at the event (IOC, 2014). This development was further accelerated in the mid-1980s when the first major broadcasting contract was signed for the 1984 Los Angeles Olympics, after which the International Olympic Committee worked on restricting the sponsorship opportunities at its events in order to signal the exclusivity of its The Olympic Partners (TOP) programme and make it more desirable to prospective sponsors.

Why do businesses choose to invest in sponsorship?

Sponsorship is becoming an increasingly important marketing communications tactic as it can have a significant impact on the sponsoring brand. This is evidenced by the unprecedented growth of sponsorship globally: sports sponsorship alone soared from $44bn in 2009 to an approximately $53.3bn in 2013 (Key Note, 2014). As a reciprocal relationship, sponsorship allows both parties involved to get what they want: an event might seek financial investment, media exposure or in kind products and services, whilst the sponsor is likely to want to achieve increased brand awareness, image enhancement, hospitality opportunities for staff and clients, or opportunities to trial new or push sales of existing products (McDonnell and Moir, 2013). Similarly, Jobber (2010) argues that sponsorship offers brands five principal opportunities:

- gaining publicity
- creating entertainment
- fostering favourable brand and company associations
- improving community relations
- creating promotional opportunities.

Whilst having the ability to significantly impact on a brand's bottom line (Cornwell *et al.*, 2001) by helping it achieve a competitive advantage (Fahy *et al.*, 2004), sponsorship should not be judged just in terms of achieving a brand's sales and profit objectives, but also in terms of relational objectives it can help achieve (Sharples *et al.*, 2014), which include creating attachment between the customer and the brand in order to support customer loyalty and business development.

Sponsorship is purported to help brands establish an emotional connection with their target audiences, which gives 'greater tangibility and depth of brand meaning' than traditional marketing tactics, such as advertising or direct marketing particularly because of its experiential component (Cliffe and Motion, 2005). Events themselves offer 'emotionally laden experiences', creating vivid imagery of the sponsoring brand (Meenaghan, 2001), linking the event experience to the brand (Cliffe and Motion, 2005) and facilitating the meaning and image transfer between the two (Chien *et al.*, 2011). As such, event sponsorship is a useful marketing communications tool to engage with the 'evolved' consumer we presented in Chapters 7 and 8.

Farrelly and Quester (2005) view sponsorship as a *co-branding alliance*, which entails the sharing of intangible brand assets, such as brand image and corporate reputation. In order for these alliances to be successful, the two entities engaging in this relationship must have a good strategic compatibility (i.e. 'fit'), a set of converging goals, a similar level of commitment to the relationship and a willingness to trust the other party. Sponsorship, they argue, has moved on from just being an economic relationship to one which supports an intense interpersonal exchange, both physically between people (e.g. attendees and brand representatives) and psychologically in terms of meanings assigned to brand characteristics and perceptions of sponsoring brands overall. Because of this, it is particularly important that the images of the sponsor and the sponsored property are *congruent*, i.e. have some inherent similarities (Meenaghan, 2001), not just in terms of *function* (e.g. sporting brands sponsoring sporting events), but also in terms of aspiration or nature of the brand, i.e. *image-related similarity* (Gwinner, 1997). For example, whilst the global logistics company DHL sponsors Formula 1 in a functional way (by transporting all the F1 gear from location to location for the duration of the event series, which is its primary business), the brand congruence runs deeper than that as DHL particularly prides itself in the speed and precision in which it conducts its operations and what better way to emphasise this characteristic than partnering with the world's epitome of speed and precision that is the F1. In addition to the functional and brand image similarities, sponsorship relationships can also be based on *target market similarities* (Howard and Crompton, 2004), such as, for example, Scavi and Ray – a high-end prosecco brand which sponsors London Fashion Week – a high-end fashion event attracting a range of affluent audiences.

In choosing properties to sponsor, Lagae (2005) argues for a logical process:

1 Brands should first establish what similarity exists between the brand's and the event's target audiences – their audience profile, geographical reach, social status, lifestyle, etc.

2 Brands should identify how the essential features of the event – event environment, media attention, experience – can support their own brand image.

3 Brands should have a clear idea of how to leverage marketing and communications opportunities offered by the sponsorship relationship.

4 Brands should decide how long they would want to be tied to a particular event (i.e. the duration of impact period).

Finding a partner with the right 'fit' is crucial in facilitating the image transfer through sponsorship, but is by no means the only element of it. The fit is often just a platform for meaning creation – it provides consumers with a set of cues (or signals) which, once interpreted, allow them to construct evaluations for relatively unobservable factors (Grau and Folse, 2007, cited in Walker *et al.*, 2011), thus enabling consumers to make up their mind as to a particular brand ('I like it', 'I love it', 'I hate it', etc.). Fleck and Quester (2007, cited in McDonnell and Moir, 2013) have identified two key variables of fit:

• Expectancy – the sponsorship relationship must meet customer expectations of the sponsoring brand (i.e. be congruent with it).

• Relevancy – the sponsorship relationship must make sense and contribute some meaning to the sponsoring brand.

Expectancy and relevancy of a sponsorship relationship are emphasised by the range of sponsorship activation activities, which we present in the following section.

Sponsorship activation

Lardinoit and Quester (2001) and Farrelly and Quester (2005) refer to sponsorship activation as a plan of marketing activities which are complementary to sponsorship and involve the application of a broad range of marketing tactics (including advertising, sales promotion, merchandising, etc.) in order to maximise the benefits from the sponsorship relationship. In other words, sponsorship activation is a comprehensive set of planned activities aimed at leveraging the value of the sponsorship relationship (Carrillat *et al.*, 2014). This means that, in order to be as effective as possible, a sponsorship involves the integration of a range of promotional elements to support the engagement of the target audiences and to facilitate the raising of brand awareness and transference of brand image between the two parties involved.

Sponsorship activation budgets are usually two to six times higher than the pure cost of rights fees and demonstrate a 'strong indication of a firm's commitment to the sponsorship relationship' (Farrelly and Quester, 2003, cited in Farrelly and Quester, 2005), which is often a long-term affair, with average sponsorship contracts lasting between two and five years, although, obviously, there are exceptions. Chadwick and Thwaites (2005) argue that currently most of the sponsorship activation is initiated by sponsoring brands, rather than the sponsored properties themselves, and this is an area that event marketers could place much more emphasis on.

Corporate hospitality is a popular part of sponsorship packages, because it has, at its heart, the physical interaction between brand representatives and their stakeholders in an environment filled with brand touch points. Corporate hospitality creates an active encounter between the attendee and the brand, which is exceptionally participative in nature, thus affecting the attendee's perception of and relationship with the brand. Sponsoring brands most often use events as platforms to reward high-performing employees or entertain current and prospective clients in the event's VIP areas. The increasing popularity of corporate hospitality has recently led to it becoming an exclusive income-generating sector of the business tourism industry and is no longer related exclusively to sponsorship.

VIGNETTE 11.2

Wagamama's sponsorship activation at festivals

Wagamama is a Japanese-inspired award-winning series of restaurants, which employs 3,500 people in 17 countries around the world. The first restaurant opened in London in 1992 and today there are over one hundred restaurants in the UK, following an aggressive expansion started in 2011, which aims to triple the current number of restaurants by 2022. To support this fast-paced expansion, the brand had to increase its efforts to raise awareness of itself with a range of target audiences, as well as create communications which will be inspiring, memorable and support brand recall, in order to increase traffic at the existing restaurants to generate future demand and profits which can then be used to expand its network across the UK. In 2011, the brand retained the services of a London-based integrated creative agency, The Tailor of Shoreditch, in order to create a three-year experiential campaign which will enable the brand to enter the festival market and thus communicate directly with its key target audiences. The campaign was launched at two festivals in 2011: the Parklife in Manchester and the Summer Sundae in Leicester.

The agency came up with the creative concept for 'the wagamama lounge', an outdoor experience of the brand's famous restaurant environment. The experience was underpinned by the three key pillars of food, art and music, which provided the framework for the design of the physical space. The lounge contained an open-plan kitchen where wagamama chefs cooked food for the hungry festivalgoers, who were entertained by the interactive graffiti wall sharing people's artwork via Facebook and by listening to the music played by the resident DJ. The design was born from the wagamama logo (red star), which was adapted into an unfolding object reflecting the changing nature of the brand. Wagamama simplified its menu to make festival meals easier to make fast, whilst still retaining the exceptional taste and quality which sets them apart from other restaurants of this type. The experience was strongly supported by an online campaign which included a dedicated wagamama lounge webpage and groups on three key social media sites: Facebook, Twitter and Foursquare, and involved the festivalgoers in online awareness-raising efforts by offering free meals at the festivals for those who 'liked' their groups or otherwise engaged with them. During the event, the attendees had the opportunity to create their own artworks on the digital graffiti wall and these were automatically uploaded onto the Facebook page and shared with them in real-time, where a photographer was available to snap photos of 'artists' next to their work, thus encouraging further engagement with the campaign's social media sites. Apart from engaging external audiences, the brand also engaged with its employees, by running internal competitions for DJs to support the experience, as well as offering employees the opportunity to work at the events.

The first event at Parklife was a huge success, attracting over 10,500 visitors and generating over £25,000 in sales, with an estimated 86 per cent of the total 26,000 Parklife visitors aware of the brand's presence at the event. Following the event, engagement continued on the campaign's social media sites, particularly YouTube, where the official video of the campaign had over 6,000 in less than three weeks from event finish.

More information about wagamama can be found at www.wagamama.com and their social media sites on: Facebook 'wagamama', Twitter @wagamama_uk and their YouTube channel 'wagamamauk'.

Case study adapted from www.festivalawards.com and a range of other sources in the public domain.

In deciding the mix, schedule and intensity of the sponsorship activation activities, one key consideration is deciding the amount of sponsorship investment the brand is willing to pay. It is important to highlight here that a sponsorship investment is not restricted only to the sponsorship rights fee that is paid to the sponsored property, but also includes additional costs, such as costs of activating the sponsorship or costs of other related campaigns brands will execute, and which will help exploit the sponsorship rights effectively (Brassington and Pettitt, 2003).

Thus, the formula can be summed up as follows:

Sponsorship Investment = Sponsorship Rights Fee + Sponsorship Activation + Ancillary Activities

For example, a brand (say, a drinks brand) might pay an event (say, a music event) a fixed sponsorship rights fee of £50,000. However, in order to really leverage this opportunity the brand will need to spend additional money on creating customised marketing materials (e.g. flyers, posters, merchandising, staff uniforms and props) that reflect that sponsorship relationship. Let's say that the brand spends an additional £90,000 on this sponsorship activation. Additionally, the brand may also want to create their own advertising campaign to promote their sponsorship of the event, which would include additional spend on buying media space and designing advertising materials (e.g. print ads, TV or radio commercials, online banners and adverts). They may also want to run an experiential marketing campaign that promotes them as the sponsor of the event. Let's say that the brand spends an extra £60,000 on these ancillary activities. Putting all these costs together, the overall value of this sponsorship investment for the brand is £50,000 + £90,000 + £60,000 = £200,000. This means that the brand has spent a whopping four times more money on this sponsorship relationship as compared to the cost of the sponsorship fee itself, in order to maximise the benefits of this relationship. This means that the ratio of sponsorship fee to sponsorship activation is 1:3 (50,000:150,000), i.e. sponsorship activation has cost the brand three times more than the sole cost of the sponsorship fee.

From the above discussion, it would be easy to think that sponsorship is only important to the sponsoring brand, but this is not entirely true – sponsored properties also receive benefits beyond just financial ones from being linked to established brands. Some evidence exists which indicates that people are more likely to attend, advocate for the event and report higher event quality based on a strong sponsor influence (i.e. sponsor being strongly related to the event brand) (Walker *et al.*, 2011). However, research in this area is still rather scant and inconclusive.

Apart from the two entities involved in the formal sponsorship relationship, some benefit from the sponsorship may be captured by the sponsors' direct competitors, who often use a tactic called **ambush marketing** to gain exposure by associating themselves with the event without having to pay the large sponsorship fees. These companies are often referred to as *pseudo-sponsors* (Meenaghan, 1998; Carrillat *et al.*, 2014), designing marketing communications activities that will indirectly associate their brand with a specific event and confuse consumers into thinking they are the event's official sponsor. Some notable examples include Nike's upstaging of Reebok at the 1996 Olympics in Atlanta, when more media attention was captured by Nike's gold sneakers, worn by American basketball star Michael Johnson, than Reebok's official sponsorship of the Games. Budweiser, the official beer of the 2010 FIFA World Cup in South Africa, experienced a similar issue when a group of 36 attractive young women dominated the TV coverage of the Holland vs Denmark match wearing bright orange dresses with the logo of their key competitor – Bavaria Beer. The group were ejected from the stadium and arrested by the South African police, but were later released (*The Guardian*, 2010).

Ambush marketing is an aggressive marketing tactic which severely dilutes the brand image transfer between the official sponsor and the event and can negatively impact on an official sponsor's return on investment (or return on objectives) from that sponsorship. Aside from these economic issues, ambush marketing also has a host of ethical (O'Sullivan and Murphy, 1998) and legal (Ellis *et al.*, 2011) implications for the companies that practise it, with a range of mega-events implementing policies aimed at minimising the opportunities for their sponsors' competitors to exploit the space to conduct ambush marketing activities.

Evaluating sponsorship

Crompton (2004) noted that an agreement amongst sponsorship researchers exists for the need for more attention to be paid to this important aspect of the relationship. For an activity of such importance both to sponsoring brands and to the properties being sponsored, it is surprising to see that there is no consensus amongst researchers or practitioners as to what makes the best, or most appropriate way, to evaluate sponsorship. O'Reilly and Madill (2012) note that this is partly because companies engaged in sponsorship are relatively wary of discussing any clear performance indicators in public, due to their sensitive nature. Thus, much of the evaluation of sponsorship – the process and the key performance indicators, as well as key stakeholders – are specific to the brand and proprietary in nature.

Although, as mentioned before, consensus does not currently exist on this topic, that is not to say that the area of sponsorship evaluation is under-researched. Indeed, O'Reilly and Madill (2012) identified no less than 52 studies focusing on evaluation of sponsorship as a whole or its individual components. They note an impressive variety of items being researched, from perceptions of various stakeholders (sponsors, sponsees, spectators and general consumers) to the quantity and quality of media space consumed by the sponsorship, to the profiling of management practice in relation to sponsorship as well as tracking the value of brand stock before, during and after sponsorship implementation. Whilst this variety is commendable and contributes to the diversity of approaches and flexibility of application in real life situations, much of the decision as to which aspects of sponsorship will be evaluated rather depends on the key objectives that the sponsorship is trying to achieve for the particular brand, as well as how it might impact the brand's relationship with a range of its stakeholders (Meenaghan *et al.*, 2013). Thus, in addition to the standard marketing-oriented indicators such as the quantity (how much airtime, how many column inches) and quality (brand awareness, image, consumer attitudes and opinions, etc.) of media exposure (Brassington and Pettitt, 2003), new metrics of return on objectives (ROO) and return on investments (ROI) have been introduced in recent years (Masterman, 2007; Meenaghan *et al.*, 2013).

More recently, focusing on recognising the key elements of sponsorship in practical terms, a next generation promotion agency based in the USA developed a statistical measure of sponsorship effectiveness, which aims to facilitate their client's decision making when deciding which properties to sponsor. In 2011, Marketing Arm introduced the Sports Property Index (SPI) – the industry's first independent index designed to quantify consumer perceptions of sponsored properties. The measurement takes into account nine key indicators: a property's appeal, avidity, awareness, breakthrough, endorsement, excitement, influence, trendsetting and trust. These indicators have been weighted based on input from industry practitioners and the SPI thus is pitched as a tool to help assess a property's success potential, as well as projected return on sponsor's objectives (Cooper, 2011).

Whilst great strides have been made in identifying the key components of sponsorship evaluation, both in terms of industry practice and in terms of academic constructs, much more research and testing is still needed in this area for the industry and academia to come to a unified approach to measuring sponsorship effectiveness. However, when we consider the speed with which the sponsorship industry is developing, it is likely that a one-size-fits-all approach is not even needed. This, then, would leave some space for new and innovative approaches to keep developing and each subsector of the sponsorship industry to come up with indicators that best represent its specific nature and address its specific needs.

Experiential marketing: live brand experiences and guerrilla marketing

Although dating back to the beginning of the twentieth century and the creative marketing practice introduced by George P. Johnson (whose name is now carried by one of the largest global experiential agencies), experiential marketing has really proliferated in the last couple of decades, as events emerged as a key interactive form that has the ability to bring brands closer to their consumers. This is due, in part, to the decreasing effectiveness of traditional marketing communications techniques, such as advertising, traditional PR and direct marketing (Ferdinand and Kitchin, 2012). Schmitt's (1999) seminal work 'Experiential Marketing' expands on Pine and Gilmore's (1999) notion of the experience economy (which we covered in detail in Chapter 3) and posits the relevance of experiential marketing in creating brands as a 'rich source of sensory, affective and cognitive associations that result in memorable and rewarding brand experiences' (p. 57). He developed a framework of five Strategic Experiential Modules (SEMs) which support the delivery of effective brand experiences, which include:

1 SENSE, or creating sensory experiences through engagement of the five senses (sight, sound, touch, taste and smell).

2 FEEL, or appealing to an individual's inner feelings and emotions, evoking affective responses.

3 THINK, or creating cognitive, problem-solving experiences that engage individuals in a creative way.

4 ACT, or providing individuals with alternative ways of doing things, alternative lifestyles and interactions.

5 RELATE, or engaging the audiences on all four levels mentioned above, with an aim of relating the individual to something outside of his/her current self.

In many ways, Schmitt's (1999) work provides a good contextualisation for the discussions about the nature of event consumer we had in Chapters 7 and 8 of this book.

Vila-López and Rodríguez-Molina (2013) view experiences as a good way to engage consumers beyond the traditional transactional relationship which dominated the marketing activities of the second half of the twentieth century. The authors argue that an emotional event experience has an impact on brand personality, as perceived by target audiences, which further impacts on overall brand reputation. Events, therefore, due to their immediate, interactive and immersive nature, provide unique platforms for consumers to willingly engage with, receive and fully comprehend a brand's marketing message – something which traditional marketing methods we discussed previously in this book are less and less able to deliver. Chanavat and Bodet (2014) note that, although traditionally the experiential consumption was primarily studied in the contexts of leisure, entertainment and the arts, it has more recently found its way into the mainstream marketing fields of retailing and hospitality. However, whichever field experiential marketing is being delivered in, there is some consensus around the fact that the quality of the event experience facilitates the creation of an (conscious or unconscious) emotional bond with the brand, which paves the way for strengthening the brand image and influencing future buying behaviour.

Experiential marketing can be considered to include three key types: sponsorship, live brand experiences and guerrilla marketing. We've discussed sponsorship at length in previous sections of this chapter, so now we turn our attention to the remaining two types: live brand experiences and guerrilla marketing.

Live brand experiences are events organised solely for the purpose of promoting one specific brand and can be considered extensions of that particular brand. As such, their key aim is to bring that brand to life and enable target audiences to RELATE (Schmitt, 1999) to the brand. The global event 'circuit' includes increasingly more events of this type. Some prominent examples include Nike's 10k run events or 3on3 basketball tournaments, Innocent's (soft drinks brand) Village Fete or the Red Bull FlugTag series of events which launched in Vienna, Austria, in 1991 and currently takes place in over 35 cities around the world.

The other type of experiential marketing is *guerrilla marketing*, which has roots in guerrilla warfare, where a technically and militarily weaker group defeats the bigger, more heavily equipped opponent through the use of creative (sometimes dubbed 'smoke and mirrors') approaches using an element of surprise. Guerrilla marketing, then, utilises an unexpected and unconventional mini-event designed to generate buzz and evoke positive feelings, which are then projected onto the brand on whose behalf the activity was organised. Hoyle (2002) argues that a successful guerrilla marketing activity has to have the element of surprise, a certain uniqueness to the concept which will generate attention, and that it needs to be delivered in an area where a large 'built-in' audience already exists. This type of marketing is often referred to as a flashmob or a publicity stunt, reflecting its key purpose of capturing audience attention for a very brief amount of time by using the element of surprise.

One of the brands that has had impressive success with its guerrilla marketing activity is the telecommunications brand T-Mobile, which has included it as a major component of its marketing communications from 2009 onwards. Many will remember the T-Mobile Dance flashmob executed at London's Liverpool Street station in early 2009, its follow-up, the T-Mobile Singalong with Pink in London's Trafalgar Square later that year, or the Heathrow Airport Welcome, done in the following year. Whilst these have been complex, large-scale productions, designed to create stories which were subsequently turned into advertising and social media campaigns, not all guerrilla marketing needs to be as complex. For example, Nike delivered a creative guerrilla campaign titled 'Run on Air' in Prague in celebration of the International Car Free Day (Dietrich and Livingston, 2012) which involved placing large cardboard cut-outs of Nike shoes and discreetly placing them on the wheels of cars parked all around Prague. These were accompanied by notices to the vehicle owners, in the style of those issued by the police, encouraging them to walk instead of using their cars and then to place the 'technical devices' (i.e. the cardboard cut-outs of Nike running shoes) on another vehicle to spread the message (Petitpr, 2007). The campaign was relatively low cost, but more effective than a major media initiative would have been (Dietrich and Livingston, 2012).

Although guerrilla marketing is considered an innovative, creative and more 'contemporary' approach to marketing, it is increasingly being used even by traditional marketers (Hoyle, 2002), thus creating a new benchmark or mainstream marketing.

Celebrity endorsement

We live in an increasingly mediatised wold in which media coverage bestows legitimacy and newsworthiness on a product or service (Wilcox *et al.*, 2015). Much of this is down to the celebrification of society (Rojek, 2001), which emphasises the role of celebrities as vehicles for humanising desire – desire for a particular lifestyle or a particular aspect of the celebrity's personality to which an ordinary individual might aspire. These aspirations stem from three key psychological factors (Wilcox and Cameron, 2007): the need for hero-worship, the need for belonging and identification with a particular social group and the need for excitement and variety in one's day-to-day life. These needs provide a thriving ground for the publicising and glorification of celebrities (Wilcox and Cameron, 2007) whose newsworthiness stems from their glamorous or notorious status within the public sphere (Rojek, 2001). In other words, celebrities are inherently newsworthy.

Rojek (2001) defines three types of celebrity (p. 17):

1 *Ascribed celebrity*, which stems from one's lineage, i.e. the status typically follows from bloodline. Good examples of this type of celebrity are Princes William and Harry, Paris Hilton, Ivanka Trump or Jayden and Willow Smith (children of Will Smith).

2 *Achieved celebrity*, derived from the perceived accomplishments of the individual in open competition and their rare talents or skills. Good examples of this type of celebrity are Michael Jackson, Serena Williams, Sean Connery or Shakira.

3 *Attributed celebrity* is the result of the concentrated representation of an individual as noteworthy or exceptional by cultural intermediaries, these are ordinary people put in the spotlight by mass media and generated in the new trend of reality TV. Good examples are the Kardashian family, or the stars of reality series such as *The Only Way Is Essex*, *The Hills* and *Bridezillas*. Rojek (2001, p. 18.) refers to these types of celebrities as *celetoids* and defines them as '*accessories of cultures organised around mass communications and staged authenticity*'. Celetoids usually have a short-term 'career', as opposed to celebrities, who tend to be more 'durable'.

Wilcox and Cameron (2007) purport that celebrity status is not officially bestowed upon these individuals by some obscure social authority, but, rather, that their value increases once they obtain a critical mass of media coverage. However, regardless of how their status is obtained – by lineage, skill, talent or pure chance – celebrities are cultural fabrications that increasingly shamelessly mediate between the products or services they endorse and the audiences these products and services are trying to reach in a 'market of sentiments' (Rojek, 2001).

Celebrity endorsement is becoming increasingly relevant with events, particularly major and mega-events which are important because of the number of attendees they are trying to attract or impacts they will undoubtedly have on their host communities and other stakeholders. Use of celebrity endorsement with events can help raise the profile of the event through generating considerable media coverage (Wilcox and Cameron, 2007). Celebrities can also help strengthen the image of the event and give it increased credibility in the eyes of the relevant stakeholders (Hoyle, 2002) by associating their own image with that of the event they are endorsing (Wilcox *et al.*, 2015). Indeed, considering three key staples of celebrity promotion are photographs, public appearances and awards (Wilcox and Cameron,

2007), celebrities are the natural next step in event promotion. So why is celebrity endorsement so important?

Wilcox *et al.* (2015, p. 268) define endorsement as 'nice things' said about a particular organisation, product or service by celebrities who are paid to do it. However, how well received these messages will be with the brand's target audiences largely depends on the credibility of the celebrity that is the source of information shared in the public domain. Wilcox *et al.* (2015) further define three sources of credibility:

- A celebrity's perceived expertise in a particular area.

- Their sincerity, i.e. whether or not they come across as believing in what they are saying about the brand they are endorsing.

- Their charisma, i.e. whether they are attractive, self-assured and articulate when talking about the brand.

Similarly to sponsorship, the right 'fit' between the event and the celebrity is crucial for a positive return on investment. Pringle (2004) argues that higher awareness of (or familiarity with) the brand will increase its favourability and likeability with its target audiences. Celebrities, therefore, increase familiarity for brands, which helps the brand to be viewed in a more favourable light by the target audiences. Once this is established, and the brand has proven itself reliable over a considerable period of time, it can hope to start cultivating consumer trust, which is the ultimate currency in twenty-first-century business. A good example of the right 'fit' is the UK's award-winning lifestyle exhibition, the Ideal Home Show. Dating back to 1908 when it was launched by the *Daily Mail*, the Ideal Home Show has grown into the UK's leading lifestyle and home design event, a brand extension of the *Ideal Home* monthly magazine. In 2016, the event is sponsored by the online property search engine Zoopla and is endorsed by a range of celebrities who are experts in the fields covered by the show: the Interiors section was endorsed by Laurence Llewelyn-Bowen, a homestyle consultant and TV personality; the Home Improvements section was endorsed by George Clarke, an architect and TV personality; the Gardens section by Alan Titchmarsh, a gardener, TV presenter and novelist; the Food and Housewares section by Jean-Christophe Novelli, a multi Michelin Star award-winning chef, etc.

Although there are many benefits to using celebrities to endorse a range of products and services and, particularly, events, there are also drawbacks to using this type of promotion (Wilcox *et al.*, 2015). First, currently there are too many celebrities endorsing too many different brands, which confuses the public as to who endorses what. Second, any celebrity endorsement carries with it a risk of over-exposure of the celebrity at the expense of the property being endorsed: the bigger the star, the harder it is to handle and control the influence he or she will have on the event (Hoyle, 2002) or what particular aspect of the relationship between the celebrity and the event (if any) the media coverage will emphasise. Another risk includes endorser's actions which can sometimes undercut the product – good examples of this are endorsements by the now disgraced cyclist Lance Armstrong and formerly much admired golfer Tiger Woods, who were both dropped by their sponsors due to negative actions and associated negative publicity. Another good example is Jeremy Clarkson, the well-known British journalist and broadcaster, who was most famous for co-presenting the hit BBC motoring programme *Top Gear*, which branched out into a series of live events that spanned five continents. Following a physical altercation with a crew member whilst filming on location, Jeremy Clarkson was informed by the BBC that his contract for the show would not be renewed (BBC, 2015). Finally, celebrity involvement in politics tends to reduce their effectiveness as endorsers of products and services because they tend to alienate segments of the consumer public who disagree with their views. Thus, celebrity endorsement can be very challenging to manage and should be carefully planned, executed and evaluated.

CASE STUDY

The Coca-Cola Company's sponsorship strategy

About the Coca-Cola Company

The Coca-Cola Company and its lead drinks brand, Coca-Cola, will be celebrating its 130 birthday in 2016. In over a century of history, the Coca-Cola Company has learned better than most the power of good storytelling and the effect it can have on brand equity: the brand has consistently been one of the world's top brands, with innovative and engaging marketing communications strategies that have inspired generations of consumers and helped to grow its fan base year on year.

Coca-Cola is one of the world's best-known and best-loved brands. Over the course of the past century, the brand has become globally ubiquitous: you can find Coke almost everywhere on the planet! In the 2015 Effie Effectiveness Index (the award for world's most effective marketing ideas), Coca-Cola was named the Most Effective Global Brand and the parent company, Coca-Cola Company, the Most Effective Global Marketer. Much of this popularity is down to the way Coca-Cola exploits its 130-year heritage and its commitment to creating visually appealing and emotionally compelling marketing communications campaigns which emphasise the brand's core values of promoting happiness, togetherness and living life to the fullest. These values are ingrained in the company's sponsorship strategy, which is tailored to each of its sub-brands: the original Coca-Cola, Coke Zero, Diet Coke, Sprite and Fanta.

Overview of the Coca-Cola drinks brands and their sponsorship strategies

The original **Coca-Cola** soft drink (introduced in 1886) follows the company's overarching ubiquity strategy: it sponsors the Olympics (since 1928), the FIFA World Cup (since 1978) and, more recently, the Rugby League World Cup (since 1995). These global mega-events have been chosen because they fit well with the brand's ubiquity strategy – they attract large numbers of audiences of different profiles, both physically to event venues, but also via global broadcasting and online presence.

Fanta (introduced in 1941) focuses on young audiences, predominantly teenagers, and is a playful brand ('there is always a time to play'). It sponsors FANTAsy (Germany) and the Jenga app, in order to reach multicultural teenage audiences, as well as the Oblivion ride at Alton Towers theme park (UK), although much of the physical sponsorship material has been removed following a petition signed by fans of Alton Towers claiming the light-hearted image of the brand is not compatible with the nature, theme and 'story' of the ride itself.

Diet Coke (introduced in 1982) was the second sister brand to the original Coca-Cola drink. As a brand, it has an upmarket, aspirational and youthful personality and focuses primarily on female audiences. Hence, the brand sponsors events such as the Oscars and the Tribeca Film Festival and has recently signed Taylor Swift as its Brand Ambassador.

Coke Zero (introduced in 2005) targets predominantly young adult male clientele, so much so that the drink has been dubbed 'Bloke Coke' in the UK. As such, this brand sponsors products and events which appeal to these audiences, such as the NASCAR championships, the ESPN College GameDays and the Riot Games (computer gaming). The brand has also had a long-standing contract with the controversial British footballer Wayne Rooney as Brand Ambassador.

Sprite (introduced in 2009) has an 'edgier', more urban image than the rest of the Coca-Cola drinks portfolio. The brand has sponsored NBA since 1994 and signed the NBA star player LeBron James as its Brand Ambassador in 2003. In early 2015, Sprite was replaced by PepsiCo as the official NBA sponsor and has since moved on to replace PepsiCo as the sponsor US Major Soccer League (MSL), following in the worldwide football sponsorship footsteps of its older sister brand Coca-Cola.

Coca-Cola's sponsorship activation at the FIFA 2014 World Cup
For the 2014 FIFA World Cup™ in Brazil, Coca-Cola pulled all the stops and created the largest ever marketing campaign in its 130-year history. The campaign titled 'The World's Cup' focused on celebrating football as a force for building a more inclusive and connected world. The key theme of the campaign was drawn from the company's core values of happiness, togetherness and living life to the fullest, which are a good fit with football as a universally popular sport based on teamwork and togetherness. This synergy of values created a strong foundation for a global campaign which was executed locally across multiple channels and tactics under one central idea: 'It's the World's Cup – Everyone's Invited!' Additionally, the visual identity of the campaign was the brainchild of the uniquely talented Brazilian artist Speto and features colours and patterns characteristic of Brazilian street art, with the faces of four young people from Brazil reproduced in Speto's signature graphic style.

The key channels and tactics used to activate the sponsorship included:

Digital media
Launched on 2 April, some two months before the events' opening ceremony, the digital campaign spanned 85 countries with activities starting in New Zealand and moving west towards Brazil. It utilised 31 social listening centres and all the relevant social media channels, including: Google+, YouTube,

BuyLocal, Facebook, Twitter, and Spotify. In the first week alone the campaign generated over 400 million impressions, with +100K photos shared across the platforms and over 90 per cent positive comments expressed by the target audiences. The digital campaign saw Coca-Cola become the most popular World Cup sponsor on social media, with its Facebook fan base growing by 2.5 million up to 85 million and the brand having the most Twitter interactions, including retweets, replies and favourites (Kimberley, 2014).

The FIFA World Cup Trophy Tour

The experiential part of the campaign – the FIFA World Cup Trophy Tour – launched in September 2014 and saw the official trophy of the competition travel 165,000 kilometres and be seen by over one million people around the globe, building up buzz and anticipation in the run up to the competition. The trophy visited 400,000 retail outlets in 85 countries and was lifted by 50 presidents. This aspect of the campaign created over $70 million worth of media value and the brand also created ten powerful films which were later on used in broadcast and digital media to continue the conversations amongst fans.

The Happiness Flag

The Happiness Flag generated for this campaign is the largest photomosaic ever created featuring fan photos and tweets. Coca-Cola used this initiative to allow its audiences to give their own personal contribution to the campaign. This component was tied in with sales promotions of Coca-Cola at a range of retail outlets, which ultimately impacted on the sales of the drink. The Flag itself was seen on pitch prior to the Opening Match in Sao Paulo on 12 June 2014.

'Where Will Happiness Strike Next'

The 'Where Will Happiness Strike Next' series of documentary-style short films were captured during stops along the FIFA World Cup™ Trophy Tour. This component of the campaign focused on grassroots sports and the sharing of stories about how football helps passionate fans and aspiring young athletes overcome adversity. Each film ends with the key protagonists having a special viewing of the original FIFA World Cup Trophy that will be awarded to the winner of the Cup. The films aim to inspire audiences around the world to use football as a means of overcoming life's challenges.

The campaign has successfully utilised a range of contemporary media channels, creating buzz and attracting unprecedented media coverage, thus cementing the popularity of the World Cup as a mega-event and Coca-Cola as a globally popular drinks brand.

To learn more about the Coca-Cola Company, its brand portfolio and its sponsorship activities, please visit their official website at www.coca-colacompany.com.

More information about the brands, as well as examples of their marketing communications activities can be found on their individual YouTube channels: 'Coca-Cola', 'Fanta', 'Diet Coke', 'Coca-Cola Zero' and 'Sprite'.

More information about Coca-Cola's 'The World's Cup' campaign at the FIFA 2014 World Cup can be found on YouTube at www.youtube.com/watch?v=hDJu1BO vRG8.

More information on Speto can be found on www.speto.com.br.

Case study questions

1 What is Coca-Cola's brand personality and how can it be used to select appropriate properties to sponsor?

2 Explain the basis of 'fit' for each of the Coca-Cola's drinks brands in selecting properties to sponsor?

3 How has Coca-Cola recognised the new role of PR in their sponsorship activation plan for the FIFA 2014 World Cup in Brazil?

4 Find some relevant videos on YouTube (or other websites) that reflect Coca-Cola's localised activities in different regions for the 'The World's Cup' campaign. You can use the search term 'coca-cola world cup trophy tour stop' in the YouTube search engine. Watch a couple of videos and interpret the impact the campaign activities have had on the brand's target audiences.

SUMMARY

This chapter explored and exemplified the emerging nature of public relations in the promotion of events in the twenty-first century. The discussion focused on four examples of experiential marketing: sponsorship, live brand experiences, guerrilla marketing and celebrity endorsement. Each of these techniques, if used effectively, can contribute to the more successful differentiation of the brand being promoted (Zdravkovic and Till, 2012). The techniques offer four key benefits of credibility, image transfer, bonding with stakeholders and customer trust and retention, which will ultimately lead to the creation of a stronger, more desirable brand, which will ultimately influence future purchasing behaviour (Aaker, 1991, cited in Zdravkovic and Till, 2012).

REVIEW QUESTIONS

1 Explain the role of the prosumer and provide some examples of this in the context of events.

2 Discuss the role of sponsorship in the promotion of events. Research some examples of event sponsorship. Identify the fit between the event and the sponsor and outline the benefits both of these enjoy from the relationship. How has this sponsorship been leveraged on behalf of the sponsor and on behalf of the event?

3 Referring back to some of our previous chapters compare and contrast the PR techniques discussed in this chapter with the traditional marketing tactics mentioned in the previous chapter.

4 Why is celebrity endorsement an increasingly popular promotional technique? Research some examples of events within your environment and explain the fit with the celebrities that are currently endorsing them. Think of some other celebrities that might be a good fit for these events and argue how the media coverage generated by their endorsement might be maximised for the event.

EVENT MARKETING SCENARIO

You are launching your city's first ever world music festival. This type of music has a small but strong following in your city, but the aim of the event is to appeal to a range of audiences from abroad and drive tourist visits to your city. Outline which key celebrities from the genre of world music you would aim to host at the event. How could their involvement be used to generate publicity for the event? Also, which companies would you aim to bring on board as sponsors for the event and why? Justify the proposed sponsor–event fit and suggest some ideas for leveraging that sponsorship, to include some examples of experiential or guerrilla marketing.

FURTHER READING

Books

Masterman, G. 2007. *Sponsorship: For a return on investment*, Oxford: Butterworth-Heinemann
This volume offers a very detailed overview of sponsorship, with interesting examples and in-depth coverage of the key aspects of sponsorship. A good introductory text.

Pringle, H. 2004. *Celebrity Sells*, Chichester: Wiley
This book provides a good discussion of celebrity in the context of marketing and promotion of third-party brands.

Rojek, C. 2001. *Celebrity*, London: Reaktion Books
An excellent introduction into the world of celebrity – how it emerged in post-modernist society and what it entails. It offers good contextualisation for some of the contemporary PR techniques discussed in this chapter.

Journals

O'Reilly, N. and Madill, J. 2012. The development of a process for evaluating marketing sponsorships, *Canadian Journal of Administrative Sciences*, 29, pp. 50–66
A good article which provides an overview of the contemporary approaches to evaluating sponsorships.

Schmitt, B. 1999. Experiential marketing, *Journal of Marketing Management*, 15(1–3), pp. 53–67
A seminal piece building on Pine and Gilmore's (1998) notion of experience economy and extending the discussion to how experiences are created.

Spry, A., Pappu, R. and Cornwell, T.B. 2011. Celebrity endorsement, brand credibility and brand equity, *European Journal of Marketing*, 45(6), pp. 882–909
One of the rare academic articles dealing specifically with celebrity endorsement, this is a good piece that contextualises the contribution of celebrity endorsement to the strengthening of brands.

Other resources

CoolBrands www.coolbrands.uk.com

CoolBrands is an annual barometer of Britain's coolest brands, people and places, derived from the opinions of members of their Expert Council and some 2,000 members of the British public.

Effie Effectiveness Index www.effieindex.com

The Effie Effectiveness Index is an annual ranking of the top global marketing communications players (agencies, marketers and brands), derived from analysing finalist and winner data from 40+ worldwide Effie Award competitions. Results are announced in April for the previous calendar year and awards are given in six categories: Individual Agency Offices, Independent Agency Offices, Agency Networks, Agency Holding Groups, Brands and Marketers. The index has been developed and implemented by Effie Worldwide (www.effie.org), a network of marketing organisations focused on promoting best case practice in marketing communications. The network is known for its awards programme which rewards exceptional effectiveness in marketing communications worldwide.

References

Bagozzi, R.P. and Nataraajan, R. 2000. The year 2000: looking forward, *Psychology and Marketing*, 17, pp. 1–11.

BBC. 2015. Jeremy Clarkson Dropped from Top Gear, BBC confirms, BBC [Online]. Available at: www.bbc.co.uk/news/entertainment-arts-32052736 [Accessed 14 February 2016].

Brassington, F. and Pettitt, S. 2003. *Principles of Marketing*, 3rd Edition, Harlow: FT Prentice Hall.

Carrillat, F.A., Colbert, F. and Feigné, M. 2014. Weapons of mass intrusion: The leveraging of ambush marketing strategies, *European Journal of Marketing*, 48(1/2), pp. 314–335.

Chadwick, S. and Thwaites, D. 2005. Managing sport sponsorship programs: Lessons from a critical assessment of English soccer, *Journal of Advertising Research*, 45(3), pp. 328–338.

Chanavat, N. and Bodet, G. 2014. Experiential marketing in sport spectatorship services: A customer perspective, *European Sport Management Quarterly*, 14(4), pp. 323–344.

Chen, K.K. 2012a. Artistic prosumption: Cocreative destruction at Burning Man, *American Behavioral Scientist*, 56(4), pp. 570–595.

Chen, K.K. 2012b. Charismatizing the routine: Storytelling for meaning and agency in the Burning Man organization, *Qualitative Sociology*, 35, pp. 311–334.

Chien, P.M., Cornwell, T.B. and Pappu, R. 2011. Sponsorship portfolio as a brand-image creation strategy, *Journal of Business Research*, 64, pp. 142–149.

Cliffe, S.J. and Motion, J. 2005. Building contemporary brands: A sponsorship-based strategy, *Journal of Business Research*, 58, pp. 1068–1077.

Cooper, D. 2011. What metrics do sponsors want from and about teams? Introducing the Sports Property Index (SPI), *The Migala Report* [online], Available from: http://migalareport.com/node/490.

Cornwell, B.T., Roy, D.P. and Steinard, E. 2001. Exploring managers' perceptions of the impact of sponsorship on brand equity, *Journal of Advertising*, 30(2), pp. 41–51.

Crompton, J.L. 1979. Motivations for pleasure vacations, *Annals of Tourism Research*, 6(4), pp. 408–424.

Crompton, J.L. 2004. Conceptualization and alternate operationalizations of the measurement of sponsorship effectiveness in sport, *Leisure Studies*, 23(3), pp. 267–281.

Derbaix, M. and Derbaix, C. 2010. Generational concerts: in quest of authenticity?, *Recherche et Applications en Marketing* (English Edition), 25(3), pp. 57–84.

Dietrich, G. and Livingston, G. 2012. *Marketing in the Round: How to develop an integrated marketing campaign in the digital era*, Indianapolis: Que Publishing.

Ellis, D., Scassa, T. and Séguin, B. 2011. Framing ambush marketing as a legal issue: An Olympic perspective, *Sport Management Review*, 14, pp. 297–308.

Fahy, J., Farrelly, F. and Quester, P. 2004. Competitive advantage through sponsorship, *European Journal of Marketing*, 38(8), pp. 1013–1030.

Farrelly, F. and Quester, P. 2005. Investigating large-scale sponsorship relationships as co-marketing alliances, *Business Horizons*, 48, pp. 55–62.

Ferdinand, N. and Kitchin, P. 2012. *Events Management: An international approach*, London: SAGE.

Gay, P. du 1995. *Consumption and Identity at Work*, London: SAGE.

Geus, S. de, Richards, G. and Toepoel, V. 2013. The Dutch Queen's Day Event, *International Journal of Event and Festival Management*, 4(2), pp. 156–172.

Gunelius, S. 2010. The shift from CONsumers to PROsumers. Forbes [Online]. Available at: www.forbes.com/sites/work-in-progress/2010/07/03/the-shift-from-consumers-to-prosumers/ [Accessed 9 April 2015].

Gwinner, K. 1997. A model of image creation and image transfer in event sponsorship, *International Marketing Review*, 14(3), pp. 145–158.

Hirschman, E.C. 1980. Innovativeness, novelty seeking and consumer creativity, *Journal of Consumer Research*, 7, pp. 283–295.

Howard, D.R. and Crompton, J.L. 2004. *Financing Sport*, 2nd Edition, Morgantown, WV: Fitness Information Technology.

Hoyle, L.H. 2002. *Event Marketing: How to successfully promote events, festivals, conventions and expositions*, New York: John Wiley & Sons.

International Olympic Committee. 2014. Olympic Marketing Factfile, 2014 Edition [Online]. Available at: www.olympic.org/Documents/IOC_Marketing/OLYMPIC_MARKETING_FACT_%20FILE_2014.pdf [Accessed 10 February 2016].

Jensen, R. 2001. *The Dream Society: How the coming shift from information to imagination will transform your business*, New York: McGraw-Hill Education.

Jobber, D. 2010. *Principles and Practice of Marketing*, 6th Edition, Maidenhead: McGraw-Hill.

Keynote. 2014. *Sports Sponsorship*, London: Key Note Ltd.

Kimberley, S. 2014. Coca-Cola most popular World Cup sponsor on social media, *Campaign* [online]. Available from: www.campaignlive.co.uk/article/1303523/coca-cola-popular-world-cup-sponsor-social-media [Accessed 15 April 2015].

Kotler, P. 1986. The Prosumer movement: a new challenge for marketers, *Advances in Consumer Research*, 13, pp. 510–513.

Lagae, W. 2005. *Sports Sponsorship and Marketing Communications: A European perspective*, Harlow: FT Prentice Hall.

Lardinoit, T. and Quester, P. 2001. Attitudinal effects of combined sponsorship and sponsor's prominence on basketball in Europe, *Journal of Advertising Research*, 41(Jan–Feb), pp. 48–58.

Masterman, G. 2007. *Sponsorship: For a return on investment*, Oxford: Butterworth-Heinemann.

McDonnell, I. and Moir, M. 2013. *Event Sponsorship*, Abingdon: Routledge.

Meenaghan, T. 1983. Commercial sponsorship, *European Journal of Marketing*, 17, pp. 1–74.

Meenaghan, T. 1998. Ambush marketing: Corporate strategy and consumer reaction, *Psychology and Marketing*, 15(4), pp. 305–322.

Meenaghan, T. 2001. Understanding sponsorship effects, *Psychology and Marketing*, 18(2), pp. 95–122.

Meenaghan, T., McLoughlin, D. and McCormack, A. 2013. New challenges in sponsorship evaluation actors, new media and the context of praxis, *Psychology and Marketing*, 30(5), pp. 444–460.

Meerman-Scott, D. 2011. *The New Rules of Marketing and PR: How to use social media, blogs, news releases, online video and viral marketing to reach buyers directly*, 3rd Edition, Chichester: John Wiley & Sons.

Nijs, D. 2003. *Imagineering: Engineering for the imagination in the emotion economy*, NHTV Breda University.

O'Reilly, N. and Madill, J. 2012. The development of a process for evaluating marketing sponsorships, *Canadian Journal of Administrative Sciences*, 29, pp. 50–66.

O'Sullivan, P. and Murphy, P. 1998. Ambush marketing: the ethical issues. *Psychology and Marketing*, 15(4), pp. 349–366.

Papadatos, C. 2006. The art of storytelling: how loyalty marketers can build emotional connections to their brands, *Journal of Consumer Marketing*, 23(7), pp. 382–384.

Petitpr 2007. Nike Guerrilla English Version. *YouTube* [Online]. Available at: https://www.youtube.com/watch?v=yFFMdi1-t6Q&feature=related [Accessed 1 September 2015].

Pine, J.P. and Gilmore, J.H. 1999. *The Experience Economy: Work is theater & every business a stage*, Boston: Harvard Business School Press.

Prahalad, C.K. and Ramaswamy, V. 2004. Co-creation experiences: the next practice in value creation, *Journal of Interactive Marketing*, 18(3), pp. 5–14.

Prindle, R. 2011. A public relations role in brand messaging, *International Journal of Business and Social Science*, 2(18), pp. 32–36.

Pringle, H. 2004. *Celebrity Sells*, Chichester: Wiley.

Ritzer, G., Dean, P. and Jurgenson, N. 2012. The coming of age of the prosumer, *American Behavioral Scientist*, 56(4), pp. 379–398.

Ritzer, G. and Jurgenson, N. 2010. Production, consumption, prosumption: the nature of capitalism in the age of the digital 'prosumer', *Journal of Consumer Culture*, 10(1), pp. 13–36.

Rojek, C. 2001. *Celebrity*, London: Reaktion Books.

Schmitt, B. 1999. Experiential marketing, *Journal of Marketing Management*, 15(1–3), pp. 53–67.

Sharples, L., Crowther, P., May, D. and Orefice, C. 2014. *Strategic Event Creation*, Oxford: Goodfellow Publishers.

Smith, K. and Wintrob, M. 2013. Brand storytelling: a framework for activation, *Design Management Review*, 24(1), pp. 36–41.

The Guardian 2010. World Cup 2010: Women arrested over 'ambush marketing' freed on bail, The Guardian [Online]. Available at: www.theguardian.com/football/2010/jun/16/fifa-world-cup-ambush-marketing [Accessed 10 February 2016].

Toffler, A. 1980. *The Third Wave*, London: Collins.

Vila-López, N. and Rodrígues-Molina, M. 2013. Event-brand transfer in an entertainment service: experiential marketing, *Industrial Management and Data Systems*, 113(5), pp. 712–731.

Walker, M., Hall, T., Todd, S.Y. and Kent, A. 2011. Does your sponsor affect my perception of the event? The role of event sponsors as signals, *Sport Marketing Quarterly*, 20, pp. 138–147.

Wilcox, D.L. and Cameron, G.T. 2007. *Public Relations Strategies and Tactics*, 8th Edition. Boston: Pearson Education Inc.

Wilcox, D.L., Cameron, G.T. and Reber, B.H. 2015. *Public Relations Strategies and Tactics*, 11th Edition, Harlow: Pearson Education Ltd.

Zdravkovic, S. and Till, B.D. 2012. Enhancing brand image via sponsorship: Strength of association effects, *International Journal of Advertising*, 31(3), pp. 113–132.

Chapter **12**

Owning, buying and earning digital spaces for events

Learning outcomes

By the end of this chapter, students should be able to:

- Appreciate the importance of the internet and social media in the context of events marketing

- Identify the range of digital media channels available to marketers and how these fit with a range of target audiences

- Understand key processes in digital marketing and how they are relevant to events

- Be critical about when and how these new channels can be utilised in the process of planning and executing event marketing activities

- Plan and deliver a social media marketing campaign for an event

> *Before the web came along, there were only three ways to get noticed: buy expensive advertising, beg the mainstream media to tell your story for you, or hire a huge sales staff to bug people one at a time about your products. Now we have a better option: publishing interesting content on the web that your buyers want to consume.*
>
> *David Meerman-Scott (2011)*

Introduction

In the preceding chapters we discussed the range of marketing strategies available to event marketers (Chapter 9) and we focused more specifically on the more 'traditional' marketing tactics of advertising, 'traditional' public relations, personal selling, sales promotion and direct marketing (Chapter 10). We contrasted the 'above the line' and 'below the line' approaches and debated when these are relevant and suitable in the context of marketing events. Chapter 11 explored more in depth the contemporary tactics of experiential marketing, sponsorship and celebrity endorsements. This chapter focuses on the now dominant realm of e-marketing, discussing the importance of having an online presence and the effective use of event's e-properties, including owned, bought and earned digital media space. This chapter concludes our discussion of the range of strategies and tactics for marketing events in the twenty-first century, in Chapter 13 we turn our attention to the role of marketing planning and in Chapter 14 we conclude by introducing a new conceptual model for the design and management of marketing activities of events.

Implications of the internet for the marketing of events

Since its penetration into mainstream business in the mid-1990s, the internet has transformed the way business is done at every level at almost lightning speed. Two key aspects of this, particularly relevant to marketing, are the speed of communications and the quantity and quality of information that can now be obtained through digital channels – these concern both the supply and the demand side of the marketing value chain. On the demand (i.e. consumer) side people are able to find information they need very quickly, which helps to speed up their decision-making process. They also have access to a much wider range of information related to any given purchase 'problem', so they are better able to assess the value of each potential 'solution' and generally feel more secure in the choices they are making. On the supply (i.e. production, or company) side, the internet facilitates the speed of communication, both internally (within the company), supporting the execution of business processes, and externally with customers. Aside from faster communication, technology has also enabled companies to know, in greater detail than ever, who their customers are and how they interact with the company's web assets, which enables them to optimise the use of these assets to increase their business revenue.

Brassington and Pettitt (2003) argue that, although the internet provides a new way for doing business, the business (and marketing) itself remains the same as it ever was. I would challenge this statement, as the internet has today created a very saturated market, where marketing messages are no longer 'loud and clear' and a much more strategic effort is needed even in this emerging space for marketers to be heard and believed. In particular, the evolution of the internet marked a seismic shift towards a two-way communication (as opposed to the one-way 'traditional' mass media approach) and has paved the way for the introduction of *permission marketing* (Godin, 2007). The internet provides consumers with a wealth of choices (Anderson, 2009): more available channels, more content available via these and more opportunities for customising this content and sharing it with own networks, and this is much of the reason why traditional marketing communications tactics, such as advertising, PR and direct marketing are proving increasingly ineffective in the twenty-first century. A new medium, therefore, requires a new approach to conceptualising and executing contemporary marketing communications, which focuses on eliminating the barriers to the consumer's adoption of a brand's marketing messages. This is accomplished, according to Meerman-Scott (2011), through designing the interaction around appropriate information and educational elements which then facilitate consumer *choice*. As intuitive and logical as this sounds, though, not many companies fully appreciate what this means for them and their bottom line and this is particularly true for events and other related experiential market offerings. One fundamental aspect of this change is the fact that brands must – to some extent – relinquish their need to control the content, timing and frequency of information about their marketing offerings (Mangold and Faulds, 2009) and embrace the increasing power of social media in the creation and management of brand perceptions with their target audiences and the wider publics.

Integrating e-marketing in your event marketing strategy

In today's business, no organisation can survive without its own digital space – however, small it may be. Much like generating value through building new houses and other infrastructure, companies can generate or increase value of their brands by building their online presence. It is, therefore, not surprising that many practitioners often refer to this space as *digital real estate*, which they often classify into owned, bought and earned digital real estate (also referred to as owned, paid and earned digital media – Chaffey, 2012).

Owned digital real estate are all the different online spaces that the organisation or brand has created themselves. These would include:

- the organisation's official website
- the organisation's official blog(s)
- its profiles on different social media channels
- any mobile applications or tools it has created to facilitate consumer engagement.

Figure 12.1 presents screenshots of the owned digital media spaces for one of the UK's leading exhibition centres – Olympia London. Owned digital spaces allow the brand to retain some control over the messages it wants to share with its audiences and maintain the desired 'look and feel' of the brand through being selective. First and foremost, these are the spaces where the brand has the ability to consistently communicate the visual aspects of its brand, such as the logo, font and official colour scheme, which are its most recognisable brand assets. This is clearly visible in all screenshots in Figure 12.1. Furthermore, these channels are also used by brands to push the desirable visuals (e.g. photos and videos) and narratives (e.g. blog posts, comments or any other type of written content), which will enable them to project a positive brand image. Because they are all *owned* by the brand, these channels present a relatively safe space for brand expression, where negative comments or negative visuals that audiences might want to share either need to be pre-approved to appear online, or (if no approval is needed) can be taken down by the brand's social media managers at any time to 'clean up' the brand's image. Although a brand's owned social media space can be argued to be less controlled than their official website, ultimately it is down to the brand to approve (or delete) which visual or narrative content contributed by the audiences appears in these spaces. It is important to note, however, that even though it is possible for a brand

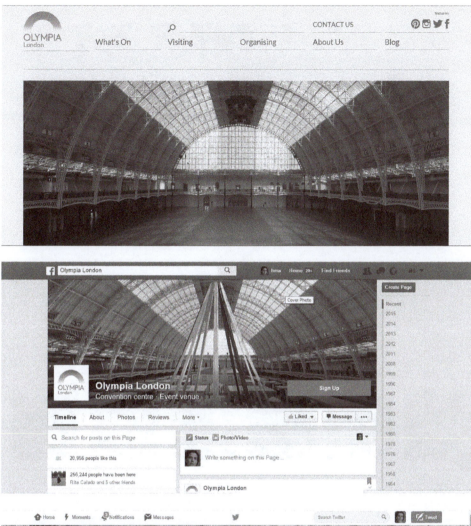

Figure 12.1 Owned digital media spaces for Olympia London exhibition centre

Source: Screenshots by author, 24 February 2016

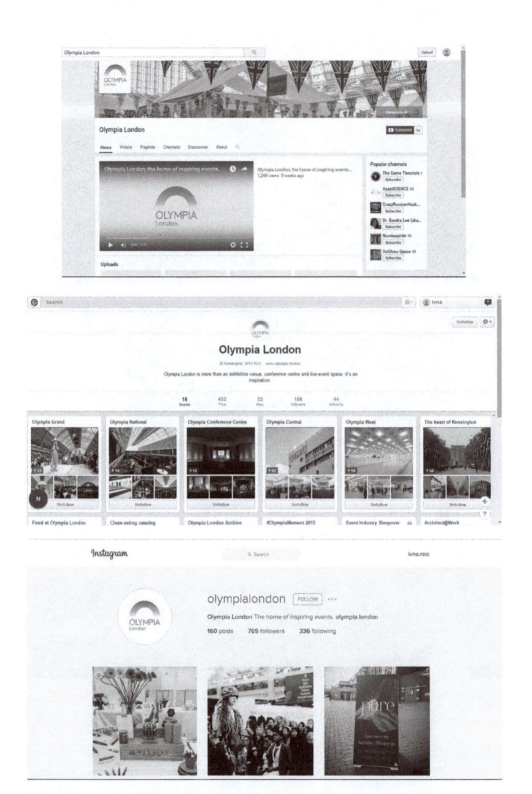

Figure 12.1 *continued*

to exercise a degree of control over the content published in its owned digital spaces, some brands, such as Olympia London, do not engage in – and often even have formal policies that specifically prevent their employees from – deleting negative comments from these. Rather than trying to be controlling and maintain a 'sterile' image, addressing consumer issues portrays a brand as being authentic and responsive to their audiences and consumers appreciate this.

Bought digital real estate (also known as paid advertising) refers to the digital space given to a particular organisation or brand which that brand has paid for. This can include paid advertisements on Google, social media sites, or elsewhere on web spaces not directly owned by that brand. Another way of obtaining bought digital media space is pursuing affiliate marketing by providing digital influencers (usually active bloggers, vloggers or other experts) with samples of own products or services in order to get them to review these products or otherwise mention them in their online posts and discussions. Although this space might not necessarily be paid for with hard cash, there is still a *quid pro quo* of the person talking about the brand getting something in return (e.g. samples of products in exchange for a review, a percentage of sales generated through this medium as a donation to the owner of the blog, or a link to their website being embedded on the brand's website and social media sites to drive traffic).

Earned digital real estate refers to all the online media space given to a particular organisation or brand based on the conversations that its target audiences and the wider publics have about them on the internet. This can include articles published in digital publications (web portals, online magazines, etc.) about the organisation or the brand based on something which is newsworthy (as opposed to being paid to do so). However, and more importantly, this particularly relates to the unprompted mentions of and conversations about the brand and/or its market offerings by the general online publics in the realms of social media, such as online blogs, comments on various communities of interest, discussion fora, or, generally, comments sent out into the ether by a range of publics commenting on particular aspects of the brand, its market offering or its specific activities.

VIGNETTE 12.1

The Samsung School of Rugby digital campaign

The world's leading electronics brand, Samsung, created the 'Samsung School of Rugby' digital campaign to celebrate their first outing as the new sponsor of the Rugby Football Union (RFU). The campaign coincided with the 2015 Rugby World Cup hosted by England and was designed to achieve three key aims:

- Raise awareness of the brand's sponsorship of the sport.
- Advertise the Samsung Galaxy S6 Edge – the brand's most recently released phone.
- Actively engage with fans over a period of eight weeks in the lead up to and during the event.

The campaign consisted of five short films which ran on TV during live event coverage and inside Twickenham stadium during the games and which were published on the Samsung UK YouTube channel. This was also supported with visuals published in print media, to increase awareness with a wide range of audiences. In the films, former England rugby team players Martin Johnson and Lawrence Dallaglio teach comedian Jack Whitehall the core elements of the rugby game: power, speed, accuracy, style and timing. A host of other England rugby legends such as Jason Leonard, Maggie Alphonsi and Jason Robinson also made their appearances, to bring the game to life. An additional short film titled 'Extra Time at The Samsung School of Rugby' included hilarious outtakes of the campaign. Conceptualised and executed by Bartle Bogle Hegarty (BBH), a creative agency co-founded by Lawrence Dallaglio, with scripts being co-written by Jack Whitehall, the campaign is based on humorous interpretation of a game often perceived as overly masculine, in order to appeal to a wide range of audiences and, particularly, those who are not necessarily avid rugby fans. In this sense, the campaign aims to broaden the appeal of the sport, as well as strengthen the image of the sponsoring brand.

Alongside an online hub created specifically to support the campaign and embedded within their UK website (www.samsung.com/uk/rugby/), Samsung also used their official Twitter (@Samsungsport) and Facebook (Samsung UK) profiles, as well as the hash tag #Samsungrugby to drive and track fan engagement with the content. This was further supported by key protagonists in the videos (Jack Whitehall, Martin Johnson and Lawrence Dallaglio) engaging with the content and sharing links to the videos on their social media profiles, thus extending the initial reach of the campaign to their extended networks.

The distinction of owned vs bought vs earned digital real estate is fairly easy to make in theory; however, in practice there is an increasing blurring of the lines between bought and earned digital real estate, although all are still considered to improve a consumer's accessibility to this content (Anderson, 2009). This accessibility is managed by the brand's digital marketing strategies which aim to define which types of content are included and shared and when, where and how. The key processes that facilitate this accessibility and which today's events marketers need to be aware of are search engine optimisation (SEO), paid search (pay-per-click), web analytics and user experience design (UX). We present these very briefly below.

Search engine optimisation (SEO) is a process by which brand's owned digital spaces (such as their website, or their official social media pages) end up listing in the *search engine results page* (SERP) on online platforms such as Google. Google uses a range of algorithms to decide where to place which particular page based on the key search terms used by the consumer doing the search. These algorithms usually scan websites for keywords and phrases that match the original search terms and then, based on how frequently these appear on particular pages, Google ranks pages in order of relevance to the search term(s) being used. In the industry this is referred to as *organic* search results (or listings) (Chaffey, 2009).

Paid search (or pay-per-click or PPC) is a form of advertising done online via a search engine platform. Google is the leading platform in paid search advertising, but other search engines such as Yahoo have their own paid advertising programmes. Although it shares these platforms with SEO, and the results of paid search depend on the search keywords and terms that the consumer is typing into the search engine which caters to organic search, paid search is much more akin to traditional advertising (Chaffey, 2009) – it's a media space bought by the brand to transmit a controlled message about itself or its market offering. The brand will spend money on buying up the space and on creating an advert which will fill that space. Once a customer types in their keywords or search terms, the brand's paid advert will be displayed based on how that advert was optimised by its creator for these particular keywords and search terms.

Web analytics is a process that enables digital marketers to track how audiences are engaging with a brand's owned, bought and (to a certain extent) earned digital spaces. It is often referred to in the industry as back-end management, because it looks at the key features of these digital spaces from the 'back', whereas the customers browsing these spaces look at these spaces from the 'front'. The reasoning here is similar to the concepts of *front-of-house* (FOH) and *back-of-house* (BOH), which form the foundation of effective delivery in tourism, hospitality and events. Normally, web analytics will report on indicators such as:

- *Acquisition*: how many visits these spaces have within a specific period of time (e.g. per day, per week, per month) and how many of these are *unique* visitors (i.e. specific individuals), as well as where these visits originated from – which can shed light on how customers find a brand's spaces, thus enabling the marketer to allocate funds for the planning and implementation of digital marketing plans. Web analytics also reports on the performance of *keywords* used in PPC to establish which of these were particularly effective in attracting audiences to the website.

- *Engagement*: how much time each of these visitors spends on the website as a whole and, more importantly, on particular areas of the website – this can indicate whether or not the website is providing its visitors with the information they are looking for or not, which will have implications for the type of content that will be included in these spaces.

- *Visitor flow*: how these visitors interact with these digital spaces – this is particularly important for websites with an *e-commerce component* (i.e. sales aspect) where the tracking of the *visitor journey* is used for website design and content development.

- *Conversion*: how many of the website visitors come to the end of the sales funnel and actually complete a purchase – this, of course, applies only to those websites that include an e-commerce component.

All of the above web analytics indicators (and many others not discussed here) are closely monitored by digital marketers to understand the nature of their target audiences. This information is then used to improve website conversion rates, which will ultimately impact the event's bottom line. Additionally, web analytics data is a good indicator of which specific digital platforms and channels generate the most traffic for the website and this information can then be used for the future allocation of marketing budgets and financial forecasting. There are a wide range of web analytics tools available today: the most popular – Google Analytics – is free and fairly simple to use, with lots of training materials readily available online, which makes it very popular. For more complex websites, paid enterprise tools such as Adobe Analytics or Webtrends offer more advanced features and are able to analyse websites on a more granular level.

User experience (UX) is an important aspect of website design which focuses on translating the characteristics of the target audiences into the structure of the website. Its purpose is to enable visitors to get to the information they need as fast as they can so that they are able to make the purchasing decision quickly and proceed with the purchase. Web analytics then helps to identify any specific issues affecting the flow of visitors on the website, so that changes can be made which will improve the customer experience of this interaction. The key to optimising the user experience on a website is to really understand who your consumers are and build content specifically tailored to their needs (Meerman-Scott, 2011). This aspect of digital marketing is particularly important for events, as the simple act of buying, for example, a ticket to attend a particular event increases the level of commitment the customer has towards the event and can be a fairly good predictor of actual physical attendance. This is especially true for events where attendance is paid for, rather than free.

Now that we've introduced the basics of digital marketing for events, we turn our attention to the nature and role of social media in this context, which we explore in further detail in the following section.

Earning social media presence for events

Since its emergence in the late 1990s (the first ever social network, SixDegrees.com, launched in 1997), there has been much debate around what social media is, with academics and practitioners alike trying to offer a comprehensive definition of the phenomenon. However, the speed of its development and the breadth of creativity involved in the creation of new social media sites, has made this task very challenging. Scholarly research on social media is still in its infancy, although there are currently several important contributions, such as those by boyd and Ellison (2008), Beer (2008), Ngai *et al.* (2015), which contextualise well the current debates in this area of study.

Research around the role of social media in the context of planning and delivering special events is still embryonic, with some notable work by Hudson and Hudson (2013) and Hudson *et al.*, (2015) related to the use of social media in the context of music festivals, as well as Rothschild (2011), who explored the use of social media in sports and entertainment venues. However, a growing body of literature exists relating to the use of social media in tourism and much of this can be related back to and discussed in the context of special events; this is presented in the following sections.

Why social media?

Although definitions of social media differ from author to author, there seems to be some consensus around the medium's key features, which include the following:

• these are online spaces, highly dependent on information technology, which

• facilitate peer-to-peer communication through user-generated content.

Much of the debate around the definition and classification of social media stems from the disagreement on how narrow (or broad) that definition should be (see Beer, 2008). Kurtz (2016) distinguishes between *social media platforms*, such as Wordpress, Facebook or LinkedIn, referring to types of software used to design interactions in the digital space, and *social media tools*, such as apps, blog posts and comments, which explain specifically how interactions occur in this space. For the purposes of this book, I acknowledge social media as a self-contained eco-system of user-generated content aimed at enabling individuals to obtain the information they need quickly through their network of interests and contacts. In this sense, social media is not just about specific social networks (e.g. Facebook, Twitter, LinkedIn, etc.) which exist for the specific purpose of connecting with others, but it also includes other digital spaces, such as forums, communities of interest, industry portals, consumer review sites and a range of other platforms offering shareable content aimed to inform, persuade or educate.

The strong proliferation of social media over the past decade is a result of its participatory nature (Leung *et al.*, 2013), which has enabled it to move from relative obscurity in its early years (late 1990s) into the cultural mainstream (Keen, 2007, cited in Beer, 2008) in the first decade of the twenty-first century. They provide an ordinary individual with an opportunity to 'type oneself into being' (Sundén, 2003, cited in boyd and Ellison, 2008), thus creating an online representation of the self (boyd and Ellison, 2008) which is controlled almost entirely by the individual. The individual's participation in and contribution to the exchanges in the sphere of social media send important identity signals and, in a sense, brand the individual themselves as the medium for connection and content creation (Leung *et al.*, 2013).

Apart from expressing parts (or the entirety) of their personality, individuals also use social media to shape their consumption choices: from learning about specific market offerings, to conducting their own research and sharing information and to making final purchasing decisions (Kurtz, 2016). Whilst every type of product or service under the sun has been the subject of online 'snooping' by consumers, this seems to be particularly important for market offerings such as travel, tourist attractions and events, which are experiential in their nature (Litvin *et al.*, 2008) and as such are well-differentiated, relatively high priced and require high levels of consumer involvement (Leung *et al.*, 2013). In these industries the traditional notion of customer service as just an aftersales add-on is not appropriate and this is where social media, with its strong focus on a 'user democracy' culture (Leung *et al.*, 2013), can make considerable contributions to a business. This means that a business is able to achieve important goals, for example increase sales of their market offerings or increase their brand awareness, at a relatively low cost, due to the fact that information about the business and its offerings is generated by its end users, not necessarily by the business itself, thus reducing the cost of 'producing' and 'distributing' this information. The current body of research of social media in tourism and hospitality reveals that tourism consumers:

- use social media in all stages of the tourist experience consumption, i.e. pre-trip, during the trip and post-trip (Leung *et al.*, 2013)

- use social media to produce and circulate *meaning* via visual and narrative content (Munar and Jacobsen, 2014)

- share their experiences for personal (e.g. gaining respect and recognition, enhancing self-esteem, increasing social ties, or augmenting social capital), as well as community-related reasons (e.g. exploring and contributing to shared norms, interests and goals, increasing solidarity and altruism) (Munar and Jacobsen, 2014).

The above characteristics of tourism consumers are easily transferrable to event audiences. Chapter 8 discussed at length consumer motivations for attending events and identified attendance at events as an aspect of expressing one's own personality and living experiences that are helping to express one's authentic self. It can, therefore, be argued that social media engagement allows individuals to buy into a *story* which reinforces their sense of self in relation to their internal needs and wants, as well as in relation to the image they want to project towards external stakeholders in their everyday life.

In Chapter 7 we presented a generic event-based consumer buying process (see Figure 7.6). Social media today contributes considerably to each of these stages, for example:

- Need recognition – social media helps consumers clarify their own existing needs and wants and can sometimes even prompt consumers to identify needs which they might not have been completely conscious of; social media today is influential in generating competitiveness between consumers and they will often make decisions to attend events based on how these are perceived (and participated in) by other members in their social networks.

- Information search – social media is now one of the key channels individuals use to gather information about possible solutions to their needs, i.e. it supports consumers in clarifying how specific products and/or brands can help satisfy their needs (i.e. which features they have and how these are compatible with their needs). As such, social media (and the internet more generally) can help in creating and strengthening awareness of events with a broad range of audiences.

- Evaluation of alternatives – social media helps consumers to establish evaluation criteria. This can be done either by asking members of their social networks for their immediate opinions or by asking for guidance on finding appropriate review sites related to the products/services being considered before making the final decision.

- Purchasing decision – once consumers have evaluated their alternatives and decided which option to go for, oftentimes the purchasing itself is done online via e-commerce platforms embedded on the event's website (e.g. shop) or via middlemen such as authorised online retailers (e.g. Ticketmaster) or packaged deals (e.g. hotel stay with theatre tickets included).

- Post-purchase (and pre-event) behaviour – social media helps events maintain a connection with their attendees and build up anticipation and excitement, which are important antecedents in the framing of the overall event experience. This is done both via visuals and via narratives contributed by the event organisers/marketers and the event's audiences consisting of confirmed attendees, as well as those who would like to go, but perhaps are (for various reasons) unable to.

- Event (or experience) – social media is increasingly used to express one's participation in events and other types of leisure activities, which contributes to the online image an individual wants to project.

- Post-experience – social media, through its visual and narrative content, provides an important tangible element which supports the recall of memories and (more importantly) feelings evoked by the event, thus facilitating continued conversations between the event and its audiences and encouraging event loyalty and repeat attendance. With events, the visual element is extremely important, as it allows event attendees to share their own experiences and tell their own *stories* which exemplify their identity and their values.

Ngai *et al.* (2015) recognised the dual role of social media: it can be used not only to facilitate simple peer-to-peer communication in a bounded social context (thus allowing individuals to co-create content and their own interpretation of it), but it can also be strategically used for professional purposes, such as building reputations (individual or corporate), helping to identify career opportunities and also generating business revenue, thus impacting on a brand's bottom line. Mangold and Faulds (2009) refer to social media as a hybrid element of the marketing communications mix which uses the traditional one-way communication (from a brand to its customers) and amplifies it through online word of mouth (or, rather, word of mouse), whereby the brand loses control of the message. Kurtz (2016) refers to this as *social media marketing* (SMM) and argues that its popularity lies in the fact that it provides ways for customers to converse with their favourite brands and to spread those brands' messages directly with their immediate and extended networks via a range of social media platforms. This, then, helps create *buzz* – the engine that drives social media marketing with the aim of achieving promotional and branding objectives, helping to deliver excellent customer service and supporting long-term relationship management (Tuten and Solomon, 2013). Although brands are highly attracted to the buzz created on social media, they are wary that they are also highly likely to lose control over what messages are shared and how frequently. Social media marketing, therefore, has become one of the key elements of a brand's integrated marketing communications (IMC) mix and one which requires to be managed by skilled staff who are strategic thinkers and in tune with the needs and wants of the brand's target audiences.

How to use social media for promoting events

Just like with the overall marketing communications, use of social media with events requires a certain amount of planning, in order to make sure that opportunities for customer engagement are identified and appropriate strategies and tactics are put in place to capitalise on these. Barker *et al.* (2013) present the essential contents of a social media marketing plan as follows:

1 *Executive summary*
   An executive summary is a short paragraph which provides a 'snapshot' of the entire report. As such it must include all the specific key points that each of the sections within the report has discussed.

2 *Overview*
   An overview should provide the contextualisation of the brand within its industry, highlight key industry trends affecting the industry and specify the need for having a social media plan, together with actions required to secure competitive advantage.

3 *Analysis of the brand's current social media presence*

This section should aim to identify what a range of audiences is currently saying about the brand in the digital space – the overall *brand health*. This *holistic* approach relies on identifying the **volume** of positive, negative or neutral comments said about the brand in the online space and their **volatility** (i.e. how they are changing over time) and the **velocity** (or speed) at which this is happening, which is impacting on the overall **visibility** of the brand – what is being said, where and by whom. On a more *granular* level, each specific digital media platform can be analysed more in depth, in terms of overall brand sentiments expressed in that space, as well as specific metrics such as its **reach** (including number of Twitter followers, Facebook fans, etc.), type and quantity of **content generated by the brand** and the **feedback** obtained **from consumers** (e.g. number of comments, number of 'likes' or replies to this content). Some examples of this can be seen in Figure 12.2.

4 *Competitive analysis*

This section should outline the key strengths, weaknesses, opportunities and threats that the brand experiences in the digital space and this is done through a detailed SWOT analysis, following which key strategic directions are chosen based on whether the brand wants to focus primarily on exploiting their strengths or improving/eliminating its weaknesses.

5 *Goals and strategies*

The goals formulated should be specific, measurable, achievable, realistic and time-bound (SMART), whilst the strategies should identify broad activities that are to be undertaken in the digital space.

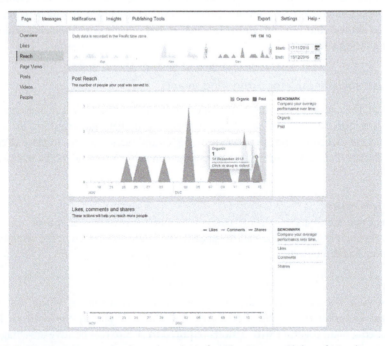

Figure 12.2 Facebook page back-end analysis for The Rotary Clubs of Northampton Duathlon's online brand presence

Source: Author's own

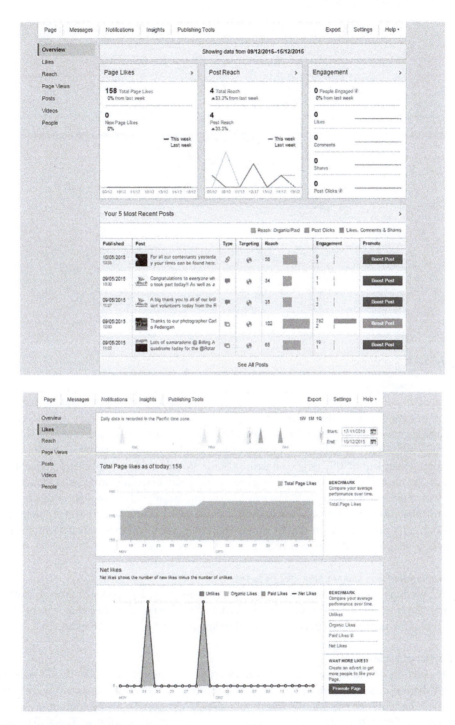

Figure 12.2 Continued

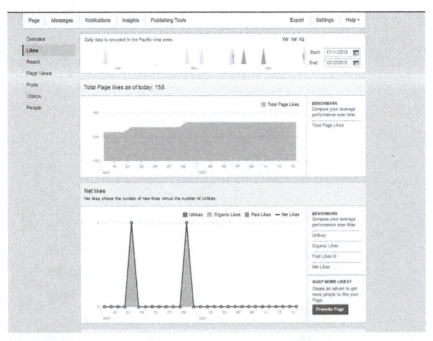

Figure 12.2 *Continued*

6 *Audience profiles/personas*

Having understood the current brand presence and identified key goals and strategies, it is important to narrow down the audience which will be targeted to drive the achievement of these goals. The audience should be profiled in depth and presented in as realistic way as possible – it needs to become a **persona**, a living, breathing 'thing' which personifies a 'typical' member of the target audience. Some brands even go as far as giving their personas human names and visualising their typical 'day in the life' in order to identify the key touchpoints that they should be using to communicate with them. Part of this process is to collate information from the brand's current social media space to understand who is currently engaging with their content the most. Some metrics which facilitate this process are presented in Figure 12.3.

7 *Choosing platforms and platform-specific tactics*

This section should outline which specific platforms (e.g. Facebook, Twitter, LinkedIn, etc.) the brand will be focusing on, as well as the specific activities that will be done through each of these platforms and the timeline to which this will be executed.

8 *Content development*

This section should focus specifically on the types of content that the brand will generate and share via its social media profiles. Good content will generate consumer interest and create the 'pull' for the brand's target audiences. A proportion of the content should be generic to facilitate its use across all the different social media platforms. This will usually involve generic information about what the brand stands for, its values, its history and/or future direction, its market offerings etc. The rest of the content should be specifically developed for each individual platform, depending on the profile of the audiences engaging

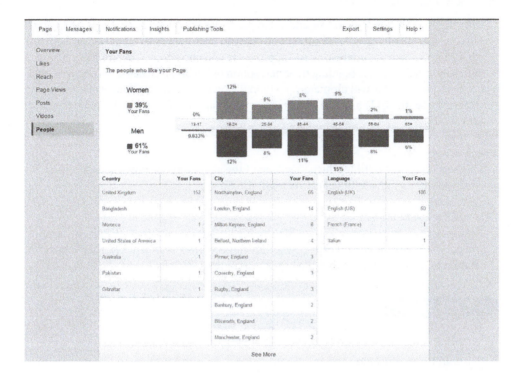

Figure 12.3 Online audiences of The Rotary Clubs of Northampton Duathlon event

with the brand on that platform and their particular content-related needs and wants. This includes providing tailored content on demand from consumers, but also anticipating what content might be interesting and appropriate and publishing it before the consumers 'officially' ask for it, thus building their perception of the brand as being in tune with their needs and wants. This will ultimately position the brand as a trusted source of information (Meerman-Scott, 2011) and will encourage return visits, as well as positive word of mouth (or eWOM).

9 *Role allocation*

This section should outline which members of the marketing team will be responsible for which specific actions outlined earlier on in the plan.

10 *Monitoring and Evaluation*

This section is crucial as it will define the *key performance indicators* (KPIs), or metrics, which will help marketers keep track of all the activities planned and their impact in relation to the overall goals that the brand is aiming to achieve.

CASE STUDY

Jogo Behaviour Conference 2015 social media campaign

About the organisation and the event

Jogo Behaviour Support is a local business which focuses on providing support in an educational setting to any professionals with the responsibility of working with children with behavioural issues. They give professionals the opportunity to learn strategies which can be implemented in any educational setting. As a small niche organisation it is therefore extremely important that Jogo Behaviour Support receives increased brand recognition from any marketing activities, specifically from social media channels. The annual Jogo Behaviour Conference in 2015 took place on Friday 20th March 2015 in Northampton and the theme of the conference was offering practical solutions to manage social, emotional and behavioural issues in children and young people.

The conference social media campaign

The social media campaign emphasised the engagement of current customers in order to encourage attendance at the conference and increase the likelihood of brand recommendation to peers, thus effecting brand ambassadorship. The campaign timeline spanned four months, from January to April 2015 (inclusive), which meant that audience engagement was supported at all stages of the event management process: pre-event, during the event and post-event.

Target audience profile

In order to successfully engage Jogo Behaviour Support's target audience using social media, it was essential to fully understand the customers whom the event (and the organisation's portfolio of services) will appeal to before planning and executing the campaign itself. Jogo Behaviour Support had identified three key market segments for their business: education professionals, healthcare professionals and the local authority. The needs of each of these segments varied slightly due to the nature in which they might utilise and implement the company's portfolio of services.

The main audience for the conference were primarily teachers and teaching assistants who work with children with behavioural issues on a regular basis. Due to this, they are more dependent on support provided by Jogo Behaviour and the theme of the conference complemented their need for continuous professional development (CPD) to be able to perform in their roles as required by the UK's national regulatory body, Ofsted (Office for Standards in Education, Children's Services and Skills).

Within this segment, the audience was further narrowed down to newly qualified professionals, as they are more likely to seek assistance and support in developing their skills, due to their limited experience. Furthermore, these were likely to be millennials who are between 20 and 30 years of age and use social media on a daily basis for both personal and professional purposes. Ideally, these would be customers who are already engaged and have some form of rapport with the Jogo Behaviour Support brand and thus would be more likely to continue this interaction with online.

Campaign aims

- Achieve an increase of 20 per cent in the number of Twitter followers.
- Achieve 150 likes of Facebook posts throughout the campaign.
- Achieve 150 clicks on the conference details page from social media platforms.

Social media channels used

A detailed profile facilitated the choice of appropriate social media platforms to be used for this campaign, as well as the creation of engaging content that will appeal to the chosen target audiences, which would raise awareness of the event itself, but also call the audiences to action by driving traffic directly to the online conference booking form.

Twitter and Facebook

Twitter and Facebook were the primary social media channels utilised by Jogo Behaviour Support in order to increase brand engagement. Messages were sent via the company's official social media accounts (@JogoBehaviour on Twitter and Jogo Behaviour Support Facebook page) and the frequency of messaging was planned to fit around the daily routines of the target audience. A key aspect of this was to engage with followers four days per week in order to ensure that consumers aren't bombarded by repetitive social media activity. The messages were scheduled on Tuesdays, Thursdays, Fridays and Saturdays and this pattern remained consistent throughout the four months of delivery. In addition to this, messages were scheduled for the periods of the day when the target audience was more likely to be active on social media. On weekdays (Tuesdays, Thursdays and Fridays) this included:

- An early morning message before classroom start time, when the majority of teachers were arriving to their workplace and preparing for the day ahead and were, therefore, more likely to be checking their smartphones.

- A lunchtime message, when the teachers are taking their breaks and able to focus on things outside their work.

- A mid-afternoon message following the completion of teaching, when the pupils will have gone home but the teachers are still at the school finishing up for the day and (again) are likely to check their social media accounts.

On Saturdays, non-work-related messages were sent out mid-morning, to engage the audience on a more personal, rather than professional level. The organisers hoped that this meaningful content would evoke positive brand associations and help build rapport with the target audience.

The *messages* focused primarily on directly advertising the conference and directing audiences to the online registration page by using a shortened link (done via bit.ly) which enabled the organisers to track the number of clicks to the page. A selection of messages included quotes from books written by industry experts and conference keynote speakers Marie Delaney and Kim Golding, as a sneak preview of the topics that will be discussed at the event, thus creating a pull factor for the audience. Another selection of messages incorporated photos from previous year's conference in an effort to engage past attendees and improve year-on-year retention. Audiences were encouraged to retweet and favourite the Twitter posts and 'Like' and 'Share' the Facebook posts, enabling the team to estimate and analyse the engagement with particular types of messages to identify which ones were particularly effective.

LinkedIn

LinkedIn is a platform that Jogo Behaviour Support uses to connect with professionals in their field and as such is particularly valuable for building the corporate brand image. Engagement on this platform involved advertising through posts published using a Bit.ly link directing professionals to the online conference booking page. Additionally, positive PR was generated by publishing book reviews written by one of the company founders and which focused on the books written by the two conference keynote speakers to provide potential attendees with deeper insight into what they can expect from the day. This platform was used less frequently than Twitter and Facebook, about once per month.

Campaign monitoring and evaluation

As with any marketing activity, it is important to monitor and evaluate the effectiveness of the social media tools that have been utilised in order to understand how much visibility the campaign has generated for the brand and how it supported audience interaction with the brand's digital spaces. The organisers of the Jogo Behaviour Support Conference 2015 used two mainstream tools to help them keep on top of the campaign; these tools were HootSuite and Bit.ly.

HootSuite

The use of HootSuite as a tool within Jogo Behaviour Support's social media campaign was extremely valuable in ensuring the smooth running and efficiency of all social media updates sent out by the organisers. HootSuite is an online service allowing businesses to promote their brand, generate leads and generally increase traffic to a company website from various social media platforms. This enabled the organisers to manage online presence across all owned and earned digital spaces for the company and the conference. All tweets and Facebook posts were planned and scheduled in advance and were automatically sent out through HootSuite on the scheduled dates and times. Additionally, HootSuite produced Twitter and Facebook analytics to track any increase in the number of Twitter followers and Facebook page fans to further identify how the target audiences engage with the company's digital real estate. This helped save the organisers a lot of time, which could then be put into other activities related to delivering a successful conference, which is very important for a small, niche and local business with limited resources.

Bit.ly

Throughout the online process, Bit.ly was being used as a URL shortening service to shorten all links that were used by the organisers in all email and social media communications. The main benefits of using Bit.ly is that they provide a free service that measures all clicks that audiences make on the shortened links and tracks their journey to the destination. In particular, this enabled the organisers to track exactly where the clicks originated from (e.g. Facebook, Twitter or direct email), as well as what geographical location the clicks have come from, providing an insight into where there is the greatest interest in attending the conference.

The main link that was tracked was the link to the conference details page, to facilitate the achievement of two key aims of the campaign: increasing the exposure for Jogo Behaviour Support as a brand and pushing the sales of the conference tickets.

To learn more about Jogo Behaviour Support and what they do, please visit the company's webpage at www.jogobehavioursupport.com, and their social media sites on Facebook: 'Jogo Behaviour Support', Twitter: @JogoBehaviour, and LinkedIn: 'Jogo Behaviour Support'.

Case study courtesy of Matilda Kelly, Jasmin Reeve and Eve Robinson, the University of Northampton.

Case study questions

1 What are the characteristics of Jogo Behaviour's target audiences? Create audience personas for this business.

2 What influenced the timing of the messages sent out via the business's social media channels? Are there any other times which may have been suitable?

3 Comment on the overall appropriateness of the social media strategy for the 2015 Jogo Behaviour Conference. Would you make any changes? Why/why not?

SUMMARY

This chapter has sought to introduce the growing importance of digital channels in the marketing of events. In particular, the chapter looked at the role of social media in this context and provided specific guidance for managing activities within this space. The chapter also introduced the key concepts in digital marketing, such as user experience, web analytics, search engine optimisation and paid search, which are all becoming increasingly important in the management of the back-end of the event experience delivery. In the following chapter, we turn our attention to the overall process of events marketing planning and the integration of the various strategies and tactics we've discussed so far in this book.

REVIEW QUESTIONS

1 What is the difference between owned, bought and earned digital spaces? Provide examples for each of these on events you are familiar with.

2 Use a couple of industry examples to identify how events use search engine optimisation (SEO) and paid search (PPC).

3 On an industry example, explore the structure of an event website and comment on its appropriateness for that event's primary target audiences. What recommendations (if any) would you make to the event marketers for changes in the website structure?

4 In what ways can events drive engagement with their target audiences in the social media space? Provide some practical examples.

5 On an industry example, explore the social media presence of an event and identify what types of content is shared about the event in this space. Which content originated from the event itself and which content was generated by consumers? What is the ratio of event-generated and consumer-generated content and what implications might that have for the marketing of the event in the future?

EVENT MARKETING SCENARIO

You are employed in a marketing communications agency which specialises in creating integrated marketing campaigns for events. The agency caters to a variety of clients of different sizes and operating in a variety of industries. Your newest client is a national charity focusing on issues of domestic abuse, which is organising a marathon to raise money for its cause. Create a profile of target audience for this event and then design a social media marketing campaign which will aim to reach this audience. Follow the ten-step model presented earlier on in this chapter.

FURTHER READING

Books

Barker, M., Barker, D., Bormann, N. and Neher, K. 2013. *Social Media Marketing: A strategic approach*, Mason, OH: South-Western Cengage Learning

This book provides an excellent overview of the context for and requirements of social media marketing. It is written in an accessible language and is easy to understand and follow. As such it is particularly suitable for students who may not have yet considered the commercial side of social media. Of particular benefit is the chapter explicating the Social Media Marketing Plan.

Kurtz, D.L. 2016. *Contemporary Marketing*, 17th Edition, Boston: Cengage Learning

This updated edition of one of the classic marketing textbooks provides a great overview of how technology has impacted the development of marketing, with particularly useful chapters on social media and the role of e-business in managing the customer experience.

Sigala, N., Christou, E. and Gretzel, U. (Eds) 2012. *Social Media in Travel, Tourism and Hospitality: Theory, practice and cases*, Farnham, Burlington: Ashgate

This edited volume provides a wealth of case studies about the use of social media within travel, tourism and hospitality, which provide a sound basis for conceptualising future research within this area. It would be particularly useful to students (both undergraduate and postgraduate) to generate ideas for potential research projects of their own as part of their studies in this area.

Journals

boyd, d. m. and Ellison, N.B. 2008. Social network sites: Definition, history and scholarship, *Journal of Computer-Mediated Communication*, 13, pp. 210–230

This *defining essay* provides a comprehensive introduction to social networks, including their historical development as well as an overview of scholarly research in this area.

Hudson, S. and Hudson, R. 2013. Engaging with consumers using social media: A case study of music festivals, *International Journal of Event and Festival Management*, 4(3), pp. 206–223

This article provides a good overview of how social media affects consumer behaviour specifically in the context of special events.

Leung, D., Law, R., van Hoof, H. and Buhalis, D. 2013. Social media in tourism and hospitality: a literature review, *Journal of Travel and Tourism Marketing*, 30(1–2), pp. 3–22

This article draws together a range of research outputs on social media in the context of tourism and hospitality and is particularly useful to understand the use of social media by both consumers and producers (i.e. companies and organisations) within this context.

Other resources

danah boyd www.danah.org
This website is owned by danah boyd, one of the leading scholars in the area of social media and its impact on consumption. The website showcases boyd's breadth of research output and is an excellent starting point for those who are interested in researching social media in greater depth.

Smart Insights www.smartinsights.com/
Smart insights is a digital marketing consultancy owned by Dave Chaffey, whose work we've mentioned in this chapter. The business offers a range of content, trainings and other business solutions related to integrating digital marketing activities. Although it is membership-based, some of the content is free resources which many will find useful.

References

Anderson, C. 2009. *The Longer Long Tail: How endless choice is creating unlimited demand*, London: Random House Business.

Barker, M., Barker, D., Bormann, N. and Neher, K. 2013. *Social Media Marketing: A strategic approach*, Mason, OH: South-Western Cengage Learning.

Beer, D. 2008. Social network(ing) sites...revisiting the story so far: a response to danah boyd & Nicole Ellison, *Journal of Computer-Mediated Communication*, 13, pp. 516–529.

boyd, d. m. and Ellison, N.B. 2008. Social network sites: Definition, history and scholarship, *Journal of Computer-Mediated Communication*, 13, pp. 210–230.

Brassington, F. and Pettitt, S. 2003. *Principles of Marketing*, 3rd Edition, Harlow: FT Prentice Hall.

Chaffey, D. (Ed.) 2009. *Internet Marketing: Strategy, implementation and practice*, 4th Edition, Harlow: Pearson Education Ltd.

Chaffey, D. 2012. The difference between paid, owned and earned digital media – 5 viewpoints, *Smart Insights* [Online]. Available at: www.smartinsights.com/digital-marketing-strategy/customer-acquisition-strategy/new-media-options/ [Accessed 25 February 2016].

Godin, S. 2007. *Permission Marketing*, London: Pocket.

Hudson, S. and Hudson, R. 2013. Engaging with consumers using social media: A case study of music festivals, *International Journal of Event and Festival Management*, 4(3), pp. 206–223.

Hudson, S., Roth, M.S., Madden, T.J. and Hudson, R. 2015. The effects of social media on emotions, brand relationship quality and word of mouth: An empirical study of music festival attendees, *Tourism Management*, 47, pp. 68–76.

Kurtz, D.L. 2016. *Contemporary Marketing*, 17th Edition, Boston: Cengage Learning.

Leung, D., Law, R., van Hoof, H. and Buhalis, D. 2013. Social media in tourism and hospitality: A literature review, *Journal of Travel and Tourism Marketing*, 30(1–2), pp. 3–22.

Litvin, S.W., Goldsmith, R.E. and Pan, B. 2008. Electronic word-of-mouth in hospitality and tourism management, *Tourism Management*, 29(3), pp. 458–468.

Mangold, W.G. and Faulds, D.J. 2009. Social media: The new hybrid element of the promotion mix, *Business Horizons*, 52, pp. 357–365.

Meerman Scott, D. 2011. *The New Rules of Marketing & PR: How to use social media, online video, mobile applications, blogs, news releases & viral marketing to reach buyers directly*, Hoboken, NJ: John Wiley & Sons.

Munar, A.M. and Jacobsen, J.K.S. 2014. Motivations for sharing tourism experiences through social media, *Tourism Management*, 43, pp. 46–54.

Ngai, E.W.T., Tao, S.S.C. and Moon, K.K.L. 2015. Social media research: Theories, constructs and conceptual frameworks, *International Journal of Information Management*, 35, pp. 33–44.

Rothschild, P.C. 2011. Social media use in sports and entertainment venues, *International Journal of Event and Festival Management*, 2(2), pp. 139–150.

Sigala, N., Christou, E. and Gretzel, U. (Eds) (2012) *Social Media in Travel, Tourism and Hospitality: Theory, practice and cases*, Farnham, Burlington: Ashgate.

Tuten, T.L. and Solomon, M.R. 2013. *Social Media Marketing*, Harlow: Pearson Education Ltd.

13

Marketing planning for events

By the end of this chapter, students should be able to:

- Identify the areas of the marketing planning function

- Understand the complexities of marketing planning and the relationships between different elements of the marketing plan

- Design a marketing plan for an event of their choice and select appropriate evaluation techniques

Marketing is still an art, and the marketing manager, as head chef, must creatively marshal all his marketing activities to advance the short and long term interests of his firm.
Borden (1964)

Introduction

Now that we have explored at length the issues of supply and demand for events, as well as the variety of marketing communications strategies and tactics available to event marketers, we turn to the role and impact of marketing planning. Marketing planning encompasses all of the concepts discussed in this book so far: the nature of events (Chapters 2 and 3) determines the approach the event marketer will take, the marketing mix and the marketing environment (Chapters 4 and 5) define the marketing 'playing field', customer profiling

(Chapters 6–8) helps define the way forward and choose the appropriate marketing strategies and tactics (Chapters 9–12). It is, thus, clear that marketing planning is no mean feat and requires time and effort. In order to create a coherent marketing plan, a focused approach is crucial and those that really want maximum impact will need to make sure they integrate their efforts across different channels. This chapter discusses the core principles of the marketing planning process and provides a practical guide for those embarking on this task. It also includes a discussion of tools for financial and other control and evaluation of the marketing plan.

The role of marketing planning with events

Marketing planning as a business function aims to provide a structured framework (Brassington and Pettitt, 2003) in which a marketer can appraise the environment of a particular product/service/event and then set appropriate goals and forecast marketing activities for a defined period of time. Looking back on the content we have covered so far in this book, we can appreciate that there are a great many variables that determine what direction a marketer will take.

The nature of the market offering is a core variable that determines its marketing. For a physical product, one of the key concerns will be the cost of production and the effectiveness and efficiency of the distribution channels by which the product will reach its intended customers. For a service, the focus will most likely be on creating and maintaining a standard of service delivery and the uniform and consistent training for the staff delivering the service; this is particularly true for services that are provided by the same brand in a variety of locations by employees of a wide range of backgrounds and professional abilities. With events, marketers must be particularly mindful of the overall event experience delivered to each individual customer, which has a strong impact on the level of audience satisfaction with the event. This presupposes that event marketers need to be aware of their event audience expectations and that they are able to ensure that the event is able to fulfil and (preferably) exceed these in order to guarantee customer satisfaction. The ephemeral nature of events and the large number of stakeholders which are vital in their delivery pose additional challenges on ensuring that the event experience (Pine and Gilmore, 1999; Berridge, 2007) is as near to perfect (or ideal) as possible for each individual attendee. This is no mean feat!

Another issue is the variety of event audiences themselves – as we have seen in Chapter 8, customer motivations can vary greatly with the type of event and with the profile of the attendee. Attendees come to the event with their own sets of expectations which are based on their motivations. Their perceptions of (and subsequently their satisfaction with) the event are shaped by the external factors under the control of the event manager/marketer, such as the ticket price, queues or entertainment offered at the event. However, a variety of personal qualities (e.g. attitude, responsiveness, openness to new experiences) also impact on the customer's perceived level of event quality. It is this clash between an attendee's expectations and perceptions that identifies the gap in service quality, as suggested by Morgan (1996). It is, therefore, the role of marketing planning to identify as closely as possible what drives people to attend events and what type of content might appeal to a particular profile of attendee, so that these elements can then be emphasised in the event's communications strategies. As such, an event's marketing plan is just one of the tools aimed at achieving the overall event objectives and so congruence between the overall event management plan and the event's marketing plan is crucial (Allen *et al.*, 2011).

In Chapters 9 to 12, we identified a wealth of marketing communications strategies and tactics that are available to event marketers. Not all channels will be suitable for all events or for all target audiences. Marketing planning, thus, helps create an 'order within a disorder' and categorise the variety of audiences and the key messages and channels that would be appropriate and effective for reaching these audiences and encouraging them to attend the event.

The marketing planning function for events

Bowdin *et al.* (2011) emphasise the need to link the marketing planning activities with the overall strategic direction of the event management process, hence the popularity of the term 'strategic marketing planning' in the context of event management. Marketing strategy, then, is grounded in the societal and business context within which an event is happening and is an essential tool in achieving the set event objectives and making sure that the event is a success in all of its different segments.

Figure 13.1 outlines the marketing planning function in the context of events, which consists of five key areas framed within the overall cycle of marketing evaluation and control. Event planning is often represented in academic literature as a linear process with clearly defined steps which lead into and follow one another. This book adopts the view that marketing planning is an ongoing phenomenon, parts of which operate continuously on a loop, whilst others shift in and out of focus repeatedly during the time frame to which the planning function applies. Thus, the terminology has been adjusted accordingly: instead of the term 'marketing planning process' we refer to the 'marketing planning function' and the term 'areas' replaces the common terms 'steps' or 'stages'. So let us then proceed to define the key areas of marketing planning.

As mentioned earlier in this book, different aspects of market research, evaluation and control permeate the planning of marketing activities, as well as their implementation. As such, they represent the backbone of the marketing function, as without these tools it would be impossible to design and implement a marketing plan or evaluate its effectiveness and efficiency.

Market research is essential in gathering the relevant information about a variety of issues in marketing planning – it helps to define the context within which an event exists (see below for more details on situational analysis) and to define target audiences' needs, wants and characteristics, thus helping the event marketer to choose an appropriate focus for the event's marketing. The event marketer needs to be able to recognise what type of information is required for making marketing decisions (Wood, 2004), including where and by which particular method that data can be obtained, as well as how this information should be interpreted.

Marketing evaluation and control mechanisms are always at the forefront of any marketing discussions. This is particularly true with events where 'hard' evaluation and control methods, such as ticket sales, attendance and profit, are not really appropriate in measuring some of the more ephemeral characteristics, such as the event experience, target market

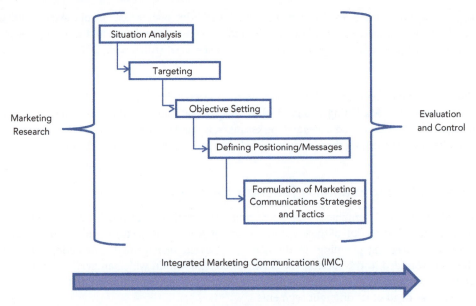

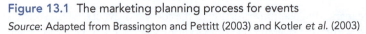

Figure 13.1 The marketing planning process for events

Source: Adapted from Brassington and Pettitt (2003) and Kotler *et al.* (2003)

awareness or attendee perceptions of the event and intention to return in the future. Specific techniques for evaluating individual marketing communications tactics have been discussed alongside them in previous chapters. However, the overall evaluation of a marketing plan as a whole is discussed in greater detail towards the end of this chapter.

Key planning area 1 – situation analysis

In this area the marketer focuses on understanding the marketing environment within which the event is happening and identifying the key issues which may impact (positively or negatively) on the event itself. The most popular tools for conducting situation analysis are the PESTLE, C-PEST and SWOT analytical frameworks – these have been discussed in detail in Chapter 5.

Key planning area 2 – targeting

This area focuses on gaining a clear understanding of the audience(s) the event is trying to attract. In other words, the event marketer must define the event's target market(s) which will provide the 'ground' on which to deliver on the event's objectives. Once all the potential target segments have been identified and the key ones chosen as focus areas, it is important to conduct a customer profiling exercise to get a vivid picture of exactly who the individuals within the target market are. This *persona development* helps the marketer to embody the target market and really drill down to a very detailed description of what a 'typical' customer is like in terms of a variety of segmentation criteria (age, gender, income level, hobbies and preferences, etc.). This persona is then used as a generalised representation of the target segment and forms the basis of decision making in relation to the preferred media channels which should be used to transmit the marketing message. An example of such a persona can be seen in Figure 13.2.

	PERSONA 'A'	PERSONA 'B'
Name	John	Diane
Age	21	24
Gender	Male	Female
Level of education	GCSEs (low skilled)	Bachelor's degree
Current occupation	Works in construction	Works in a charity
Level of income	Approx. £22,000 pa	Approx. £24,000 pa
Lives in	With parents	In a flat share
Owns a vehicle	No	No
Interests	Football, going out on weekends, hanging out with friends	Music gigs, fringe theatre and dance

Figure 13.2 An example of persona development for a careers fair

For an event such as a careers fair, the audience base will be quite wide, as can be seen in the sample personas developed. Therefore, the marketing manager of such an event will need to really develop these personas in such depth so that certain overlaps begin to emerge. Whilst it may appear that the two personas presented may not have almost anything in common, their age range suggests that they will most likely be very active on social media, so one strategy that would make sense to use, which could reach both of these 'people' at the same time, would be Facebook and/or Twitter and/or Instagram or similar.

Persona development helps marketers to identify which channels would be most suitable to the chosen target audiences and, in particular, which channels would be more effective than others because they might be used by a number of audiences at the same time. It is then the role of the event marketer to 'make the target audience feel excited, interested, and catered to' (Saget, 2006, p. 35) so that they are interested in attending (or, indeed, being connected in some other way) with the event. Persona development relies on qualitative research with real people who are part of the intended target segment for the marketer: interviews are thought to be particularly useful for this purpose (Meerman Scott, 2011). Although personas do not represent any particular individual *per se*, their characteristics are used to form a generalised view of the target market segment as a whole. Persona development is a popular concept in online marketing, where it is particularly pertinent to the optimisation of user experience on webpages and social media outlets, although the concept is now finding its place in 'offline' marketing as well (Meerman Scott, 2011).

Key planning area 3 – objective setting

Once the environment has been thoroughly analysed and the marketing context has been fully understood, it is time to define the objectives (goals) of the event's marketing strategy. Objectives are the 'guiding lights' of any marketing plan and need to be well defined. The usual rule of SMART objectives (Jackson, 2013) applies – all objectives should be:

Specific

Measurable

Achievable

Realistic

Time-framed

Event marketing objectives can often be confused with the overall event objectives, so it is important to make this distinction and emphasise it. Event marketing objectives focus on what is to be achieved with the actual marketing activities for the event. This can be anything from setting a target number of audience members to be reached through a particular channel and persuaded to attend to the specific indicators of how brand awareness of the event will be raised through the chosen mix of marketing communications strategies and tactics. Masterman and Wood (2006) identify four key purposes of communications objectives in relation to events marketing:

- providing information and (through that) creating brand awareness

- changing perception of an event and enhancing positive attitudes toward it

- facilitating purchase decisions by target audiences, and

- increasing or stabilising the demand for an event.

Event objectives, on the other hand, refer specifically to what the event itself will achieve and these can include setting a target number for the event contact database to be built post-event, setting the desired level of customer satisfaction to be achieved by the event or, indeed, a particular amount of profit to be made by the event. In either case, the objectives are also one of the tools of evaluating event success – if they are SMART-ly defined, it should be reasonably easy to identify whether or not they have been achieved. Some hypothetical examples of marketing objectives can be seen in Vignette 13.1.

VIGNETTE 13.1

Setting marketing objectives for the Fiesta Mexicana 2010

Fiesta Mexicana was a local community event that took place in Portsmouth's Gunwharf Quays in the period of 11–29 October 2010. It was conceptualised and delivered by a partnership of four organisations:

- Takepart Arts – an organisation set up and headed by Daniel Bernstein, specialising in participation and education in the arts.

- Same Sky – the largest community arts charity in the southeast of England specialising in participatory events.

- Copperdollar theatre company.

- Gunwharf Quays shopping centre.

These organisations were further supported financially by a grant awarded by Arts Council England and a variety of other sponsors.

The event itself was conceptualised focusing on celebrating life by organising the traditional Mexican celebration of the Day of the Dead. In addition to offering creative arts and dance workshops for children and young people over the last four days of the event, the event's centrepiece was the evening parade through the event site on the last day. The event had a very strong local focus and the organisers were particularly interested in developing connections with local schools, considering part of the event overlapped with the autumn half-term holiday, meaning it provided a great opportunity to engage local families. As such, the event could have defined its marketing objectives as follows:

1 To have at least eight local school teams participate in the final event procession.

2 To attract at least 20 workshop providers across the final four days of the event.

3 To sign up at least ten acts to provide entertainment during the event.

4 To achieve at least 15 mentions of the event in the local media and three mentions in the national media between 1 September and 31 December 2010.

5 To raise £5,000 of sponsorship to cover the costs of the event, to be received up to three weeks prior to the event.

As can be seen above, the objectives suggested are specific, measurable, achievable, realistic and time-framed. Objectives should, ideally, be related to the various target audiences and provide an instant indicator against which the performance of the event can be measured.

More information on the Fiesta Mexicana 2010 can be found on the following websites:

- Take Part Arts webpage at: www.takepartarts.co.uk/web/projects/fiesta-mexicana/.

- Event Facebook page at: www.facebook.com/events/145395388835306/.

Key planning area 4 – defining positioning strategy and key messages

Once the objectives have been set and the key target markets have been identified, it is time to define the basis of positioning of the event in the eyes and minds (and hearts) of the chosen target audiences. More specifically, it is the time to decide what perceptions an event's target audiences do, should and/or will have of the event (Allen *et al.*, 2011; McCabe 2009). A variety of positioning strategies available to event marketers has been discussed in detail in Chapter 5. Key communication messages narrow down the specific ideas and perceptions that the event marketer wants to evoke with the chosen target audiences. Think of Nike's classic 'Just Do It', Coca-Cola's 'Always Coca-Cola' from the early 1990s and 'Open Happiness' from 2009 or Disney Parks' 'Where Dreams Come True'. In the event world, slogans are just as important: Saget (2006) highlights the need to communicate an event's message in 25 words or less. Some examples of event slogans can be seen in Table 13.1.

Table 13.1 Some examples of event taglines (slogans)

Event name	Location	Profile	Tagline
TED	various	Series of inspirational and educational talks	'Ideas worth spreading'
International Confex	UK	Event industry trade show	'The UK's leading exhibition for the events industry'
Rio de Janeiro Carnival	Brazil	Carnival	'The greatest show on earth'
2010 FIFA World Cup	South Africa	Football competition	'KeNako' – 'Celebrate Africa's Humanity'
London 2012 Olympics	UK	Sporting competition	'Inspire a generation'
Sochi 2014 Olympics	Russia	Sporting competition	'Hot. Cool. Yours.'
Turku Capital of Culture	Finland	Series of cultural events	'Turku on Fire'
2014 Formula 1 Petronas Malaysia Grand Prix	Malaysia	Formula 1 race	'Sepang Comes Alive!'
Tour de France 2014	France	Cycling race	'Attraction Universelle'

Key planning area 5 – formulation of marketing communications strategies and tactics

This area builds on the previous four in the sense that the choice of communications strategies and tactics stems from the extensive understanding of an event's target audiences and their preferred media channels. It is pointless to market your event via radio if the majority of your target audience largely uses social media or mobile applications to keep up-to-date with the news. A full range of strategies and tactics has been discussed in Chapters 9–12; however, how these strategies and tactics will be combined in order to achieve specific marketing objectives will be determined by the event marketer.

Integrating your event marketing efforts

We have highlighted in a number of places within this book the importance of choosing appropriate channels to reach your chosen target audiences. Similarly, another crucial element in creating an effective marketing plan is the event marketer's skill of integrating the marketing efforts across a variety of channels that will reach a variety of audiences. We have mentioned in Chapter 6 the wide variety of potential audiences for an event and the fact that an event will *always* have to appeal to at least two different target audiences. This poses quite a challenge on limited marketing resources and creates the need for a coherent marketing campaign that will be focused enough to be recognisable, but will also appeal to a variety of audiences. Thus, an event marketing plan must ensure congruence of all the relevant elements which make it up. In particular, the key message(s) being transmitted across the variety of media channels must be consistent. Seitel (2004) refers to this principle as 'One Voice'. A coherent marketing plan and communication messages will:

- create a strong image/identity of the event

- ensure consistency of messages across different media channels

- help build reputation and trust amongst target audiences

- inspire audience engagement and (later on) loyalty (which is particularly important for recurring events).

Brassington and Pettitt (2003) identify five key elements of any communication effort between two parties – the sender and the receiver. These elements are as follows:

1 The sender phrases the message (a process called *encoding*).

2 The sender chooses a **channel**(s) by which the message will be communicated.

3 The receiver of the message *decodes* (interprets) the message.

4 The receiver of the message provides *feedback* to the sender – this is usually measured by whether or not a customer will buy a particular product or service and how quickly, or how often this will be done.

5 Steps 1–4 are done in an environment which can create more or less *noise* – factors which will influence how the receiver will interpret the message, but also whether or not he or she will even receive the message in the first place.

With events, the complexity of coding and decoding a marketing message is even more pronounced due to the variety of audiences an event has to attract at the same time (Chapter 7). With such differences amongst different segments, it can be a very challenging task to ensure that the 'One Voice' (Kitchen *et al.*, 2004) principle mentioned above is successfully implemented and is yielding results in each segment. It is debatable, however, how applicable the 'One Voice' principle is with the range of target audiences events are likely to attract and the versatility of motivations they will have for attending that particular event. For instance, would the same key message work for both B2C and B2B audiences – likely not! So yes, whilst the concept of 'One Voice' provides some focus for marketers in terms of integrating their marketing efforts, it is important to always be conscious of the variety of audiences that are being targeted. Whilst the overall message can be unified, the mix of marketing channels used and the language utilised to phrase the message can differ amongst audiences, as far as is reasonably practicable.

Evaluating marketing plans

In Chapters 10 to 12 we mentioned a range of techniques which can be used to evaluate specific marketing communications techniques. This *micro*-evaluation enables the marketer to specifically investigate what marketing communications techniques were effective in communicating the messages set and to what extent. It is, however, also important to evaluate the marketing plan as a whole, on a *macro* level, to establish:

a) what the impact was of the specific mix of techniques that were used on the attainment of the initial marketing objectives that were set at the beginning of the planning process; and

b) if this mix was both cost-effective and time-efficient.

It should, therefore, come as little surprise that marketing objectives, budgets and timelines are the three primary tools which are used for evaluation purposes on this *macro* level. The concept of marketing evaluation is visually presented in Figure 13.3.

As can be seen in Figure 13.3, evaluation is a process that is not linear in nature, i.e. it does not specifically precede or follow other aspects of the marketing planning and implementation cycle; rather, it is usually conducted on an ongoing basis, throughout the planning, implementation and wrap-up (recommendation) stages of any marketing activity. Indeed, the evaluation process is often so integral to the rest of marketing planning and implementation that it can become almost completely indistinguishable from these. Still, there is a good amount of deliberateness that goes into the process of evaluating marketing activities and usually marketers will have a set cycle of evaluation with specific deadlines for completing these types of activities in order to monitor how the planned marketing activities are meeting the overall deliverables.

Financial marketing control

Financial control is the cornerstone of evaluation, not just in marketing, but in a range of general business and management activities. In terms of marketing, three key types of financial control are utilised: budgeting, cost-benefit analysis and cash flow control.

Figure 13.3 The role of marketing evaluation

Budgets

The purpose of a budget is to set out all the relevant specific costs for materials and activities which form part of the overall marketing plan. A marketing budget will contain an outline of marketing income, as well as expenses related to executing the planned marketing activities. A sample marketing budget can be seen in Figure 13.4.

As can be seen in Figure 13.4, it is important to break the budget down as much as possible, so that it reflects all the relevant income and cost items, no matter how small they might be. Marketing *income* can involve a range of categories, such as grants, ticket sales, merchandise sales and similar, and if these are being completely retained for the purpose of financing marketing activities they should be presented in detail within the budget. The income can also, however, be made up primarily of the monies allocated to the marketing function from the company's master budget (i.e. the budget that covers all aspects of business activity – with events this will usually include event operations, staffing, technical support and a range of other areas). There are a number of ways to calculate the sum that will be awarded to the marketing function: the CFO (Chief Financial Officer) or other person responsible for the event's finances can decide to allocate to the marketing function income by using one of the following approaches:

1 *Inertia based* (or '*as last year*') – matching what was spent last year, adjusted for the current rate of inflation.

2 *Business-based* – basing it on a proportion of profit that the company/event has made in the previous year or is projected to make in the current year.

3 *Media-based* – basing it on the amount of projected costs of marketing/media outlets planned for the current edition of the event (cost-driven).

4 *Competition-based* – basing it on what a direct competitor is spending on their more recent campaign (this approach is rarely used, for the simple reason that it is very difficult to get the exact information about how much competitors are spending on their marketing activities).

5 *Dynamic* – using a combination of the above approaches to come up with a figure that would 'work'.

Budgeting is the key element of financial control, whether it is used by an agency-based event manager working on behalf of an external client, or by in-house event managers based within a company. It is a tool for ongoing evaluation: an event manager begins with the initial *projected* (or planned) budget which includes the income and costs as they are initially planned, but this is regularly updated as and when changes are made. At the end, following the event delivery and shutdown, the manager then consolidates the *actual* budget, which contains entries of every single income and cost item – this final budget represents the totality of income and costs that the event has achieved and provides a clear financial picture of the event's success. Considering this fluidity of the budget as an evaluation tool, a pertinent question arises: how does one estimate the projected income and costs? Contrary to what some may think, it is not just a matter of 'plucking a number out of the sky', as this is more likely than not to lead to frequent revisions and amendments to the budget, which adds more work to the event manager. The key is to estimate the numbers as close as possible

Income	£	Expenditure	£
1. Grants	**2,000.00**	**1. Print marketing**	**15,700.00**
1.1 Local council	2,000.00	1.1 Magazines	5,600.00
		1.1.1 Magazine 1	2,500.00
2. Ticket sales	**7,000.00**	1.1.2 Magazine 2	3,100.00
2.1 Early bird tickets	3,000.00	1.2 Newspapers	4,500.00
2.2 Family tickets	4,000.00		
		2. E-marketing	**1,000.00**
3. Sponsorships	**23,000.00**	2.1 Online banners	
3.1 Sponsor 1	10,000.00	2.1.1 Banner design	250.00
3.2 Sponsor 2	8,000.00	2.1.2 Banner space	750.00
3.3 Sponsor 3	5,000.00		
		3. Guerrilla marketing	**2,900.00**
4. Concessions	**7,700.00**	3.1 Leaflets (3000 pcs)	150.00
4.1 Concession 1	3,200.00	3.2 Costumes/props	750.00
4.2 Concession 2	4,500.00	3.3 Staff	2,000.00
Total	**39,700.00**		**19,600.00**
Profit (loss)	**20,100.00**		

Figure 13.4 A sample marketing budget

to what will actually be received and spent in the context of event marketing. Estimating costs is relatively easily managed by doing proper market research, identifying appropriate providers for each of the cost items and requesting a number of them (usually three) to provide cost estimates specific to the event manager's requirements; this can make estimating costs fairly straightforward. Estimating income is much more complicated than that. For events that have been taking place over a period of time, past figures related to ticket sales, merchandise sales, sponsorship income, etc. can provide a fairly sound guide to estimating income in these categories. For events that are in their first edition, estimating income can often feel like guesswork. It is, therefore, advisable to be conservative with initial budget estimates: slightly over-estimate the costs and slightly under-estimate the income, as this can provide a much-needed buffer to absorb the financial impact in case of deviations of the actual marketing income and spend from the projected ones.

Cost-benefit analysis

Another method frequently used in evaluating marketing activities is the cost-benefit analysis. In broad terms, this involves a detailed outline of costs associated with the marketing activities being conducted, which are easily identifiable from the marketing budget. On the other end of the spectrum is the overview of the benefits generated by the marketing activities, which may be trickier to pinpoint due to a host of non-tangible and non-financial items that can be included in this analysis. For example, a lot of marketing (particularly advertising) activities focus on raising awareness of a particular product or service, or changing consumer perceptions of and preferences with regards to these. These can be difficult to express in financial terms, which is why cost-benefit analysis is often based on guessing and estimating the value of the benefits being generated.

Cash flow control

Controlling the event marketing cash flow is an important activity which complements event budgeting. Budgets present the snapshot of the overall amount of money that will be spent on marketing activities, but they do not help the marketer establish *when* particular sums will be coming into and – more importantly – going out of the event's business account. Whilst it is always important to make sure that the overall budget of the marketing campaign finishes with a profit (or at least breaks even), it is even more important to make sure that all the cost items can be paid out when they become due without delay. Thus, the event marketer is responsible not only for generating marketing income, but also making sure that this income is received in the event's business account *before* the marketing expenses are due to be paid out. The dynamics of income versus expenses is usually monitored on a monthly, and often even weekly, basis. Anticipating when monies will be coming into the account can help the event marketer negotiate payment terms with suppliers. For example, some suppliers will require payments in advance of delivering their products or services, whilst with others payments can be made days or even weeks after the event has taken place. Negotiating extended payment terms can also help the event marketer keep control of the quality of the marketing materials being produced, as payments can be delayed or even withheld if the quality delivered is not as agreed beforehand, but these are usually offered by suppliers to customers with whom they have a good professional relationship. Therefore, those working with specific suppliers for the very first time might need to be ready to pay for most goods and services in advance, with the prospect of getting some more 'wiggle room' with future ventures.

Controlling marketing time-efficiency

Controlling time-efficiency in relation to marketing activities encompasses a detailed tracking of all time-scales related to the event. Every marketing plan should include a detailed timeline of activities which outlines exactly when each activity needs to be carried out. This initial plan is then tracked throughout the process of planning and delivering the event and amendments are made as and when required (e.g. moving particular deadlines due to circumstances, adding new activities and deadlines, etc.). Like with budgets, timelines need to be regularly checked and updated throughout the process of planning and delivering the event, to make sure no important tasks are missed. Timelines can be presented in a range of different ways, but Gantt charts seem to be the most popular. Whilst Gantt charts are fairly straightforward to create and they do provide a quick visual overview of the tasks, for more complex events they may be too long and cumbersome to manage when using the MS Excel software. For more complex event management processes, the more sophisticated MS Project software may be helpful as it can facilitate linking specific tasks together and updating any linked tasks as other changes are made within the software. An example of an Excel Gantt chart can be seen in Figure 13.5.

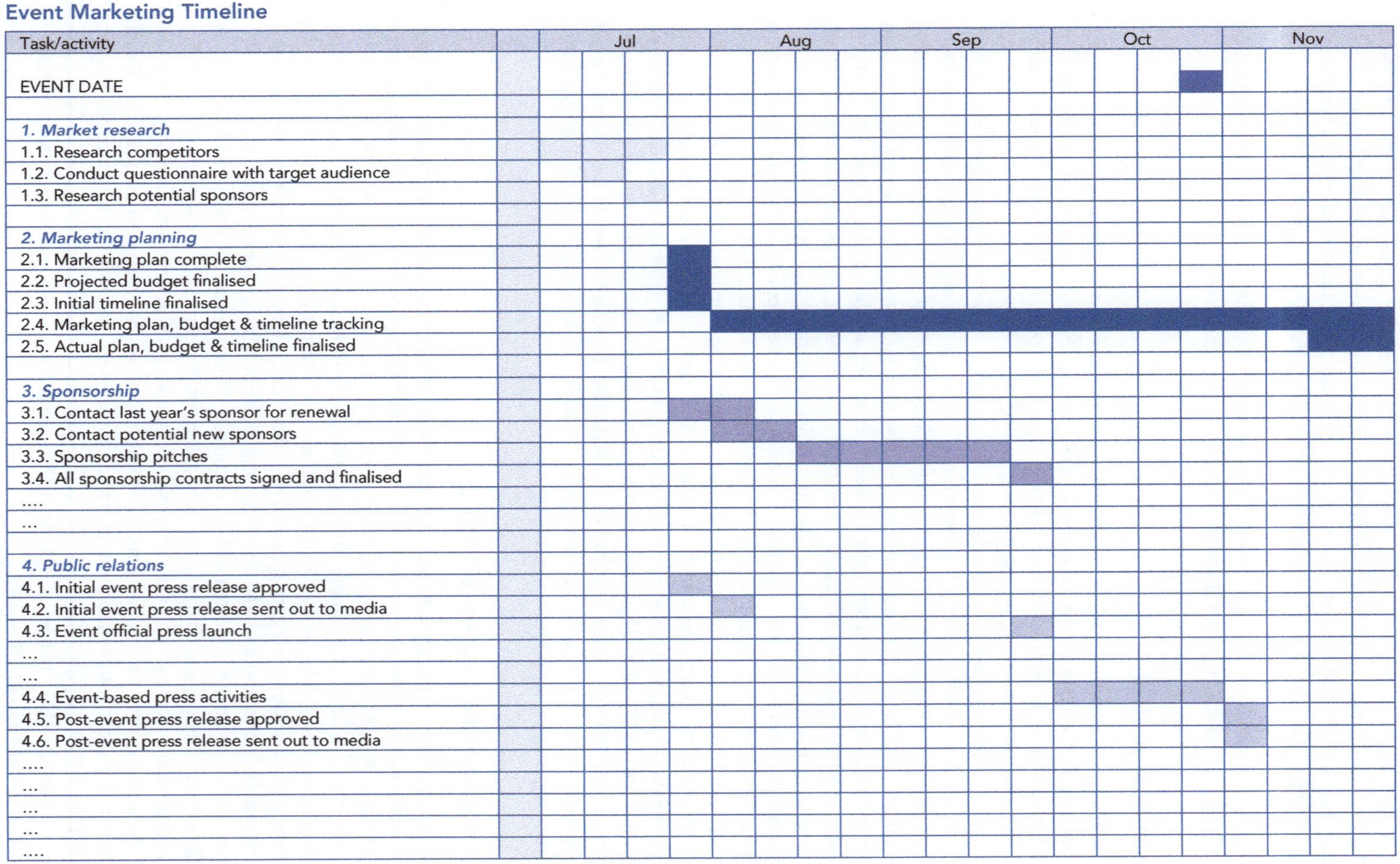

Event Marketing Timeline

Task/activity		Jul		Aug		Sep		Oct		Nov
EVENT DATE										
1. Market research										
1.1. Research competitors										
1.2. Conduct questionnaire with target audience		▓								
1.3. Research potential sponsors										
2. Marketing planning										
2.1. Marketing plan complete										
2.2. Projected budget finalised										
2.3. Initial timeline finalised										
2.4. Marketing plan, budget & timeline tracking		███							███	
2.5. Actual plan, budget & timeline finalised										
3. Sponsorship										
3.1. Contact last year's sponsor for renewal				▓						
3.2. Contact potential new sponsors				▓						
3.3. Sponsorship pitches					▓					
3.4. All sponsorship contracts signed and finalised						▓				
...										
...										
4. Public relations										
4.1. Initial event press release approved										
4.2. Initial event press release sent out to media				▓						
4.3. Event official press launch						▓				
...										
4.4. Event-based press activities								▓		
4.5. Post-event press release approved								▓		
4.6. Post-event press release sent out to media									▓	
...										
...										
...										
...										

Figure 13.5 A marketing Gantt chart created in MS Excel software

Contents of a marketing plan for events

Whilst there is no 'perfect' template for a marketing plan (and this is particularly true for events which can vary greatly in size, scope, nature and concept), there is a general consensus amongst marketers that the structure of the marketing plan should be a holistic reflection of the various factors that determine the market position of a particular market offering. Figures 13.6 and 13.7 provide a detailed outline of the sections recommended to be included in an event's marketing plan. The only difference between the two is in the model used to define the event as a market offering – Figure 13.6 incorporates an adapted model of the Marketing Mix, whilst Figure 13.7 outlines the newly proposed VITER approach, which we discuss in Chapter 14. These two templates can be used to guide the write-up of the marketing plan for almost any type of event.

Executive summary

Your plan should start off with a one paragraph executive summary. An executive summary is not an introduction nor is it a table of contents written in sentence form; it is a summary of the key points, main goals, highlights, outcomes and recommendations of your plan.

Overview of the parent company and event

Briefly explain the primary motivations of the organisation.
• What are the primary objectives of the Parent Company; what is the reason for its existence
• Identify and define the strategic objectives of the organisation

Event overview

• Provide a brief overview of the event, including historical development
• Explain how the event delivers or supports the strategic objectives of the company

Marketing overview

You should consider the following:
• **Event productivity**
  ▪ Describe the productivity of the event
  ▪ Describe the productivity of the segments/territories served
• **The marketing organisation**
  ▪ Describe the organisational structure of the marketing operations

Marketing audit

SWOT/PEST/PESTEL analysis
• Use an appropriate method(s) to define strengths and weaknesses against the competition in the market, and the opportunities and threats that are available or may impact on the firm. It also identifies 'environmental' issues impacting upon the firm.

Competitor analysis

• Identify and define the primary competitors within the marketplace; include details of the competitor event dates, venue, attendance, and organiser.

Key issues

• Identify and define the key issues that need to be addressed for the coming event and/or future events
• Examples could include; increasing visitor numbers, breaking into a new market segment etc.

Key objectives and issues

Having reviewed any issues arising from the earlier sections and having identified and considered the strengths, weaknesses, opportunities and threats; decide the objectives for the coming year, and explain the issues that affect them.
• Include a definition of target markets, and the basis for segmentation
  ▪ For example, you might plan to increase event visitor numbers by 25%, but where are these extra visitors going to come from?
• Include a definition of any intended changes in positioning, and the basis for positioning

Key messaging

- Define the key messages that you want to attach to the event, that shall be communicated through the marketing plan
- For example; 'Get Up Close to Your Show', 'The original outdoor event show' etc.

Strategic marketing initiatives

This section identifies and introduces the strategic marketing techniques that shall be used to deliver the planned targets, objectives and issues.
- Identify and explain the strategic marketing techniques

Market segmentation

- Define how your market can be segmented and define the target market(s) for the event
- Define the market segment/particle and identify the messaging to each segment

Marketing Mix

Product, programming and packaging: the visitor experience
- Define the Visitor Experience using appropriate methodology
- Define how Physical Evidence will be incorporated

Marketing Communications Mix

- Define specific tactics for the marketing communications mix for EACH segment/particle (target market)
- Explain how each action within the mix addresses the issues and objectives you identified earlier in the plan

Place

- Define where the event shall take place
- Define the locations for distribution of marketing material

People and Promotional Partners

- Define the range of stakeholders in the event, and their role and purpose
- Define any Sales Promotion strategies

Pricing

- Define the prices for each segment/particle – such as ticket prices, exhibition space prices and sponsorship
- Define any Sales Promotion prices

Controls

This section explains methods to implement controls to monitor progress of the marketing plan; typically the targets for monitoring are stated monthly or quarterly.

Marketing budget

The budget should detail everything that you plan to spend on the project.

Action programmes

Using techniques such as Media Plans, Time Lines and Gantt Charts; detail when elements of the marketing plan shall be delivered. Include identification of:
- WHAT needs to be done
- WHEN it will be done
- WHO will do it

Summary of outcomes

This section to confirm the key outcomes expected by the plan.

Figure 13.6 Guidelines for Event Marketing Plans – focus on marketing mix

Source: Adapted from Kotler *et al.* (2005)

Executive summary

Your plan should start off with a one paragraph executive summary. An executive summary is not an introduction nor is it a table of contents written in sentence form; it is a summary of the key points, main goals, highlights, outcomes and recommendations of your plan.

Overview of the parent company and event

Briefly explain the primary motivations of the organisation.
- What are the primary objectives of the Parent Company; what is the reason for its existence
- Identify and define the strategic objectives of the organisation

Event overview

- Provide a brief overview of the event, including historical development
- Explain how the event delivers or supports the strategic objectives of the company

Marketing overview

You should consider the following:
- Event productivity
  - Describe the productivity of the event
  - Describe the productivity of the segments/territories served
- The marketing organisation
  - Describe the organisational structure of the marketing operations

Competitor analysis

- Identify and define the primary competitors within the marketplace; include details of the competitor event dates, venue, attendance, and organiser

Key issues

- Identify and define the key issues that need to be addressed for the coming event and/or future events
- Examples could include; increasing visitor numbers, breaking into a new market segment etc.

Key messaging

- Define the key messages that you want to attach to the event, that shall be communicated through the marketing plan
  - For example; 'Get Up Close to Your Show', 'The original outdoor event show' etc.

SWOT/PEST/PESTEL analysis

- Use an appropriate method(s) to define strengths and weaknesses against the competition in the market, and the opportunities and threats that are available or may impact on the firm. It also identifies 'environmental' issues impacting upon the firm

Key objectives and issues

Having reviewed any issues arising from the earlier sections and having identified and considered the strengths, weaknesses, opportunities and threats; decide the objectives for the coming year, and explain the issues that affect them.
- Include a definition of target markets, and the basis for segmentation
  - For example, you might plan to increase event visitor numbers by 25%, but where are these extra visitors going to come from?
- Include a definition of any intended changes in positioning, and the basis for positioning

Strategic marketing initiatives

This section identifies and introduces the strategic marketing techniques that shall be used to deliver the planned targets, objectives and issues.
- Identify and explain of the strategic marketing techniques

Segmentation

- Define how your market can be segmented and define the target markets for the event
- Define the market segment/particle and identity the messaging to each segment

The VITER Model

Value
- Cost and pricing models, including cost of effort, and opportunity cost as they apply to consumers.
- Define the prices for each segment/particle – such as ticket prices, exhibition space prices and sponsorship
- Define any Sales Promotion prices

Information
- Define specific tactics for marketing communications to each segment/particle (target market)
- Explain how each tactic addresses the issues and objectives you identified earlier in the plan
- Define the places of dissemination, and messages and language used

Tangibles
- Define strategies for providing evidence that overcome the intangible, variable, and perishable characteristics of events
- Define event service elements that enhance tangibility, and explain how this relates to the Experience element

Experience
- Define the Event Experience; include a description of programming, packaging, and the visitor experience
- Define positioning and differentiation
- Define the place of distribution, location and emotional attachment to the place

Relationships
- Define the people as stakeholders in event marketing
- The processes that support relationships with customers, partners such as sponsors

Controls and evaluation

This section explains methods to implement controls to monitor progress of the marketing plan; typically the targets for monitoring are stated monthly or quarterly.

Marketing budget

The budget should detail everything that you plan to spend on the project.

Action programmes

Using techniques such as Media Plans, Time Lines and Gantt Charts; detail when elements of the marketing plan shall be delivered. Include identification of:
- WHAT needs to be done
- WHEN it will be done
- WHO will do it

Summary of outcomes

This section to confirm the key outcomes expected by the plan.

Figure 13.7 Guidelines for Event Marketing Plans – focus on VITER model

The role of a marketing plan is primarily to create a coherent overview of how a particular brand will be promoted to its target audiences. It takes into account the key segments that the brand is trying to achieve and important factors within the internal and external environment of the event that frame its marketing activities. It sets clear goals that must be achieved with the marketing activities planned, presents strategies and tactics that will be used to achieve these objectives and identifies key performance indicators that will be used to measure the effectiveness and efficiency of the strategies and tactics employed. In many ways, designing a marketing plan for an event requires using a holistic and integrated approach between these various elements.

CASE STUDY

WOMAD Abu Dhabi

The WOMAD (World of Music, Arts and Dance) festival was founded in 1980 by Peter Gabriel, Thomas Brooman and Bob Hooton, but the very first edition of the festival was organised only two years later in 1982 in Shepton Mallet, Somerset, UK. After a financial challenge in meeting the costs of the festival, the event was franchised around the world and over the past 30 years has been organised in countries such as Australia, New Zealand, Spain, Russia and many others. The core ethos of the event focuses on presenting music that 'is of excellence, passion and individuality, regardless of musical genre or geographical origin' (WOMAD, 2014).

On 23–25 April 2009, WOMAD was introduced in Abu Dhabi, UAE, under the patronage of the Abu Dhabi Authority for Culture & Heritage (ADACH) who decided the event was to be a gift to the people of Abu Dhabi: a cultural celebration of the 200+ nationalities living in the city. The event was organised at two locations: the Corniche and the Al Jahili Fort at Al Ain. The organisers, the leading branding agency in the UAE, The Media House (TMH), brought together 20 artists over the three days of the festival. The key challenges faced by the festival organisers were the following:

- The event was a free event, which meant that significant attention needed to be paid to the crowd management and security issues in the delivery of the event.

- Previous cultural and music events had either been focusing on attracting expatriate Westerners, expatriate Asians, expatriate Arabs or UAE nationals, but until 2009 no event had ever tried to bring all of these audiences together at the same time.

- Music events held in the UAE up until 2009 had mainly featured Western artists, thus focusing primarily on attracting expatriate Westerners under 30 years of age.

- The event, apart from being an inclusive cultural celebration reflecting the fabric of the Abu Dhabi society, also had to promote Abu Dhabi globally and build its brand as a tourist destination and a cultural hub.

- Awareness of the WOMAD brand in Abu Dhabi was extremely low, which posed a severe risk of event failure if the event's communications efforts had not been delivered successfully.

Thus, the organisers, TMH, had the challenging task of designing a marketing campaign that would not only inform, excite and engage the intended target audiences for the event, but also raise awareness of the event on a global level. The following objectives were then set for the marketing campaign:

- Attendee base to be made up of: at least 5 per cent UAE nationals, at least 20 per cent expatriate Arabs, at least 20 per cent expatriate Asians and at least

- 20 per cent expatriate Westerners. These figures were chosen to reflect the overall structure of the UAE population.

- At least one-third of attendees to be over the age of 30.

- To achieve the total attendance of at least 16,000 over the three days: 5,000 per night on the main festival site (Corniche in Abu Dhabi) and an additional 1,000 people at the one-off event at Al Jahili Fort in Al Ain.

The objectives were informed by extensive research: the first two were formulated so as to reflect the overall structure of society in Abu Dhabi and the third objective was informed by looking at attendance figures for recent music concerts held in Abu Dhabi, as well as attendance figures for WOMAD Singapore, as Singapore is quite similar to Abu Dhabi in terms of population size and diversity. In creating the image for the event, TMH were heavily influenced by two particular editions of WOMAD, those in Singapore and Spain, which were both free events focusing on the celebration of local cultures, and which inspired the event's tagline – 'a festival uniting cultures through music'.

In designing the event's marketing plan and communications strategy, a great deal of effort was put into understanding exactly who the audiences were. To that end, the organisers conducted informal focus groups with UAE nationals, expatriate Arabs and expatriate Asians, and discovered that the key motivator for these audiences was the extent to which the event was family-friendly and offering a good learning experience for their children. Another important factor was the line-up of the festival, which needed to really reflect the cultures that live within Abu Dhabi. The final key factor was the way in which the event communicated with these ethnic groups – it was identified that these groups would feel more involved and excited about the event if the event's communications were conducted both in English and in their mother tongues. Expatriate Westerners were considered well aware and positively inclined towards this type of event, due to the large number of music events targeting this particular audience organised in Abu Dhabi over the years, so no specific research was organised with them.

The marketing communications for the event were split into three stages, which layered one on top of the other to build up excitement and interest in the lead-up to the festival, followed by a loud call for action. The first stage lasted from mid-February to mid-March and focused on building awareness of and educating audiences about the WOMAD concept. The second stage lasted from mid-March to mid-April and focused on creating interest with the target audiences. The final stage took place in the week leading up to the event with loud marketing activity voicing a call to action, i.e. making sure people had the event in mind and are making plans to attend with family and friends. The key marketing communications strategies and tactics used to promote the event included:

- A strong web presence, including a dual language (English and Arabic) event webpage www.womadabudhabi.ae with contact details inviting audiences to engage with the festival in case of any queries, as well as online banners on key regional and global websites and 'eye blasters', supported by geo-targeted banner advertising on social media (Facebook and Twitter).

- Press activity in daily newspapers and glossy periodicals, supported by providing journalists direct access to signed acts for interviews, as well as buying inserts in regional dailies in the 'call to action' stage.

- Radio time on both Arabic and English language stations was used to promote the artists and music genres that will be displayed at the event, as well as doing interviews with artists in the 'call to action' stage.

- Outdoor media towards the end of the campaign.

- Direct mail using the mailing list of the event patron ADACH, as well as commercial purchased mailing lists.

- Partnerships with Starbucks, Borders and Virgin Megastores in Abu Dhabi and Dubai to distribute flyers and concert programmes in exchange for promotional space at the event.

- Collaborating with the WOMAD foundation to deliver music, arts and crafts workshops in schools across Abu Dhabi, inviting children to be part of the event by participating in the first performance on stage at the Corniche and the children's procession on the final day of the event.

- Internal marketing with staff to ensure they understand the nature of the event and are able to promote it effectively.

- VIP invitations to key members of the press, encouraging them to attend the event and, hopefully, write about it in their media outlets.

The evaluation of the success of the marketing campaign was done through exit interviews conducted towards the end of each event day. These indicated that the structure of the attendee base included 7 per cent UAE nationals, 24 per cent expatriate Westerners, 23 per cent expatriate Asians and 46 per cent expatriate Arabs. Additionally, 44 per cent of attendees were over 30, and an impressive 89 per cent of respondents rated the event as either 'very good' or 'excellent' and 99 per cent said they would attend again and recommend the event to their friends or relatives. This was a great success compared to the initial marketing objectives. The research also showed that over 66 per cent of people learned about the event via traditional media channels, whilst 27 per cent had heard about the event through word-of-mouth, indicating that all the PR efforts conducted for the event (and estimated at AED 1.5 million) had been successful. In the end the event attracted 82,000 people, five times more than the originally projected 16,000.

Case study adapted from Prakash Vel and Sharma (2010) and online media

Case study questions

1 What criteria were used for setting the event's communications objectives?

2 How do the objectives reflect the nature of the event?

3 What key insights were gained through market research and how have they informed the creation of the marketing plan for the event?

4 How did the chosen marketing communications strategies and tactics support the successful delivery of the event?

5 What aspect of the WOMAD Abu Dhabi marketing plan was the most important and why?

SUMMARY

This chapter has presented the role of marketing planning in the successful marketing of events. It has tied in several concepts already discussed in this book into a holistic unit. The key to successful event marketing planning is to not treat it as a linear process with clearly defined steps, but rather as a function in which a variety of areas randomly intertwine as and when necessary over the required time period. The chapter has presented the various areas of the marketing planning function and has also argued the importance of a coherent approach to it. Marketing plan templates have also been outlined to facilitate the process. Although events are challenging due to the multiplicity of their stakeholders, the 'One Voice' principle should be the guiding light for any event marketer that wishes to successfully promote their events, regardless of their size, scope or complexity.

REVIEW QUESTIONS

1 What is the role of marketing planning? How would you explain its importance?

2 Discuss the relevance of the concept of persona development in event marketing. What are its benefits and drawbacks?

3 What types of market research need to be undertaken to support the preparation of a marketing plan?

4 How is the principle of 'One Voice' relevant to today's event marketing? What does it imply?

EVENT MARKETING SCENARIO

You are the marketing manager of your university. It is the beginning of the academic year and you are in the process of defining your marketing strategy for a series of Open Day events which target potential future applicants to your institution. Of particular importance to your university, in terms of student recruitment, are the undergraduate and postgraduate programmes within the Business School focusing on tourism and events management and you need to come up with a marketing plan for this group of programmes. As a marketing manager, you now need to:

- identify and profile your potential target audiences

- decide which marketing communications strategies and tactics you will use to reach these audiences

- define how the success of your marketing plan will be evaluated.

Use the two templates we presented in this chapter and discuss the usefulness of each of them for your specific task.

FURTHER READING

Books

Jobber, D. 2010. *Principles and Practice of Marketing*, 6th Edition, Maidenhead: McGraw-Hill
This is a useful core text for any student familiarising themselves with the key concepts in marketing. The topic of marketing planning is covered in great detail and is written in a clear and understandable manner.

Morgan, M. 1996. *Marketing for Leisure and Tourism*, Harlow: FT Prentice Hall
This is an excellent starting resource for those who need to get acquainted with the nature of the leisure and tourism sectors and its impact on their marketing. It is written by one of the leading UK thinkers in this area.

Wood, E. 2004. Marketing information for the events industry, in Yeoman, I., Robertson, M., Ali-Knight, J., Drummond, S. and McMahon-Beattie, U. (Eds), *Festival and Events Management: An international arts and culture perspective*, Oxford: Butterworth-Heinemann, pp. 130–157
This is a very useful chapter which explores in detail the role of information mining in the marketing of events, as well as what particular applications such information can have.

Journals

Ardley, B. 2011. Marketing theory and critical phenomenology: Exploring the human side of management practice, *Marketing Intelligence and Planning*, 29(7), pp. 628–642
This is a great article which contextualises the role of marketing professionals in the running of marketing activities.

Kitchen, P.J. and Schultz, D.E. 2009. IMC: New horizon/false dawn for a marketplace in turmoil? *Journal of Marketing Communications*, 15(2–3), pp. 197–204
This is a good article discussing the role of integrated marketing communications in twenty-first-century marketing. A particularly useful feature of the article is the recognition of the relevance of the concept in the context of changing consumer preferences and dire economic conditions.

Prakash Vel, K. and Sharma, R. 2010. Megamarketing an event using integrated marketing communications: The success story of TMH, *Business Strategy Series*, 11(6), pp. 371–382
This article provides a detailed overview of the marketing plan for the 2009 WOMAD Abu Dhabi. The case study within this chapter is based on this article.

Other resources

CIM. 2014. The Marketing Expert. *CIM* [Online]. Available at: www.cimmarketingexpert.co.uk/ [Accessed 31 January 2014]
This is a useful contemporary resource by the UK Chartered Institute of Marketing, the leading marketing industry body. It offers a wealth of practical information to help guide you through the process of marketing planning and execution.

Mplans www.mplans.com
Mplans is part of the Palo Alto Software network, and has been designed as a free resource to support entrepreneurs in delivering their marketing. It has some very useful features and samples of marketing plans for a variety of organisations, but do approach it with a critical mind.

References

Allen, J., O'Toole, W., Harris, R. and McDonnell, I. 2011. *Festival and Special Event Management*, 5th Edition, Milton: John Wiley & Sons Australia.

Berridge, G. 2007. *Events Design and Experience*, Oxford: Butterworth-Heinemann.

Borden, N.H. 1964. The concept of the Marketing Mix, in Schwartz, G. (Ed.), *Science in Marketing*, New York: John Wiley & Sons.

Bowdin, G., Allen, J., O'Toole, W., Harris, R. and McDonnell, I. 2011. *Event Management*, 3rd Edition, Oxford: Butterworth-Heinemann.

Brassington, F. and Pettitt, S. 2003. *Principles of Marketing*, 3rd Edition, Harlow: FT Prentice Hall.

Jackson, N. 2013. *Promoting and Marketing Events: Theory and practice*, 1st Edition, Abingdon: Routledge.

Kitchen, P.J., Schultz, D.E., Kim, I., Han, D. and Li, T. 2004. Will agencies ever 'get' (or understand) IMC?, *European Journal of Marketing*, 38(11/12), pp. 1417–1436.

Kotler, P., Bowen, J. and Makens, J. 2003. *Marketing for Hospitality and Tourism*, 3rd Edition, Harlow: Pearson Education Ltd.

Kotler, P., Wong, V., Saunders, J. and Armstrong, G. 2005. *Principles of Marketing*, 4th Edition, Harlow: Pearson Education Ltd.

McCabe, S. 2009. *Marketing Communications in Tourism and Hospitality: Concepts, strategies and cases*, Oxford: Butterworth-Heinemann.

Masterman, G. and Wood, E. 2006. *Innovative Marketing Communications: Strategies for the events industry*, Oxford: Butterworth-Heinemann.

Meerman Scott, D. 2011. *The New Rules of Marketing and PR: How to use social media, online video, mobile applications, blogs, news releases and viral marketing to reach buyers directly*, 3rd Edition, Hoboken, NJ: John Wiley & Sons.

Morgan, M. 1996. *Marketing for Leisure and Tourism*, Harlow: FT Prentice Hall.

Pine and Gilmore 1999. *The Experience Economy: Work is theater and every business a stage*, Boston: Harvard Business School Press.

Prakash Vel, K. and Sharma, R. 2010. Megamarketing an event using integrated marketing communications: The success story of TMH, *Business Strategy Series*, 11(6), pp. 371–382.

Saget, A. 2006. *The Event Marketing Handbook: Beyond logistics & planning*, Chicago: Kaplan Publishing.

Seitel, F.P. 2004. *The practice of Public Relations*, 9th Edition, Harlow: Pearson Prentice Hall.

WOMAD 2014. Our WOMAD Story. *WOMAD* [Online]. Available at: http://womad.org/about/ [Accessed 29 January 2014].

Wood, E. 2004. Marketing information for the events industry, In Yeoman, I., Robertson, M., Ali-Knight, J., Drummond, S. and McMahon-Beattie, U. (Eds) *Festival and Events Management: An international arts and culture perspective*, Oxford: Butterworth-Heinemann, pp. 130–157.

Chapter **14**

The future of events marketing
An alternative model that puts the consumer at the centre of marketing activities

By the end of this chapter, students should be able to:

- Reflect on what has been discussed so far in this book and highlight the needs of consumers in terms of receiving marketing information from events

- Identify the key aspects of marketing relevant to events

- Appreciate the reasoning behind the proposed new model for the marketing of events and identify its benefits and drawbacks

Introduction

This short chapter collates all the key concepts discussed previously in this book and presents an argument for a change in approach to the marketing of events and other experiential market offerings, thus providing a natural conclusion to our discussion. In particular, the chapter draws on the dilemmas discussed in Chapter 4 and presents in detail the constructs of the proposed new model which aims to eliminate these dilemmas by putting the consumer at the centre of event marketing activities. The chapter presents in some detail the main constructs of the model, drawing on topics covered in previous chapters of this book. No case study has been included, as it is hoped that the discussions around the applicability of the model will be taken up by academics and practitioners alike, to test the validity of the constructs and their manifestations and implications within an industry context.

The need to rethink the marketing communications for events

In the early chapters of this book we discussed the distinctive nature of events as market offerings and why it is important to distinguish them from regular products and services offered in the market. We defined events as unique market offerings that represent an amalgamation of products and services and which support the delivery of the event experience and have argued that they do not (nor should they) neatly fit into the dominant definitions of products and services. In Chapter 4, in particular, we discussed the limitations of the dominant concept of the Marketing Mix and we stressed the fact that this conceptual model looks at marketing from the supply side (Grönroos, 1997; Rosenbloom and Dimitrova, 2011), with little regard given to the consumer perspective. This was the main motivation behind publishing this work – the time has come to put more emphasis on the consumer in the conceptualisation and delivery of marketing activities. Events as market offerings are a particularly fruitful ground to do this, considering that they are in their very nature consumer-focused and rely heavily on individual consumer experiences. Therefore, rather than trying to rehash the Ps of the Marketing Mix, I opt for a complete change of perspective and propose a completely new model for the marketing of events which comprises five interrelated elements:

- value
- information
- tangibles
- experience
- relationships.

Figure 14.1 presents a visual conceptualisation of the model and each of the model's constructs is discussed in greater detail in the following sections.

Value

In Chapter 2 we discussed the unique characteristics of events and the contribution of their experiential component to the overall creation of value. Grönroos (2000) emphasised that successful value delivery stems from a thorough understanding of the consumers perceptions of quality and value and an effective allocation of resources within the process of creating that value. His earlier work (see Grönroos, 1994) defined relationship marketing as a process by which a brand–consumer relationship should successfully fulfil the objectives of both parties involved, which opened the door to the notion that value is not only created on the supply side, but that consumers themselves can (and should) contribute to the definition of value, thus paving the way for the introduction of co-creation into contemporary marketing thought. Extending this work, Prahalad and Ramaswamy (2004) and Prahalad (2004)

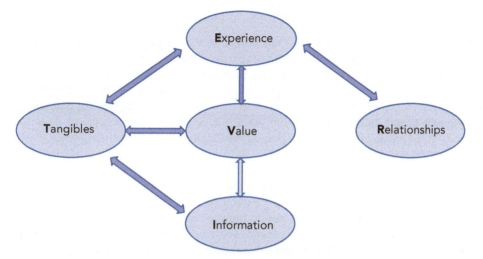

Figure 14.1 The proposed new model for the marketing of events

defined co-creation of value as a function of individual consumer experiences, which marked a shift from the view of value creation as internal to a brand (or company) to a more externally focused view which emphasises the contribution of meaning-creation to a consumer's definition of value. This shift in viewpoint, then, has an impact on the definition of the value chain: if value is created 'inside the firm' (Prahalad and Ramaswamy, 2004) and the customer is perceived to be 'on the outside', production and consumption would naturally be two separate and distinct processes. However, as we've seen in Chapter 3 (see Figure 3.5), with events the production and consumption of the experience are merged, which is vital to the co-creation of value. From this we further argued that the term 'supply chain' does not really accurately reflect the complexities of the supply concept for events and we introduced the terms 'supply matrix' or 'supply network' as its potentially appropriate replacements.

Aside from the divergent views of *where* value is created, another stumbling block in the discussion of value is *what* actually constitutes value. There is some agreement in marketing literature that with products and services value is often evaluated in relation to perceived customer cost (or sacrifice) of obtaining the benefits offered by a particular product or service (Ravald and Grönroos, 1996). This results in companies wishing to provide greater value almost always resorting to a reduction in the price of a product or service to reflect this. With events, however, precisely because of their uniqueness, their experiential nature and the important role that co-creation plays in value creation from a consumer's perspective, this notion of cost (or sacrifice) becomes increasingly difficult to ascertain. Therefore, a simple reduction in price (of an event ticket, or other aspect of the event which is being charged) will not necessarily have an impact on perceived value. This means (perhaps) that defining value itself in the context of event delivery and its implications for events marketing presents a challenging yet attractive area for future research where Chaffey and Ellis-Chadwick's (2012) *value proposition* and Kotler *et al.*'s (2013) emphasis on differentiation and positioning as key parameters of value creation are likely to present an interesting direction in which this research might develop.

Information

Because of its focus on interpreting marketing from the perspective of the brand, the P for promotion within the Marketing Mix is not able to adequately reflect the changing nature of the communications between brands and their consumers. Even the very definition of marketing implies that brands are responsible for the satisfaction of customer's needs and wants. Therefore, the conventional term 'marketing communications mix' (or promotion) is inherently unable to communicate the value that consumers increasingly co-create with brands. It is because of this that I propose a much broader construct of Information as one of the key elements of the new model.

As we've seen in Chapters 11 and 12, the rules of the game have changed considerably. The internet has enabled consumers to have a wealth of information at their fingertips which makes them less dependent on messaging provided directly by the brand. Indeed, today, information coming directly from the brand is less and less persuasive, whilst information obtained through individuals' personal networks of contacts, whether in their physical or in their virtual environment carry much more weight than ever before. Furthermore, there is now even some empirical evidence (see Smith, 2008) that – specifically in the context of tourism and events – there is a mismatch between the channels that events use to push their marketing messages (i.e. traditional marketing communications mix) and the channels which consumers actually use to obtain information about the event, which he terms 'the information mix'. It seems, therefore, ineffective to continue to use terms and constructs which are unable to account for this changing nature in consumer-brand interactions.

This would imply that Information should be distributed through a range of different touchpoints relevant to the consumers, facilitating a dialogue between the event and the consumer and thus supporting the co-creation of value (Prahalad and Ramaswamy, 2004; Frigo, 2010), but also facilitating consumer-to-consumer (C2C) communication via word of mouth, either in the physical or in a virtual setting. Information should, also, be meaningful to the consumers, which makes *content* crucial in enabling consumers to construct their own meaning and in doing so contribute to the co-creation of their own experience. This, in turn contributes to the overall value a consumer will derive from their participation in (or engagement with) an event. Payne *et al.* (2009) define co-creation as dialogue and interaction between the consumer and the supplier. Information should, then, also refer to the touchpoints where this interaction takes place, which makes it another important part of the consumer's overall value chain.

Tangibles

The construct of Tangibles within this newly proposed model needs no particular debate, as it is fairly self-explanatory. Tangibles aid the delivery of the event experience by providing sensory stimuli which, when experienced and interpreted by the consumer, frame their overall event experience making it engaging and memorable. Due to the transient and ephemeral nature of events (which we discussed in detail in Chapters 2 and 3), tangibles are particularly important in providing a form of physical interaction between the event and the consumer in all stages of the event delivery: pre-event, during the event and post-event.

Experience

In Chapter 8 we contextualised humans as balancing on a thin line between individualism and belonging to a community. We also asserted that the role of events as leisure experiences encompasses providing individuals with a space for hedonic consumption which contributes to their understanding and expression of their authentic self within a specific social interaction. Drawing on the work of Holbrook and Hirschman (1982), who emphasised emotions, contexts and symbolic aspects of experiences, we further emphasised that experiences should evoke emotional responses by focusing on fantasies, feelings, emotion, social interaction and fun. Without going into a deep discussion of this (as we have already done so in Chapter 8), I propose the third key construct of the new model for the marketing of events: the Experience.

Whilst it can often be an overlooked aspect of event planning and delivery, the event experience can have far reaching implications for the marketing of events. First, the nature of the Event Life Cycle (discussed in Chapter 2, see Figures 2.5a–e) and the specific characteristics of the different stages within it mean that the nature and delivery of the event experience might *have* to differ from stage to stage in order to meet the evolving consumer expectations of it. Key considerations will likely range from the simple 'ironing out the kinks' in the introduction and growth stages, to major changes in the maturity stage to keep the event 'fresh' and interesting in order to retain attendance numbers, to the potential complete overhaul of the experience to prevent consumer boredom in the decline stage, thus preventing event abandonment and supporting rejuvenation and relaunch.

Furthermore, in Chapter 4 we presented the societal marketing concept and consumers operating within their own, unique context, which frames their experiences and facilitates meaning-making. Relating this to the levels of product (see Vignette 4.2) it seems reasonable to consider that one potential product of an event is the meaning the consumer will derive from their experience at the event and how that will contribute to the construction of their own identity. In this sense, it is particularly pertinent to examine the role of *stories* in supporting the co-creation of the experience, their contribution to the self and, subsequently, to own interpretation of event value and enhancing the emotional connection with the event (Payne *et al.*, 2009). In the words of Prahalad (2004), *the brand (or in our case: the event) itself becomes the experience*, but in order for this to really happen, event organisers and marketers need to think through what kinds of experiences they want to offer and how these can be sustained outside of the physical boundaries of the event (i.e. pre- and post-event). One of the particularly useful tools that could facilitate an event organiser's decision in this respect is Sharples *et al.*'s (2014) model of the six dimensions of the experience which includes: sensory stimuli, feelings, knowledge, doing, being and belonging. Future research into event experience and its impact on events marketing should definitely consider how the dimensions of the experience relate to the specific consumer motivations and drivers to attend and what specific impact they have on overall satisfaction with the event and perception of event value.

Relationships

The final construct in the newly proposed model for the marketing of events are relationships. Ravald and Grönroos (1996) for the first time addressed the lack of integration of the relational aspect into the overall product or service being offered, and their ground-breaking work helped to establish value as the very foundation of brand relationships, but also contextualised relationships as building blocks of value. This interdependence of value and relationships is particularly visible with events for two key reasons: the fact that the consumer actively participates in the co-creation of the event experience and the fact that this co-creation starts from the very first moment the consumer learns about the event and this can be well before the event takes place. Therefore, it can be argued that, in the context of events, relationships serve the following purposes:

- Inspiring trust – this is particularly important in the pre-event phase to encourage consumer commitment to attending the event and overcome any apprehension about what the event can be expected to deliver by way of its content and the associated experience.

- Co-creating meaning and own experience – co-creation is impossible to achieve without some form of relationship, as it requires frequent exchange, validation and verification of information.

- Fostering emotional connectivity which helps build consumer loyalty – this is crucial for events, as a positive experience can lead to an emotional connection, which will impact on repeat attendance and positive word-of-mouth (see Chapter 7, Figure 7.6).

Relationships are formed and reinforced through personalised experiences in a range of 'encounters' (Payne *et al.*, 2009) or 'moments of truth' (Grönroos, 1990), which provide consumers with information about the event. Sometimes (but not always) this happens in a related tangible setting which supports the consumer's creation of meaning and co-creation of value. Similarly to the Experience construct, relationships formed between the event and its consumers will have a direct impact on the management and marketing of the event during the various stages of the Event Life Cycle. For instance, in the early stages of introduction and growth the relationships will still be fairly new and therefore clear and consistent communication with consumers is important to make consumers feel heard and to inspire trust. In the maturity stage, the nature of the conversations will be different, as consumers are now familiar with the event and are more in charge of where and how they interact with the event, so it is likely that social media will be their preferred choice of channel. Relationships with event audiences are also crucial in ensuring that any crises or other negative episodes are managed with care so that they do not adversely affect the event brand.

Creating and sustaining good quality relationships with consumers will impact on the overall perception consumers have of the event and their understanding of event value. Event marketers should be mindful of where and how their target audiences prefer to obtain their information and make sure they cater to these particular channels. But relationships involve more than just the mere choice of information channels, they also need to take into consideration what motivates consumers to engage with the event, as well as how they co-create their experience. Event marketers should be particularly mindful to reduce the relationship 'cost' for the consumer, which is likely to impact their perception of value (Ravald and Grönroos, 1996).

As can be seen from Figure 14.1 all the constructs within the new model are interrelated and no one construct exists in a complete vacuum. This implies that changes in one construct will have an impact on the interpretation and delivery of other constructs, which will depend on the specificities of the event being considered. In this sense, this model is more dynamic and more holistic than the conventional Marketing Mix model, as it allows the marketers to understand the overlap between the constructs and how changes (whether intentional or not) in one construct might bring about changes in others and the implications this will have on the overall marketing of the event.

SUMMARY

This chapter sought to build on the discussions we presented earlier on in this book and introduce an alternative model for the marketing of events in the twenty-first century. The chapter introduced the constructs of Value, Information, Tangibles, Experience and Relationships. The key contribution of this chapter to contemporary marketing thought is the departure from the traditional model of the Marketing Mix, which presents its constructs largely as independent silos, and a move towards a more integrated and holistic approach to the marketing of events. This approach is highly reliant on the consumer's co-creation of their own experience which is why the VITER model puts the consumer at the very centre of event's marketing activities and each of the constructs is explored with an emphasis on its implications for event consumers' engagement with the event.

REVIEW QUESTIONS

1 What is your opinion on the author's call for a change in approach to the marketing of events? Is it needed? Justify your answer.

2 How do the constructs of the VITER model relate to the 'old' constructs of the Marketing Mix? Use a few different examples of the Marketing Mix model from Chapter 4 to illustrate your points.

REFERENCES

Chaffey, D. and Ellis-Chadwick, F. 2012. *Digital Marketing: Strategy, implementation and practice*, 5th Edition, Harlow: Pearson Education Ltd.

Frigo, M.L. (2010. How enterprises can drive new value creation, *Strategic Finance*, December, pp. 17–18 and 69.

Grönroos, C. 1990. *Service Management and Marketing – Managing the Moments of Truth in Service Competition*, Lexington, MA: Lexington Books.

Grönroos, C. 1994. From marketing mix to relationship marketing. Toward a paradigm shift in marketing, *Management Decision*, 32(2), pp. 4–32.

Grönroos, C. 1997. Keynote paper: From marketing mix to relationship marketing – towards a paradigm shift in marketing, *Management Decision*, 35(4), pp. 322–339.

Grönroos, C. 2000. Creating a relationship dialogue: Communication, interaction and value, *The Marketing Review*, 1(1), pp. 5–14.

Holbrook, M.B. and Hirschman, E.C. 1982. The experiential aspects of consumption: Consumer fantasies, feelings and fun, *Journal of Consumer Research*, 9, pp. 132–140.

Kotler, P., Harris, L.C., Armstrong, G. and Piercy, N. 2013. *Principles of Marketing*, 6th European Edition, Harlow: Pearson Education Ltd.

Payne, A., Storbacka, K., Frow, P. and Knox, S. 2009. Co-creating brands: Diagnosing and designing the relationship experience, *Journal of Business Research*, 62, pp. 379–389.

Prahalad, C.K. 2004. The co-creation of value, *Journal of Marketing*, 68(1), p. 23.

Prahalad, C.K. and Ramaswamy, V. 2004. Co-creation experiences: The next practice in value creation, *Journal of Interactive Marketing*, 18(3), pp. 5–14.

Ravald, A. and Grönroos, C. 1996. The value concept and relationship marketing, *European Journal of Marketing*, 30(2), pp. 19–30.

Rosenbloom, B. and Dimitrova, B. 2011. The marketing mix paradigm and the Dixonian systems perspective of marketing, *Journal of Historical Research in Marketing*, 3(1), pp. 53–66.

Sharples, L., Crowther, P., May, D. and Orefice, C. (Eds). 2014. *Strategic Event Creation*, Oxford: Goodfellow Publishers.

Smith, K.A. 2008. Information mix for events: A comparison of multiple channels used by event organisers and visitors, *International Journal of Event Management Research*, 4(1), 24–37.

Index

Items in *italic* relate to figures and tables.